An Urban History of the Plague

As a medical, economic, spiritual and demographic crisis, plague affected practically every aspect of an early modern community whether on a local, regional or national scale. Its study therefore affords opportunities for the reassessment of many aspects of the pre-modern world.

This book examines the incidence and effects of plague in an early modern Scottish community by analysing civic, medical and social responses to epidemics in the north-east port of Aberdeen, focusing on the period 1500–1650. While Aberdeen's experience of plague was in many ways similar to that of other towns throughout Europe, certain idiosyncrasies in the city make it a particularly interesting case study, which challenges several assumptions about early modern mentalities.

Karen Jillings is Senior Lecturer in History at Massey University, New Zealand, where she has taught since 2004. She has published on aspects of medicine and society in pre-modern Scotland.

Perspectives in Economic and Social History
Series Editors: Andrew August and Jari Eloranta

44 A History of Drink and the English, 1500–2000
Paul Jennings

45 Rural–Urban Relationships in the Nineteenth Century
Uneasy Neighbours?
Edited by Mary Hammond and Barry Sloan

46 A History of Professional Economists and Policymaking in the United States
Irrelevant Genius
Jonathan S. Franklin

47 Merchants and Trade Networks in the Atlantic and the Mediterranean, 1550–1800
Connectors of Commercial Maritime Systems
Edited by Manuel Herrero Sánchez and Klemens Kaps

48 Property Rights in Land
Issues in Social, Economic and Global History
Edited by Rosa Congost, Jorge Gelman and Rui Santos

49 Working-Class Community in the Age of Affluence
Stefan Ramsden

50 Culture, Philanthropy and the Poor in Late-Victorian London
Geoffrey A. C. Ginn

51 The Economic and Business History of Occupied Japan
New Perspectives
Edited by Thomas French

52 An Urban History of the Plague
Socio-Economic, Political and Medical Impacts in a Scottish Community, 1500–1650
Karen Jillings

For more information about this series please visit
www.routledge.com/series/PESH

An Urban History of the Plague

Socio-Economic, Political and Medical Impacts in a Scottish Community, 1500–1650

Karen Jillings

Routledge
Taylor & Francis Group
LONDON AND NEW YORK

First published 2018
by Routledge
2 Park Square, Milton Park, Abingdon, Oxon OX14 4RN

and by Routledge
711 Third Avenue, New York, NY 10017

Routledge is an imprint of the Taylor & Francis Group, an informa business

British Library Cataloguing-in-Publication Data
A catalogue record for this book is available from the British Library

Library of Congress Cataloging-in-Publication Data
A catalog record has been requested for this book

ISBN: 978-1-138-19282-9 (hbk)
ISBN: 978-1-315-63966-6 (ebk)

Typeset in Bembo
by Swales & Willis Ltd, Exeter, UK

Contents

Maps

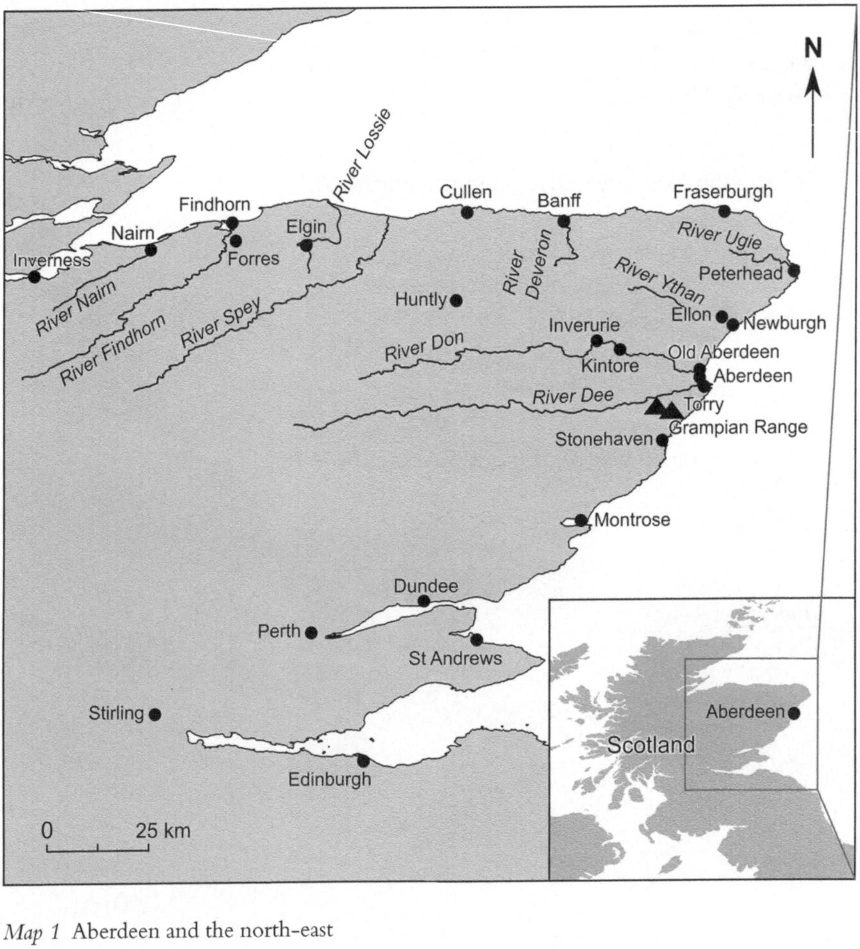

Map 1 Aberdeen and the north-east

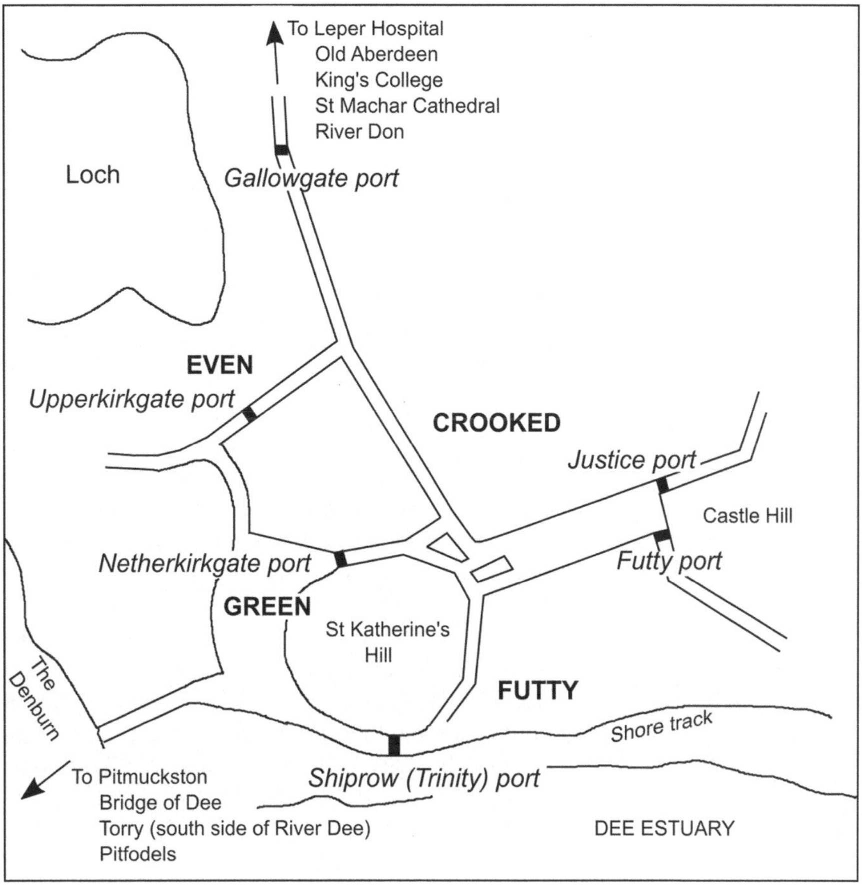

Map 2 Layout of early modern Aberdeen

Abbreviations

ACL	L. Taylor (ed.), *Aberdeen Council Letters*, vols 1-4 (London: Oxford University Press, 1942–54) [volume, page number]
ACR	Aberdeen City and Aberdeenshire Archives, CA1/1: Aberdeen City Council Registers [volume, page number]
AGA	Aberdeen City and Aberdeenshire Archives, CA7/2/1: Aberdeen Guildry Account Book, vol. I, 1453–1650 [not paginated]
ATA	Aberdeen City and Aberdeenshire Archives, CA6/1/1: Aberdeen Treasurer's Accounts, vol. I: 1578–1652 [page number]
Dundee CMB	Dundee City Archives, Dundee Council Minute Book [volume, folio number]
Edinburgh CMB	Edinburgh City Archives, SL1/1: Edinburgh Council Minute Book [volume, folio number]
Edinburgh Extracts	National Library of Scotland, Adv.MS.31.4.9: Extracts from the Minutes of Edinburgh Town Council, 1442–1579 [folio number]
Elgin BCB	Local Heritage Services, Moray Council, Elgin, B2: Elgin Burgh Court Book [volume, page number]
Inverness CMB	Highland Archive Centre, Inverness, BI/1/7: Inverness Council Minute Books [volume, folio number]
KS	National Archives of Scotland, CH2: Kirk Session minutes [preceded by NAS catalogue, volume, folio number] (Aberdeenshire, Angus, Banffshire, Kincardineshire, Inverness-shire, Moray, Nairnshire) Except those for Old Machar (held at St Machar Cathedral, Old Aberdeen)

NAS	National Archives of Scotland
Old Ab CMB	Aberdeen City and Aberdeenshire Archives, OA/1: Old Aberdeen Council Minute Book [volume number, page number]
Records of Old Aberdeen	A.M. Munro (ed.), *Records of Old Aberdeen* (Aberdeen: New Spalding Club, 1899) [volume, page number] (including Old Machar Kirk Session accounts, which are now mislaid)
RPC	John Hill Burton *et al.* (eds.), *Register of the Privy Council of Scotland* (Edinburgh: H.M. General Register House, 1898–) [series, volume, page number]
RPS	Records of the Acts of Parliament [online at: www.rps.ac.uk]

Preface

Like many monographs dealing with a historical issue, this study was inspired by an intriguing conundrum; in my case, one which I first stumbled across a few months into my doctoral research at the University of Aberdeen. When I began my studies, I knew I wanted to indulge my longstanding fascination with slightly macabre topics by looking more closely at plague (though from the safely immune distance of several centuries) and it suited me to focus on my native Scotland, about which I had already come to realise little had been written concerning historical epidemics. But I was unsure which aspect of this broad topic I wanted to focus on. The answer jumped out at me one day as I sat reading *A History of Epidemics in Britain*, an eminently detailed chronological survey by the medical historian Charles Creighton and one which remains a fascinating and authoritative text despite its age. In his section on 'Plague in Scotland, 1495–1603', Creighton noted that 'in the foregoing records of plague in Scotland, the absolute immunity of Aberdeen in the latter half of the sixteenth century is remarkable'.[1] My interest was immediately sparked. Then, as now, Aberdeen was one of Scotland's largest towns and an important centre of commercial, intellectual, political and social interactions. Yet it avoided plague outbreaks for a significant length of time; at least a ninety-eight-year period, in fact, unparalleled in the British Isles. How could this have been the case? I had found my thesis topic. Twenty years later, the book you are now holding in your hands (or reading on a screen) is a substantially revised version of the doctorate which resulted.

The city of Aberdeen experienced only three recorded outbreaks of plague: in 1514, 1545 and 1647. It was not struck by the severe epidemics that spread through much of Scotland's more populous central belt in the 1560s and 1580s, or by the plagues which afflicted many surrounding settlements in the first decade of the seventeenth century. It even remained immune in 1608 when the disease ravaged what was then the separate burgh of Torry, which lay only a short distance away on the southern side of the river Dee, and when it apparently caused the death of a resident in Sheddocksley on the western fringes of the modern city. Creighton followed up his comment recalled above by noting that this prolonged absence of plague from Aberdeen 'does not depend on any imperfection of the records'. The city archives are blessed to possess an almost unbroken run of council registers (a rich source for so many aspects of burgh life) from 1398, the first eight volumes of which were recently recognised by being placed on UNESCO's UK Register of Important Documentary Heritage.[2] Accordingly, various aspects of the city's well-documented history have been the focus of much scholarship, including several valuable recent overviews which have given me a sturdy basis on which to build my study of the impact of plague on the urban community.[3]

It is possible that a misreading of these extensive archival sources has been responsible for certain assertions made about plague in Aberdeen by those few historians who have given tangential consideration to the topic within their own specialisms. Even though it has been acknowledged that the city avoided plague for a remarkably long time, some scholars have assumed outbreaks to have occurred on occasions when, as this book will show, they simply did not. In addition to two epidemics for which there is incontrovertible evidence, Robert Tyson stated that plague also broke out in Aberdeen in 1499–1500 and 1549, while Margo Todd reckoned it to have been present in the city in 1608 and Michael Flinn asserted that it struck in 1649.[4] These misidentifications may have arisen from a failure to establish the context of certain civic proclamations, from a misinterpretation of the evidence, or by extrapolating from the experience of other places. It certainly was the case that on each of these occasions, measures were put into place by Aberdeen's council to tackle infection. However, when these orders are comprehensively contextualised, it is apparent that there is no evidence that plague was actually present in the burgh. Rather, these actions were entirely precautionary, not reactionary. As such, they stand as testimony to the city's immunity and invite consideration of how this came about.

As a study of the impact of plague on a Scottish community, this book is unique despite the academic recognition of the inherent value of its subject matter.[5] It joins a growing corpus of scholarship that focuses on the impact of epidemics on areas north of the Alps, rather than on Italy which was the locus of the origins of plague control in a western European context and which therefore tended to be the setting for earlier case studies.[6] Historical epidemics remain a source of enduring fascination that continues to spawn a plethora of books focusing on various aspects of the impact of plague, but the constraints of space have meant that comparisons with other places made throughout this book are limited to those considered most pertinent. The same is regrettably true of some important aspects of Aberdeen's civic life, such as the minutiae of the day-to-day decisions made by the council and the price fluctuations of various commodities, except where these are concerned directly with plague.

Before we begin to consider the impact of plague in Aberdeen, we ought to address one contentious issue. What do we mean today when we talk of past plagues? Historians and clinicians continue to debate the issue extensively, particularly in light of new findings resulting from the development of scientific methods and technologies, including DNA extraction and GIS-based spatial analysis.[7] The assumption that bubonic plague was solely to blame for the mid-fourteenth century Black Death and subsequent epidemics has increasingly been discredited; its spread relies on the vector of rats and their fleas, which can blinker historians to other possible methods of transmission and so leave them open to criticism.[8] A classic example of this concerns Aberdeen. In his history of what he assumed to be bubonic plague in the British Isles, the bacteriologist John Shrewsbury was unequivocal in his explanation of Aberdeen's comparative immunity to outbreaks. 'Basically', he opined,

> that immunity resulted from the fact that the house-rat population of Aberdeen was not dense enough to support an epizootic of rat-plague, and this sparseness of rodents resulted in turn from the early use of stone for the building material of the ordinary dwelling-house in Aberdeen and the contemporaneous absence of thatch as the roofing material.

He went on to note that most places in Scotland hit by plague were ports situated either on the coast or alongside a river, and so, 'it is obvious that these Scottish visitations by bubonic plague were almost entirely consequential upon the maritime importations of [the bacillus] *P*[*asteurella*] *pestis* from English and European ports, most often in all probability from Baltic ports'.[9] But perhaps it stretches credulity to accept that a significant seaport that maintained some of Scotland's best established connections with the Baltic (where, apparently, plague 'most often' came from) was saved from the disease largely because its buildings were constructed from stone from an early time (which, in any case, for much of the period the majority were not). This also neglects consideration of other factors that may plausibly be brought to bear, including: climate; cramped living conditions within individual dwellings; and the relative distance of the north-east from the more populous central belt of Scotland. While bubonic plague might well have been responsible for a proportion of deaths in a given outbreak, it has been persuasively posited that also often present was a specifically airborne virus that spread directly from person to person causing swellings, fevers and haemorrhaging, and which perhaps exacerbated the natural mortality caused by endemic ailments such as typhus and influenza. Though problematic, the identification of the north-east's pre-modern plagues cannot be ignored in explaining Aberdeen's comparative immunity, so we will return to the issue in the concluding chapter.[10]

In an age before the identification of the *Pasteurella pestis* bacterium (which became renamed *Yersinia pestis* in honour of Alexandre Yersin, the Swiss-French physician who had discovered it in 1894[11]), how did contemporaries who encountered plague interpret it? From its initial appearance in the mid-fourteenth century, they were aware that it was something which had 'never been heard of by man'. In the earliest Scottish description of the disease, John of Fordun (who probably served as a chantry priest in Old Aberdeen's St Machar Cathedral) highlighted those characteristics that were to become synonymous with many subsequent outbreaks: it could kill quickly, kill many and kill horribly.[12] In the civic records that constitute the main source for urban governmental efforts to assuage it, the nomenclature of the disease could reflect these aspects: the Aberdeen council described it as 'this violent and contageous suord of pestilence' when it first broke out.[13] Furthermore, contemporaries recognised that not every outbreak of plague was entirely the same: in 1439 individuals in Dumfries and elsewhere (though not Aberdeen) were afflicted with a particularly virulent plague described as the 'pestilence but [that is, without] mercy'.[14] In 1538 and 1539 many places, Aberdeen included, were threatened by 'a contagious disease, callit the boiche', a likely derivative of the term for a swelling, 'botch'.[15] Just as importantly, the Borders-born, Edinburgh-based physician John MakLuire showed in his *Tractatus de febre pestilente* (*Treatise on the Pestilent Fever*) published in Edinburgh in 1630 that medical personnel could be as clear about what plague was *not* as what it *was*.[16]

This book considers responses to what contemporaries in Aberdeen and the north-east identified as the specific disease of plague, and analyses these in accordance with how the concepts of contagion and infection were understood at the time. It adopts a largely chronological approach. Chapter 1 sets the scene for the subsequent discussion by contextualising Aberdeen's location within the north-east and considering those geographical and topographical features that, as will be shown, might have had a bearing on the incidence of plague. It will also sketch the salient features of contemporary urban life, highlighting aspects including the articulation of piety and civic notions of belonging. Chapter 2 then considers responses to plague from a variety of perspectives, including theories about the origins, prevention and cure of the disease espoused by the Aberdeen physician Gilbert Skene in Scotland's only plague treatise, and the place of this text in medical writing. It also highlights the interpretation of plague, in common with other crises, as the manifestation of divine wrath and contextualises government measures to tackle repeated outbreaks at both the local and national levels. Chapters 3 and 4 provide a chronological analysis of these responses in Aberdeen and across the north-east from the end of the fifteenth century to the occasion of the city's (and the country's) final outbreak in the 1640s, which is the subject of Chapter 5. During this 150-year period, the story of plague in Aberdeen itself is one of two halves: before 1550 it was afflicted by two prolonged outbreaks, whereas after 1550 it went almost a century without experiencing the presence of the disease within its bounds at all. Chapter 6 provides an epilogue discussing responses in the north-east to subsequent epidemics further afield (which were almost entirely focused on quarantine and divine appeasement), before considering some possible explanations for Aberdeen's prolonged immunity. In so doing, this book offers a reconsideration of some important aspects of pre-modern urban life as viewed through the lens of plague, including both the challenges and triumphs of the implementation of civic measures during the most trying of times, and the effects of crisis on the articulation of piety and community cohesion.

Notes

1 Charles Creighton, *A History of Epidemics in Britain, vol. I: from A.D. 664 to the Great Plague* [1891] (New York: Barnes and Noble, second edition, 1965), p. 370.
2 UNESCO, *2012 Memory of the World Register*: www.unesco.org.uk/2012-uk-memory-of-the-world-register/#aberdeen.
3 These include: E. Patricia Dennison, David Ditchburn and Michael Lynch (eds.), *Aberdeen Before 1800: A New History* (East Linton: Tuckwell Press, 2002); Alison S. Cameron and Judith A. Stones (eds.), *Aberdeen: An In-depth View of the City's Past* (Edinburgh: Society of Antiquaries of Scotland, 2001); Jane Geddes (ed.), *Medieval Art, Architecture and Archaeology in the Dioceses of Aberdeen and Moray* (Abingdon: Routledge, 2016); and Diane Morgan's *Lost Aberdeen* series, including *Lost Aberdeen: Aberdeen's Lost Architectural Heritage* (Edinburgh: Birlinn, 2004) and *Lost Aberdeen: The Freedom Lands* (Edinburgh: Birlinn, 2009).
4 Robert E. Tyson, "People in the two towns", in Dennison *et al.* (eds.), *Aberdeen Before 1800*, pp. 111–128, at p. 113; Margo Todd, *The Culture of Protestantism in Early Modern Scotland* (New Haven: Yale University Press, 2002), p. 181; M. Flinn (ed.), *Scottish Population History from the Seventeenth Century to the 1930s* (Cambridge: Cambridge University Press, 1977), p. 146.
5 Articles that have discussed plague in Scotland include: Richard D. Oram, "'It cannot be decernit quha are clean and quha are foulle': responses to epidemic disease in sixteenth- and seventeenth-century Scotland", *Renaissance and Reformation* 30:4 (2007), pp. 13–39; Audrey-Beth Fitch, "Assumptions about plague in late medieval Scotland", *Scotia* 11 (1987), pp. 30–40; Charles F. Mullett, "Plague policy in Scotland, 16th–17th centuries", *Osiris* 9 (1950), pp. 435–456; and T.C. Smout, "Coping with plague in sixteenth and seventeenth century Scotland", *Scotia* 2 (1978), pp. 19–33. I should like also to recognise the work of the medical historian John Ritchie, some of whose articles on aspects of plague in Scotland are cited in this book. At the time of his death in 1959 he was working on a manuscript of the subject, now in the archives of the Royal College of Physicians of Edinburgh, which provided the inspiration for some of the section titles in Chapter 3.
6 Among the extensive literature, the following are selected examples of recent case studies: Zlata Blažina Tomič and Vesna Blažina, *Expelling the Plague: The Health Office and the Implementation of Quarantine in Dubrovnik, 1377–1533* (Montreal: McGill-Queens' University Press, 2015); Kristy Wilson Bowers, *Plague and Public Health in Early Modern Seville* (Rochester: University of Rochester Press, 2013); Jane L. Stevens Crawshaw, *Plague Hospitals: Public Health for the City in Early Modern Venice* (Farnham: Ashgate, 2012); Karl-Erik Frandsen, *The Last Plague in the Baltic Region, 1709–1713* (Copenhagen: Museum Tusculanum Press, 2010); Alexandra Parma Cook and Noble David Cook, *The Plague Files: Crisis Management in Sixteenth-Century Seville* (Baton Rouge: Louisiana State University Press, 2009).
7 There is an extensive literature on the topic, to which additions are regularly made in light of new findings. For a comprehensive account of the various theories and arguments surrounding the issue, see Ole Benedictow, *What Disease Was Plague? On the Controversy over the Microbiological Identity of Plague Epidemics of the Past* (Leiden: Brill, 2011). To cite but two examples of the technologies used: Pierre Galanaud, Anne Galanaud and Patrick Giraudoux, "Historical epidemics cartography generated by spatial analysis: mapping the heterogeneity of three medieval 'plagues' in Dijon", *PLoS ONE Online Journal* 10:12 (2015); and M. Thomas, P. Gilbert, Ian Barnes, Matthew J. Collins *et al.*, "Absence of Yersinia pestis-specific DNA in human teeth from five European excavations of putative plague victims", *Microbiology* 150 (2004), pp. 341–354.
8 See, for example, Samuel J. Cohn Jr's sole criticism of Blažina Tomič and Blažina's *Expelling the Plague: The Health Office and the Implementation of Quarantine in*

Dubrovnik, 1377–1533, in which he notes that while the authorities acknowledged this to a 'communicable' disease, the authors discuss it in terms of rats and fleas even though these are not documented in contemporary accounts; Samuel K. Cohn Jr, "Review of Zlata Blažina Tomič and Vesna Blažina, *Expelling the Plague: The Health Office and the Implementation of Quarantine in Dubrovnik, 1377–1533* (Montreal: McGill-Queen's University Press, 2015)", *Bulletin of the History of Medicine* 90:2 (2016), pp. 322–325.

9 J.F.D. Shrewsbury, *A History of Bubonic Plague in the British Isles* (Cambridge: Cambridge University Press, 1970), p. 263.

10 As Vivian Nutton has pointed out: 'after all, if one knows the parameters of a disease, one might be able to draw conclusions about how the disease may have worked in the past'; Vivian Nutton, "Pestilential complexities: understanding medieval plague", *Medical History* Supplement 27 (2008), pp. 1–16.

11 Barbara J. Hawgood, "Alexandre Yersin (1863–1943): discoverer of the plague bacillus, explorer and agronomist", *Journal of Medical Biography* 16:3 (2008), pp. 167–172.

12 W.F. Skene (ed.), *The Historians of Scotland, Vol. IV: John of Fordun's Chronicle of the Scottish Nation* (Edinburgh: Edmonston and Douglas, 1872), p. 359.

13 ACR.9.338 [24 Apr 1514].

14 Robert Chambers, *Domestic Annals of Scotland, from the Reformation to the Revolution*, vol. I (Edinburgh: W. and R. Chambers, third edition, 1874), p. 57.

15 ACR.15.732 [20 Sep 1538].

16 MakLuire concluded from clinical experience of a disease outbreak in 1624 that 'true' plague differed from pestilent (or plague-like) fever because plague (proper) 'afflicts more [individuals]; is more contagious; always affects [the glands in] the groin or axilla; and sometimes causes carbuncles behind the ears or indeed anywhere throughout the body'. Pestilent fever, on the other hand, 'is diagnosed by other symptoms' such as heart palpitations and delirium. Both diseases arose from similar internal and external factors, including the impurity of the air and stagnant waters, and hence could be prevented by similar means including the cleansing of water supplies and the use of vinegar-infused water for washing; James F. McHarg (with a historical introduction by Helen Dingwall), *In Search of Dr John MakLuire: Pioneer Edinburgh Physician Forgotten for Over 300 Years* (Glasgow: Wellcome Unit for the History of Medicine, University of Glasgow, 1997), pp. 74–78.

Bibliography

Benedictow, Ole, *What Disease Was Plague? On the Controversy over the Microbiological Identity of Plague Epidemics of the Past* (Leiden: Brill, 2011).

Blažina Tomič, Zlata and Vesna Blažina, *Expelling the Plague: The Health Office and the Implementation of Quarantine in Dubrovnik, 1377–1533* (Montreal: McGill-Queens' University Press, 2015).

Bowers, Kristy Wilson, *Plague and Public Health in Early Modern Seville* (Rochester: University of Rochester Press, 2013).

Cameron, Alison S. and Judith A. Stones (eds.), *Aberdeen: An In-depth View of the City's Past* (Edinburgh: Society of Antiquaries of Scotland, 2001).

Chambers, Robert, *Domestic Annals of Scotland, from the Reformation to the Revolution*, vol. I (Edinburgh: W. and R. Chambers, third edition, 1874).

Cohn, Samuel K., Jr, "Review of Zlata Blažina Tomič and Vesna Blažina, *Expelling the Plague: The Health Office and the Implementation of Quarantine in Dubrovnik, 1377–1533*

(Montreal: McGill-Queen's University Press, 2015)", *Bulletin of the History of Medicine* 90:2 (2016), pp. 322–325.

Cook, Alexandra Parma and Noble David Cook, *The Plague Files: Crisis Management in Sixteenth-Century Seville* (Baton Rouge: Louisiana State University Press, 2009).

Crawshaw, Jane L. Stevens, *Plague Hospitals: Public Health for the City in Early Modern Venice* (Farnham: Ashgate, 2012).

Creighton, Charles, *A History of Epidemics in Britain, Vol. I: from A.D. 664 to the Great Plague* [1891] (New York: Barnes and Noble, second edition, 1965).

Dennison, E. Patricia, David Ditchburn and Michael Lynch (eds.), *Aberdeen Before 1800: A New History* (East Linton: Tuckwell Press, 2002).

Fitch, Audrey-Beth, "Assumptions about plague in late medieval Scotland", *Scotia* 11 (1987), pp. 30–40.

Flinn, M. (ed.), *Scottish Population History from the Seventeenth Century to the 1930s* (Cambridge: Cambridge University Press, 1977).

Frandsen, Karl-Erik, *The Last Plague in the Baltic Region, 1709–1713* (Copenhagen: Museum Tusculanum Press, 2010).

Galanaud, Pierre, Anne Galanaud and Patrick Giraudoux, "Historical epidemics cartography generated by spatial analysis: mapping the heterogeneity of three medieval 'plagues' in Dijon", *PLoS ONE Online Journal* 10:12 (2015).

Geddes, Jane (ed.), *Medieval Art, Architecture and Archaeology in the Dioceses of Aberdeen and Moray* (Abingdon: Routledge, 2016).

Hawgood, Barbara J., "Alexandre Yersin (1863–1943): discoverer of the plague bacillus, explorer and agronomist", *Journal of Medical Biography* 16:3 (2008), pp. 167–172.

McHarg, James F. (with a historical introduction by Helen Dingwall), *In Search of Dr John MakLuire: Pioneer Edinburgh Physician Forgotten for Over 300 Years* (Glasgow: Wellcome Unit for the History of Medicine, University of Glasgow, 1997).

Morgan, Diane, *Lost Aberdeen: Aberdeen's Lost Architectural Heritage* (Edinburgh: Birlinn, 2004).

Morgan, Diane, *Lost Aberdeen: The Freedom Lands* (Edinburgh: Birlinn, 2009).

Mullett, Charles F., "Plague policy in Scotland, 16th–17th centuries", *Osiris* 9 (1950), pp. 435–456.

Nutton, Vivian, "Pestilential complexities: understanding medieval plague", *Medical History* Supplement 27 (2008), pp. 1–16.

Oram, Richard D., "'It cannot be decernit quha are clean and quha are foulle': responses to epidemic disease in sixteenth- and seventeenth-century Scotland", *Renaissance and Reformation* 30:4 (2007), pp. 13–39.

Shrewsbury, J.F.D., *A History of Bubonic Plague in the British Isles* (Cambridge: Cambridge University Press, 1970).

Skene, W.F. (ed.), *The Historians of Scotland, Vol. IV: John of Fordun's Chronicle of the Scottish Nation* (Edinburgh: Edmonston and Douglas, 1872).

Smout, T.C., "Coping with plague in sixteenth and seventeenth century Scotland", *Scotia* 2 (1978), pp. 19–33.

Thomas, M., P. Gilbert, Ian Barnes, Matthew J. Collins *et al.*, "Absence of Yersinia pestis-specific DNA in human teeth from five European excavations of putative plague victims", *Microbiology* 150 (2004), pp. 341–354.

Todd, Margo, *The Culture of Protestantism in Early Modern Scotland* (New Haven: Yale University Press, 2002).

Tyson, Robert E., "People in the two towns", in E. Patricia Dennison, David Ditchburn and Michael Lynch (eds.), *Aberdeen Before 1800: A New History* (East Linton: Tuckwell Press, 2002), pp. 111–128.

UNESCO, *2012 UK Memory of the World Register*: www.unesco.org.uk/2012-uk-memory-of-the-world-register/#aberdeen.

Acknowledgements

Writing this book has entailed my reacquaintance with Aberdeen, the city in which I lived and studied for a decade after my arrival as a first-year undergraduate in 1992. Some of my favourite memories and most enduring friendships were made during those years, and it is a pleasure to have rekindled them in the course of my research for this project. I'm fortunate that, eased by the wonders of technology, many have stood the test of both time and distance since my relocation to the other side of the globe, where a combination of family connections and a well-timed academic career opportunity brought me in 2004. My time in New Zealand has been substantially enriched by the forging of many important new relationships, both personally and professionally. I would like particularly to thank the following for their support, encouragement and convivial respite on both sides of the world: Anette and Hughie; Fiona; everyone at GEMS; Gretchen and her wonderful family; Joyce; Louise; Rowena; Sally-Anne; Sarah; and Sue and Annie. I'd like also to make special mention of Andrea, Irvin, Yasmin and Dylan (my Manchester family), and of Ali, Seth, Daniel and Lily (my Stirling family). At Massey University, welcome distractions have been provided by many of my colleagues, particularly those who have graciously tolerated my modest contribution to solving the morning quiz on a daily basis. My biggest academic debt is to Professor William Naphy of the University of Aberdeen; I couldn't have asked for a better doctoral supervisor than Bill, and he has unwaveringly supported my academic endeavours ever since. My research for the book was boosted by a Massey University Women's Award in 2007 and has since been facilitated enormously by the generosity of the College of Humanities and Social Sciences thanks to the unstinting support of James Watson and Kerry Taylor, successive Heads of the School of Humanities in its various incarnations. My regular research trips to Scotland were eased by the helpfulness of the staff at each of the archives I visited. I would like especially to thank Phil and his team at Aberdeen City and Aberdeenshire Archives for their immense support during my many visits to their offices. The staff at the University of Aberdeen's Special Collections Centre were equally invaluable. I would also like to record my appreciation of the staff of the following repositories: Edinburgh City Archives; the National Library of Scotland; the National Archives of

Scotland; Dundee City Archives; Local Heritage Services, Elgin; the Highland Archive Centre, Inverness; Special Collections, Mitchell Library, Glasgow; and the Edinburgh and Scottish Collection, Edinburgh Central Library. I would like to extend special thanks to Sandy Riddell for allowing me to consult the archives of St Machar Cathedral, Old Aberdeen. I'd like to thank Jane Richardson for her invaluable mapmaking skills, the editorial staff at Routledge for all their help in the preparation of this book, and Janka Romero (now at CUP) for recognising its potential in the first place. I'm grateful for the insightful comments of the two anonymous referees for Routledge and of the audiences at conferences and seminars to whom I have presented various aspects of this project. Given the all-consuming nature of this book, particularly in its final stages, I'd like to thank the wonderful staff at WES for their understanding, particularly Brigid for her after-hours care, as well as Singing Hands, Mr Tumble and the Wiggles, who all provided the soundtracks to some of the less intellectual aspects of its preparation in their entertainment (and valuable distraction) of one enraptured little boy. Grateful thanks to my parents and Nyree, who have always been my biggest supporters; Mum and Dad both diligently proofread several drafts of the book, and I owe a special debt to Mum, whose grandparental care has far exceeded the call of duty. I would also like to acknowledge Stephen, who in some form or another has lived with the spectre of plague in his midst for the last twenty-one years but, like his pre-modern ancestors, has borne his plight with good grace, forbearance and faith that it could be overcome. Most importantly, this book is dedicated with all my love to Lenny, this little light of mine.

1 Setting the scene

Aberdeen and the north-east

The city of Aberdeen dominated the north-east corner of Scotland, a landmass which contained meandering rivers, boggy marshes and dense woodlands, bounded on two sides by the North Sea. The relatively inhospitable topography of the region's interior naturally made early societies look to seaborne travel as a means of communication and commerce, with settlements being clustered along its coast and along the major rivers such as the Don, the Dee and the Spey.[1] Aberdeen itself grew up between the mouths of the Dee and the Don, and quickly eclipsed neighbouring Old Aberdeen (which lay to the immediate north near the mouth of the Don), even though the latter was the seat of a bishopric whose incumbent, William Elphinstone, was the driving force behind the founding in the burgh of Scotland's third university in 1495. Under this powerful and active churchman and diplomat Old Aberdeen was elevated by the Crown to burgh of barony status, in contrast to Aberdeen proper which, like many of Scotland's ports, was a royal burgh that flourished through its monopoly on overseas trade in the area. Many of the royal burghs that were founded throughout the north-east formed a chain of settlements along the Moray coast as well as along major rivers, but none ever approached Aberdeen in terms of size. Elgin, the largest burgh and seat of government in Moray, had a population of only around 2,500 by 1660,[2] while others such as Inverurie, Kintore and Cullen were 'simply large villages',[3] 'barely distinguishable in size or function' from other rural settlements,[4] over two-thirds of which comprised no more than one hundred inhabitants.[5] Despite periodic checks, Aberdeen's population grew to an estimated 5,500 in the late 1570s and increased to 8,300 just before the final plague outbreak hit in 1647, when it was perhaps double that which it had been in 1500. Thereafter, mirroring a wider trend, it declined to around 7,000 just before the onset in 1695 of a devastating nationwide famine, after which it remained depressed well into the eighteenth century.[6] Though plague constituted one of the periodic checks on population levels prior to 1650, this was to a far lesser extent than elsewhere. This chapter will consider the factors that might have determined the comparatively low incidence of plague outbreaks in Aberdeen and the north-east: regional communications by land and sea; the city's topography, layout and defences; and its administration and governance. Furthermore, the possible social and psychological impact of plague on successive generations will be contextualised by considering notions of community and belonging within the urban environment, in addition to the expression of popular piety and the role of the Church in the north-east.

Communications by land

Aberdeen was connected to its vast hinterland by a network of roads that facilitated myriad land-based interactions between the north-east's major city and the region's other settlements, which ranged from other royal burghs to burghs of barony (founded and controlled by a baron by means of a grant from the monarch) and of regality (over which leading noblemen maintained distinctive judicial powers), down to tiny parish settlements comprising only a handful of houses. The pattern of roads connecting these was dictated by the rivers, boggy ground and hill ranges that abounded throughout the region and which early modern maps clearly indicate loomed large in contemporary mentalities.[7] The river Spey bisected the northern coast of Moray, inhibiting easy access between the north-western burghs of Elgin, Forres, Nairn and Inverness and those on the eastern side of the country such as Peterhead and Fraserburgh, while almost any approach to Aberdeen necessitated crossing either the Dee or the Don. Passage over the Don located to the immediate north of Old Aberdeen was afforded by the fourteenth-century Brig of Balgownie, though this frequently fell into a dilapidated state in spite of the considerable public funds channelled into its upkeep and its status, in the words of Aberdeen's provost in 1605, as 'the most special brig and passage to this town' from Buchan and 'vther pairtis there-abouts'.[8] The Don also impeded the route between Inverurie and Kintore (and on to Aberdeen), and could only be crossed via a suitable ford before the eventual construction of a bridge in 1797.[9]

The same was true of the Dee, whose location presented a considerable obstacle to travel between Aberdeen and the south. Due to that river's size, crossing it was a hazardous undertaking in times of spate, whether by ford or by ferry. Three fords across the Dee existed near Aberdeen, one at Hilldowntree, one opposite the Ruthrieston Burn, and one by the modern Duthie Park. There were also two ferry routes, named Upper and Lower, the former situated at the Crag (or Craig) Lug and now immortalised in the eponymous Ferryhill area of the city,[10] the latter near the mouth of the Dee between the settlements of Torry on the south side of the river and Futty on the north. Each of these means of crossing the Dee gradually fell out of use after 1527 with the completion of a stone bridge, begun under the direction of Bishop William Elphinstone, in which the city council regularly invested in terms of both manpower and materials.[11] In Moray, crossing the Spey had been possible since the thirteenth century by means of ferries whose locations were determined by favoured fording places commemorated today in place names such as Boat of Garten and Boat o' Brig.[12] Other regional rivers including the Nairn, the Findhorn, the Lossie, the Ythan and the Deveron similarly impeded easy land travel, being in most cases passable only by ford throughout the entire plague period.[13]

Whether facilitated by means of a timber or stone bridge, therefore, land travel throughout the north-east was hindered by the various rivers that meandered through the region. Travellers, either on foot or on horseback, were hampered still further by the woeful state of the roads they were required to use. The provision of roads north of the river Forth has been described as 'markedly inferior' compared with those in Scotland's central belt,[14] and their poor condition hindered speedy travel particularly during bouts of inclement weather, when heavy rain could make even major routes difficult to traverse. Aside from the weather, progress could be obstructed by natural barriers such as the large overhanging trees which were required to be moved from the northern end of the Brig o' Balgownie in 1632.[15] The roads throughout Moray and Nairnshire have been described as 'little more than dirt tracks across open moorland, which were muddy at best and impassable at worst', with the 'only well-defined' route in the region for many centuries being the great King's High Way that linked all of the larger settlements from Inverness east to Banff and then down to Aberdeen.[16] Smooth passage between the north-east and the more populous southern centres was impeded by the 'formidable obstacle' of the mountainous region known as the Mounth, which stretched inland between Aberdeen and Stonehaven.[17] Crossing this range could be a 'veritable undertaking' on the poorly maintained roads, with even the most significant of the eight passes in existence being often waterlogged and sometimes impassable.[18]

The various hazards and obstructions to smooth overland travel inconvenienced the individuals who used the north-east's network of roads for a myriad of commercial, social, diplomatic and spiritual pursuits. Such impediments had a significant bearing on responses to plague throughout the region, particularly those in the city of Aberdeen. Efficient travel was crucial for the ability of landowners, civic and Kirk officials alike to exchange timely news and advice about the spread of plague, but for most of Scotland's plague era this had necessarily to be done on an *ad hoc* basis by hired messengers, for whom the average journey between Aberdeen and the administrative capital Edinburgh was still expected in the later seventeenth century to take three days.[19] Even via major routes, travel by land could take a relatively long time: an entire day to traverse the length of the King's High Way on a fast horse with favourable ferry crossings, or three days on foot.[20] So, *prima facie* it would appear that the impracticalities of overland travel hindered individuals and settlements alike in their efforts to establish and extend networks of information regarding plague. However, these aspects were in any case a fact of life no matter the reason for the journey and were obviously surmountable. The extensive links maintained between inhabitants of Aberdeen and their counterparts in other regional burghs clearly show that this network of roads throughout the north-east was 'well-traversed'.[21] As we will see, in the event efficient communications regarding plague were nevertheless maintained and, in fact, built on over time both throughout the region and further afield.

Communications by sea

These communications were maintained not only through land travel but also by sea, the dominant cultural force as the mainstay of the economy and society for those living in the north-east's numerous coastal communities. The region's relative isolation, it has been claimed, meant that inhabitants of these settlements maintained a host of ties that were 'more closely bound up with the continent than with England or even with southern Scotland'.[22] The historiographical annals of Aberdeen's foreign contacts often laud the city's self-attribution in a mid-fourteenth-century letter to the merchants of Bruges as one of the four 'great towns' of Scotland, the others being Dundee, Perth and Edinburgh.[23] On a national level, Aberdeen certainly did rank as an eminent trading port due primarily to two factors, both of which arose from its idiosyncratic location. Firstly, it was sufficiently isolated so as to have no real competition from other royal burghs (for whom overseas trade was a statutory privilege until 1672) that were situated on the coast. What might be termed the entrepôt for the Moray region was Findhorn, which acted as the port for Elgin but whose size both relatively and absolutely meant that it could never have competed commercially with Aberdeen. The city was also situated significantly further north of the other east coast ports through which foreign trade was conducted, with its closest neighbour Dundee located nearly sixty nautical miles to the south.[24] Despite the monopoly on overseas trade enjoyed by Aberdeen and Elgin, there was additionally extremely modest participation in foreign commerce by 'those dwelling to land'[25] in certain burghs of barony and regality (such as the bishop of Moray's haven at Spynie on the river Lossie), which was one aspect of wider animosity between major towns and their hinterlands over the perceived encroachment of each other upon their respective administrative, judicial and commercial affairs.[26] Within a north-east context, therefore, Aberdeen had no commercial competition. The second factor in the city's status as the economic hub of the entire region is the total dominance it had over an agriculturally rich hinterland that was markedly more extensive than that of any other Scottish town.[27] This enabled it to act as the 'central distribution point'[28] for the region's abundant agricultural produce, particularly wool, woolfells, hides and skins, and fish, mainly salmon.[29] The cloth that was produced throughout the north-east was another lucrative product, particularly coarse woollen plaiding of which Aberdeen remained Scotland's main exporter well into the seventeenth century.[30]

For much of the Middle Ages these export commodities found ready markets across the North Sea in Scandinavia, the Baltic, the Low Countries and northern France, making Aberdeen the second busiest Scottish port in the mid-fifteenth century after Edinburgh's port of Leith.[31] Leith's dominance was consolidated as it became the national entrepôt through which merchandise from the north-east and throughout the country was increasingly channelled to be on-sold by foreign middlemen.[32] While smaller and inland burghs continued to send certain produce to be shipped abroad directly from larger ports including Aberdeen, Dundee and Montrose, by the 1530s Leith was exporting a disproportionate amount of most of the nation's staple produce, including some 90% of its wool and 80% of its cloth. Salmon was the sole commodity that continued to be exported mainly from Aberdeen, though the quantity was 'only of modest international importance'.[33] Increasingly this trade was channelled through Leith and by the 1590s many of Aberdeen's merchants were relocating there to make the most of that port's 'superior infrastructure and connections'.[34] By the early sixteenth century, 'very few ships left Aberdeen for either Scandinavia or the Baltic', particularly after the establishment of the Scottish staple at Veere in 1541 drastically reduced the number of the city's direct foreign trading partners. In the absence of statistics it can only be conjectured that more vessels probably arrived into Aberdeen than departed from it, as was the case with Dundee.[35] Nevertheless, by the early seventeenth century there were 'relatively few' ports with which Aberdeen traded; indeed, it has been observed that by this time, 'this was hardly a town with regular international contacts'.[36]

Aside from Veere, the Baltic port of Danzig (modern-day Gdansk) remained the major focus of Aberdeen's overseas exchanges and was the port most frequently identified in civic plague legislation. Flax, used in the production of linen, was a particular target: it was a ubiquitous component of imported cargoes arriving from Danzig to the city (one which comprised 60% of imports to Scotland from the Baltic port in the early sixteenth century);[37] and its organic nature was believed to render it particularly susceptible to harbouring infection. Strong commercial links with the Baltic led many Scots (including Aberdonians) to settle profitably in the region, perhaps as many as 500 in Danzig alone between 1588 and 1649.[38] The funnelling of most Scottish commodities through Leith meant that overseas merchants did not tend to establish communities in many burghs outside of Edinburgh, the north-east included. Aberdeen's direct continental contacts were increasingly 'eclipsed' by extensive inter-regional commercial links, which were maintained both by sea with Moray and east coastal ports as far south as Berwick, and by land with larger burghs such as Forres, Elgin and Banff.[39] The city's businessmen (into whose activities the case study of John Rutherfurd offers valuable insight)[40] focused heavily on inland trade, which was 'the basis of Aberdeen's wealth'.[41] In the early seventeenth century, for example, only about seventy-five of the city's 350 members of the merchant guild traded overseas in any one year.[42] Archaeological finds demonstrate that craftsmen in both Aberdeen and Elgin exploited the resources of their surrounding environments, with the result that the range of crafts practised in Aberdeen was 'remarkably narrow', while Elgin's output was 'small and unexceptional'.[43]

In economic terms, therefore, Aberdeen dominated the north-east but can be considered a comparatively large fish in a rather shallow pond, as within a European context 'Scotland was a relatively small market and Aberdeen only one of its ports'.[44] In national terms, it was perennially one of the country's busiest and most affluent ports, after Leith and Dundee, thanks to its near-monopolisation of the abundant agricultural produce of its hinterland. An evaluation of prices in Aberdeen has indicated that before the mid-sixteenth century it did not experience economic decline to the same extent as other burghs, though in the seventeenth century religious conservatism and the relative lack of mobility into the city's merchant guild might have precipitated a comparative decline in prosperity, which was exacerbated by nationwide political upheaval and plague in the 1640s and the republican government's ban on wool, hide and skin exports for much of the following decade. Nevertheless, the balance of overall trade was such that imports to the north-east included not only necessary raw materials like salt, pitch, iron and wheat but also luxury items such as the satins and velvets sent to Elgin from Edinburgh in 1553, as well as exotic foodstuffs such as spices, almonds and rice.[45]

Although 'it was easier and perhaps safer to travel by sea than by land',[46] vessels wishing to dock in Aberdeen faced a number of challenges. The approach to the harbour from the mouth of the river Dee was notoriously difficult to navigate, with the anchorage being both narrow and shallow. The river's tidal basin was only 600 yards wide and was frequently subject to drifting sand, which created islands known generally as inches and specifically by names such as the Raik and the Flock Pott.[47] The majority of these became submerged at high tide, creating a water level which contemporary historian John Spalding reported as being only thirteen feet high in 1637.[48] Larger vessels at risk of being grounded had therefore to anchor off Torry, a burgh of barony on the south bank of the Dee under the administrative jurisdiction of Aberdeen. Here cargoes would be transferred into smaller boats and transported up the river to the quay head, where from 1582 they would be unloaded by a purpose-built crane.[49] Smaller vessels would commonly anchor at the fishing settlement of Futty closer to the mouth of the Dee from where wares were then transferred by foot or horse and cart up Futty Wynd, passing through the Futty port into the bounds of the city and its commercial heart, the marketplace. A series of efforts were made to improve access for vessels to the harbour, including the creation in 1607 of a bulwark of stone blocks and oak beams to overcome the fluctuating sand bar which further impeded the passage of vessels on the northern approach to the quay, and the removal several years later of a sunken boulder embedded in the centre of the navigable channel.[50] As with other ports with which Aberdeen traded, persistent silting and stormy weather proved endlessly challenging and the harbour required regular upkeep, administered by the council under the charge of the master of harbour work.[51] These conditions may have hindered the efficient conduct of seaborne commerce, but conversely they proved a significant aid in situations where it was desirable to impede the entry of vessels. There were two scenarios in which this was the case: security against enemy attack and efforts to prevent seaborne infection. On such occasions the council made additional use of a round stone Blockhouse constructed in 1532 on the north side of the harbour mouth to replace a smaller wooden defensive structure dating from

1477. The new building was usually used to store weapons and was therefore extremely fortified, having walls that were six feet thick and a lookout on the roof.[52] During plague it acted as a vantage point from which to monitor vessels entering the harbour, and as a relatively isolated building in which to quarantine crews and cargoes suspected of infection. Furthermore, the sandy inches which impeded the smooth passage of larger vessels were used by the council to its advantage to ground ships deemed suspicious. By 1715 Aberdeen's harbour was said to 'afford[s] a most safe station to ships from all winds and tempest',[53] but this book contends that for the majority of the city's plague era the challenges of arrival by sea were to play a significant role in its avoidance of disease.

Aberdeen: topography, layout, defences

Essentially, this was also the case for arrivals to Aberdeen by land. The topography of the region that dictated the course and accessibility of major roadways conspired with the narrow harbour to be a significant help, rather than hindrance, to the city's plague prevention. Indeed, while plague spread extensively throughout the north-east of Scotland and killed indwellers of large burghs and tiny parish settlements alike, on only three occasions did the disease spread throughout the bounds of Aberdeen itself. The fundamental starting point for any settlement in its efforts to prevent the intrusion of plague was to monitor the arrival of every person and every item in order that only those deemed 'clean' (that is, free from infection) could gain entry. Aberdeen's medieval growth around a harbour at the mouth of the Dee was dictated by the surrounding natural features that delineated both its boundaries and its defences, for, in common with most other burghs, it was not walled. To the west lay the Den burn, whose estuary ran into the sea at the Dee to the south. The land to the south-west was comprised of clayhills and marshes, while to the north-east lay a loch which was the city's main water supply.[54] Expansion, therefore, took place to the east and north-east across topographical features such as the Castle Hill and St Katherine's Hill, though the burgh remained fairly compact, extending only to approximately 800 acres in the late seventeenth century.[55]

These natural features also dictated the establishment of the arterial routes leading out of the city, which were mapped together with its street layout in James Gordon's *Description of Bothe Touns of Aberdeene* (1661).[56] The thoroughfare known as the Gallowgate headed north before splitting in two, one branching west to Kintore, Inverurie and points further north-west and the other to Old Aberdeen and from there over the river Don (via the Brig o' Balgownie) to the north where the royal burghs of Peterhead and Fraserburgh were situated. Another road ran to the immediate west through the freedom lands of the Stocket forest and out along Deeside,[57] while another provided an alternative route north to the immediate east of the city close to the coastline. The main route going south out of the city, which has been described as 'the most interesting historic highway in all the north country',[58] first veered south-west and crossed the Den burn by means of the Bow Brig, a sturdy wooden construction rebuilt in stone with a double bow design in 1556.[59] The section between here and the Bridge of Dee was known as the Hardgate, and once it crossed the river it wended its way south over the Mounth to Stonehaven and beyond.

Visitors arriving at Aberdeen via one of these roads typically entered the city through one of six official entrances known as ports (from the French word for gateway), all of which were in existence by 1443. Those journeying from the north or north-west arrived at the port located on the Gallowgate, with the eponymous gallows being situated outside the port to the east. Crossing the Den burn via the Bow Brig from the south, visitors could skirt round St Katherine's Hill either by veering right towards the quay through the Green until they reached the Shiprow (or Trinity) port, or by heading left from where they could enter the city either through a port situated on the Netherkirkgate or, if they continued past the great parish Kirk of St Nicholas, one situated on the Upperkirkgate. These two streets ran down from the Broadgate, leading from that important thoroughfare, as their names suggest, to the church. Approaching the city from the north-east, arrivals entered through the Justice port situated at the top right corner of the burgh's administrative and commercial centre, the Castlegate; it was so named due both to its proximity to an execution site known as the Heading Hill and to its role as the gateway through which condemned criminals could be taken on their final journey to the gallows. The sixth entrance, the Futty port, stood in the south-eastern corner of the Castlegate and provided a check to arrivals from Futty, a fishing village which came under the administrative purview of Aberdeen. Written descriptions indicate that the ports were stone-built archways, perhaps twelve feet wide and fitted with wooden doors which, when closed, could be locked with iron chains, bolts and padlocks. They could be variously embellished: the Gallowgate port boasted the royal arms in colour in the early sixteenth century, while the Justice port was often adorned with the heads of executed criminals as a warning to would-be offenders. Above each archway was a porch that provided a protected vantage point for those on guard duty.[60]

The monitoring of these ports was the first line of defence implemented by Aberdeen's civic authorities when the city came under threat, whether from regional or national enemies, or from plague. This was the case with all arrivals at the city's official entrances, both for those returning home from distant destinations and for those seeking entry to the burgh for any one of myriad purposes, legitimate or otherwise. The ports loomed large in contemporary mentalities about issues of identity and belonging: in addition to serving as 'physical and judicial boundaries' which 'lay at the heart of the definition of a burgh', they were 'a psychological barrier between the town and those outside'.[61] Getting through the port gave the individual access not just to the physical city, but also to the many advantages on offer through participation in the collective common weal of the urban environment. During crises such as plague, when it was crucial to exclude elements which might imperil the social no less than the physical wellbeing of the community, strict restrictions were put in place to delineate very markedly those whose presence ought to be considered legitimate. As a result, 'the monopolisation of the legitimate means of movement by states entailed their successful assertion of the authority to determine who "belonged" and who did not'.[62] The various topographical and geographical idiosyncrasies of the city noted so far – the inhospitable surrounds, the hemmed-in location, the restricted access points, the natural defences – eased considerably the civic duty of monitoring entrance and egress during times of plague (and in so doing embodied contemporary ideologies about social belonging), though as we will see this task was not without its own challenges due not least to the ability to enter the city illicitly given its lack of an outer wall.

Administration and governance

An important aspect of plague prevention was the monitoring not only of comings and goings of individuals and their goods through the burgh's official entrances, but also within the city itself. The town was quartered for administrative purposes, which provided an important conduit for the easier implementation of various aspects of civic plague policy. The south-western quarter, named Green, encompassed the eponymous area extending to the banks of the Dee and was bounded by the Upperkirkgate and Broadgate, while the smallest quarter in terms of size, Futty in the south-east, took in the fishing settlement of the same name as well as St Katherine's Hill and the south side of the Castlegate. In the north-western area of the city, the Even quarter covered the quadrant between the Gallowgate and the marshy loch, while the largest quarter, Crooked, extended east bounded by the Castlegate and Broadgate.[63]

The group of men who formulated, implemented and supervised Aberdeen's plague policy were drawn from a similar socio-economic background as in other towns throughout Scotland and further afield. The principles underlying the make-up of burgh councils were confirmed in nationwide legislation passed in the later fifteenth century: the election of the new council by the old, the choice of officers by both the old and the new incumbents, and the continuation of four members of the old council, a process which resulted in successive councils becoming 'revolved around an in-bred clique of self-perpetuating oligarchs'. Aberdeen provided Scotland's 'most extreme example' of this for much of the pre-modern period, exemplified by the dominance of the Menzies family whose members held the prime post of provost for all but six years between 1507 and 1590.[64] They 'formed the central link in an exceedingly complex chain of power, kinship and patronage' that, together with leading families such as the Gordons, epitomised the symbiotic relationship between the burgh and the hinterland in the political no less than the economic sphere.[65] As we will see, despite the ramifications of ongoing power disputes this situation engendered, there were advantages to be gained from landed involvement in urban politics, particularly concerning the exchange of information throughout the region about plague. This paradigm changed significantly in the second half of the seventeenth century in the wake of the city's final plague outbreak, when the political disruptions of the Cromwellian regime and subsequent Restoration of the Stuart monarchy conspired to prevent the dominance of one particular family and instead created a situation in which fifty-one reconstitutions of the council's make-up occurred between 1649 and 1699.[66]

A significant administrative dimension to burgh affairs was created in the form of a Kirk Session in every parish after the Reformation of 1560. The membership of these Sessions typically overlapped with those of successive councils, with two positive results. Firstly, it enabled a greater degree of participation by the enfranchised minority of the privileged burgess and merchant classes (perhaps one in every twelve of eligible citizens)[67] and, secondly, it engendered close co-operation between the two bodies. This was particularly manifested in the area of social control, albeit for different impetuses, that of the council being the maintenance of public order and the upholding of the ideal of the common weal, while that of the Kirk Session being the enforcement of godly discipline and the reform of moral indiscretions. These apparently distinct concerns became conflated significantly during crises such as plague, which as we will see was interpreted through a lens of providentialism in which infection had a moral no less than a medical genesis. In Aberdeen, political factionalism during the 1640s and 1650s created a fissure between the predominantly royalist council and the Kirk Session dominated by the ardent Presbyterian covenanting minister Andrew Cant.[68] While it has been stated that this rift undermined the efficiency of local administration, Chapter 5 will show that it did not have a significant impact on responses to the city's final outbreak in the late 1640s and that, generally speaking, councils and Kirk Sessions throughout the north-east worked together effectively in the implementation and supervision of measures against plague.

By the time plague first troubled Aberdeen at the end of the fifteenth century its council was well-established, consisting of between twelve and twenty-four members with a dominant inner circle of executive positions: five magistrates, four baillies (each with responsibility for overseeing one of the city's quarters), the dean of guild (who managed commercial affairs) and the treasurer (who controlled the burgh's public accounts), all of whom were presided over by a provost (also known as an alderman). In Scotland's burghs of barony and regality the administration of civic affairs was 'largely at the whim' of their landowner, such as the earl Marischal in the case of Peterhead and in Old Aberdeen the bishop, whose control of civic appointments undermined its council's role as a democratic corporate body.[69] Royal burghs were those upon which the Crown directly bestowed legal, political and commercial privileges such as a monopoly on trade, and the right to hold weekly markets and to regulate their own legal affairs. Councillors in these burghs were ultimately representatives of the monarch and were therefore responsible for the implementation locally of nationally-applicable legislation decreed by the Convention of Royal Burghs, a 'forum for the common interests of towns' which met regularly from the mid-sixteenth century to decide on matters of protection, privilege and proportional taxation, and which aspired to uniformity in the enforcement of its laws.[70] Plague regulations were often decreed at the local level ostensibly within a co-ordinated national framework, but the relative distance of the north-east from the central belt meant that the Edinburgh-based parliament and Privy Council could not always execute their laws effectively, with the result that in that region more so than the central belt measures during outbreaks were characteristically local initiatives implemented in response to specific circumstances. Laws pertaining to local circumstance were formulated at the weekly burgh court, which was presided over by the baillies and attended by all burgesses whose collective assent ('all in one voice') to all laws and statutes was a requirement and to which every member of the community was bound.[71] All governmental, legal and commercial business was conducted in, or supervised from, the tolbooth, which was 'the physical expression of the burgh community' and 'the architectural symbol of corporateness'.[72] Aberdeen's was rebuilt in stone in the late 1610s a short distance along the Castlegate from its earlier, wooden incarnation and naturally sited beside the market which was the focal point of burgh life. New legislation was invariably publicised by being read out at the market cross, to which a copy was subsequently affixed 'so that no man may pretend ignorance'. The emphasis on collective assent and public dissemination of civic decrees legitimised its enforcement for the good of the common weal and ensured no comeback in the event of contravention.

Community and belonging

The formulation of legal statutes for the collective good actualised the early modern emphasis on the importance of collective identity, of belonging to a community united by certain fundamental values and beliefs regardless of variants among its individual members. Within communities throughout the north-east such differences abounded, fuelled by myriad circumstances: neighbourly fallouts over a dilapidated boundary wall or an unpaid debt; professional disputes such as that between Aberdeen's merchants and craftsmen, whose simmering feud over commercial privileges reached its zenith in the 1580s;[73] or deep-rooted kinship allegiances which periodically pitted powerful landed men against the incumbent council and their kinsmen for municipal control. Falconer has drawn attention to the nuances inherent in notions of 'belonging' to a given community, the contestable definition of which might be equated with the notion of the common weal.[74] What constituted the pre-modern burgh is equally debateable, though Dennison has reminded us that contemporaries clearly recognised what differentiated it from other settlements, both as a physical entity and by its 'liberties, privileges [and] power [which] set it apart from the surrounding countryside'.[75] Aberdeen's domination of its hinterland may have amplified these understandings.

Essentially, the privilege of participation in civic life was conferred through being deemed to belong to it, and the benefits of this were jealously protected by its members against external encroachment, which engendered an inherent antagonism towards outsiders. Perhaps the most fundamental division within the urban community was that between migrant incomers and established residents, the criteria for which in Aberdeen were to have been born in the town or to have lived in it for at least seven years. As Winter has shown with regard to the duchy of Brabant, civic leaders might often have wrestled with the tensions between 'the desire for a viable and competitive labour force, on the one hand, and one free of those who would draw on public funds for relief, on the other'.[76] A visitor judged to be 'ane strangear in this cuntra [with] na freyndis' could find him or herself with few rights in Aberdeen, even if their cause was just.[77] There was, after all, considerable variance within the membership of a community between the 'haves' and the 'have-nots', even if one was considered an Aberdonian (or any other demonym). While the social, political and commercial privileges accorded to those residents who were free (a status conferred by merchant or craft guild membership) were denied to those who were unfree (who had no skilled trade and were likely unemployed or unemployable), the unfree who 'belonged' to Aberdeen at least had the vital right to remain there and to claim the community's protection and support during crises such as plague when resources were stretched, bonds of solidarity were strained, and notions of communal entitlement and legitimacy took on particular significance. It is discernible that in Aberdeen, as in German towns, 'such exclusionary policies implied, and consequently fostered, the notion of the trustworthy resident versus the untrustworthy outsider, or the dubious foreigner'.[78] This notwithstanding, McCallum's recent important work on post-Reformation poor relief has shown how Kirk Sessions throughout Scotland could extend their charitable efforts to individuals who did not identify with the parish, but who nevertheless were deemed 'morally worthy of support' through some other criterion such as religious confessional identity.[79]

Piety and the Church in the north-east

The communal identity conferred upon those who 'belonged' to a burgh was but one of multiple overlapping affinities that united individuals at every level of life, taking in family, guild, burgh, parish, diocese and nation.[80] One aspect that provided a sense of unity to each of these collectivities was religious faith; while the Reformation fractured this, at least at the national level, it did not overturn the established ecclesiastical administrative structure of parishes and dioceses. On the contrary, it has been argued that the parish 'remained a dynamic institution long after the Reformation, possibly stimulated rather than enfeebled by the climate of religious and social change' in becoming 'the sole legitimate focus of collective activity'.[81] Within the framework of ecclesiastical administration the north-east of Scotland comprised two dioceses, those of Aberdeen and Moray, each of which was overseen by a bishop from his cathedral seat in Old Aberdeen and in Elgin respectively. Each diocese was subdivided into parishes, each of which acted as a further geographical mechanism by which identity and belonging could be socially and ideologically demarcated, a mode of apportioning responsibility for individuals that was to come to the fore in the treatment of the poor during economic crises such as plague by which traditional forms of support were disrupted. At the heart of each parish was its church, the 'most obvious centre of communal religious experience' and the 'only public building intended for the assembly of the entire local community'.[82] Aberdeen's parish church of St Nicholas dominated the west end of the burgh in the Green quarter and was the largest in Scotland, being more than 200 feet long and 100 feet wide by the early sixteenth century.[83] The parish church provided a vital unifying physical location for all inhabitants, particularly within Scotland's burghs, each one of which (with the exception of Edinburgh) comprised only one parish. The same did not necessarily apply in the rural north-east, where parishes contained many scattered settlements and could be so large that it was difficult to reach the church at all.[84] The diocese of Aberdeen contained something in the region of ninety parishes and that of Moray only seventy-one, significantly fewer than St Andrews with 282, though nevertheless covering a fifth of Scotland's landmass.[85] This presented particular difficulties in the dissemination of orders for fasts from the early seventeenth century, which undermined the ideal of appeasing the omnipotent God during times of plague through a unified show of contrition.

Fasting was one spiritual response to plague epidemics that straddled religious change, which continued to emphasise the importance of repentance to assuage the divine wrath at communal sin that manifested itself as plague and other crises. Two out of three of Aberdeen's outbreaks occurred prior to the Reformation, at a time when believers expressed their faith within the parameters of traditional Catholic teaching: they venerated saints and their relics; went on pilgrimage; participated in the liturgical rituals of the Eucharist; and regarded as crucial the performance of good works to atone for sin and earn divine favour. Each of these was concerned fundamentally with maintaining a correct, ordered relationship with God thereby to improve one's own circumstances both in the present life and for all eternity in the afterlife. Churchmen such as John Watson, employed in 1547 to preach regularly both at St Machar Cathedral in Old Aberdeen and at churches throughout the diocese, pressed these points home in their sermons.[86] Through these, believers understood the efficacy both of preparing for their own death through atonement and of praying for the souls of beloved decedents to alleviate their sufferings after death in purgatory. Sufficiently wealthy individuals could ensure their soul would be remembered by bestowing generous endowments on the Church. There was a 'proliferation' of such endowments in the fourteenth and fifteenth centuries that represented 'the dynamics for change and internal renewal within the later medieval Church'.[87] Commonly this was through the foundation of an altar, chaplainry or chantry, at least thirty of which were founded in St Nicholas Kirk.[88] To give a typical example, in return for Sir John Prat's perpetual endowment of the altar of Saints Thomas and George in the church in 1503, on the anniversary of his death each year residents throughout the burgh were to be admonished to pray for his soul and those of his ancestors, a sung mass was to be celebrated by two clerks, and the Office of the Dead was to be recited 'for the health of my soul, and of the souls aforesaid'.[89] This was a ritualistic prayer cycle for the departed that was commonly celebrated as part of the funeral service, and which was performed in fifteenth-century Aberdeen by clerics wearing black vestments adorned with death's heads.[90] One of its central refrains, 'Timor mortis conturbat me' ('the fear of death unsettles me'), was echoed in William Dunbar's titular poem, which highlighted the ability of sickness to make the prospect of death a stark reality.[91]

While historiography has since tempered the paradigm espoused particularly by Huizinga that medieval Christians were obsessed with death, it is rational to assume that the persistent awareness of this inevitable aspect of one's life was sharpened by epidemics and the other mortality crises which were earthly manifestations of divine wrath.[92] A poem written by Walter Cullen, a sixteenth-century vicar and reader of Aberdeen, begged God to be merciful through its refrain, 'Lord, towrn thy wrathe away'.[93] It was prudent to prepare for a 'good death' by making amends with Him through sincere contrition and repentance. The cleansing of sin through the deathbed sacrament of extreme unction could be administered 'in whatever sickness fear of death is entertained'.[94] Archbishop John Hamilton's *Catechism* (1552) warned Scots that death might come 'as theif cummis on nycht',[95] a prospect which was of particular concern, 'that we suld thus be haistely put doun, and de as beistis without confessioun', as Robert Henryson had described it in his early sixteenth-century poem, 'Ane Prayer for the Pest'.[96] Plague could kill quickly and indiscriminately; it therefore heightened believers' anxiety about dying unprepared and further imperilled their prospects for the afterlife by denying them the associated rituals (not to mention the dignity) of a proper Christian burial, some of which straddled the Reformation.[97]

Representations of death reminded the laity of the seriousness of their plight and the need for the benefits of the Passion.[98] Christ's human suffering through these events was a source of artistic inspiration throughout the north-east, being depicted symbolically by a flaming heart on a pillar in the chapter house of Elgin Cathedral dedicated by Bishop Andrew Stewart (1482–1501), on an exterior wall of Castle Fraser in 1576, and on the seventeenth-century ceiling of Provost Skene's house in Aberdeen.[99] St Nicholas Kirk was home to a large tabernacle depicting the 'most elaborate' of Scotland's visual reminders of the Passion.[100] The tabernacle was a box used to store the Eucharist, which was the central sacramental aspect of the mass in which transubstantiation was believed to occur and which every Christian was supposed to receive at least once a year.[101] The consecrated Host could also be stored in so-called sacrament houses, with that at Cullen being adorned with an inscription reminding believers that the bread and wine contained within were a spiritual food and a source of salvation, while the sacrament houses at Kintore and Auchindoir combined the monograms of Jesus and Mary to remind the faithful of Mary's role in the bringing of the Saviour of humanity.[102]

Mary's status as mother and nurturer of Christ placed her in closest proximity to God and in highest regard among saints given her multiple roles, expressed by the poet William Dunbar as 'oratrice, mediatrice, salvatrice'.[103] The Madonna and Child were depicted in the burgh arms of Banff and Cullen, as well as on the front cover of the fifteenth-century prayer book produced by the Arbuthnott family for use in their parish church dedicated to St Ternan south of Aberdeen.[104] Mary was also celebrated in a play performed in Aberdeen in the early sixteenth century entitled 'The Salutation of the Virgin' and dedications to her were made in a chapel erected at the Bridge of Dee by 1531, and in a number of foundations in Old Aberdeen including the parish church of St Mary ad Nives and a hospital founded beside St Machar Cathedral, while King's College had at least four Marian statues.[105] Individuals displayed their own Marian devotion by funding dedications to her in the form of altars, vestments, statues and paintings.[106] Additionally, a host of other saints were venerated as having an intercessory role between believers and God, and throughout Christendom many gained associations with particular circumstances and ailments due either to their earthly actions or the nature of their specific martyrdom. The parish church of St Nicholas contained altars to at least thirty saints, while St Machar Cathedral in Old Aberdeen possessed the relics of at least fourteen beatified individuals.[107] During the later medieval period there was a rise throughout much of Scotland in the worship of 'an exotic pantheon' of saints that reflected 'the development of new pan-European cults' such as that of the Holy Blood.[108] However, while the Aberdeen Breviary, printed in 1510 under the charge of Bishop William Elphinstone, gave Scotland its own 'large-scale national hagiography',[109] the array of saints to whom believers in the north-east remained devoted reveals a dominant adherence to local figures which reflects an inward, rather than outward, looking spirituality. It would appear that few people embarked on pilgrimages beyond the local area (though scallop shells provide archaeological evidence that there were exceptions),[110] while there is no evidence of adherence to fashionable saints' cults such as those of Catherine of Siena or Birgitta of Sweden which were prevalent elsewhere in Scotland.[111]

One way in which the veneration of saints was manifested in urban centres across Europe was through the staging of religious plays and processions, which were sources of entertainment, didacticism and communal bonding.[112] From at least the mid-fifteenth century, these were regularly put on in

Aberdeen to celebrate particularly the feasts of Corpus Christi and Holy Blood, and were evidently lavish affairs in which considerable time, effort and money were invested by a broad section of inhabitants. The feast of Corpus Christi, a highlight of Aberdeen's urban community calendar, 'may be viewed as the expression of urban unity and wholeness' even if the ideal did not always accord with the reality.[113] It had special resonance through its focus on the physical body and the connotation this had with the ordered social body. Plague was another manifestation of this: physical ailments were interpreted as 'the result of sins, lapses or crimes which had inflicted harm on the social body'.[114] The plays can be read as 'genuine community expressions of religious identity'[115] in which each guild, representing a saint whose earthly life or martyrdom was seen to correlate to the nature of the particular guild's industry, processed through the burgh in reverse order of status (a contentious issue despite statutory regulation)[116] in a symbolic acknowledgement of the central tenets of the Catholic faith. Processions and plays served an important didactic function, being 'excellent forums' for impressing on participants (both active and passive) the role of saints as intercessors and exemplars, the perils of sin and the significance of the Passion to human salvation.[117] The plays in Aberdeen came to be supervised by the local figures of 'unreason' and 'bon accord', who assumed various titular roles including Lord and Abbot and in so doing combined a sign of authority with a purview of misrule.[118] They acted as 'a kind of anti-provost' in charge of a controlled period of revelry that provided inhabitants of all social strata with an outlet for simmering disaffection with the burgh.[119] The banning of these figures in 1555 was part of a wider concern by authorities in Aberdeen and elsewhere to suppress any hint of disorder, which also saw the council restricting carnivalesque festivities as being 'neither profitable nor godly'.[120] There is also evidence that the popularity of religious plays in Aberdeen declined during the first half of the sixteenth century, which forced the council on several occasions to compel craft participation. While this has been attributed to the expense involved, it is arguably another indication of the relatively muted adherence in Aberdeen to outward civic piety.[121]

The Reformation swept away many of these fundamental tenets of Catholic belief, with the most radical change being the elimination of the doctrine of purgatory and the shunning of good works in favour of a focus on faith alone as a means to secure a contented afterlife.[122] By the time of Aberdeen's third and final outbreak, the Reformation had officially gained widespread acceptance throughout the north-east, though this was a relatively slow and uneven process which helped to ensure that the region remained 'a centre of recusant Roman Catholicism and became the heartland of Scottish Episcopalianism'.[123] This was thanks in part to the Gordons of Huntly and other powerful Catholic landowning families, who during the early decades provided 'a regional bulwark' against the spread of Protestantism.[124] A reluctance to accept the Reformed faith might also have been due to the ongoing programme of liturgical reform that had been set in motion decades previously by Bishop

William Elphinstone and a cohort of local clergy and laymen termed 'Aberdeen Liturgists', whose efforts 'laid the foundations for the enduring and distinctive religious culture of north-east Scotland'.[125]

Scholarship on the Reformation in Aberdeen itself has shown that the city authorities accepted the Reformed faith 'only reluctantly and under considerable political pressure'; the newly established Kirk Session contained several known Catholics into the 1570s and 'genuine conversion' within some families might have taken generations.[126] It was Reformers from the south who were responsible for much of the 'orgy of vandalism' of ecclesiastical buildings in the Aberdeen area, including most of its friaries and chapels as well as St Nicholas Kirk and St Machar Cathedral.[127] These two most important ecclesiastical structures were remodelled to accommodate the liturgical demands of the Reformed faith, with St Nicholas Kirk being split into two preaching churches by the end of the sixteenth century and St Machar Cathedral relegated to the parish church of Old Machar, superseding that of St Mary ad Nives.[128] The Reformation also led to the appropriation for secular purposes of the property belonging to the city's four orders of friars, the same fate which befell the convents of Dominicans and Observant Franciscans in Elgin and Inverness, among other burghs.[129] The buildings owned by the Trinitarians in the Green were used by William Guild in 1631 to build a hospital and meeting house for the city's seven Incorporated Trades,[130] while the lands of the other three – those of the Observant Franciscans, the Dominicans and the Carmelites – passed through the hands of various owners including the council before being put towards the Protestant college founded by George Keith in 1593 to rival King's in Old Aberdeen.[131]

The health of the people

The former Carmelite friary mentioned above is but one of the numerous sites in pre-modern Aberdeen to have undergone extensive excavation in recent decades under the charge of the city council's Archaeology Service (formerly the Archaeological Unit). Its exciting findings have been garnered from meticulous digs spread throughout many significant areas of the built-up environment including the Gallowgate, the Upperkirkgate, the Green, the Shiprow, Broadgate and, more recently, the east chapel of St Nicholas Kirk and on the site of the present Robert Gordon University.[132] Aberdeen is just one of the many burghs (including others across the north-east) to have been subjected to archaeological investigation as part of the Scottish Burgh Survey first embarked upon in the 1970s, the results of which have been published in an ongoing series.[133] Falconer has drawn attention to the increasing historiographical recognition of the 'crucial' value of archaeological findings in augmenting the documentary evidence for life in Scotland's pre-modern burghs.[134] These have enabled an exponential understanding of many aspects of urban living, from the sorts of buildings in which inhabitants lived and worked to the kinds of clothes they wore and the different foods they ate, all of which impinged upon their health.[135]

The evidence indicates that Aberdonians and their counterparts across the north-east lived in conditions typical of the pre-modern urban environment. Many of Aberdeen's poorer residents lived cheek by jowl in cramped post-and-wattle dwellings several storeys tall, the upper floors of which were reached by wooden forestairs. Stretching away behind each building were the backlands, used for various purposes from orchards to cesspits, forming a distinctive aerial herringbone pattern evident from maps of the burgh such as that created in 1661 by James Gordon. Then as now, the rich fared better than the poor and relatively spacious and opulent standards of living were enjoyed by those who lived in Aberdeen's better quality houses, clustered along such streets as the Castlegate, the Gallowgate and the Upperkirkgate. Some of these contained well-tended gardens and archaeology has revealed little evidence here of the midden deposits that were common in areas such as Broadgate, where most craft activity – such as pottery, tanning, leatherwork and butchery – took place.[136] The relatively large number of animal bones excavated throughout the town is testament to the variety of animals many households had, which included pigs, sheep, chickens, horses and cows. Most of these roamed freely and mixed with individuals from every social strata; the magistrate hurrying to his weekly council meeting, passing the servant on her way to collect her master's new shoes from the cordwainer, the fruit seller carrying her basket of apples to market and the ragged cripple hoping she might take pity on him and drop one in his begging bowl. Each had his or her own concerns and preoccupations, and in his or her own way each belonged to the community and contributed to its fluctuating fortunes.

To whom did these people turn for medical care? The hospitals that were scattered throughout the north-east (including in Rathven, Turriff, Elgin and Newburgh as well as Old and New Aberdeen) were characteristically small and catered to pilgrims, passing travellers, the elderly and the crippled. None of them, even the leper house dedicated to St Peter, which stood midway between Old and New Aberdeen, offered little in the way of healthcare as we would understand it today; as McCallum has cautioned, 'it is misleading to focus too closely on medical treatment when examining the early modern hospital'. His recent pioneering work has shown that the characteristics of the Scottish hospitals in this period fell somewhere between those of the Middle Ages, which typically were 'ecclesiastical institutions with obvious charitable intentions' whose proprietors were concerned with healing the spiritual as much as the physical body, and the eighteenth-century forerunners of modern centres providing 'professional medical care in a secular rather than ecclesiastical setting'.[137] If hospitals could not be relied upon as a source of healthcare, what (or who) could? As Chapter 2 will show, the endowment by King James IV of a Chair in Medicine (known as mediciner) at the newly-founded King's College in Old Aberdeen entailed the presence from the early sixteenth century of a learned physician in the vicinity of Aberdeen. But aside from the first incumbent there is no evidence that any of them combined their employment at the university with operating a private practice in the city; even if they did, their services would have been unaffordable to all but the richest inhabitants. There were occasional references to the presence in the city of other qualified physicians aside from the mediciner, including Mr Quintine Prestoun, 'professor of phisick' who in 1596, with the aid of an assistant, opened the city's first apothecary shop 'for the better furneising of this burgh and of the cuntrie of all sort of physicall and chirurgicall medicamentis'.[138] Most inhabitants of Aberdeen, and perhaps of other larger burghs throughout the north-east, would have turned to the resident barbers, who used their blades not only for depilation but also to perform regular bloodletting both for prophylactic and remedial purposes in the face of a host of ailments, as well as to heal ('leiche') injuries. Though the number of barbers in Aberdeen was always modest, their presence (and perhaps popularity) grew exponentially from the outset of the sixteenth century, leading in 1537 to their guild incorporation, which gave them the same rights of self-regulation as other crafts.[139]

The traditional paradigm of the pre-modern urban environment is one of noxious filth, though Skelton and others have emphasised that recorded instances of unhygienic practices might have been the exception rather than the rule and that civic authorities were by no means disinterested in the regulation of sanitation.[140] Nevertheless, such efforts only sometimes coincided with the threat or presence of disease, and were also made in consideration of special occasions such as the visit of James IV's queen Margaret, whose sojourn to 'blyth and blisfull' Aberdeen in 1511 was celebrated in verse by William Dunbar.[141] Street-cleaning was occasionally called for, supervised in the burgh from the later fifteenth century by a specially appointed council official, but this appears to have been motivated by a desire to ease access rather than a concern with hygiene; to clear the streets rather than cleanse them.[142] Over time the council made attempts to enhance their condition through rudimentary cobbling or paving and guttering, and further regulated the state of the environment through orders for the removal of midden deposits, the restraining of domesticated animals such as 'swyne tyke [and] catte', and the control of unclean trades such as butchery and tanning.[143] But these were perhaps more concerned with limiting anti-social behaviour and improving the appearance of the environment rather than the cleanliness of it.[144] This is not to deny a perceived causal link between dirt and disease, as Chapter 2 will show; however, civic efforts to prevent plague were rather more focused on preventing external sources of infection from entering the environment rather than tackling those potential generators within it. In this regard Aberdeen's councillors had much in common with their counterparts in England, for whom a concern with cleanliness informed government rhetoric more so than practical action and was in any case 'as much about order as about medicine'.[145]

As studies of the relationship between epidemics and the built environment have shown, unsanitary conditions naturally had adverse implications for the health of the people.[146] Archaeological finds indicate that for many Aberdonians, 'life must have been short, brutal and painful'.[147] Childhood mortality was high, with diseases such as influenza, diphtheria, whooping cough and measles routinely proving fatal to many youngsters. Almost half of the skeletons excavated on the site of the Carmelite Friary were under twenty-five, while 53% of those buried in one of Aberdeen's medieval graveyards had died before the age of six and only 3% of the almost 900 articulated skeletons uncovered in the east chapel of St Nicholas Kirk lived past the age of fifty.[148] Many of those who survived childhood found themselves beset by chronic conditions including poor dental health, arthritis, and osteoporosis leading to fractures. In addition to chronic conditions tuberculosis, leukaemia and cancerous tumours also afflicted individuals. Fish, chicken and grains such as barley and oats were staples of the typical diet, which offered little variety. Endemic parasitic infection, especially in conjunction with poor standards of hygiene and nutrition, may have been have been 'an important factor' in the susceptibility of people to illness.[149]

It is not inconceivable that this inherent susceptibility extended to plague, regardless of which modern clinical identification one might attribute to it, particularly when compounded by other diseases such as typhus and by inclement weather producing episodic food shortages. Additionally, this chapter has considered various other factors that might have had a different kind of bearing on the susceptibility of Aberdonians to plague. The city's coastal location and the topography of its hinterlands conspired to inhibit easy access whether by sea or by land, and facilitated civic efforts to monitor those who sought entrance for a host of economic, diplomatic, spiritual, intellectual or social purposes. Its relative distance from the central belt engendered a sense of semi-autonomous self-reliance that was enhanced by its total dominance of an extensive hinterland, with which it necessarily maintained a symbiotic relationship. From across the north-east the encroachment of landed men and rural migrants alike could variously enhance and endanger civic harmony among its urban community, members of which remained largely united in spiritual belief and expression, as well as by a determination to protect the rights and privileges of those deemed to belong to the common weal. It remains in the rest of this book to investigate how these aspects were affected by the repeated threat of plague throughout the north-east and beyond.

Notes

1 Richard Oram, "The medieval Church in the dioceses of Aberdeen and Moray", in Jane Geddes (ed.), *Medieval Art, Architecture and Archaeology in the Dioceses of Aberdeen and Moray* (Routledge: Abingdon, 2016), pp. 16–32, at p. 17.

2 Bruce B. Bishop, *Lost Moray and Nairn* (Edinburgh: Birlinn, 2010), p. 103.

3 Oram, "The medieval Church in the dioceses of Aberdeen and Moray", p. 16.
4 Ian Whyte, "Agriculture in Aberdeenshire in the seventeenth and early eighteenth centuries: continuity and change", in David Stevenson (ed.), *From Lairds to Louns: Country and Burgh Life in Aberdeen, 1600–1800* (Aberdeen: Aberdeen University Press, 1986), pp. 10–31, at pp. 18–19.
5 Daniel MacCannell, *Lost Banff and Buchan* (Edinburgh: Birlinn, 2012), p. 14.
6 Robert E. Tyson, "People in the two towns", in E. Patricia Dennison, David Ditchburn and Michael Lynch (eds), *Aberdeen Before 1800: A New History* (East Linton: Tuckwell Press, 2002), pp. 111–128, at p. 112.
7 See, for example, Christopher Fleet, Margaret Wilkes and Charles W.J. Withers, *Scotland: Mapping the Nation* (Edinburgh: Birlinn, 2011), particularly the maps of the north-east created by Robert Gordon of Straloch and his son James Gordon of Rothiemay in the seventeenth century.
8 Alexander Smith, *The History and Antiquities of New and Old Aberdeen* (Aberdeen: Alexander Murray, 1882), p. 138.
9 Robert Gourlay and Anne Turner, *Historic Inverurie: The Archaeological Implications of Development* (Glasgow: Scottish Burgh Survey, 1977), p. 5.
10 William Kennedy, *Annals of Aberdeen, from the Reign of King William the Lion, to the End of the Year 1818* (London: Brown, 1818), p. 416.
11 Stewart D. Redwood, "The history of the ferries across the river Dee at Aberdeen", *Northern Scotland* 14:1 (1994), pp. 1–25, at pp. 1–8, 21; Fenton Wyness, *City by the Grey North Sea: Aberdeen* (Aberdeen: Impulse Books, 1972), p. 58; G.M. Fraser, *The Bridge of Dee: Its History, its Structural Features and its Sculptures* (Aberdeen: Bon-Accord Press, 1913).
12 G.W.S. Barrow, "Land routes: the medieval evidence", in Alexander Fenton and Geoffrey Stell (eds), *Loads and Roads in Scotland and Beyond: Land Transport over 6000 Years* (Edinburgh: John Donald, 1984), pp. 49–66, at p. 60.
13 A stone bridge was built over the river Nairn in 1631, but it and later replacements were frequently damaged by flooding. The river Findhorn was passable via the eponymous Waterford to the north-west of Forres, while the Lossie could be crossed via a seventeenth-century bridge at Oldmills which brought the traveller to Elgin; Bishop, *Lost Moray and Nairn*, p. 228. The Deveron, which delineated the eastern boundary of Banff, was only crossable by ferry or ford until 1763; Robert Gourlay and Anne Turner, *Historic Banff: The Archaeological Implications of Development* (Glasgow: Scottish Burgh Survey, 1977), p. 5. See also Ted Ruddock, "Bridges and roads in Scotland: 1400–1750", in Fenton and Stell (eds), *Loads and Roads in Scotland and Beyond*, pp. 67–91.
14 Barrow, "Land routes: the medieval evidence", p. 55.
15 ACR.52:1.51 [18 Apr 1632].
16 Bishop, *Lost Moray and Nairn*, p. 227.
17 Wyness, *City by the Grey North Sea*, p. 57; Michael Lynch and David Ditchburn, "Economic development", in Peter G.B. McNeill and Hector L. MacQueen (eds), *Atlas of Scottish History to 1707* (Edinburgh: The Scottish Medievalists and Department of Geography, University of Edinburgh, 1996), pp. 231–328, at p. 238.
18 Wyness, *City by the Grey North Sea*, p. 58; Barrow, "Land routes: the medieval evidence", p. 55.
19 This included overnight stops in Montrose and Dundee; Gordon DesBrisay, *Authority and Discipline in Aberdeen, 1650–1700* (University of St Andrews, unpublished PhD thesis, 1989), p. 236.
20 Bishop, *Lost Moray and Nairn*, p. 230.
21 David Ditchburn, "Locating Aberdeen and Elgin in the later Middle Ages: regional, national and international paradigms", in Geddes (ed.), *Medieval Art, Architecture and Archaeology in the Dioceses of Aberdeen and Moray*, pp. 1–15, at p. 9.

22 Wyness, *City by the Grey North Sea*, p. 57.
23 For example, this is mentioned on four separate occasions in Dennison *et al.* (eds), *Aberdeen Before 1800*, pp. xxvi, 111, 160, 348.
24 Edda Frankot, *'Of Laws of Ships and Shipmen': Medieval Maritime Law and its Practice in Urban Northern Europe* (Edinburgh: Edinburgh University Press, 2012), p. 54.
25 As the council complained to the king in 1502; Ditchburn, "Locating Aberdeen and Elgin in the later Middle Ages", p. 9.
26 For more on the complexities of regional trading patterns in the north-east, see Andrew Gibb and Ronan Paddison, "The rise and fall of burghal monopolies in Scotland: the case of the north east", *Scottish Geographical Magazine* 99:3 (1983), pp. 130–140, which traces the rise of non-burghal markets and the steady erosion of the trading monopolies enjoyed by royal burghs in the region that were increasingly 'seen as obstacles to the free development of commerce' (p. 136).
27 Edda Frankot, "Aberdeen and the east coast of Scotland: autonomy on the periphery", in Wim Blockmans, Mikhail Krom and Justyna Wubs-Mrozewicz (eds), *The Routledge Handbook of Maritime Trade around Europe, 1300–1600: Commercial Networks and Urban Autonomy* (Abingdon: Routledge, 2017), pp. 411–427, at pp. 412–414.
28 Frankot, *'Of Laws of Ships and Shipmen'*, p. 54.
29 'Sales of salmon [in particular] contributed towards the conspicuous consumption of the leading members of Aberdeen society': David Ditchburn, "Salmon, salt and the internationalization of Aberdeen's economy in the later Middle Ages", in Jesús Ángel Solórzano Telechea, Beatriz Arízaga Bolumburu and Michel Bochaca (eds), *Las Sociedades Portuarias de la Europa Atlántica en la Edad Media* (Logroño: Instituto de Estudios Riojanos, 2016), pp. 49–66, at p. 58; Ditchburn, "Locating Aberdeen and Elgin in the later Middle Ages", p. 5; David Ditchburn, "Cargoes and commodities: Aberdeen's trade with Scandinavia and the Baltic, c.1302–c.1542", *Northern Studies* 27 (1990), pp. 12–22, at p. 16; David Ditchburn, "The pirate, the policeman and the pantomime star: Aberdeen's alternative economy in the early fifteenth century", *Northern Scotland* 12 (1992), pp. 19–34.
30 Whyte, "Agriculture in Aberdeenshire", p. 20; Ian Blanchard, Elizabeth Gemmill, Nicholas Mayhew and Ian D. Whyte, "The economy: town and country", in Dennison *et al.* (eds), *Aberdeen Before 1800*, pp. 129–158, at pp. 157–158. It was briefly even exported via Dutch traders across the Atlantic to Brazil; Gordon DesBrisay, "Aberdeen and the Dutch Atlantic: women and woollens in the seventeenth century", in Douglas Catterall and Jodi Campbell (eds), *Women in Port: Gendering Communities, Economies, and Social Networks in Atlantic Port Cities, 1500–1800* (Leiden: Brill, 2012), pp. 69–102.
31 Frankot, "Aberdeen and the east coast of Scotland", p. 413.
32 Ditchburn, "Locating Aberdeen and Elgin in the later Middle Ages", pp. 9–10.
33 Ditchburn, "Salmon, salt and the internationalization of Aberdeen's economy in the later Middle Ages", p. 65.
34 Frankot, "Aberdeen and the east coast of Scotland", p. 416.
35 Ditchburn, "Cargoes and commodities", pp. 19–20.
36 Duncan MacNiven, "Merchants and traders in early seventeenth century Aberdeen", in Stevenson (ed.), *From Lairds to Louns*, pp. 57–69, at p. 59; Ditchburn, "Locating Aberdeen and Elgin in the later Middle Ages", p. 9.
37 Frankot, "Aberdeen and the east coast of Scotland", p. 415.
38 Waldemar Kowalski, *The Great Immigration: Scots in Cracow and Little Poland, circa 1500–1660* (Leiden: Brill, 2016), p. 8; Jaroslav Miller, *Urban Societies in East-Central Europe, 1500–1700* (Farnham: Ashgate, 2008), p. 52, notes that 30–40,000 Scots immigrated to Poland during the first half of the seventeenth century; see

also Peter Paul Bajer, *Scots in the Polish-Lithuanian Commonwealth, 16th to 18th Centuries: The Formation and Disappearance of an Ethnic Group* (Leiden: Brill, 2012); David Dobson, *Scots in Poland, Russia and the Baltic States: 1550–1850* (Baltimore: Clearfield, 2000); Maria Bogucka, "Scots in Gdansk (Danzig) in the seventeenth century", in Allan I. Macinnes, Thomas Riis and Frederik Pedersen (eds), *Ships, Guns, and Bibles in the North Sea and Baltic States, c. 1350–c. 1700* (East Linton: Tuckwell, 2000), pp. 39–46.

39 Ditchburn, "Locating Aberdeen and Elgin in the later Middle Ages", p. 10.

40 Harold W. Booton, "Sir John Rutherfurd: a fifteenth century Aberdeen burgess", *Scottish Economic & Social History* 10:1 (1990), pp. 21–37.

41 Frankot, "Aberdeen and the east coast of Scotland", p. 413; Harold W. Booton, "Inland trade: a study of Aberdeen in the later Middle Ages", in Michael Lynch, Michael Spearman and Geoffrey Stell (eds), *The Scottish Medieval Town* (Edinburgh: John Donald, 1988), pp. 148–160.

42 MacNiven, "Merchants and traders in early seventeenth century Aberdeen", p. 57.

43 Ditchburn, "Locating Aberdeen and Elgin in the later Middle Ages", pp. 8–9.

44 Frankot, "Aberdeen and the east coast of Scotland", p. 413.

45 Nicholas Mayhew and Elizabeth Gemmill, *Changing Values in Medieval Scotland: A Study of Prices, Money, and Weights and Measures* (Cambridge: Cambridge University Press, 1995), especially Chapter 3, "Prices in medieval Aberdeen", pp. 25–80; Ditchburn, "Salmon, salt and the internationalization of Aberdeen's economy in the later Middle Ages", pp. 58, 62; Lynch and Ditchburn, "Economic development", pp. 231–328; MacNiven, "Merchants and traders in early seventeenth century Aberdeen", pp. 57–69; Gordon Jackson, "The economy: Aberdeen and the sea", in Dennison *et al.* (eds), *Aberdeen Before 1800*, pp. 159–180, at pp. 165–168; Ditchburn, "Locating Aberdeen and Elgin in the later Middle Ages", p. 10.

46 Wyness, *City by the Grey North Sea*, p. 57.

47 Louise B. Taylor, *Aberdeen Shore Works Accounts, 1596–1670* (Aberdeen: Aberdeen University Press, 1972), p. 2.

48 Smith, *The History and Antiquities of New and Old Aberdeen*, p. 37.

49 Case studies show that shallow waters were a problem for many ports, from the south of England to the Baltic, which also required larger vessels to unload their cargoes into smaller boats in the road for transferral to the quayside; Przemysław Smolarek, "Ships and ports in Pomorze", pp. 51–60, at p. 59; C.G. Henderson, "Exeter", pp. 119–122, at p. 119: both in Gustav Milne and Brian Hobley (eds), *Waterfront Archaeology in Britain and Northern Europe* (London: Council for British Archaeology, Research Report no. 41, 1981). There was even a short-lived and fanciful scheme proposed in 1636 to straighten the river Forth at its narrower reaches, which 'vessels of goode burden are hindered to go up'; David Stevenson, "A note on a scheme to straighten the river Forth in 1636", *Scottish Economic and Social History* 17:1 (1997), pp. 65–68, at p. 67.

50 Wyness, *City by the Grey North Sea*, pp. 201–202.

51 Angus Graham, "Archaeological notes in some harbours in eastern Scotland", *Proceedings of the Society of Antiquaries of Scotland* 101 (1968–69), pp. 200–285. Shifting sand banks forced Banff's harbour to be relocated from the mouth of the river Deveron to the immediate west of it, a prolonged process which took well over a century after its commencement in 1625; Laura Bailey, Tim Holden, Julie Franklin, Catherine Smith and Ruby Cerón-Carrasco, "An archaeological excavation of a medieval fishermen's midden at Castle Hill Pumping Station, Banff", *Scottish Archaeological Journal* 36–37:1 (2014–15), pp. 1–35, at p. 8.

52 It was thirty-six feet in length and eighteen feet wide; ACR.14.118 [20 Feb 1532].
53 [Sir Samuel Forbes of Foveran], "Description of Aberdeenshire, by Sir Samuel Forbes of Foveran, MDCCXVI–MDCCXVII", in Joseph Robertson (ed.), *Collections for a History of the Shires of Aberdeen and Banff* (Aberdeen: Spalding Club, 1843), pp. 31–59, at p. 47.
54 These features gave the city 'a considerable degree of natural defence'; J.C. Murray, "Conclusions", in J.C. Murray (ed.), *Excavations in the Medieval Burgh of Aberdeen, 1973–81* (Edinburgh: Society of Antiquaries of Scotland, 1982), pp. 244–249, at p. 246.
55 Wyness, *City by the Grey North Sea*, p. 17; E.P.D. Torrie, "The early urban site of New Aberdeen: a reappraisal of the evidence", *Northern Scotland* 12:1 (1992), pp. 1–18, at p. 15; DesBrisay, *Authority and Discipline in Aberdeen*, p. 132.
56 James Gordon, *Abredoniae Utriusque Descriptio Topographica: A Description of Bothe Touns of Aberdeene* [1661] [edited by C. Innes] (Edinburgh: Spalding Club, 1842).
57 For more on Aberdeen's freedom lands, first granted by royal charter in 1319, see Diane Morgan, *Lost Aberdeen: The Freedom Lands* (Edinburgh: Birlinn, 2009).
58 G.M. Fraser, *The Old Deeside Road (Aberdeen to Braemar): Its Course, History, and Associations* (Aberdeen: Aberdeen University Press, 1921), p. 4.
59 ACR.22.458 [2 Jan 1556].
60 Diane Morgan, *Lost Aberdeen: Aberdeen's Lost Architectural Heritage* (Edinburgh: Birlinn, 2004), pp. 87–88; Wyness, *City by the Grey North Sea*, pp. 67–69.
61 Ranald MacInnes, *The Aberdeen Guide* (Edinburgh: Birlinn, 2000), p. 144; E. Patricia Dennison, "Power to the people? The myth of the medieval burgh community", in Sally M. Foster, Allan I. Macinnes and Ranald MacInnes (eds), *Scottish Power Centres: From the Early Middle Ages to the Twentieth Century* (Glasgow: Cruithne, 1998), pp. 100–131, at p. 102.
62 John Torpey, *The Invention of the Passport: Surveillance, Citizenship and the State* (Cambridge: Cambridge University Press, 2000), p. 20.
63 Notwithstanding considerable fluctuations over time, stent and valuation rolls indicate that the highest taxpayers were evenly distributed throughout the burgh and that Aberdeen 'did not have a genuine poor quarter'; Lynch and Ditchburn, "Economic development", p. 316; Tyson, "People in the two towns", pp. 124–128.
64 DesBrisay, *Authority and Discipline in Aberdeen*, p. 257; Allan White, "The Menzies era: sixteenth-century politics", in Dennison *et al.* (eds), *Aberdeen Before 1800*, pp. 224–237.
65 Dennison, "Power to the people?", p. 111.
66 DesBrisay, *Authority and Discipline in Aberdeen*, p. 259. Aberdeen's local governance in this period might be likened to that of Oxford, about which the epithets of 'accessible hierarchy' and 'porous oligarchy' have been used; Carl I. Hammer Jr, "Anatomy of an oligarchy: the Oxford town council in the fifteenth and sixteenth centuries", *Journal of British Studies* 18:1 (1978), pp. 1–27, at p. 11.
67 DesBrisay, *Authority and Discipline in Aberdeen*, p. 42.
68 DesBrisay, *Authority and Discipline in Aberdeen*, pp. 296–297.
69 Anne Turner Simpson and Sylvia Stevenson, *Historic Peterhead: The Archaeological Implications of Development* (Glasgow: Scottish Burgh Survey, 1982), p. 2; Wyness, *City by the Grey North Sea*, pp. 110–111.
70 Ian H. Adams, *The Making of Urban Scotland* (London: Croom Helm, 1978), p. 45; Theodora Pagan, *The Convention of the Royal Burghs of Scotland* (Glasgow: Glasgow University Press, 1926), pp. 2–4.
71 Frankot, *'Of Laws of Ships and Shipmen'*, p. 56.
72 Torrie, "The early urban site of New Aberdeen", p. 8.

73 Pagan, *The Convention of the Royal Burghs of Scotland*, p. 80; Harold Booton, "The craftsmen of Aberdeen between 1400 and 1550", *Northern Scotland* 13:1 (1993), pp. 1–19. Stephen Bowman's recent examination of the power wielded by the crafts in the burghs concluded that, across the board, they 'were attempting to reconcile social and commercial realities with what they regarded as their rightful status and authority within burgh society'; Stephen Bowman, "'By hammer in hand all arts do stand': the protection and projection of craft privilege in the early modern Scottish burgh", in Kate Buchanan and Lucinda H.S. Dean, with Michael Penman (eds), *Medieval and Early Modern Representations of Authority in Scotland and the British Isles* (Abingdon: Routledge, 2016).

74 J.R.D. Falconer, *Crime and Community in Reformation Scotland: Negotiating Power in a Burgh Society* (London: Pickering and Chatto, 2013), p. 24; Dennison, "Power to the people?", *passim*; Elizabeth Ewan, *Townlife in Fourteenth-Century Scotland* (Edinburgh: Edinburgh University Press, 1990), pp. 136–160 traces the development of such notions in line with the establishment of individual burghs. Many different types of 'community' may be identified within early modern societies, but it is above all important to recognise 'both the complexity and, in many cases, the unexpected flexibility of community definitions and boundaries in early modern Europe'; Karen E. Spierling and Michael J. Halvorson, "Introduction: definitions of community in early modern Europe", in Michael J. Halvorson and Karen E. Spierling (eds), *Defining Community in Early Modern Europe* (Ashgate: Aldershot, 2008), pp. 1–23, at p. 1. It is equally important to acknowledge that, in the classification of marginal groups, 'social boundaries were not necessarily a "top down" initiative and were often contested by many of the groups considered to be marginal to society in the past'; Jane L. Stevens Crawshaw, "Introduction", in Andrew Spicer and Jane L. Stevens Crawshaw (eds), *The Place of the Social Margins, 1350–1750* (Abingdon: Routledge, 2017), pp. 1–17, at p. 4.

75 Dennison, "Power to the people?", pp. 102–103;

> if the medieval burgh is to be recognised as a power centre it must be assessed as a force not solely within the confines of its own urban space, defined by the burgh ports, but also within its wider geographical context

76 Leslie Page Moch, "Conclusions", in Bert De Munck and Anne Winter (eds), *Gated Communities? Regulating Migration in Early Modern Cities* (Farnham: Ashgate, 2012), pp. 241–244, at p. 243, referencing from the same collection Anne Winter, "Regulating urban migration and relief entitlements in eighteenth-century Brabant", pp. 175–196.

77 Because he was defined in this way, John Rakay was forbidden from pursuing a resident named John Ross for monies owed and dismissed from the burgh; ACR.14.592 [2 Jul 1535].

78 Maria R. Boes, "Unwanted travellers: the tightening of city borders in early modern Germany", in Thomas Betteridge (ed.), *Borders and Travellers in Early Modern Europe* (Aldershot: Ashgate, 2007), pp. 87–111, at p. 100.

79 John McCallum, "Charity doesn't begin at home: ecclesiastical poor relief beyond the parish, 1560–1650", *Journal of Scottish Historical Studies* 32:2 (2012), pp. 107–126, at p. 119.

80 Audrey-Beth Fitch, *The Search for Salvation: Lay Faith in Scotland, 1480–1560* [edited by Elizabeth Ewan] (Edinburgh: John Donald, 2009), p. 102.

81 Nick Alldridge, "Loyalty and identity in Chester parishes, 1540–1640", in S.J. Wright (ed.), *Parish, Church and People: Local Studies in Lay Religion, 1350–1750* (London: Hutchinson, 1988), pp. 85–124, at p. 117; G. Rosser, "Communities of

parish and guild in the later Middle Ages", in Wright (ed.), *Parish, Church and People*, pp. 29–55, at p. 44.

82 Mairi Cowan, *Death, Life, and Religious Change in Scottish Towns, c.1350–1560* (Manchester: Manchester University Press, 2012), pp. 86–88; D.M. Palliser, "Introduction: the parish in perspective", in Wright (ed.), *Parish, Church and People*, pp. 5–28, at p. 8.

83 Cowan, *Death, Life, and Religious Change in Scottish Towns*, pp. 86–88; Morgan, *Lost Aberdeen: Aberdeen's Lost Architectural Heritage*, p. 132; Wyness, *City by the Grey North Sea*, p. 25.

84 Cowan, *Death, Life, and Religious Change in Scottish Towns*, pp. 85–86.

85 Oram, "The medieval Church in the dioceses of Aberdeen and Moray", p. 16.

86 Gilbert Hill, "The sermons of John Watson, canon of Aberdeen, with a note on John Royaerts, O.F.M.", *Innes Review* 15:1 (1964), pp. 3–34.

87 Richard D. Oram, "Lay religiosity, piety, and devotion in Scotland, c.1300 to c.1450", *Florilegium* 25 (2008), pp. 95–126, at p. 116.

88 Wyness, *City by the Grey North Sea*, p. 25.

89 James Cooper (ed.), *Cartularium Ecclesiae Sancti Nicholai Aberdonensis*, vol. II (Aberdeen: New Spalding Club, 1892), pp. 91–92.

90 Cowan, *Death, Life, and Religious Change in Scottish Towns*, p. 18; C. Innes (ed.), *Registrum episcopatus Aberdonensis: Ecclesie cathedralis Aberdonensis*, vol. II (Edinburgh: Spalding Club, 1845), p. 190.

91 Harriet Harvey Wood (ed. and intro.), *William Dunbar: Selected Poems* (New York: Routledge, 2003), p. 98: "Lament for the Makaris", lines 9–12: 'The stait of man dois change and vary/Now sound, now seik, now blith, now sary/Now dansand mery, now like to dee;/Timor mortis conturbat me'.

92 Johan Huizinga, *The Waning of the Middle Ages: A Study of the Forms of Life, Thought and Art in France and the Netherlands in the Dawn of the Renaissance* (Garden City: Doubleday Anchor, 1956), p. 138: 'no other epoch has laid so much stress as the expiring Middle Ages on the thought of death'; Joëlle Rollo-Koster (ed.), *Death in Medieval Europe: Death Scripted and Death Choreographed* (Abingdon: Routledge, 2017); Bruce Gordon and Peter Marshall (eds), *The Place of the Dead: Death and Remembrance in Late Medieval and Early Modern Europe* (Cambridge: Cambridge University Press, 2000); Edelgard E. DuBruck and Barbara I. Gusick (eds), *Death and Dying in the Middle Ages* (New York: Peter Lang, 1999); Paul Binski, *Medieval Death: Ritual and Representation* (Ithaca, NY: Cornell University Press, 1996).

93 [Walter Cullen], "The Chronicle of Aberdeen, M.CCCC.XCI–M.D.XCV", in *Miscellany of the Spalding Club*, vol. II (Aberdeen: Spalding Club, 1842), pp. 29–70, at pp. 47–50.

94 Cooper, *Cartularium Ecclesiae Sancti Nicholai Aberdonensis*, vol. II, p. 36.

95 Fitch, *The Search for Salvation*, p. 28.

96 Robert L. Kindrick (ed.), *The Poems of Robert Henryson* (Kalamazoo: Medieval Institute Publications, 1997), p. 239; 'Ane Prayer for the Pest', lines 20–21.

97 Practices that were 'retained, if repurposed' after the Reformation included the use of a dead bell to announce a death, of staging of 'lyke-wakes' and the excessive lamentation of the dead; Gordon D. Raeburn, "Death, superstition, and common society following the Scottish Reformation", *Mortality* 21:1 (2016), pp. 36–51, at p. 40; Andrew Spicer, "'Rest of their bones': fear of death and Reformed burial practices", in William G. Naphy and Penny Roberts (eds), *Fear in Early Modern Society* (Manchester: Manchester University Press, 1997), pp. 167–183; Andrew Spicer, "'Defyle not Christ's kirk with your carrion': burial and the development of burial aisles in post-Reformation Scotland", in Gordon and

Marshall (eds), *The Place of the Dead, pp. 149–169. Medieval and Early Modern Europe* (Cambridge: Cambridge University Press, 2000), pp. 149–169.

98 Fitch, *The Search for Salvation*, p. 27.

99 Fitch, *The Search for Salvation*, p. 154; Audrey-Beth Fitch, "Paving the road to salvation: Scottish images of the afterlife, 1450–1560", in Macinnes et al. (eds), *Ships, Guns and Bibles in the North Sea and the Baltic States,* pp. 206–234, at p. 221. pp. 206–234, at p. 221. The ceiling in Provost Skene's house has been identified as forming part of a secret Catholic chapel painted c.1626 during the occupancy of Patrick Lumsden, a 'crypto-Catholic' and baillie of Aberdeen who was killed fighting for the Covenanters' cause at the battle of Justice Mills in 1644; David McRoberts, "Provost Skene's house, in Aberdeen, and its Catholic chapel", *Innes Review* 5:2 (1954), pp. 119–124, at p. 122.

100 Cowan, *Death, Life, and Religious Change in Scottish Towns*, p. 75.

101 Cooper, *Cartularium Ecclesiae Sancti Nicholai Aberdonensis*, vol. II, p. 33.

102 Fitch, *The Search for Salvation*, pp. 159–160; Fitch, "Paving the road to salvation", p. 222.

103 Audrey-Beth Fitch, "Maternal mediators: saintly ideals and secular realities in late medieval Scotland", *Innes Review* 57:1 (2006), pp. 1–35, at p. 6; Mary was particularly lauded for her 'pious, nurturing, compassionate, forgiving, protective, and mediating characteristics'; Audrey-Beth Fitch, "Mothers and their sons: Mary and Jesus in Scotland, 1450–1560", in Steve Boardman and Eila Williamson (eds), *The Cult of Saints and the Virgin Mary in Medieval Scotland* (Woodbridge: Boydell, 2010), pp. 159–176, at pp. 159–160.

104 Fitch, *The Search for Salvation*, p. 142; Marlene Villalobos Hennessy, "The Arbuthnott book of hours: book production and religious culture in late medieval Scotland", in Geddes (ed.), *Medieval Art, Architecture and Archaeology in the Dioceses of Aberdeen and Moray*, pp. 212–238, argues that the prayer book 'reflects very early evidence of the dissemination of Maria in sole (Virgin in the Sun) iconography and of devotion to the rosary' (p. 212).

105 Fitch, *The Search for Salvation*, p. 142; Fraser, *The Bridge of Dee*, p. 36; D.H. Evans, J.C. Murray and J.A. Stones (eds), *A Tale of Two Burghs: The Archaeology of Old and New Aberdeen* (Aberdeen: Aberdeen Art Gallery and Museums, 1987), pp. 49–50; Richard W.K. Bain, *Bishop Gavin Dunbar's Hospital: Memorandum Dealing with the History and Records from the Foundation of the Benefaction and List of Title Deeds and Other Writs Relating Thereto* (Aberdeen: Rosemount Press, 1931); David Ditchburn, "The 'McRoberts thesis' and patterns of sanctity", in Boardman and Williamson (eds), *The Cult of Saints and the Virgin Mary in Medieval Scotland,* pp. 177–194, at p. 181.

106 Fitch, *The Search for Salvation*, p. 154.

107 Cowan, *Death, Life, and Religious Change in Scottish Towns*, pp. 61, 69, 71.

108 Oram, "Lay religiosity, piety, and devotion in Scotland, c.1300 to c.1450", p. 116; Tom Turpie, *Kind Neighbours: Scottish Saints and Society in the Later Middle Ages* (Leiden: Brill, 2015), pp. 92–93; Richard Oram, "Holy Blood devotion in later medieval Scotland", *Journal of Medieval History* (2017), pp. 1–17. [doi: 10.1080/03044181.2017.1377104]

109 Alan Macquarrie, "Scottish saints' legends in the Aberdeen Breviary", in Boardman and Williamson (eds), *The Cult of Saints and the Virgin Mary in Medieval Scotland*, pp. 143–157, at p. 146.

110 Alison S. Cameron and Judith A. Stones, "Excavations within the East Kirk of St Nicholas, Aberdeen", in Geddes (ed.), *Medieval Art, Architecture and Archaeology in the Dioceses of Aberdeen and Moray*, pp. 82–98, at pp. 87, 91.

111 Ditchburn, "Locating Aberdeen and Elgin in the later Middle Ages", p. 8; for contextual surveys of Scots' fluctuating participation in pilgrimage, see Peter

Yeoman, *Pilgrimage in Medieval Scotland* (London: B.T. Batsford Ltd, 1999) and David Ditchburn, "'Saints at the door don't make miracles'? The contrasting fortunes of Scottish pilgrimage, c.1450–1550", in Julian Goodare and Alasdair A. MacDonald (eds), *Sixteenth-Century Scotland: Essays in Honour of Michael Lynch* (Leiden: Brill, 2008), pp. 69–98.

112 They enabled people to belong, as through them the town was made 'a stage, on which the identity of social groups and institutions was displayed'; Jose Antonio Mateos Royo, "All the town is a stage: civic ceremonies and religious festivities in Spain during the golden age", *Urban History* 26:2 (1999), pp. 165–189, at p. 167. Furthermore, they were 'intended to bring God's intervention and to affirm the religious and social solidarity of the community'; Fitch, *The Search for Salvation*, p. 101.

113 Dennison, "Power to the people?", p. 113.

114 Mervyn James, "Ritual, drama and social body in the late medieval English town", *Past and Present* 98 (1983), pp. 3–29, at p. 7.

115 Cowan, *Death, Life, and Religious Change in Scottish Towns*, p. 113.

116 Booton, "The craftsmen of Aberdeen between 1400 and 1550", p. 7.

117 Fitch, "Paving the road to salvation", p. 212.

118 Cowan, *Death, Life, and Religious Change in Scottish Towns*, pp. 196–197.

119 MacInnes, *The Aberdeen Guide*, p. 144.

120 Cowan, *Death, Life, and Religious Change in Scottish Towns*, pp. 200–201.

121 Denis McKay, "Parish life in Scotland, 1500–1560", *Innes Review* 10:2 (1959), pp. 237–267, at pp. 259–260; Margo Todd, *The Culture of Protestantism in Early Modern Scotland* (New Haven: Yale University Press, 2002), pp. 186–187.

122 Cooper, *Cartularium Ecclesiae Sancti Nicholai Aberdonensis*, vol. II, p. 10.

123 Stephen Mark Holmes, *Sacred Signs in Reformation Scotland: Interpreting Worship, 1488–1590* (Oxford: Oxford University Press, 2015), p. 146.

124 Oram, "The medieval Church in the dioceses of Aberdeen and Moray", p. 27. Haws identified Bishop Patrick Hepburn as exerting a 'conservative influence' over the two hundred clerics in the diocese of Moray during the early years of the Reformation, the majority of whom paid lip service to the Reformed faith in return for retaining their benefices with only a 'small minority ... actively serv[ing] the reformed Church'; Charles H. Haws, "Continuity and change: the clergy of the diocese of Moray, 1560–74", *Northern Scotland* 5:1 (1982), pp. 91–98, at pp. 91, 94.

125 Holmes, *Sacred Signs in Reformation Scotland*, Chapter 2: "Used books and networks: the Aberdeen Liturgists and Catholic reform in Scotland", pp. 51–77, at p. 51.

126 Todd, *The Culture of Protestantism*, p. 196; Michael Lynch and Gordon DesBrisay, "The faith of the people", in Dennison *et al.* (eds), *Aberdeen Before 1800*, pp. 289–308, at p. 296; Allan White, "The impact of the Reformation on a burgh community: the case of Aberdeen", in Michael Lynch (ed.), *The Early Modern Town in Scotland* (London: Croom Helm, 1987), pp. 81–101; Charles H. Haws, "The diocese of Aberdeen and the Reformation", *Innes Review* 22 (1971), pp. 72–84; Bruce McLennan, "The Reformation in the burgh of Aberdeen", *Northern Scotland* 2 (1977), pp. 119–144.

127 David Stevenson, *St Machar's Cathedral and the Reformation: 1560–1690* (Aberdeen: Friends of St Machar's Cathedral, 1981), p. 3.

128 Morgan, *Lost Aberdeen: Aberdeen's Lost Architectural Heritage*, p. 132; Evans *et al.* (eds), *A Tale of Two Burghs*, pp. 49–50.

129 Oram, "The medieval Church in the dioceses of Aberdeen and Moray", p. 28.

130 Morgan, *Lost Aberdeen: Aberdeen's Lost Architectural Heritage*, pp. 16–17; Alexander A. Cormack, *Poor Relief in Scotland* (Aberdeen: D. Wylie, 1923), p. 6.

131 G.D. Henderson, *The Founding of Marischal College, Aberdeen* (Aberdeen: Aberdeen University Press, 1947); Steven Reid, "Aberdeen's 'Toun College': Marischal College, 1593–1623", *Innes Review* 58:2 (2007), pp. 173–195; Evans *et al.* (eds), *A Tale of Two Burghs*, pp. 49–50; Morgan, *Lost Aberdeen: Aberdeen's Lost Architectural Heritage*, pp. 132–133.

132 Cameron and Stones, "Excavations within the East Kirk of St Nicholas, Aberdeen"; A. Cameron, C. Croly, A. Johnston and J. Stones, *Five Sites in the Environs of the Medieval Burgh of Aberdeen* (Aberdeen: Aberdeen City Council Archaeology Service, 2016); Alison S. Cameron and Judith A. Stones (eds), *Aberdeen: An In-depth View of the City's Past* (Edinburgh: Society of Antiquaries of Scotland, 2001); J.C. Murray (ed.), *Excavations in the Medieval Burgh of Aberdeen, 1973–81* (Edinburgh: Society of Antiquaries of Scotland, 1982); J.A. Stones (ed.), *Three Scottish Carmelite Friaries: Aberdeen, Linlithgow and Perth, 1980–86* (Edinburgh: Society of Antiquaries of Scotland, 1989); J. Charles Murray, "The archaeological evidence", in J.S. Smith (ed.), *New Light on Medieval Aberdeen* (Aberdeen: Aberdeen University Press, 1985), pp. 10–19; A. Cameron, A. Johnson and J. Stones, "Excavations at two sites in Old Aberdeen", *Proceedings of the Society of Antiquaries of Scotland* 126 (1996), pp. 911–927.

133 J.C. Murray, "The Scottish Burgh Survey: a review", *Proceedings of the Society of Antiquaries of Scotland* 113 (1983), pp. 1–10; Elizabeth P.D. Torrie, "The work of the Scottish Medieval Burgh Survey", *Review of Scottish Culture* 4 (1988), pp. 45–51.

134 J.R.D. Falconer, "Surveying Scotland's urban past: the pre-modern burgh", *History Compass* 9:1 (2011), pp. 34–44, at p. 36. Surveys of pre-modern burgh life include: Maureen M. Meikle, *The Scottish People, 1490–1625* (Raleigh: Lulu, 2013); Edward J. Cowan and Lizanne Henderson (eds), *A History of Everyday Life in Medieval Scotland, 1000–1600* (Edinburgh: Edinburgh University Press, 2011); E. Foyster and C. Whatley (eds), *A History of Everyday Life in Scotland, 1600–1800* (Edinburgh: Edinburgh University Press, 2010); Michael Lynch, Michael Spearman and Geoffrey Stell (eds), *The Scottish Medieval Town* (Edinburgh: John Donald, 1988); Michael Lynch (ed.), *The Early Modern Town in Scotland* (London: Croom Helm, 1987); Derek Hall, *Burgess, Merchant and Priest: Burgh Life in the Scottish Medieval Town* (Edinburgh: Birlinn, 2002); Margaret H.B. Sanderson, *A Kindly Place? Living in Sixteenth-Century Scotland* (East Lothian: Tuckwell Press, 2002); Ewan, *Townlife in Fourteenth-Century Scotland*. Emily Cockayne, *Hubbub: Filth, Noise and Stench in England, 1600–1770* (New York and London: Yale University Press, 2007) offers a wonderfully evocative (if selective) survey of the sights, sounds and smells encountered in the typical early modern English town.

135 Archaeology can yield particularly valuable information about such aspects of public health as 'population make-up, longevity, stature, robustness, and disease'; P.V. Addyman, "The archaeology of public health at York, England", *World Archaeology* 21:2 (1989), pp. 244–264, at p. 261.

136 Murray, "Archaeological evidence", p. 14.

137 John McCallum, "'Nurseries of the poore': hospitals and almshouses in early modern Scotland", *Journal of Social History* 48:2 (2014), pp. 427–449, at p. 428. Hospitals in the vicinity of Aberdeen, in addition to the leper house, included foundations dedicated to Saints Thomas, Mary and Anne, while throughout the north-east twelve hospitals and almshouses were established before the sixteenth century by rich benefactors, including five leper houses the largest of which was St Peters at Rathven; Oram, "The medieval Church in the dioceses of Aberdeen and Moray", pp. 20–22.

138 ACR.36.598 [2 Sep 1596].
139 ACR.15.352 [12 Jun 1537]; ACR.15.353 [14 Jun 1537]; at this time craft membership numbered five, compared for example to the nine names recorded as being 'the haill baxteris of this guid toune' in Oct 1533; ACR.14.290 [17 Oct 1533].
140 See, for example: Leona J. Skelton, *Sanitation in Urban Britain, 1560–1700* (Abingdon: Routledge, 2016); J. Harrison, "Public hygiene and drainage in Stirling and other early modern Scottish towns", *Review of Scottish Culture* 11 (1998–1999), pp. 67–77; R. Houston, "Fire and filth: Edinburgh's environment, 1660–1760", *The Book of the Old Edinburgh Club*, new series, vol. III (1994), pp. 25–36; Dolly Jørgensen, "'All good rule of the citee': sanitation and civic government in England, 1400–1600", *Journal of Urban History* 36:3 (2010), pp. 300–315.
141 William Dunbar, "Blyth Aberdein", in John Small (ed.), *The Poems of William Dunbar*, vol. II (Edinburgh: Scottish Text Society, 1893), pp. 251–253; ACR.8.1180 [30 Apr 1511]; ACR.8.1182 [4 May 1511]; ACR.8.1183 [10 May 1511].
142 For example, John Chalmer was ordered to remove his dirty clothes from the gutter, so 'that the wattir mycht heff passage'; ACR.16.729 [14 Feb 1541].
143 ACR.8.753 [8 Aug 1507]; ACR.9.036–037 [17 Oct 1511]; ACR.9.268 [7 Oct 1513]; ACR.9.377 [22 Dec 1514]; ACR.9.594 [9 Jun 1516]; ACR.10.072 [2 May 1519]; ACR.10.300 [22 Apr 1521]; ACR.14.219 [7 Jul 1533]; ACR.14.499 [15 Jan 1535]; ACR.15.215 [2 Oct 1536]; ACR.15.230 [17 Oct 1536]; ACR.16.036 [25 Oct 1538]; ACR.16.445 [26 Jan 1540]; ACR.19.061 [19 Mar 1546]; ACR.20.310 [16 Oct 1549]; ACR.53/2.1457 [27 Apr 1647].
144 C.P. Croly, *'Privies and other Filthiness…': The Environment of Late Medieval Aberdeen, c.1399–1650* (Aberdeen: Aberdeen City Council, Archaeology Unit, 2003), pp. 6–9.
145 Andrew Wear, *Knowledge and Practice in English Medicine, 1550–1680* (Cambridge: Cambridge University Press, 2000), p. 316.
146 Mary J. Dobson, *Contours of Death and Disease in Early Modern England* (Cambridge: Cambridge University Press, 1997); Justin Champion, "Epidemics and the built environment in 1665", in J.A.I. Champion (ed.), *Epidemic Disease in London* (London: Institute of Historical Research, Centre for Metropolitan History Working Papers Series no. 1, 1993), pp. 35–52.
147 Evans *et al.* (eds), *A Tale of Two Burghs*, p. 32.
148 Ibid.; Elizabeth Ewan, "'Hamperit in ane hony came': sights, sounds and smells in the medieval town", in Cowan and Henderson (eds), *A History of Everyday Life in Medieval Scotland*, pp. 109–144, at p. 129; Cameron and Stones, "Excavations within the East Kirk of St Nicholas, Aberdeen", p. 95.
149 Evans *et al.* (eds), *A Tale of Two Burghs*, pp. 35–36.

Bibliography

Adams, Ian H., *The Making of Urban Scotland* (London: Croom Helm, 1978).

Addyman, P.V., "The archaeology of public health at York, England", *World Archaeology* 21:2 (1989), pp. 244–264.

Alldridge, Nick, "Loyalty and identity in Chester parishes, 1540–1640", in S.J. Wright (ed.), *Parish, Church and People: Local Studies in Lay Religion, 1350–1750* (London: Hutchinson, 1988), pp. 85–124.

Bailey, Laura, Tim Holden, Julie Franklin, Catherine Smith and Ruby Cerón-Carrasco, "An archaeological excavation of a medieval fishermen's midden at Castle Hill Pumping Station, Banff", *Scottish Archaeological Journal* 36–37:1 (2014–15), pp. 1–35.

Bain, Richard W.K., *Bishop Gavin Dunbar's Hospital: Memorandum Dealing with the History and Records from the Foundation of the Benefaction and List of Title Deeds and Other Writs Relating Thereto* (Aberdeen: Rosemount Press, 1931).

Bajer, Peter Paul, *Scots in the Polish-Lithuanian Commonwealth, 16th to 18th Centuries: The Formation and Disappearance of an Ethnic Group* (Leiden: Brill, 2012).

Barrow, G.W.S., "Land routes: the medieval evidence", in Alexander Fenton and Geoffrey Stell (eds), *Loads and Roads in Scotland and Beyond: Land Transport over 6000 Years* (Edinburgh: John Donald, 1984), pp. 49–66.

Binski, Paul, *Medieval Death: Ritual and Representation* (Ithaca, NY: Cornell University Press, 1996).

Bishop, Bruce B., *Lost Moray and Nairn* (Edinburgh: Birlinn, 2010).

Blanchard, Ian, Elizabeth Gemmill, Nicholas Mayhew and Ian D. Whyte, "The economy: town and country", in E. Patricia Dennison, David Ditchburn and Michael Lynch (eds), *Aberdeen Before 1800: A New History* (East Linton: Tuckwell Press, 2002), pp. 129–158.

Boes, Maria R., "Unwanted travellers: the tightening of city borders in early modern Germany", in Thomas Betteridge (ed.), *Borders and Travellers in Early Modern Europe* (Aldershot: Ashgate, 2007), pp. 87–111.

Bogucka, Maria, "Scots in Gdansk (Danzig) in the seventeenth century", in Allan I. Macinnes, Thomas Riis and Frederik Pedersen (eds), *Ships, Guns, and Bibles in the North Sea and Baltic States, c. 1350–c. 1700* (East Linton: Tuckwell, 2000), pp. 39–46.

Booton, Harold W., "Inland trade: a study of Aberdeen in the later Middle Ages", in Michael Lynch, Michael Spearman and Geoffrey Stell (eds), *The Scottish Medieval Town* (Edinburgh: John Donald, 1988), pp. 148–160.

Booton, Harold W., "Sir John Rutherfurd: a fifteenth century Aberdeen burgess", *Scottish Economic & Social History* 10:1 (1990), pp. 21–37.

Booton, Harold, "The craftsmen of Aberdeen between 1400 and 1550", *Northern Scotland* 13:1 (1993), pp. 1–19.

Bowman, Stephen, "'By hammer in hand all arts do stand': the protection and projection of craft privilege in the early modern Scottish burgh", in Kate Buchanan and Lucinda H.S. Dean, with Michael Penman (eds), *Medieval and Early Modern Representations of Authority in Scotland and the British Isles* (Abingdon: Routledge, 2016).

Cameron, A., A. Johnson and J. Stones, "Excavations at two sites in Old Aberdeen", *Proceedings of the Society of Antiquaries of Scotland* 126 (1996), pp. 911–927.

Cameron, Alison S. and Judith A. Stones (eds), *Aberdeen: An In-depth View of the City's Past* (Edinburgh: Society of Antiquaries of Scotland, 2001).

Cameron, Alison S. and Judith A. Stones, "Excavations within the East Kirk of St Nicholas, Aberdeen", in Jane Geddes (ed.), *Medieval Art, Architecture and Archaeology in the Dioceses of Aberdeen and Moray* (Routledge: Abingdon, 2016), pp. 82–98.

Cameron, A., C. Croly, A. Johnston and J. Stones, *Five Sites in the Environs of the Medieval Burgh of Aberdeen* (Aberdeen: Aberdeen City Council Archaeology Service, 2016).

Champion, Justin, "Epidemics and the built environment in 1665", in J.A.I. Champion (ed.), *Epidemic Disease in London* (London: Institute of Historical Research, Centre for Metropolitan History Working Papers Series no. 1, 1993), pp. 35–52.

Cockayne, Emily, *Hubbub: Filth, Noise and Stench in England, 1600–1770* (New York and London: Yale University Press, 2007).

Cooper, James (ed.), *Cartularium Ecclesiae Sancti Nicholai Aberdonensis*, vol. II (Aberdeen: New Spalding Club, 1892).

Cormack, Alexander A., *Poor Relief in Scotland* (Aberdeen: D. Wylie, 1923).

Cowan, Edward J., and Lizanne Henderson (eds), *A History of Everyday Life in Medieval Scotland, 1000–1600* (Edinburgh: Edinburgh University Press, 2011).
Cowan, Mairi, *Death, Life, and Religious Change in Scottish Towns, c.1350–1560* (Manchester: Manchester University Press, 2012).
Crawshaw, Jane L. Stevens, "Introduction", in Andrew Spicer and Jane L. Stevens Crawshaw (eds), *The Place of the Social Margins, 1350–1750* (Abingdon: Routledge, 2017), pp. 1–17.
Croly, C.P., *'Privies and Other Filthiness…': The Environment of Late Medieval Aberdeen, c.1399–1650* (Aberdeen: Aberdeen City Council, Archaeology Unit, 2003).
Cullen, Walter, "The Chronicle of Aberdeen, M.CCCC.XCI–M.D.XCV", in John Stuart (ed.), *Miscellany of the Spalding Club*, vol. II (Aberdeen: Spalding Club, 1842), pp. 29–70.
Dennison, E. Patricia, "Power to the people? The myth of the medieval burgh community", in Sally M. Foster, Allan I. Macinnes and Ranald MacInnes (eds), *Scottish Power Centres: From the Early Middle Ages to the Twentieth Century* (Glasgow: Cruithne, 1998), pp. 100–131.
DesBrisay, Gordon, *Authority and Discipline in Aberdeen, 1650–1700* (University of St Andrews, unpublished PhD thesis, 1989).
DesBrisay, Gordon, "Aberdeen and the Dutch Atlantic: women and woollens in the seventeenth century", in Douglas Catterall and Jodi Campbell (eds), *Women in Port: Gendering Communities, Economies, and Social Networks in Atlantic Port Cities, 1500–1800* (Leiden: Brill, 2012), pp. 69–102.
Ditchburn, David, "Cargoes and commodities: Aberdeen's trade with Scandinavia and the Baltic, c.1302–c.1542", *Northern Studies* 27 (1990), pp. 12–22.
Ditchburn, David, "The pirate, the policeman and the pantomime star: Aberdeen's alternative economy in the early fifteenth century", *Northern Scotland* 12 (1992), pp. 19–34.
Ditchburn, David, "'Saints at the door don't make miracles'? The contrasting fortunes of Scottish pilgrimage, c.1450–1550", in Julian Goodare and Alasdair A. MacDonald (eds), *Sixteenth-Century Scotland: Essays in Honour of Michael Lynch* (Leiden: Brill, 2008), pp. 69–98.
Ditchburn, David, "The 'McRoberts thesis' and patterns of sanctity", in Steve Boardman and Eila Williamson (eds), *The Cult of Saints and the Virgin Mary in Medieval Scotland* (Woodbridge: Boydell, 2010), pp. 177–194.
Ditchburn, David, "Locating Aberdeen and Elgin in the later Middle Ages: regional, national and international paradigms", in Jane Geddes (ed.), *Medieval Art, Architecture and Archaeology in the Dioceses of Aberdeen and Moray* (Routledge: Abingdon, 2016), pp. 1–15.
Ditchburn, David, "Salmon, salt and the internationalization of Aberdeen's economy in the later Middle Ages" in Jesús Ángel Solórzano Telechea, Beatriz Arízaga Bolumburu and Michel Bochaca (eds), *Las Sociedades Portuarias de la Europa Atlántica en la Edad Media* (Logroño: Instituto de Estudios Riojanos, 2016), pp. 49–66.
Dobson, David, *Scots in Poland, Russia and the Baltic States: 1550–1850* (Baltimore: Clearfield, 2000).
Dobson, Mary J., *Contours of Death and Disease in Early Modern England* (Cambridge: Cambridge University Press, 1997).
DuBruck, Edelgard E. and Barbara I. Gusick (eds), *Death and Dying in the Middle Ages* (New York: Peter Lang, 1999).

Dunbar, William, "Blyth Aberdein", in John Small (ed.), *The Poems of William Dunbar*, vol. II (Edinburgh: Scottish Text Society, 1893), pp. 251–253.

Evans, D.H., J.C. Murray and J.A. Stones (eds), *A Tale of Two Burghs: The Archaeology of Old and New Aberdeen* (Aberdeen: Aberdeen Art Gallery and Museums, 1987).

Ewan, Elizabeth, *Townlife in Fourteenth-Century Scotland* (Edinburgh: Edinburgh University Press, 1990).

Ewan, Elizabeth, "'Hamperit in ane hony came': sights, sounds and smells in the medieval town", in Edward J. Cowan and Lizanne Henderson (eds), *A History of Everyday Life in Medieval Scotland, 1000–1600* (Edinburgh: Edinburgh University Press, 2011), pp. 109–144.

Falconer, J.R.D., "Surveying Scotland's urban past: the pre-modern burgh", *History Compass* 9:1 (2011), pp. 34–44.

Falconer, J.R.D., *Crime and Community in Reformation Scotland: Negotiating Power in a Burgh Society* (London: Pickering and Chatto, 2013).

Fitch, Audrey-Beth, "Paving the road to salvation: Scottish images of the afterlife, 1450–1560", in Allan I. Macinnes, Thomas Riis and Frederik Pedersen (eds), *Ships, Guns and Bibles in the North Sea and the Baltic States, c.1350–c.1700* (East Linton: Tuckwell Press, 2000), pp. 206–234.

Fitch, Audrey-Beth, "Maternal mediators: saintly ideals and secular realities in late medieval Scotland", *Innes Review* 57:1 (2006), pp. 1–35.

Fitch, Audrey-Beth, *The Search for Salvation: Lay Faith in Scotland, 1480–1560* [edited by Elizabeth Ewan] (Edinburgh: John Donald, 2009).

Fitch, Audrey-Beth, "Mothers and their sons: Mary and Jesus in Scotland, 1450–1560", in Steve Boardman and Eila Williamson (eds), *The Cult of Saints and the Virgin Mary in Medieval Scotland* (Woodbridge: Boydell, 2010), pp. 159–176.

Fleet, Christopher, Margaret Wilkes and Charles Withers W.J., *Scotland: Mapping the Nation* (Edinburgh: Birlinn, 2011).

[Forbes, Sir Samuel, of Foveran], "Description of Aberdeenshire, by Sir Samuel Forbes of Foveran, MDCCXVI–MDCCXVII", in Joseph Robertson (ed.), *Collections for a History of the Shires of Aberdeen and Banff* (Aberdeen: Spalding Club, 1843), pp. 31–59.

Foyster, E. and C. Whatley (eds), *A History of Everyday Life in Scotland, 1600–1800* (Edinburgh: Edinburgh University Press, 2010).

Frankot, Edda, *'Of Laws of Ships and Shipmen': Medieval Maritime Law and its Practice in Urban Northern Europe* (Edinburgh: Edinburgh University Press, 2012).

Frankot, Edda, "Aberdeen and the east coast of Scotland: autonomy on the periphery", in Wim Blockmans, Mikhail Krom and Justyna Wubs-Mrozewicz (eds), *The Routledge Handbook of Maritime Trade around Europe, 1300–1600: Commercial Networks and Urban Autonomy* (Abingdon: Routledge, 2017), pp. 411–427.

Fraser, G.M., *The Bridge of Dee: Its History, its Structural Features and its Sculptures* (Aberdeen: Bon-Accord Press, 1913).

Fraser, G.M., *The Old Deeside Road (Aberdeen to Braemar): Its Course, History, and Associations* (Aberdeen: Aberdeen University Press, 1921).

Gibb, Andrew and Ronan Paddison, "The rise and fall of burghal monopolies in Scotland: the case of the north east", *Scottish Geographical Magazine* 99:3 (1983), pp. 130–140.

Gordon, Bruce and Peter Marshall (eds), *The Place of the Dead: Death and Remembrance in Late Medieval and Early Modern Europe* (Cambridge: Cambridge University Press, 2000).

Gordon, James, *Abredoniae Utriusque Descriptio Topographica: A Description of Bothe Touns of Aberdeene* [1661] [edited by C. Innes] (Edinburgh: Spalding Club, 1842).

Gourlay, Robert and Anne Turner, *Historic Banff: The Archaeological Implications of Development* (Glasgow: Scottish Burgh Survey, 1977).

Gourlay, Robert and Anne Turner, *Historic Inverurie: The Archaeological Implications of Development* (Glasgow: Scottish Burgh Survey, 1977).

Graham, Angus, "Archaeological notes in some harbours in eastern Scotland", *Proceedings of the Society of Antiquaries of Scotland* 101 (1968–69), pp. 200–285.

Hall, Derek, *Burgess, Merchant and Priest: Burgh Life in the Scottish Medieval Town* (Edinburgh: Birlinn, 2002).

Hammer, Carl I., Jr, "Anatomy of an oligarchy: the Oxford town council in the fifteenth and sixteenth centuries", *Journal of British Studies* 18:1 (1978), pp. 1–27.

Harrison, J., "Public hygiene and drainage in Stirling and other early modern Scottish towns", *Review of Scottish Culture* 11 (1998–99), pp. 67–77.

Harvey Wood, Harriet (ed. and intro.), *William Dunbar: Selected Poems* (New York: Routledge, 2003).

Haws, Charles H., "The diocese of Aberdeen and the Reformation", *Innes Review* 22 (1971), pp. 72–84.

Haws, Charles H., "Continuity and change: the clergy of the diocese of Moray, 1560–74", *Northern Scotland* 5:1 (1982), pp. 91–98.

Henderson, C.G., "Exeter", in Gustav Milne and Brian Hobley (eds), *Waterfront Archaeology in Britain and Northern Europe* (London: Council for British Archaeology, Research Report no. 41, 1981), pp. 119–122.

Henderson, G.D., *The Founding of Marischal College, Aberdeen* (Aberdeen: Aberdeen University Press, 1947).

Hill, Gilbert, "The sermons of John Watson, canon of Aberdeen, with a note on John Royaerts, O.F.M.", *Innes Review* 15:1 (1964), pp. 3–34.

Holmes, Stephen Mark, *Sacred Signs in Reformation Scotland: Interpreting Worship, 1488–1590* (Oxford: Oxford University Press, 2015).

Houston, R., "Fire and filth: Edinburgh's environment, 1660–1760", *The Book of the Old Edinburgh Club*, new series, vol. III (1994), pp. 25–36.

Huizinga, Johan, *The Waning of the Middle Ages: A Study of the Forms of Life, Thought and Art in France and the Netherlands in the Dawn of the Renaissance* (Garden City: Doubleday Anchor, 1956).

Innes, C. (ed.), *Registrum episcopatus Aberdonensis: Ecclesie cathedralis Aberdonensis*, vol. II (Edinburgh: Spalding Club, 1845).

Jackson, Gordon, "The economy: Aberdeen and the sea", in E. Patricia Dennison, David Ditchburn and Michael Lynch (eds), *Aberdeen Before 1800: A New History* (East Linton: Tuckwell Press, 2002), pp. 159–180.

James, Mervyn, "Ritual, drama and social body in the late medieval English town", *Past and Present* 98 (1983), pp. 3–29.

Jørgensen, Dolly, "'All good rule of the citee': sanitation and civic government in England, 1400–1600", *Journal of Urban History* 36:3 (2010), pp. 300–315.

Kennedy, William, *Annals of Aberdeen, from the Reign of King William the Lion, to the End of the Year 1818* (London: Brown, 1818).

Kindrick, Robert L. (ed.), *The Poems of Robert Henryson* (Kalamazoo: Medieval Institute Publications, 1997).

Kowalski, Waldemar, *The Great Immigration: Scots in Cracow and Little Poland, circa 1500–1660* (Leiden: Brill, 2016).

Lynch, Michael (ed.), *The Early Modern Town in Scotland* (London: Croom Helm, 1987).
Lynch, Michael, Michael Spearman and Geoffrey Stell (eds), *The Scottish Medieval Town* (Edinburgh: John Donald, 1988).
Lynch, Michael and David Ditchburn, "Economic development", in Peter G.B. McNeill and Hector L. MacQueen (eds), *Atlas of Scottish History to 1707* (Edinburgh: The Scottish Medievalists and Department of Geography, University of Edinburgh, 1996), pp. 231–328.
Lynch, Michael and Gordon DesBrisay, "The faith of the people", in E. Patricia Dennison, David Ditchburn and Michael Lynch (eds), *Aberdeen Before 1800: A New History* (East Linton: Tuckwell Press, 2002), pp. 289–308.
MacCannell, Daniel, *Lost Banff and Buchan* (Edinburgh: Birlinn, 2012).
MacInnes, Ranald, *The Aberdeen Guide* (Edinburgh: Birlinn, 2000).
MacNiven, Duncan, "Merchants and traders in early seventeenth century Aberdeen", in David Stevenson (ed.), *From Lairds to Louns: Country and Burgh Life in Aberdeen, 1600–1800* (Aberdeen: Aberdeen University Press, 1986), pp. 57–69.
Macquarrie, Alan, "Scottish saints' legends in the Aberdeen Breviary", in Steve Boardman and Eila Williamson (eds), *The Cult of Saints and the Virgin Mary in Medieval Scotland* (Woodbridge: Boydell, 2010), pp. 143–157.
Mayhew, Nicholas and Elizabeth Gemmill, *Changing Values in Medieval Scotland: A Study of Prices, Money, and Weights and Measures* (Cambridge: Cambridge University Press, 1995).
McCallum, John, "Charity doesn't begin at home: ecclesiastical poor relief beyond the parish, 1560–1650", *Journal of Scottish Historical Studies* 32:2 (2012), pp. 107–126.
McCallum, John, "'Nurseries of the poore': hospitals and almshouses in early modern Scotland", *Journal of Social History* 48:2 (2014), pp. 427–449.
McKay, Denis, "Parish life in Scotland, 1500–1560", *Innes Review* 10:2 (1959), pp.237–267.
McLennan, Bruce, "The Reformation in the burgh of Aberdeen", *Northern Scotland* 2 (1977), pp. 119–144.
McRoberts, David, "Provost Skene's house, in Aberdeen, and its Catholic chapel", *Innes Review* 5:2 (1954), pp. 119–124.
Meikle, Maureen M., *The Scottish People, 1490–1625* (Raleigh: Lulu, 2013).
Miller, Jaroslav, *Urban Societies in East-Central Europe, 1500–1700* (Farnham: Ashgate, 2008).
Morgan, Diane, *Lost Aberdeen: Aberdeen's Lost Architectural Heritage* (Edinburgh: Birlinn, 2004).
Morgan, Diane, *Lost Aberdeen: The Freedom Lands* (Edinburgh: Birlinn, 2009).
Murray, J.C., "Conclusions", in J.C. Murray (ed.), *Excavations in the Medieval Burgh of Aberdeen, 1973–81* (Edinburgh: Society of Antiquaries of Scotland, 1982), pp. 244–249.
Murray, J.C., "The Scottish Burgh Survey: a review", *Proceedings of the Society of Antiquaries of Scotland* 113 (1983), pp. 1–10.
Murray, J. Charles, "The archaeological evidence", in J.S. Smith (ed.), *New Light on Medieval Aberdeen* (Aberdeen: Aberdeen University Press, 1985), pp. 10–19.
Oram, Richard D., "Lay religiosity, piety, and devotion in Scotland, c.1300 to c.1450", *Florilegium* 25 (2008), pp. 95–126.
Oram, Richard, "The medieval Church in the dioceses of Aberdeen and Moray", in Jane Geddes (ed.), *Medieval Art, Architecture and Archaeology in the Dioceses of Aberdeen and Moray* (Routledge: Abingdon, 2016), pp. 16–32.
Oram, Richard, "Holy Blood devotion in later medieval Scotland", *Journal of Medieval History* (2017), pp. 1–17 [doi:10.1080/03044181.2017.1377104].

Pagan, Theodora, *The Convention of the Royal Burghs of Scotland* (Glasgow: Glasgow University Press, 1926).
Page Moch, Leslie, "Conclusions", in Bert De Munck and Anne Winter (eds), *Gated Communities? Regulating Migration in Early Modern Cities* (Farnham: Ashgate, 2012), pp. 241–244.
Palliser, D.M., "Introduction: the parish in perspective", in S.J. Wright (ed.), *Parish, Church and People: Local Studies in Lay Religion, 1350–1750* (London: Hutchinson, 1988), pp. 5–28.
Raeburn, Gordon D., "Death, superstition, and common society following the Scottish Reformation", *Mortality* 21:1 (2016), pp. 36–51.
Redwood, Stewart D., "The history of the ferries across the river Dee at Aberdeen", *Northern Scotland* 14:1 (1994), pp. 1–25.
Reid, Steven, "Aberdeen's 'Toun College': Marischal College, 1593–1623", *Innes Review* 58:2 (2007), pp. 173–195.
Rollo-Koster, Joëlle (ed.), *Death in Medieval Europe: Death Scripted and Death Choreographed* (Abingdon: Routledge, 2017).
Rosser, G., "Communities of parish and guild in the later Middle Ages", in S.J. Wright (ed.), *Parish, Church and People: Local Studies in Lay Religion, 1350–1750* (London: Hutchinson, 1988), pp. 29–55.
Royo, Jose Antonio Mateos, "All the town is a stage: civic ceremonies and religious festivities in Spain during the golden age", *Urban History* 26:2 (1999), pp. 165–189.
Ruddock, Ted, "Bridges and roads in Scotland: 1400–1750", in Alexander Fenton and Geoffrey Stell (eds), *Loads and Roads in Scotland and Beyond: Land Transport over 6000 Years* (Edinburgh: John Donald, 1984), pp. 67–91.
Sanderson, Margaret H.B., *A Kindly Place? Living in Sixteenth-Century Scotland* (East Lothian: Tuckwell Press, 2002).
Simpson, Anne Turner and Sylvia Stevenson, *Historic Peterhead: The Archaeological Implications of Development* (Glasgow: Scottish Burgh Survey, 1982).
Skelton, Leona J., *Sanitation in Urban Britain, 1560–1700* (Abingdon: Routledge, 2016).
Smith, Alexander, *The History and Antiquities of New and Old Aberdeen* (Aberdeen: Alexander Murray, 1882).
Smolarek, Przemysław, "Ships and ports in Pomorze", in Gustav Milne and Brian Hobley (eds), *Waterfront Archaeology in Britain and Northern Europe* (London: Council for British Archaeology, Research Report no. 41, 1981), pp. 51–60.
Spicer, Andrew, "'Rest of their bones': fear of death and Reformed burial practices", in William G. Naphy and Penny Roberts (eds), *Fear in Early Modern Society* (Manchester: Manchester University Press, 1997), pp. 167–183.
Spicer, Andrew, "'Defyle not Christ's kirk with your carrion': burial and the development of burial aisles in post-Reformation Scotland", in Bruce Gordon and Peter Marshall (eds), *The Place of the Dead: Death and Remembrance in Late Medieval and Early Modern Europe* (Cambridge: Cambridge University Press, 2000), pp. 149–169.
Spierling, Karen E. and Michael J. Halvorson, "Introduction: definitions of community in early modern Europe", in Michael J. Halvorson and Karen E. Spierling (eds), *Defining Community in Early Modern Europe* (Ashgate: Aldershot, 2008), pp. 1–23.
Stevenson, David, *St Machar's Cathedral and the Reformation: 1560–1690* (Aberdeen: Friends of St Machar's Cathedral, 1981).
Stevenson, David, "A note on a scheme to straighten the river Forth in 1636", *Scottish Economic and Social History* 17:1 (1997), pp. 65–68.

Stones, J.A. (ed.), *Three Scottish Carmelite Friaries: Aberdeen, Linlithgow and Perth, 1980–86* (Edinburgh: Society of Antiquaries of Scotland, 1989).

Taylor, Louise B., *Aberdeen Shore Works Accounts, 1596–1670* (Aberdeen: Aberdeen University Press, 1972).

Todd, Margo, *The Culture of Protestantism in Early Modern Scotland* (New Haven: Yale University Press, 2002).

Torpey, John, *The Invention of the Passport: Surveillance, Citizenship and the State* (Cambridge: Cambridge University Press, 2000).

Torrie, Elizabeth P.D., "The work of the Scottish Medieval Burgh Survey", *Review of Scottish Culture* 4 (1988), pp. 45–51.

Torrie, E.P.D., "The early urban site of New Aberdeen: a reappraisal of the evidence", *Northern Scotland* 12:1 (1992), pp. 1–18.

Turpie, Tom, *Kind Neighbours: Scottish Saints and Society in the Later Middle Ages* (Leiden: Brill, 2015).

Tyson, Robert E., "People in the two towns", in E. Patricia Dennison, David Ditchburn and Michael Lynch (eds), *Aberdeen Before 1800: A New History* (East Linton: Tuckwell Press, 2002), pp. 111–128.

Villalobos Hennessy, Marlene, "The Arbuthnott book of hours: book production and religious culture in late medieval Scotland", in Jane Geddes (ed.), *Medieval Art, Architecture and Archaeology in the Dioceses of Aberdeen and Moray* (Routledge: Abingdon, 2016), pp. 212–238.

Wear, Andrew, *Knowledge and Practice in English Medicine, 1550–1680* (Cambridge: Cambridge University Press, 2000).

White, Allan, "The impact of the Reformation on a burgh community: the case of Aberdeen", in Michael Lynch (ed.), *The Early Modern Town in Scotland* (London: Croom Helm, 1987), pp. 81–101.

White, Allan, "The Menzies era: sixteenth-century politics", in E. Patricia Dennison, David Ditchburn and Michael Lynch (eds), *Aberdeen Before 1800: A New History* (East Linton: Tuckwell Press, 2002), pp. 224–237.

Whyte, Ian, "Agriculture in Aberdeenshire in the seventeenth and early eighteenth centuries: continuity and change", in David Stevenson (ed.), *From Lairds to Louns: Country and Burgh Life in Aberdeen, 1600–1800* (Aberdeen: Aberdeen University Press, 1986), pp. 10–31.

Wyness, Fenton, *City by the Grey North Sea: Aberdeen* (Aberdeen: Impulse Books, 1972).

Yeoman, Peter, *Pilgrimage in Medieval Scotland* (London: B.T. Batsford Ltd, 1999).

2 Responses to plague in Scotland

Shock and awe: interpreting disasters

Plague took its place alongside fires, floods, droughts and famines as one of many disasters with the potential to impact a significant proportion of a given community, and which therefore loomed large in both the individual and collective memory. For local vicar William Cullen, one of the most significant events to have taken place in early modern Aberdeen was the devastation by fire in 1529 of the wooden dwelling in the Castlegate owned by the provost Gilbert Menzies.[1] No doubt the illustrious ownership of that particular residence increased the notoriety of the event and contributed to the subsequent redevelopment of the building as the 'first stone house of any size' in the city.[2] As devastating as individual calamities could be, historians have increasingly recognised what those affected by them had long understood: that such events evoked a range of emotions from fear to panic and had the power not only to destroy but also to transform (or, crucially in the minds of contemporaries, to reform).[3] Emphasis on this latter aspect in particular accords with the sociological approach to disasters, which has rejected their characterisation as 'events' and instead analysed them as processes that tend to be neither sudden nor simply destructive.[4] Scholarship on historic catastrophes now places less emphasis on their 'destructive potential' and instead acknowledges the 'constructive operations of disaster management' that could result, particularly with regard to positive legislative action.[5]

As the example of Gilbert Menzies's home indicates, urban fires could destroy structures and 'recalibrat[e] architectural history from that date', but in the long term this destruction brought about tangible benefits in terms of better building construction, as well as notions of both public safety and civic liability.[6] The devastating fires that had been recorded in Aberdeen since the thirteenth century led eventually to the implementation of civic regulations concerning various aspects of fire reduction and response, specifically the safer storage of fuel and the better preparedness of citizens to help tackle a blaze, as well as the procurement of fire-fighting equipment, including thirty leather water buckets purchased in the aftermath of a fire at Marischal College and later a water engine which was sourced from London.[7] Subsequently, following 'many dreadful and fatal instances' of accidental urban blazes a severe instance on Broadgate in 1741 led the council to outlaw timber as a building material in preference for stone or brick, with slate or tile to be used in future roofing construction rather than heather or straw.[8] Thereafter it is probable that in real terms the incidence of urban fire decreased, as has been shown to have been the case across England from the second half of the eighteenth century.[9]

While accidental fire could most easily be attributed to human error, other types of natural disaster were interpreted as arising from fundamental moral failings as much as from aberrations in the workings of nature. Calamities that contradicted the natural order could be rationalised according to understandings of how the natural world worked – Aristotelian thought attributed earthquakes to a build-up of steam in underground cavities, while the flooding of the Tiber which killed nearly 1,000 people in Rome on Christmas Eve 1599 was identified as resulting from melting snow.[10] However, it was rare at least before the later seventeenth century that such occurrences were interpreted purely in natural terms.[11] Rather, natural events – including plague – were believed to arise from secondary, temporal causes which were dictated fundamentally by primary, spiritual causes at the will of an omnipotent God. He controlled the natural world and hence manipulated it to convey to believers His anger with sin, whether of a specific individual or more broadly of a faction, locality or nation. At the heart of these beliefs was an acceptance of providence, characterised by Alexandra Walsham as 'an ingrained parochial response to chaos and crisis'.[12] The author of a pamphlet about an earthquake in Glasgow noted that 'we being Christians, must always acknowledg a Supernatural Intendency from the Divine Prerogative',[13] while the Edinburgh reprint of a similar treatise emphasised that although the 'Efficient & Matterial causes' of such phenomena were 'natural', the ultimate cause 'is the signification of an Angry GOD, moved by the execrable Crimes of a wicked people'.[14] Essentially irrespective of the confessional divide, such events regardless of scale – from a so-called monstrous birth to a plague outbreak, famine, flood, earthquake or volcano – were regarded as calls to reform and invitations to sincere contrition and repentance, enabling the faithful to make amends and thereby smooth the path to joyous eternity. Contemporaries, therefore, were compelled to respond to such occurrences not only with the instinctive terror that accompanies any threat but also with due deference to God's inherent benevolence and with awestruck wonder at such marvellous evidence of His omnipotence.

Instances of unnatural phenomena increased in line with the severity of divine anger and could be prodigious warnings of worse to come in the face of continued immorality. Hence, plague was often presaged by a volcano, earthquake, comet or other event which contradicted the natural order. In his history of the Scottish Church, David Calderwood recorded that in 1597 plague broke out in Edinburgh shortly after a notable earthquake had 'made all the north parts of Scotland to tremble', while an earthquake which accompanied the severe outbreak of 1608 was felt throughout the north-east 'to the great terror of the people'.[15] One late seventeenth-century discourse provided both a natural and a supernatural rationale for earthquakes: the severing of land masses as a result of a quake created clefts in which new water sources rose up from the bowels of the earth, as did 'poisonous fume [which] infects the Air and the Air us'. Equally, however, the absence of 'Morality and Charity' in society made 'the Earth to reel too and fro, like a Drunkard: flinging out its Inhabitants in some places in other places swallowing them down', and giving rise to the 'unseparable consequents' of famine, war and 'sweeping pest'.[16] Modern interpretations provide ample explanations for the concurrency of disasters: the movement and garrisoning of troops during conflict is widely regarded as a prime factor in the spread of disease, while Germany's central military involvement in the Thirty Years War (1618–1648) diverted funds away from crucial dike reconstruction, precipitating regional flooding that affected many of its North Sea coastal communities.[17] The tsunami and localised fires that followed some of the worst earthquakes in history (including Basel in 1356, Lisbon in 1755 and San Francisco in 1906) are today recognised as scientific phenomena, but to contemporaries they served as particularly forceful reminders of divine wrath.

Disasters 'required explanation and incited reflection'.[18] Contemporaries who debated the particular sins precipitating a given event attributed them most commonly to factionalism in accordance with their own biases. Not surprisingly, they often identified a sharp increase in such occurrences during periods of particular political, religious or social turmoil such as the Reformation, around which time there were reported sightings in Scotland of hailstones 'as big as Pigeons Eggs', comets and fiery dragons, as well as whales 'of a huge bigness' being washed up along the Firth of Forth.[19] Similarly, disasters could be metaphors for concurrent events, with one Italian contemporary interpreting the eruption of Vesuvius in 1631 as an embodiment of the political unrest between Neapolitan citizens and their Habsburg rulers: 'in its fashion, then, the volcano spoke for the city'.[20] In this context, we can better appreciate the awestruck fascination with which the Italian 'two-headed boy' Lazarus Colloredo and his parasitic brother John Baptiste were greeted when their tour of Europe brought them to Aberdeen for a week in the midst of civil war in 1642.[21] The same prurient undertones probably characterised the reception five years later of the pamphlet *Strange Newes from Scotland*, which related the birth near Edinburgh of a 'terrible and prodigious Monster' that provoked a 'quaking terrour' in all those who witnessed it.[22] The timing of the birth in September 1647 resonated with a readership in the central belt reeling from years of war and plague, and occurred right in the midst of Aberdeen's final, devastating epidemic. That particular birth was attributed to its mother's errant fissure from Presbyterianism, while an earthquake in Glasgow in July 1679 was attributed by a royalist commentator to divine wrath over the failed uprising at Bothwell Bridge of a group of militant Covenanters resistant to the imposition by James VII of Episcopacy.[23] Nationwide factionalism was further identified as a leading cause of earthquakes, which were said to occur because 'the Bible suffers more abuse in Scotland nor [that is, than] any Kingdom of the World'.[24]

It has been observed with regard to early modern France that the interpretation of natural disasters as 'manifestations of God's wrath and punishment for human transgressions' enabled the Church to categorise them 'so as to replace chronic anxiety about survival with the fear of divine retribution for sin'.[25] However, this worldview not only threatened death but also offered hope and agency in the face of calamity. Inhabitants of Aberdeen or Elgin in the seventeenth century might well have been duly shocked and awed at the prospect of plague, but their belief in divine benevolence as well as divine wrath gave them the crucial ability to help themselves through redemption. Epidemics were disastrous, but the fact of their occurrence was entirely comprehensible. They had an established place within a coherent apocalyptic worldview in which providence underpinned natural causality, but which still allowed space for effective temporal efforts to assuage calamity. In many European cities responses to successive outbreaks ultimately brought about the establishment of hospitals and public health boards, an aspect of natural disasters which echoes their transformative potential noted at the start of this section. Smaller urban centres and sufficiently effective civic government at the local level made such developments redundant in Aberdeen and the north-east (as indeed in Scotland more generally). Nevertheless, in settlements throughout the nation civic responses to disasters – fires and plagues alike – shared a number of positive elements, particularly the mobilisation of the citizenry for the collective good and the acknowledgement of a civic responsibility to those worst affected.

Aberdeen's plague treatise: Gilbert Skene's *Ane Breve Descriptioun of the Pest* (1568)

At the outset, it might be expected that plague policy in Aberdeen and its vicinity – both in the formulation of legislation and in the practical care of sufferers – would have benefited significantly from the existence of King's College located in Old Aberdeen a few miles to the north of the city proper. However, this would be a misleading assumption. Scotland's third university was founded in 1495 by Bishop William Elphinstone, a prominent humanist for whom it has been claimed medicine was 'the least important subject'.[26] Study of the subject might well have languished, as it did at Scotland's two other universities, St Andrews and Glasgow,[27] were it not for the intervention of James IV (in whose honour the college was named), a Renaissance king famed for his active interest in medical matters.[28] In May 1497 he set aside royal revenues to provide an annual salary for an ongoing post of professor of medicine at Aberdeen, a position known as 'mediciner'.[29] Regius chairs in medicine were only established at England's two universities well into the sixteenth century (at Cambridge in 1540 and at Oxford six years later[30]), and the endowment at Aberdeen has been celebrated in both scholarly and popular histories of the university and city as the 'oldest chair of medicine in [the British Isles]'.[31] Historians of medical education have failed to acknowledge such an apparently auspicious development, however, and it could be argued that this reflects the fact that the existence of the professorship did not herald regular teaching in the subject, far less a thriving faculty.[32] Elphinstone struggled to secure two of the requirements necessary for this – suitably-qualified candidates to fill the post, prestigious though it was, and students for him to teach. It seems likely that an arrangement was made with each of the early mediciners, whereby King's financed the remainder of their studies to enable them to gain suitable medical qualifications on the continent, after which time they returned to Aberdeen to take up the post. The first mediciner, James Cumming, combined his duties at the college with employment as official physician to the burgh of Aberdeen, a move enacted in October 1503 shortly before his arrival at King's and possibly engineered by Elphinstone as an added inducement to entice Cumming to accept the chair. His appointment provided him with a yearly salary of ten merks and various fishing rights, on the condition that he and his family came to live in the town and that he visited the sick.[33] Despite the theoretical comfort in having to hand learned physicians to call upon, there is no evidence that either Cumming or any of his successors were ever explicitly consulted by the local council either in the formulation of plague policy or in the diagnosis and care of sufferers, though as Chapter 3 will show the first mediciner was at least in magistrates' employ when they passed legislation concerning sufferers of the Great Pox.

However, the efforts of the third mediciner at King's College, Gilbert Skene, have ensured that Aberdeen will forever retain a significant association with learned discourses on plague and its prevention. Born in Bandodle to the west of Aberdeen about the year 1522, Skene had studied at King's College before completing his medical education abroad at Paris and Louvain. Returning to Aberdeen to take up the mediciner's post in the early 1560s, he would have taught few, if any, students and most likely combined his employment at King's with operating a private practice in the city. This arrangement would have allowed him time to focus on composing *Ane Breve Descriptioun of the Pest*, published at Edinburgh in 1568. This treatise occupies a significant place in early modern medical print culture: it was the first medical work to be printed in Scotland, the first to be written in the vernacular, and the only one specifically to deal with plague that was authored by a Scotsman (and a native of Aberdeenshire at that). In the first half of the sixteenth century Scotland had been hit by major outbreaks, during which numerous burghs over a fairly wide area were infected in every decade with particularly severe epidemics occurring in the 1510s and the 1540s; indeed, these were the only two which struck the city of Aberdeen itself. Even though communities throughout the nation had become used to recurrent outbreaks by the mid-sixteenth century, this did not mean that the impact of plague on any given locality was lessened. Far from it; the overall tone of Skene's treatise makes it clear that the disease remained the most feared affliction some two centuries after it had first broken out.

The threat of plague naturally made consumers wish to have the ability to discuss matters relating to health with their medical practitioner on a mutual footing, particularly when it came to such a frightening and intractable disease. Before the publication of Skene's vernacular treatise readers in much of Scotland seeking medical information had been reliant on Latin texts that were brought back by students returning home after completing their medical training on the continent, such as those owned by the mediciners at King's College.[34] Latin works naturally had a very limited readership and vernacular medical literature provided a more accessible alternative, as well as enhancing the patient–practitioner relationship.[35] Skene's treatise was written at a time when, aided by the advent of printing, the production and availability of vernacular texts in England, not least those concerning medical beliefs, were increasing exponentially and exceeding those written in Latin, 'the international language of scholarship'.[36] In 1485 the first vernacular plague treatise had been printed in England, and during the century or so after the appearance of the *Litill Boke* attributed to Canutius, over forty editions of twenty different plague tracts were published to help English society cope with continued outbreaks. This output particularly rose after the middle of the sixteenth century, making plague one of the most popular medical topics.[37] A particularly severe epidemic had broken out in many parts of the British Isles in 1563 and over the course of the following three years ravaged communities from London to Edinburgh. The devastation it caused saw a surge in the production of plague treatises in England, including William Bullein's *Dialogue against the feuer Pestilence*, a particularly popular work first published in 1564. Even though this epidemic did not reach Aberdeen, it may have been the virulence of plague in Edinburgh and the south that prompted Skene to commence the writing of his treatise.

By the time the disease next broke out it was late in 1568 and the *Breve Descriptioun* was issued by the king's official printer Robert Lekpreuik's press in Edinburgh, a city which was then in the grip of plague. The epidemic ravaged many towns in Scotland's central belt and, notwithstanding the measures implemented by the city's magistrates, killed almost a fifth of Edinburgh's inhabitants.[38] Those who remained wanted to know both how and why this had occurred, and how best they could safeguard their own health in the face of such imminent and overwhelming disaster.[39] Skene sought to unravel the mysteries of the disease he termed a 'cruell miserable tiran and manslayar' through a comprehensive yet straightforward analysis of its causes, symptoms, treatment and cure.[40] His views on plague were typical, and most of his comments are easily identifiable in other treatises produced both before and after his own.[41] The vast majority of works on plague were derivative and therefore unremarkable, and some were identical translations of foreign texts.

Thomas Lodge's *A Treatise of the Plague* of 1603, for example, has been judged the 'most comprehensive English work on plague to that date',[42] but it was essentially a direct translation into English of a little-known French treatise from 1566.[43] Rather than being largely derived from an earlier, foreign work, Skene's own treatise was an 'original' composition, bearing in mind that this is something of a misnomer when discussing sixteenth-century plague tracts. His treatise is divided into eight chapters of varying length. It begins by describing the nature and causes of plague and advising how best the disease might be recognised, before moving on to discuss the environmental and physiological conditions conducive to infection. It concludes with several chapters detailing how plague might be avoided, treated and cured.

In the hierarchy of diseases, plague was the most feared due to its intractability and the high mortality it could cause in a relatively short space of time. It was believed to be generated by environmental corruption and to spread in two interrelated ways: through polluted airborne vapours (miasma) and by contact, both direct and indirect, with sources of infection (contagion). Skene emphasised that plague was particularly malevolent because it spread through the medium of the air, the one thing that was 'necessar for mannis lyfe'.[44] It had a hidden, venomous quality which Skene believed had 'strenthe and wikitnes above al natural putrifactioun'. The airborne plague poison subtly entered the body through the pores, corrupting the humours and putrefying the organs, before attacking the principal organ, the heart. It was particularly dangerous to patients and challenging to practitioners because it was so insidious and invasive; 'theiflie' is how Skene described it.[45]

In describing plague as 'ane scurge and punischment of the maist iust God', Skene echoed contemporary understanding about the origins of all disasters as manifestations of divine wrath because of society's sins. Naturally, then, the most effective way to counter plague was to appease God: 'to return to [Him], quha is maist puissant with ane affectionat and ardent will and hart, to imploir the support of his Maiestie ... to pacifie his wrathe aganis vs'.[46] The overarching, spiritual cause of plague in no way precluded the efficacy of secondary, natural causes of plague through which God worked, just as civic efforts to fight fires and prevent floods were imperative despite these occurrences being earthly manifestations of divine wrath. Physicians were evidently optimistic that plague could be treated and cured, and treatises, including that by Skene, contained long sections on how this might be achieved.

This reflects the intended purpose of Skene's book. Plague treatises catered to a captive market and were produced as convenient, usually pocket-sized self-help manuals for everyday use by better-off patients and the practitioners who attended them. These manuals were designed as easy reference guides, deliberately jargon-free and to the point. While some writers offered longer expositions – Humfre Lloyd's translation of *The Treasuri of Helth* attributed to Pope John XXI being one notable example[47] – most plague treatises were focused on providing straightforward, practical guidance in prevention, treatment and cure. The majority were between twenty and seventy pages long,[48] so Skene's own *Breve* [brief] *Descriptioun*, at forty-five pages, was of average length. Ideas about the identification, prevention and treatment of plague were based on classical assumptions about the workings of the human body and the way that disease attacked it, and, as with all plague treatises his book was couched in terms that assumed a familiarity among its readers with Galenic humoural theory which dominated clinical understanding.

This overarching system cast each individual as essentially a microcosm of the universe that he inhabited; as a result he functioned in the same way as it, being similarly influenced by external factors such as planetary movements. The universe was comprised of the four elements of fire (which had the qualities of being hot and dry), water (cold and wet), earth (cold and dry) and air (hot and wet); so the human body was made up of four corresponding principal fluids known as humours – choler or yellow bile, phlegm or mucus, black bile and blood respectively. It followed logically that each season of the year shared similar properties with a particular bodily humour and with each stage of a person's life cycle. Each individual's body contained a unique mix of these humours, which determined their own particular state of wellbeing. Skene noted that, ideally, good health would be maintained by ensuring humoural equilibrium and the body would naturally be purged of any excess or harmful humours through 'the Intestines, Vrines, Exercise, Sueit, fasting, and difflatioun'. However, when the workings of the body broke down or were upset the composition of the humours could become unbalanced, leading to illnesses which corresponded to the characteristics of the dominant humour.[49] An excess could be expelled through bleeding, purging, sweating or enemas as appropriate. This was necessary because too much of a particular humour predisposed the individual to a corresponding temperament, such as melancholic, and more importantly increased their susceptibility to a corresponding illness or disease. Diagnoses were necessarily case specific, as physicians sought to identify what precisely was attacking the individual body by 'seeing through' (the literal translation of *diagnosis*) certain observable 'signs', or 'tokens' manifested in a particular individual. There were, therefore, many different variables that could affect internal personal health, and the sections in Skene's *Breve Descriptioun* on the prevention and treatment of plague reflect the problematic nature of catering for a readership comprised of individuals whose particular humoural circumstances varied so widely.

The influence of the humoural system also determined external factors in the spread of plague. The disease spread through the agency of the air so it was related directly to the qualities of heat and humidity, which Skene acknowledged were 'the parentis of corruptioun'.[50] Such meteorological conditions were portents of plague, and locations deemed particularly susceptible were south-facing coastal places, exposed to warm southern winds.[51] It followed that excessive north winds counteracted the spread of disease. The chronicler John Leslie, writing in the 1570s, commented upon the north winds which blew 'oft verie vehement, swifte, and with a horrable sound' across Scotland, claiming that as a result the country suffered 'fewar seiknessis'.[52] Skene, too, remarked on the danger of 'greit sowthin wynde, or the samin blawand from pestiferous placis'.[53] The qualities of being hot and wet particularly predisposed children and youths to infection,[54] and also dictated that blood was the humour most associated with plague. It was particularly important to prevent blood from dominating the body's humoural composition, and this was true both for individuals who had already succumbed to plague and as a precaution against infection for others. Skene advised draining blood through either bleeding or cupping, particularly 'befoir or efter that ony persone hes bene in suspect place'.[55] Bleeding involved the strategic opening of a vein according to seasonal or environmental conditions and the draining of a predetermined amount of blood depending on factors such as the patient's age, constitution or severity of infection. Cupping was the application of a heated glass to various parts of the body, which created a vacuum and drew the blood to the surface of the skin. If the patient was already infected, similar methods could be used to draw out the poison. Skene concurred with other writers in recommending doing this by using blistering plasters made from a concoction of egg, flour, honey and turpentine. He made no mention of the efficacy of applying live animals like snakes, toads and even chickens to the affected area, though this was a popular method recommended in many English vernacular treatises from Thomas Phaer's *Treatyse of the Pestylence* to Nathaniel Hodges' eighteenth-century treatise *Loimologia*.[56]

Pills and potions for both the prevention and cure of plague contained similar ingredients, which ranged from the mundane to the fantastic. Some that Skene recommended like theriac ('treacle') or mithridate and garlic (the poor man's medicine)[57] were popular all-round medicines, while his advocacy of scorpions and powdered unicorn horn reflects a respect for tradition and classical authority.[58] Few writers offered any rationale for their particular choice of ingredients, and explanations that were given were usually based on humoural theory, with, for example, cold and dry herbs being used to counteract hot and moist diseases such as plague, and others like rue being considered to drive out poison and prevent corruption.[59]

Corruption was the key to plague causation and so also to plague prevention. Heat and humidity caused decay which produced foul odours and corrupted the environment, generating the plague poison. All writers understood the association between pollution and plague and acknowledged the environmental factors that were likely to generate infection. Skene's list of these included 'standand vatter, sic as Stank, Pule, or Loche moste corrupte, and filthie: Erd, dung, stinkand Closettis, [and] deid Cariounis vnbureit'. Furthermore, plague broke out as a result of 'stinkand corruptioun and filth, quhilkis occupeis the commune streittis and gaittis', and the 'greit reik of colis without vinde to dispache the sam'.[60] Stamping out noxious everyday practices such as giving free rein to swine and other dirty animals, along with the casual discarding of butchers' offcuts and the steeping of hides in water, would help to cleanse the environment.[61] So too would countering the noxious odours with pleasant ones. The use of sweet-smelling herbs was considered an important prophylactic measure, for plants such as saffron, juniper and thyme 'temperis & correctis all pestilenciall corruptioun of air'.[62] They were to be used 'vniuersalie or priuatlie be fyre & suffumigatioun maid be aromatical materialis', particularly in the homes of infected people. Skene used classical precedent to support this, noting that Hippocrates had used perfumed fire to rid Athens of plague as it caused the air to become dry 'and of gude odour', and was 'ane Antidote contrarie the pest and all corruptioun'.[63] Skene recommended that when visiting the sick, sponges or handkerchiefs should be soaked in vinegar or rosewater and used to cover the mouth. Anointing the ears, face and neck with these liquids also helped to prevent noxious fumes being absorbed through the pores, as did the avoidance of baths and laborious exercise, which caused sweating.[64] In order to freshen the breath and prevent vapours being inhaled, he recommended chewing substances like citron, cloves and angelica, and sufferers were to turn their faces away during conversation. Windows should be left open to facilitate the circulation of the air, except if they faced south. Skene also stressed the importance of a holistic approach in preventing plague by attending correctly to each of the Galenic six non-naturals, which included maintaining the right mental attitude, eating a healthy diet and practising temperance in all activities.[65]

If these methods failed and infection took hold its effects were devastating. Since Skene's treatise was to be consulted as a diagnostic tool, he included a chapter on the symptoms shown by a typical sufferer in order that they could be treated before it was too late. Bleeding, for example, had to be done within twenty-four hours of infection or it would be ineffective.[66] The noxious nature of plague defined its ghastly symptoms. Skene's list of these included stinking, feverish sweating and detestable breath, with laboured breathing, racing pulse, and an aching body that was subject to fainting, vomiting, tiredness and spitting blood. The patient would have an intolerable thirst but no appetite. Most notably his body might show swellings around the lymph nodes, the most distinctive tokens of plague.[67] Rather disconcertingly for the reader, most of these awful symptoms were also noted by Skene in the following chapter, which identified the signs of impending death in sufferers. Additional symptoms included black- or lead-coloured urine, a black tongue and cramps, and were a grim indication that infection had advanced too far to be treatable. It was thought possible to tell whether the heart had been infected by drinking a mixture of bole armeniac (a type of clay-like earth), wine and rosewater, with death imminent if the patient subsequently vomited.[68]

Traditional views about the causes, prevention and treatment of plague were very long-lasting, and were not seriously challenged until the later seventeenth century, by which time plague had receded from pre-modern Scotland for good.[69] Innovations in plague discourses, such as they were, concerned controversial aspects including the efficacy of prayer and the morality of flight by physicians and clerics.[70] The ethics of flight were much debated, though most physicians recognised that the best way to avoid polluted air was to flee from it; as Gideon Harvey succinctly put it in his *Discourse of the Plague*, 'Flee quick, Go far, and Slow return'.[71] Skene likewise advised his readers to '[remove] thame self fra cuntrey, town, and Air, infectit or suspect', while noting that flight was less acceptable for citizens with civic responsibilities.[72] Magistrates and clergy in particular had a moral obligation during epidemics to remain.[73] There was general agreement that it was acceptable for physicians themselves to flee, with one defence being that their duty of patient care had been fulfilled sufficiently through their composition of helpful medical texts.[74] Skene, however, scorned those physicians who fled, accusing them of being 'mair studious of thair awine helthe' than that 'of the commoun weilthe'.[75] He was able to take the moral high ground because plague did not break out during his time in Aberdeen, so he never had to face the dilemma of flight himself.

The influence of Skene's *Breve Descriptioun*

Skene's plague treatise occupies a significant place in early modern print culture in Scotland, not least because it was the first medical text of Scottish origin to be written in the vernacular. Like other medical writers, Skene was clearly very proud of his academic training in medicine, boasting that he had spent his entire youth 'in the Sculis', and he noted that it would have befitted his learned background to have written his treatise in Latin. He was, however, conscious that his audience in Scotland had no vernacular medical work of its own available to illuminate the principles of bodily health, let alone one that concentrated specifically on such an immediate and frightening disease as plague. He recognised that Latin medical texts had 'bene nothing profitable to the commoun and wulgar people', and so he 'thocht it expedient and neidfull to express the sam in sic language as the vnlernit may be als weil satisfyit as Masteris of Clargie'.[76]

This apparent desire to inform society at large, expressed by many writers of English vernacular medical texts, drew criticism from within the medical profession and played out what has been termed 'the politics of open access to knowledge'.[77] Writing in the mid-sixteenth century, John Caius 'thought it beste to auiode the iudgement of the multitude, from whome in maters of learning a man shalbe forced to dissente'; indeed, he asserted that 'the common setting furthe and printing of euery foolish thing in englishe, both of physicke unperfectly, and other matters undiscretly, diminishe the grace of thynges learned set furth in thesame'.[78] Likewise, John Securis argued that making medical works more widely accessible diluted the information they contained, and devalued the money and effort that physicians had invested in their medical education. What was the point in investing so much time and finance into studying the subject at university if vernacular texts enabled anyone – even 'pouchemakers, threshers, ploughmen and coblers' – to practice medicine?[79]

Despite these objections vernacular medical writers professed a desire to better inform the general population about matters pertaining to their own health, believing that to write in Latin served only to 'haue the people ignoraunt', as Thomas Phaer put it.[80] Skene himself emphasised the philanthropic impetus for writing in the vernacular and stressed how the physician worked for the 'aduancement of the commoun weilth', particularly the poor, the social group with which plague was by then the most firmly associated.[81] This echoed earlier vernacular writers on plague such as Thomas Moulton, whose *This is the Myrrour or Glasse of Helth* (c.1531) was 'set in printe in Englysh [so] that euery man both lerned & lewde ryche and pore may the better understande it'.[82]

To a large extent, however, such sentiments were rhetorical. Even with the relative rise in literacy the evidence from England indicates that the vast majority of readers of medical works were medical professionals and the social elite; therefore 'the statement of the "unlearned" as the target audience ... cannot be taken at its face value'.[83] This is particularly evident given the bilingual nature of Skene's treatise. In spite of his grand claims to benevolence he followed many vernacular medical texts and wrote his recipes and instructions for administering them in Latin, maintaining that they could not 'goodly be put in vulgar language'.[84] Such bi- or multi-lingualism was a strategy employed in many medical works from the period, particularly in conveying what might be regarded as the more technical aspects of medicine such as the names of medicines which English vocabulary could not adequately express; Humfre Lloyd, for example, noted in his introduction to *The Treasuri of Helth* (1556) that 'in the natures of herbes and symples ... we be eyther ignorant or destitute of Englyshe names for a great sorte of them'.[85] As a practical handbook, the sections on the treatment and cure of plague amounted to a significant proportion of Skene's treatise, in which Latin prescriptions were interspersed throughout the later chapters with comment written in the vernacular on the treatment and cure of plague. In writing most of his handbook in the vernacular but his recipes in Latin, Skene's rationale appeared to accord with many of his English counterparts who 'helped to create a medical culture that was based on the transformation of learned medicine into a popularly accessible medicine, whilst still preserving the impression that there was a learned medicine, a higher level of expertise'.[86]

The influence on sixteenth-century society of Skene's vernacular treatise must also take into account the necessary distinction between audience and readership. As plague was of universal concern its potential audience was restricted only by the extent of literacy or aurality, and was heterogeneous in terms of social status, education and profession, including both lay readers and medical professionals of various levels.[87] However, the issue of who actually did read his text is rather different; unfortunately, explicit evidence of possession or purchase, 'the real test of readership', is non-existent.[88] It is not known how many copies were even printed and to this day only one has been preserved; octavo plague tracts were relatively few in number and were rarely bound, which lessened their ability to survive.[89] The *Breve Descriptioun* was not reprinted, nor was it listed in the inventories of any other booksellers in

Scotland aside from that of the printer himself, Robert Lekpreuik. The issue of affordability is similarly problematic but the evidence for comparable texts in England indicates that, although Skene promoted his work as offering medical advice on plague to the unlearned, the treatise itself would most likely still have been beyond the financial means of the majority of society. Its possible price tag of four to six shillings is substantially greater than the average price of a book sold on the Scottish market during the 1570s (1*s* 5*d*).[90] Nevertheless, it remains the case that 'vernacular medical literature is of wider interest than its limited circle of readers might suggest'.[91] Even if its ownership was restricted to the wealthiest urban households, the information and advice it contained might have circulated amongst both citizens and magistrates within Scotland's burghs, perhaps particularly in Aberdeen and Edinburgh, and might have helped to inform subsequent measures taken to prevent plague at the individual – if less so the communal – level. The publication of the *Breve Descriptioun* did bring Skene some fame, and probably played a part in his subsequent move to Edinburgh and in his appointment in 1581 as royal physician to James VI.[92] By the time of his death in 1599 Skene's treatise had found its way to London, being listed (without a price) in the bookseller Andrew Maunsell's *Catalogue of English Printed Bookes* of 1595.[93] London's social elite would have found its information about plague useful, if familiar. To that end at least, Skene's *Breve Descriptioun of the Pest* made an important contribution to the growing corpus of vernacular discourses on plague, which itself constituted an immensely significant part of early modern medical writing.

The place of the *Breve Description* in medical writing in Scotland

As a plague treatise of Scottish origin Skene's *Breve Descriptioun* had no precedent. While sources including chronicles and burgh records provide written evidence for both localised and nationwide outbreaks that occurred before the publication of Skene's text, the written medical response to plague within Scotland appears to have been limited to several translations into the vernacular of the smaller of two celebrated plague texts written by John of Burgundy around 1365.[94] Close-knit monastic communities were particularly susceptible to high fatalities from plague and manuscripts of John of Burgundy's treatise, called in translation *Ane Tretyse Agayne the Pestilens*, are known to have been owned by three Scottish abbeys – those of Kelso, Paisley and Inchcolm. Those belonging to the latter two were appended to mid-fifteenth-century manuscripts of the chronicler Walter Bower's *Scotichronicon*, which itself recorded notable epidemics including the notorious Black Death, which Bower reported as having killed twenty-four canons of St Andrews.[95] The more renowned of the two is the manuscript known as the Black Book of Paisley, possibly the earliest composition of those named and owned by the Abbey of Paisley well into the sixteenth century.[96] It has been suggested that the inclusion of the tract *De Pestilentia* in the Black Book of Paisley was made as a consequence of a visitation of plague either in 1455 or in 1474, during which time 'the pestilence raged in Scotland most fearfully'.[97] A translation of the smaller treatise, entitled *A Nobyl Tretyse Agayne the Pestilens*, is also attached to the Register of the Abbey of Kelso.[98] The abridged treatise provides advice on how to recognise and treat symptoms of plague, including the correct way to bleed the patient and the formula of concoctions to be administered, noting that ultimately his fate will be decided by the 'grace of god'.[99]

In terms of printed texts in Scotland, medical works comprised only a small fraction of the total number produced since the advent of printing in 1508. The subject matter of these, written in either Latin or in the vernacular and numbering just over four hundred in total, ranged from devotional and confessional works to parliamentary proclamations, poetry and grammar books.[100] Of these, *The Complaynt of Scotland* (1548), possibly attributed to Robert Wedderburn of Dundee, conveys a certain understanding of the cosmological, meteorological and spiritual causes of the plague which was then raging.[101] But only two texts are explicitly concerned with matters of health –the *Breve Descriptioun* and a short treatise called *Ane Breif descriptioun of the qualiteis and effectis of the well of the woman hill besyde Abirdene*, which extolled the medicinal virtues of a healing well at Aberdeen. Though published anonymously in 1580, it was probably also authored by Gilbert Skene, who retained links with his native city despite having moved to Edinburgh five years previously. From the turn of the seventeenth century a number of popular English medical texts were printed north of the border, making them more accessible to a Scottish audience.[102] Other works associated with health and healthcare composed and printed in Scotland during the seventeenth century included a treatise on pestilent fever, the virtues of tobacco and several texts praising the healing properties of various Scottish spas including that of Aberdeen.[103] Only two other works specifically on plague were printed in pre-modern Scotland. The first was issued by the official Edinburgh University printer James Lindsay's press in 1645, during what was to be the nation's final epidemic and the most severe since the Black Death of the mid-fourteenth century. The text, entitled *Medicines against the pest. Or An advice set down by the best learned in physick within the kingdome of England*, was a short compendium of octavo size that had originally been authorised by James VI and I during a nationwide outbreak in 1603 across each of his kingdoms, and as the title makes clear, it had an English origin. This work contrasts sharply with Skene's in its narrow focus on practical measures for self-preservation from plague, particularly as it articulated much more effectively the *Breve Descriptioun*'s apparent altruistic intention to advise the poor of society by eschewing inaccessible Latin remedies and providing specific alternatives aimed at those with limited finances. The other printed work on plague was likewise an English publication subsequently printed in Scotland, in this instance a treatise written by members of the English College of Physicians in 1665 which was printed in Edinburgh in 1721 in response to the outbreak of plague in the French port of Marseilles.[104] Private papers provide an indication that medical recipes and advice concerning plague circulated among the upper echelons of society; for example, the *Directions against the Plague* advocated by a Dr Burgess were copied out and enclosed with a letter from Sir John Hope of Craighall to his friend Sir George Mowatt of Bucholly in Caithness during the epidemic of 1645,[105] and eighty years later were also procured by Archibald Grant of Monymusk in the wake of the Marseilles outbreak.[106] Sections of the Englishman Thomas Moulton's *This is the Myrrour or Glasse of Helth* (first published c.1531), which attributed the plague then raging to a conjunction of Saturn and Jupiter, were included in a handwritten book owned by Dame Lilias Ruthven of Stobhall (afterwards Lady Drummond) in the later sixteenth century.[107] It seems plausible to conjecture that the advice contained in Skene's *Breve Descriptioun* might also have been similarly circulated.

It might appear *prima facie* that Gilbert Skene's treatise would have been of great practical benefit to civic authorities in Aberdeen and elsewhere in their fight against plague. Although such texts tended to contain advice directed towards the private client rather than the body politic, they could include comment relevant to collective action. While Skene did not state that his advice ought to be followed by magistrates, other writers such as Thomas Lodge in his *Treatise of the Plague* (1603) addressed governments directly and offered advice as though it were novel.[108] But in actuality the measures advocated by Skene and his fellow medical writers for avoiding infection simply reflected legislation that governments in many of Scotland's major burghs (helped to a significant extent at the parochial level by Kirk Session elders after the Reformation) had been implementing for over a century to counter the recurrent impact of plague in the communities under their jurisdiction.

Miasma and contagion

Miasma and contagion were the two methods by which plague was believed to spread that informed the way in which magistrates as well as physicians tackled the spread of the disease and treated its victims. To early modern minds, these dual concepts were not so much viewed as separate explanations for the generation and transmission of infection but rather as two sides of the same coin. Miasma was a non-specific infelicity in the general environment, which could produce plague. Contagion concerned the spread of the disease from one host (be it animals, people, or inanimate objects such as cloth) to another through indirect as well as direct contact, and the concept thus had a far broader meaning to early modern minds than does its modern usage. Miasma, as a general corruption, was regarded as the nature or general 'cause' of the disease and contagion the particular way it spread. The two theories were therefore interdependent. When physicians wrote of 'contagion' and chroniclers of spreading plague through contact with inanimate objects, both had underpinning their definition the idea of transmission through corrupt vapours.[109] The terms 'plague' and 'contagion' became almost synonymous in contemporary medical treatises but, again, this was because 'contagion' entailed general infection, whether spread through the air, touch or sight.[110] Skene himself noted that 'ane pest is the corruptioun or infectioun of the Air . . . the Heauine blawis that contagioun vpoune the face of the Earth'.[111] Similarly, it was believed that miasma could also be transported in clothes or bedding, or on the bodies of domestic animals (especially dogs, cats and pigs).

From its initial implementation by governments in Aberdeen and elsewhere, plague legislation reflected a belief in both miasma and contagion as integrated rather than mutually exclusive vectors of transmission. While the specific disease, such as plague, might be contagious (in its wider early modern sense), officials also believed that diseases, of which plague was one, could arise from a corrupt environment. Thus plague might enter the urban area by means of a person or their goods, or it might also arise from a polluted environment gradually worsening as the wider environs became afflicted. As contagion and miasma were essentially interchangeable concepts, either theory (or both) could motivate officials to implement exactly the same course of action. For example, if it was believed that plague was the result of a miasmic pollution of the environment endeavours would be made to clean the air through the removal of bad-smelling refuse and the control of noxious industrial activities (such as tanning). If, on the other hand, a contagion theory were solely to be promoted then it might be decided that the specific disease was being spread in a locale and the way to eliminate the danger was to clean the place. In other words, exactly the same course of action would be pursued. Furthermore, for any enthusiast of a miasmic theory, once a corruption existed, how individuals actually became diseased was not really different from the methodology of contagion theorists. In a miasmic situation, a person became diseased or ill because of the environment. In a contagion model a disease entered an area and was transmitted to specific individuals, since a contagion could also be passed by the air (in a rather vague manner). Thus, two alternative processes of reasoning produced the same result and informed plague policies implemented in Aberdeen as elsewhere.

In any case, the precise reasoning behind the way they spread is of less significance than the practical ways in which such beliefs motivated authorities to respond. Regardless of whether Aberdeen's government did consult learned medical men in the formulation of legislation, the theoretical justification for the implementation of policy was of little relevance to magistrates, whose concerns were far more pragmatic. They had to decide which actions were most likely to deal with the health crisis while not making the situation worse by severely damaging or unsettling the economy or the society more generally. As today, for early modern governments the chief concerns were cost, public opinion and demand rather than medical theories. Indeed, the chances were that the state would try everything and anything that might work. Adherence to any particular medical theory came a poor second to the perceived necessity of trying anything that the situation demanded. The decisive factor as to when a particular response might be tried largely depended on realities wholly divorced from medical theory. The wealth of a state, its social cohesion, its level of governmental sophistication and the depth of the crisis were more likely to dictate policy and action than theories of contagion and/or miasma.

Controlling plague, controlling people

For the social theorist Michel Foucault, early modern 'plague management was the political dream',[112] as the powers this gave for the civic control over the movements of everyone into and within the town, under the guise of a concern for public health, created what he regarded as 'the utopia of the perfectly governed city'.[113] While the isolation of sufferers, for example, was justified according to notions of both contagion and miasma, social control was not only a consequence but also a very real intention of such a policy given that plague threatened public order as much as public health. The same can be said for many of the other policies implemented in Aberdeen as elsewhere ostensibly as a result of plague: conducting house-to-house enquiries to ascertain the occupants of a given dwelling; enclosing and guarding entire households; ejecting from the bounds of the burgh those deemed a threat; and forcibly identifying certain categories of individual.

These policies were additionally informed and justified by the widespread acceptance of plague as a manifestation of divine wrath. Governors acknowledged as emphatically as physicians, chroniclers and clergy that the ultimate cause of plague and other diseases was divine punishment of sinful intent. In the causal hierarchy of a wide variety of afflictions, therefore, personal characteristics and moral behaviour were equally as important as environmental and physiological conditions in dictating an individual's particular disposition to infection. Regarding plague victims as particularly sinful helped to explain why within any given community some people were killed by the disease, some eventually recovered and others were completely left untouched. Society's moral leaders used the unequivocal fear of God's wrath as a tool to encourage an end to sinful and improper actions, while civic leaders were able to mould plague legislation to fit their own wider desires for the preservation of social order in a variety of ways. By the end of the fifteenth century, when Aberdeen was first seriously threatened with plague, the notion already existed that some persons within society were more likely than others to harbour infection. This was the case with regard to those whose lives were, for occupational or other reasons, socially promiscuous: soldiers, itinerant pedlars, gypsies, prostitutes and, particularly, the poor.

For magistrates in Florence and other towns whose plague legislation has been studied in detail, plague and poverty became regarded as particularly 'close companions' over the course of the sixteenth century.[114] Empirical observation taught governors that the disease flourished in places that were dirty, malodorous and overcrowded, and was associated with spoilt food and contaminated water. Not only did poverty force the destitute to endure such things, it further predisposed them to plague by robbing them of the ability to escape it. Like many of his fellow physicians Gilbert Skene advocated flight from sources of contamination, adding that those 'quha may not do the samyn, or mowit be Christiane Cheritie will not', were to ensure that they took suitable precautions against infection.[115] While many residents in Aberdeen did indeed flee when plague broke out, the poor could not afford to do this and hence became more likely to succumb.

The interpretation of plague as divine punishment for sin might also have emphasised the apparent predisposition of the poor to infection. Studies have stressed the traditional classification of the poor as fundamentally either deserving or undeserving, with commentators from Juan Luis Vives and Cornelius Agrippa to Erasmus and Thomas More denouncing the latter as lazy and immoral. These individuals were accused of 'feign[ing] being cripple or lame' and of wandering 'idly, lasciviously and dissolutely' about, spreading their 'sundry and diverse diseases, contagions and infections' indiscriminately.[116] They were not only deprived but also depraved and, as such, they particularly threatened social stability during the economic, spiritual and medical crisis of an outbreak.[117] In many places urban governments made a discernible effort to restrict support to orphans, the aged and the infirm who were considered deserving of it. After the Reformation in Scotland, it was more typical that civic governments and Kirk authorities worked together rather than in opposition, to continue in a restructured and reinvigorated way to dispense support to such individuals through sources typical of the earlier period: the collection of alms, offerings at church, fines paid to both secular and ecclesiastical authorities, and individual instances of benevolence (even though with the advent of Protestantism this no longer guaranteed salvation).[118] It has been argued that the process of religious reform in many countries influenced the increasing intolerance of the undeserving poor, which contributed to the punishment and rehabilitation of sinful behaviours that led to impoverishment, such as idleness and gambling. Studies of poor relief in Scotland (a recently reinvigorated historiographical topic) have likewise shown that poor relief and ecclesiastical discipline were 'two sides of the same coin', not surprising given the Kirk's natural concern with moral reform.[119] On the other hand, it is perhaps equally likely that secular and ecclesiastical bodies alike were simply responding more ruthlessly to the growing dimensions of the problem of the poor, regardless of confessional beliefs.[120] Either way, both in urban areas and throughout the parishes plague enabled the moral and physical control of people, particularly the poor, whether by casting them as recipients of charitable support according to moral suitability or as subjects of restrictive measures.

The ramifications of plague and other crises emphasised the fact that there were many causes of poverty and the poor were far from a homogenous social group. Just as today, within practically any community there was an omnipresent group of long-term dependent paupers, regardless of the precise circumstances of the individual. The lack of concern shown by Aberdeen's governors about these individuals during times of relative stability indicates that usually they were considered supportable, most likely through the informal charitable networks which went unrecorded but which McCallum has shown were an integral aspect of wider poor relief.[121] In addition to this, at any given time support could be required on a temporary basis by 'extraordinary' poor as the result of an adverse situation, such as a broken leg or an accidental fire, which brought about a short-term need for help. Again, it is likely that such individuals (and their families) tended to be sufficiently supported by private benevolence or a portion of the collection from church.

While an outbreak was also a temporary crisis, it was on a much wider and more burdensome scale, affecting not only those within a given urban locality or parish but also outsiders who were drawn to it by the prospect of receiving support. To make matters worse, the economic dislocation which gave rise to this trend also meant 'the bringing down of the formerly self-sufficient lower income groups to the ranks of the destitute'. During crises they became so-called 'shamefaced' poor, for whom poverty was shameful as well as unpleasant.[122] They were able typically to eke out a precarious living, but they could be tipped into poverty by the cancellation of the regional market one week or the failure of their regular supplier to come up with the goods necessary to supplement their craft. Plague entailed such scenarios and it was in the face of economic downturn coupled with a rise in the number of poor that both Kirk and civic authorities were forced to be particularly discerning about deciding eligibility. Such crises 'tested "the effectiveness and thus the legitimacy of political power", and during such shocks the priorities and efficiency of local and national institutions become apparent'.[123] This was as true in Aberdeen as elsewhere.

Civic responses to plague in their national and international contexts

As this chapter has outlined, civic responses to plague in Aberdeen, as in Scotland's other major burghs, might or might not have been formulated in conjunction with advice taken from physicians or other medical practitioners. Policy might have been based on the interchangeable transmission theories of miasma and contagion, or it might simply have been implemented as a pragmatic reaction to empirical observation and the social and financial circumstances of the locality at that particular time. While magistrates acknowledged plague as resulting from divine wrath due to human sin, their treatment of the poor and other minority groups was very likely dictated by practical concerns of social control and cost as much as a desire to eliminate infection by propitiatory acts and the removal from the community of sinful people and behaviours.

Notwithstanding these variables, what is certain is that the responses of local governments to plague were formulated long before the height of the written intellectual discourse amongst the medical profession about the nature of the disease in the later sixteenth century, of which Gilbert Skene was a part. In a

European context, Aberdeen's response (in common with other burghs in Scotland) is remarkably innovative. That the Italian city states led the way in the formation of civic plague policy is reflected in the large historiography devoted to case studies of plague legislation in Ragusa (modern Dubrovnik), Florence, Bologna and elsewhere from the later fourteenth century. Measures from quarantine to the issuing of bills of health were subsequently adapted (or were perhaps formulated independently) by governments north of the Alps, in towns across France, Germany, central and eastern Europe and in Russia over the course of the following century or two.

England was anomalous in this pattern. The first plague measures were implemented only in January 1518, when a royal proclamation of Henry VIII set out strategies to control what were termed 'contagious infections', which were likely to continue if 'remedy by the sufferance of Almighty God' was not provided. But these had a concern with protecting the stability of the government and Crown, being aimed specifically at protecting London, the seat of government, and Oxford, where the royal court then was. A handful of English towns made efforts to implement their own preventative measures, but these were rather *ad hoc* and most councils might have been content to adopt the view taken by the London aldermen in 1535, who 'trusting to God that the sickness shall cease', as they put it, waited several weeks before taking action to curb the latest outbreak within their city.[124] While a national order for fasting in response to plague was issued in 1563, it was not until 1578 that nationwide legislation was passed to tackle the temporal causes of the disease, 'to be executed throughout the Counties of this Realme, in such Townes, Villages, and other places as are, or may be hereafter infected with the plague'. These became the model for the legislation implemented by successive English governments: leading plague historian Paul Slack noted that 'until almost the last breath of the disease in England, the Orders of 1578 dictated policy from one end of the kingdom to the other'.[125] He has further remarked that 'by comparison with Italy or France', England was 'a benighted, backward country' in the implementation of plague legislation.[126] As the example of Aberdeen alone shows, it also lagged far behind Scotland. In his recent survey of maritime quarantine John Booker noted that 'measures against plague in Scotland were being vigorously undertaken while England was still groping for some kind of effective response' and drew particular attention to the way in which the identification in various Scottish records of certain goods as being susceptible to infection 'quite significantly' pre-dated a recognition of this in equivalent measures adopted in England.[127]

But whether we can truly talk of a 'nationwide' plague policy in Scotland is another matter. And so, a caveat before the next section: when considering plague measures, no less than other orders issued by the national parliament from its base in Edinburgh, it is wise to realise that the tentacles of central government by no means always reached throughout the nation effectively. From at least the mid-sixteenth century, the Privy Council issued a number of regulations designed to staunch overseas sources of infection from infiltrating Scotland's boundaries. These efforts were naturally aimed at coastal settlements, particularly those situated on the east which engaged in the bulk of seaborne interactions with potentially infected ports. Aberdeen was comparatively removed from the administrative centre of Edinburgh, however, and therefore tended to respond somewhat later (and sometimes not at all) to orders addressed to 'heid burrowes of this kingdome' or 'all places neidfull' as did burghs situated either side of the Forth and on the eastern coast to the immediate north as well as south of the capital.[128] More pertinently, oftentimes Privy Council orders were only concerned with those burghs situated either side of the Forth and in Fife. They did not address Aberdeen or settlements located in its hinterland at all, despite Aberdeen being one of the nation's major ports engaged in overseas trade.[129] The issuing of these central directives by the Privy Council (from the mid-sixteenth century) coincided with Aberdeen's plague-free period, so it could be said that with the passage of time central governors accepted that Aberdeen's councillors were doing a successful job in staunching plague without their interference. More often than not, Aberdeen's magistrates were proactive in efforts to prevent seaborne infection throughout the region independently of central government directives, and concerned themselves not only with the major port of the city itself but also the numerous small harbours and coves dotted around the north-east coast.

Nationwide plague policy

Responses to plague at the urban and parochial level were underpinned by a legislative framework comprised of two particular statutes: the Rule of the Pestilence (1456) and the letter of James IV (1513). The first of these might be said to have been issued nominally at the national level, while the second was certainly not (though a copy was sent to burghs throughout the kingdom, including Aberdeen). Nevertheless, both statutes were significant efforts made by the national parliament to tackle sources of plague. The disease had broken out in 1455, causing death 'per universum regnum Scocie'.[130] Notwithstanding this exaggeration (to begin with, there is no evidence that Aberdeen and its vicinity were affected) the epidemic clearly caused sufficient concern for parliament to respond with the implementation of what has been identified as 'the first attempt by any central body in Scotland to codify the methods of dealing with plague'.[131] The statute, passed in October 1456, was known as the Rule of the Pestilence and contained four clauses which are of interest both in confirming established practices in Scotland and in regulating responses to plague by magistrates and clergy alike that would continue in the coming years, decades and centuries.[132]

The first clause of the Rule stipulated that any person with sufficient means to support themselves and their household was able to be enclosed within their own house, with removal from the burgh the consequence for anyone who chose to disobey their 'nychtbouris' (that is, the wider community including the civic authorities). It was not explicitly stated that removal from the burgh entailed relocation to a designated isolation area, though this might be assumed given that the notion of civic responsibility for the protection of the common weal would not have allowed the reckless unchecked release of anyone suspected or confirmed to be infectious. This is demonstrated by the second part of this clause, which stated that anyone found within a burgh who did not have the means to be self-sufficient was considered to be the responsibility of that particular community, and it was up to its members to ensure that that individual should not be permitted to leave it 'to fyle the cuntre about thame'. Two notable observations may be made concerning this first clause of the Rule. To begin with, the notion of social control is evident in the latter stipulation in the restriction of an individual's movements, particularly since this applied to 'pure folkis' with no resources of their own. Secondly, the clause makes it apparent that two methods of segregation were recognised in Scotland by this time: enclosure within one's own house along with one's household (which could effectively entail a death sentence for all enclosed) or removal to a designated isolation area outside the town boundaries. As the Rule makes clear, the primary criterion in deciding which of these methods was to be chosen was the extent of the individual's assets and self-sufficiency. Pragmatism – in this case consideration of the consequent financial burden – was of paramount concern to the state. During more extensive outbreaks the numbers of those who were forcibly enclosed within their own houses was most likely greater than the number removed to purpose-built quarantine camps, so as to lessen the financial and administrative burden this placed on the local government to establish, supervise and sustain those in isolation. Nevertheless, inherent in this prescription is the acknowledgement of the obligation of the state in the care and sustenance of the infected or those suspected of it. This was an obligation recognised in Scottish legislation concerning lepers since the twelfth century; but while the leper was permitted to beg (within certain figurative and literal limits), no such leniency was granted to plague victims.[133]

The second clause of the Rule of the Pestilence continued to acknowledge civic obligation in the care of the community, with regard to both confirmed plague victims and those still free from infection. It stipulated that in the event of any sick person escaping after they had been 'put out of ony towne' – presumably for the purpose of quarantine rather than banishment – it was the responsibility of officials from his or her place of residency to locate them, bring them home and punish them for their 'awaie passing'. This places a certain obligation on a community for the whereabouts of any person under its jurisdiction. The expulsion of plague victims, though a convenient way of ridding the community of a source of physical (and moral) corruption, was clearly a practice harmful to healthy society. Despite this, it had been a punishment meted out to criminal lepers that had been enshrined in legislation such as the Act *Anent Lipper Folk* of 1427 and was also sometimes inflicted on plague victims who broke the law in various burghs including Aberdeen. While the protection of the wider common weal was important, magistrates prioritised civic responsibility and the maintenance of social order within the bounds of the local community.

The third and fourth clauses of the Rule related to particular practices undertaken during outbreaks; firstly, the prohibition on burning another's house unless this could be done without any damage and, secondly, the stipulation that clergymen were to be pardoned to process throughout their diocese twice a week 'for stanching of the pestilence'. As already discussed, the use of fire (whether through the scorching of internal walls or the burning of heather and other aromatic materials) was one perceived method of eliminating infection, but it carried with it the very real danger of a resultant blaze. Indeed, a number of properties were razed to the ground in this way (including in Belhelvie north of Aberdeen in 1608) and the Rule urged care to be exercised in carrying out fumigation during outbreaks. The final clause highlights the way in which spiritual responses were as important as temporal ones in tackling plague, and the role of the clergy in the care of their parishioners during outbreaks prior to the Reformation remained consistent (albeit differently organised and with different emphases) as part of the post-1560 Kirk.

While the Rule was not acknowledged by the Aberdeen authorities at the time of its promulgation, this was most likely because the city had not then experienced plague. In fact, it was to be a further fifty years before the disease even threatened the burgh and longer still before the second set of plague precautions was issued by the state. They took the form of a letter 'anent the pest' written in the name of King James IV 'with the avys of our counsale'. This was issued on 17 January 1513, still five years before the first public precautions against plague appeared in England, and came in response to a severe epidemic which had broken out in Edinburgh and its vicinity some months earlier. Though the statutes themselves were addressed to magistrates in Edinburgh, they were ordered to be distributed to each major burgh, so in that sense they were aimed at civic authorities nationwide.[134] As with the Rule of the Pestilence they might be thought of as confirmatory rather than innovative, as they essentially reiterated measures which were then in place in Edinburgh and which local authorities in Aberdeen and throughout much of Europe had been implementing for years (over a century in the case of the Italian city states). Each of their recommendations was designed to prevent, contain and eliminate plague in accordance with the interrelated theories of transmission via both miasma and contagion. Broadly speaking, they were concerned with targeting all possible sources of infection both internal and external to a locality. No infected goods were to be imported either by sea or by land. No one suspected of infection was to interact in any way with 'clene folkis'. Anyone who had been enclosed was forbidden from breaking their quarantine, whether this was in their own home or in a designated segregated area. All 'vile and suspect beistis' such as dogs, cats and swine were to be restrained or else could lawfully be slain. Concerted efforts were to be made to clean up the environment both at the individual and the local level. Residents were to clean their own 'rewes, windis, closis, and guttaris, bayth on baksyd and foresyd', while governments were to ensure that no middens could build up at official entrances to a burgh. No beggars were permitted to remain within the burgh unless they were deemed to be 'impotent aged or blind folkis, that ar nocht abill to wyn thari leving within the realme vtherwayis'; they were to be given a token of the town to prove their right to remain.

Demonstrating consistency with the earlier Rule of the Pestilence, notions of both civic and communal responsibility continued to be stressed in various ways in the letter of James IV. It stipulated that local governments were answerable to higher authorities if they happened to be negligent in their enforcement of the plague statutes, and reiterated that the regulations applied to everyone within 'the boundis of your office'. The letter further warned that citizens were to be held to account for the actions of their servants, though this did not preclude the overarching emphasis that each individual was responsible for his or her own adherence to the legislation.

A development that can be identified in the letter of 1513 – bearing in mind that this should be interpreted as a measure that was to some extent innovative though not necessarily 'better' (that is, demonstrably more successful) – included a staggered quarantine process. Through this, any plague victim deemed to have recovered, 'if God relevis thame of pestilence and givis thame heall', was free to mix with healthy society on the condition that they were clearly identifiable for the fifteen days following their reintroduction. This was to be achieved either by carrying a white stick or wearing a square of white cloth on their chest in order that 'vther clane folkis may eschew thame'. Anyone who disobeyed this clearly threatened the health of others and was to be quarantined immediately once more 'amang vtheris suspectit personis'. In this way, their previously 'clean' status reverted to one of being 'suspected' and they once more posed a risk to public health. This might have been an indication that learned medical advice was to be sought in discerning the symptoms of an infected individual, though it could just as easily have been the case that officials were to be expected to use their own judgement in this matter. This aspect of James IV's statutes was specifically cited by the Aberdeen authorities in the legislation they passed the following year to deal with the epidemic which had broken out within the burgh by April 1514, when they undertook the reintroduction to healthy society of recovered residents after their time in quarantine in the designated plague camp first constructed the same year.[135]

The nationwide orders of 1513 were designed for the 'stancheing of the contagious plaige of pestilence now ringing in dyvers places within this our realm' and, as the letter reiterated several times, were to be adhered to not only on that occasion but also 'in tyme cuming'. Over the course of the following two centuries similar regulations were implemented throughout Scotland's burghs, both to prevent the appearance of plague within the locality and to eliminate it if these efforts failed. While public health boards were never set up by local authorities, in many towns a designated body of workers was appointed as circumstances demanded, in order both to carry out the tasks necessary for the prevention of plague (e.g., searchers, cleansers and watchers) as well as for the practical ramifications of quarantine (e.g., carpenters, guards and alms distributors) and of mass mortality (e.g., grave diggers, porters and coffin bearers). Because ideas about the transmission of plague via contagion and miasma changed very little during the entire time Scotland was subjected to outbreaks of plague, neither the Rule of the Pestilence nor James IV's letter become obsolete with the passage of time. Indeed, in response to the severe epidemic in Marseilles in 1720, which was to be the last occasions on which plague broke out in pre-modern Europe, the Convention of Royal Burghs recalled both pieces of legislation in promulgating quarantine measures for seaborne vessels arriving at Scotland's ports, including Aberdeen.

Responses to plague in Scotland

The imposition of quarantine measures was a rational way for governments to respond to the renewed threat of plague in the eighteenth century, just as it had been in the mid-fifteenth century. In addition to an acknowledgement that the disease could be brought into a house, burgh, region or nation from outside, it was also recognised that it could originate within each of these locations given the existence of corrupted, polluted conditions. The belief that plague was transmitted by the interrelated concepts of miasma and contagion led physicians to advocate, and magistrates to implement, measures both to tackle existing sources of infection and to prevent external sources of the disease from invading the locality. The extent to which governments implemented these regulations in consultation with learned medical input in Aberdeen varied over the centuries during which plague assailed Scotland. The establishment of the post of mediciner at King's College in the late fifteenth century more or less entailed the consistent presence thereafter of at least one learned medical practitioner in the vicinity of the city. A formal arrangement between the council and the first mediciner (perhaps to entice him to accept the post) might have given way with subsequent incumbents to an informal arrangement in which successive local governments might have received much, some or no learned medical advice in the formulation of plague policy.

Understandings of the disposition of an individual to plague were based on both internal and external factors. Humoural theory dictated that susceptibility was determined by the state of the four humours within the body as well as to considerations such as the various stages of life and the seasons of the year. Governing bodies, though not medically trained, appreciated this: in their debate in 1567 over the future dates of sittings for the Lords of Session, parliament determined the unsuitability of July by noting that it was 'the moneth of all the yeir maist dangerous and men abillest to contract seiknes thairintill, speciallie thay being in burrowis, townis not weill airit'.[136] Equally important in an individual's disposition to afflictions such as plague were external considerations including the moral dimension of infection, which was recognised and emphasised by magistrates as much as by physicians and preachers. In various sources the notion of 'plague' became (as it remains today) a common verb to represent the annoyance or torment of another party, and contemporaries emphasised its relation to divine anger at communal sin. During the widespread epidemic of the 1640s parliament noted that the granting of remissions to criminals provoked God's 'wrath to plague the land and to doe justice upon the inhabitantis theirof becaus of the neglect of the magistrat heerin'.[137] The disease of plague was, after all, 'not merely an impersonal natural force'.[138] Its incidence was effected not only by medical skill and bureaucratic competence, but equally by society's inherent moral behaviour.

It was certainly not the case that either the intellectual discourse on plague or the government measures that were implemented remained totally static throughout the entire period in which the disease threatened Scotland. Adaptations could be made to policy in accordance with the particular circumstances at the time due to variables such as the financial situation, and there were also shifts in intellectual argument particularly from the late seventeenth century.[139] But, in general, ideas about and responses to plague were very long-lasting. Consequently, there is much continuity apparent in both local and nationwide governmental measures to tackle the disease from the fifteenth to the eighteenth century. In the promulgation of regulations to ward off plague in 1720, parliament cited the Rule of the Pestilence (1456) and also told local governments that 'it may be expedient to search your records for discovering the procedure of your predecessors in the like caices'.[140] The renewal in 1779 of nationwide government orders concerning possible plague outbreaks, which were received by magistrates in Aberdeen, included the stipulation that a health questionnaire was to be completed by the captain of any vessel arriving from a suspected port. The form was to be dipped in vinegar and fumigated before being returned to the authorities in a slit stick.[141] Four hundred years after plague legislation had first been decreed in Scotland, notions of transmission through miasma and contagion, and the consequent treatment of potential infection with the use of strong odours and avoiding touch, continued to be common approaches to eschew plague. The remainder of this study analyses the way in which these responses were implemented in Aberdeen and throughout the north-east, and the impact this had on life in those communities.

Notes

1 Walter Cullen, "The Chronicle of Aberdeen, M.CCCC.XCI-M.D.XCV", in John Stuart (ed.), *Miscellany of the Spalding Club*, vol. II (Aberdeen: Spalding Club, 1842), pp. 29–70, at p. 32 [24 Aug 1529].

2 Fenton Wyness, *City by the Grey North Sea: Aberdeen* (Aberdeen: Impulse Books, 1972), p. 65.

3 See, for example: Jennifer Spinks and Charles Zika (eds), *Disaster, Death and the Emotions in the Shadow of the Apocalypse, 1400–1700* (London: Palgrave Macmillan, 2016); Robert Peckham (ed.), *Empires of Panic: Epidemics and Colonial Anxieties* (Hong Kong: Hong Kong University Press, 2015); William G. Naphy and Penny Roberts (eds), *Fear in Early Modern Society* (Manchester: Manchester University Press, 1997); Gordon D. Raeburn, "Plague", in Susan Broomhall (ed.), *Early Modern Emotions: An Introduction* (Abingdon: Routledge, 2017), pp. 205–208.

4 Franz Mauelshagen, "Disaster and political culture in Germany since 1500", in Christof Mauch and Christian Pfister (eds), *Natural Disasters, Cultural Responses: Case Studies toward a Global Environmental History* (Lanham: Lexington Books, 2009), pp. 41–75, at p. 42.

5 Mauelshagen, "Disaster and political culture in Germany since 1500", p. 56.

6 E.L. Jones, S. Porter and M. Turner, *A Gazetteer of English Urban Fire Disasters, 1500–1900* (Norwich: Geo Books, 1984), pp. 61, 63; see also John E. Morgan, "The representation and experience of English urban fire disasters, c.1580–1640", *Historical Research* 89:244 (2016), pp. 268–293; Penny Roberts, "Agencies human and divine: fire in French cities, 1520–1720", in Naphy and Roberts (eds), *Fear in Early Modern Society*, pp. 9–27 reminds us that while accidental fires could have positive effects, arson had the potential to engender suspicion and create scapegoats.

7 Fuel: ACR.8.864 [21 Aug 1508]; citizens: ACR.9.293 [30 Dec 1513]; buckets: ACR.52:1.512-513 [4 Dec 1639]; ACR.52:1.514 [18 Dec 1639]; water engine: ACR.59.013 [5 Dec 1721].

8 ACR.60.707 [17 Aug 1741].

9 Jones *et al., A Gazetteer of English Urban Fire Disasters*, p. 63.

10 Henrik Svensen, *The End is Nigh: A History of Natural Disasters* (London: Reaktion Books, 2006), p. 24; Sean Cocco, "Contesting Vesuvius and claiming Naples: disaster in print and pen, 1631–1649", in Michael J. Halvorson and Karen E. Spierling (eds), *Defining Community in Early Modern Europe* (Ashgate: Aldershot, 2008), pp. 307–326, at p. 313.

11 The Scientific Revolution and the Enlightenment have both been posited as heralding the epoch when 'scientific rationality' displaced 'religious explanations of natural phenomena with scientific theories'; Mauelshagen, "Disaster and political culture in Germany since 1500", p. 58; Svensen, *The End is Nigh*, p. 30; Jan Kozák and Vladimír Čermák, *The Illustrated History of Natural Disasters* (Dordrecht: Springer, 2010), pp. 15, 47.

12 Alexandra Walsham, *Providence in Early Modern England* (Oxford: Oxford University Press, 1999), p. 3; for a specific discussion of providence in relation to plague, see pp. 156–166.

13 [J.W.], *Strange and wonderful news from Glasgow in Scotland, being a full and true account of a terrible earthquake* (London, 1679), p. 7.

14 *Gods voice to Christendom, or, Alarum to Europe by the remarkable earthquakes, with the several kinds thereof, two hundred years before the birth of Christ. The causes and kinds, antecedents, and consequents, (pestilence, sword, famine) following thereupon, the nature of meteors, effective, and productive of an earthquake. Some part whereof was delineated by the great and vertuous Robert Boyle Esquyer, in the year 1681, relating to the dreadful comet. The impending judgements and causes of Gods wrath against a sinful people, seasonably and particularly applyed to the sons of Levi. By a minister of Christ* (Edinburgh, 1693), p. 6.

15 David Calderwood, *The History of the Kirk of Scotland*, vol. V [edited by Thomas Thomson] (Edinburgh: Wodrow Society, 1844), p. 655 [23 Jul 1597]; Aberdeen KS.2.324-325 [13 Nov 1608].

16 *Gods voice to Christendom*, pp. 12, 15.
17 Mauelshagen, "Disaster and political culture in Germany since 1500", p. 50.
18 Cocco, "Contesting Vesuvius and Claiming Naples", p. 308.
19 [R.B.], *Admirable Curiosities, Rarities and Wonders in England, Scotland & Ireland: Being an Account of many Remarkable Persons and Places* (London, 1697), pp. 180–181.
20 Cocco, "Contesting Vesuvius and Claiming Naples", pp. 321, 323.
21 Karen Jillings, "Monstrosity as spectacle: the *Two Inseparable Brothers*' European tour of the 1630s and 1640s", *Popular Entertainment Studies* 2:1 (2011), pp. 54–68; Jan Bondeson, *The Two-Headed Boy and Other Medical Marvels* (Ithaca and London: Cornell University Press, 2000), pp. vii–xix; Luca Baratta, *A Marvellous and Strange Event: Racconti di nascite mostruose nell'Inghilterra della prima età moderna* (Florence: Firenze University Press, 2016), pp. 181–201.
22 *Strange newes from Scotland, or, a strange relation of a terrible and prodigious monster borne to the amazement of all those that were spectators, in the Kingdome of Scotland, in a village neere Edenborough, call'd Hadensworth, Septem. 14. 1647, and the words the said monster spoke at its birth* ([London], 1647), pp. 2, 3, 5.
23 [J.W.], *Strange and wonderful news from Glasgow in Scotland*, p. 7.
24 *Gods voice to Christendom*, p. 16.
25 René Favier and Anne-Marie Granet-Abisset, "Society and natural risks in France, 1500–2000: changing historical perspectives", in Mauch and Pfister (eds), *Natural Disasters, Cultural Responses*, pp. 103–136, at pp. 104–105.
26 Leslie J. Macfarlane, "William Elphinstone's library revisited", in A.A. MacDonald, Michael Lynch and Ian B. Cowan (eds), *The Renaissance in Scotland: Studies in Literature, Religion, History and Culture offered to John Durkan* (Leiden: Brill, 1994), pp. 66–81, at p. 69; Roger French, "Medical teaching in Aberdeen: from the foundation of the university to the middle of the seventeenth century", *History of Universities* 3 (1983), pp. 127–157, at p. 128.
27 Theoretical provision had been made for the teaching of medicine at St Andrews, as it was one of the faculties mentioned in the university's foundation Bull issued in 1413 and was thereafter 'at least occasionally represented'; R.G. Cant, *The University of St Andrews: A Short History* (Edinburgh: Scottish Academic Press, 1970), p. 10. Glasgow University, founded in 1451, had plans approved for student bursaries in the 1570s but it was found that 'the university could offer no formal instruction' in medicine; John Durkan and James Kirk, *The University of Glasgow, 1451–1577* (Glasgow: University of Glasgow Press, 1977), p. 328.
28 Douglas Guthrie, "King James the fourth of Scotland: his influence on medicine and science", *Bulletin of the History of Medicine* 21 (1947), pp. 173–192; A.I. Short and T.W.J. Lennard, *James IV of Scotland: Sovereign and Surgeon* (Durham: Thomas Harriot Seminar, Occasional Paper no. 7, 1992).
29 Leslie J. Macfarlane, *William Elphinstone and the Kingdom of Scotland, 1431–1514: The Struggle for Order* (Aberdeen: Aberdeen University Press, 1985), p. 301.
30 Vern Bullough, "Medical study at medieval Oxford", *Speculum* 36 (1961), pp. 600–612; Vern Bullough, "The mediaeval medical school at Cambridge", *Mediaeval Studies* 24 (1962), pp. 161–168; A.H.T. Robb-Smith, "Medical education in Cambridge before 1600", in A. Rook (ed.), *Cambridge and its Contribution to Medicine* (London: Wellcome Institute of the History of Medicine, New Series, vol. XX, 1971), pp. 1–25; L.R.C. Agnew, "Scottish medical education", in C.D. O'Malley (ed.), *The History of Medical Education* (Los Angeles: University of California Press, 1970), pp. 251–261, at p. 254.
31 French, "Medical teaching", p. 127; for example, Alexander Keith, *A Thousand Years of Aberdeen* (Aberdeen: Aberdeen University Press, 1972), p. 128: 'the mediciner was the first professor of medicine to be appointed in Britain'. Articles

that specifically discuss early medical education at Aberdeen, aside from French noted above, include: Karen Jillings, "Humanism and medicine in sixteenth-century Aberdeen", *Intellectual History Review* 18 (2008), pp. 31–40; Douglas Guthrie, "Aberdeen's contribution to the progress of medicine", *Aberdeen University Review* 32 (1945), pp. 137–141; G.A.G. Mitchell, "The medical history of Aberdeen and its universities", *Aberdeen University Review* 37 (1958), pp. 225–238; W.P.D. Wightman, "The growth of medical education in Aberdeen", *Zodiac: A Journal of Aberdeen University Medical Society* 4 (1957), pp. 66–72; W. Stephenson, "Four centuries of medicine in Aberdeen", in P.J. Anderson (ed.), *Studies in the History and Development of the University of Aberdeen* (Aberdeen: Aberdeen University Press, 1906), pp. 303–318.

32 For example, Robb-Smith, "Medical education in Cambridge", p. 1: 'until about 1750 [Oxford and Cambridge] were the only places offering medical education in the British Isles, for it was not until the eighteenth century that the Scottish universities were organised for the mass-production of doctors'.

33 ACR.8.278 [20 Oct 1503].

34 For example, texts owned by Skene included Galen's *Ars parva* as well as works by Dioscorides, Nicholas of Salerno, Mesue and Albucasis, and possibly also Avicenna's *Canon*; French, "Medical teaching", pp. 135–136. The Gaelic-speaking areas of the nation were the notable exception to this paradigm, fostering their own tradition of medical theory and practice with the help of translations into Gaelic of classical medical works; R. Black, "Manuscripts, medical", in Derick S. Thomson (ed.), *The Companion to Gaelic Scotland* (Glasgow: Gairm, 1994), pp. 195–196.

35 Paul Slack, "Mirrors of health and treasures of poor men: the uses of the vernacular medical literature of Tudor England", in Charles Webster (ed.), *Health, Medicine and Mortality in the Sixteenth Century* (Cambridge: Cambridge University Press, 1979), pp. 237–273, at p. 260.

36 Andrew Wear, *Knowledge and Practice in English Medicine, 1550–1680* (Cambridge: Cambridge University Press, 2000), p. 40.

37 Forty-two editions of these twenty-three separate titles were published before 1605, with plague the most popular subject matter after anatomy and surgery, reflections on theory and practice, and herbals; Slack, "Mirrors of health", pp. 239, 243.

38 Edinburgh CMB.4.443-458 [13 Oct–22 Dec 1568].

39 J.F.D. Shrewsbury, *A History of Bubonic Plague in the British Isles* (Cambridge: Cambridge University Press, 1970), p. 209.

40 Gilbert Skene, *Ane Breve Descriptioun of the Pest, quhair in the causis, signis and sum speciall preseruatioun and cure thairof ar contenit* (Edinburgh, 1568), p. 8.

41 For example, Caroline Proctor has identified similarities between Skene's writing and the section on plague in the *Regimen* of Maino de Maineri, a fourteenth-century Italian physician who treated Robert I; Caroline Proctor, "Physician to the Bruce: Maino de Maineri in Scotland", *Scottish Historical Review* 86:1 (2007), pp. 16–26, at pp. 23–25.

42 Lauren Kassell, *Medicine and Magic in Elizabethan London. Simon Forman: Astrologer, Alchemist and Physician* (Oxford: Oxford University Press, 2005), p. 104.

43 R.S. Roberts, "A note on Thomas Lodge's *A Treatise of the Plague* (1603)", *Medical History* 22:1 (1978), p. 89.

44 Skene, *Breve Descriptioun*, p. 6.

45 Skene, *Breve Descriptioun*, pp. 4–5. The patient could appear to be well 'but interiorly is most heavily vexed', which complicated his or her treatment and cure.

46 Skene, *Breve Descriptioun*, pp. 5, 17.

47 Lloyd had however explained in his preface that 'I dyd adde before euery chapter as brefely as I coulde, the causes and sygnes of the sycknesses, and diseases, trusting therby both to gratify and somwhat ease the paynes of the reader'; Pope John XXI, *The Treasuri of Helth Contaynynge Many Profytable Medicines, Gathered out of Hipocratz, Gale[n] [and] Auicen by One Petrus Hyspanus [and] tra[n]slated into Englysh by Hu[m]fre Lloyd who Hath Added Therunto the Causes [and] Sygnes of Euer[y] Disease...* ([London], 1556).
48 Wear, *Knowledge and Practice*, p. 78.
49 Skene, *Breve Descriptioun*, p. 18.
50 Skene, *Breve Descriptioun*, p. 8.
51 Skene, *Breve Descriptioun*, pp. 7–8, 11. Plague was particularly heralded by spring (the corresponding season) being continuously wet and hot, as humid conditions were more likely to be infectious.
52 John Leslie, *The Historie of Scotland*, vol. I [edited by E.G. Cody] (Edinburgh: Scottish Text Society, 1888), p. 5. This was also his explanation for why Scotland was not apparently affected by the 'sueit of Britannie', that is, the 'English Sweats' which broke out periodically in England between 1485 and 1551 after which the disease mysteriously disappeared. It was characterised by 'a grete swetying and stynking, with redness of the face and of all the body, and a contynual thirst with a grete hete and hedache because of the fumes and venoms', as one observer noted in 1490; John A.H. Wylie and Leslie H. Collier, "The English Sweating Sickness (*Sudor Anglicus*): a reappraisal", *Journal of the History of Medicine and Allied Sciences* 36 (1981), pp. 425–445, at pp. 425, 427.
53 Skene, *Breve Descriptioun*, p. 6.
54 Skene, *Breve Descriptioun*, p. 12.
55 Skene, *Breve Descriptioun*, p. 18.
56 E.A. Heinrichs, "The live chicken treatment for buboes: trying a plague cure in medieval and early modern Europe", *Bulletin of the History of Medicine* 92:2 (2017), pp. 210–232.
57 Wear, *Knowledge and Practice*, p. 337.
58 Skene, *Breve Descriptioun*, p. 26.
59 Slack, "Mirrors of health", pp. 251, 262, 264–265; Paul Slack, *The Impact of Plague in Tudor and Stuart England* (Oxford: Oxford University Press; 1985), p. 30.
60 Skene, *Breve Descriptioun*, p. 6, echoed by Stephen Bradwell in *A Watch-Man for the Pest* (London, 1625), p. 4: '*contagious* Aire' was caused by 'noysome vapours arising from filthy sincks, stincking sewers, channels, gutters, privies, sluttish corners, dunghills and uncast ditches', as well as from stagnant water and 'dead rotting carrions'.
61 Skene, *Breve Descriptioun*, p. 6; 'ledder steipit in Vater' was a major source of corruption.
62 Skene, *Breve Descriptioun*, p. 21.
63 Skene, *Breve Descriptioun*, pp. 18–19.
64 Skene, *Breve Descriptioun*, p. 37; once the patient had succumbed, however, sweating was advocated in order to 'purge al superflew flewme as may redunde in all naturall partis' of the body.
65 Skene, *Breve Descriptioun*, p. 25.
66 Skene, *Breve Descriptioun*, p. 37.
67 Skene, *Breve Descriptioun*, pp. 12–14.
68 Skene, *Breve Descriptioun*, p. 14.
69 Wear, *Knowledge and Practice*, p. 349.
70 Kassell, *Medicine and Magic in Elizabethan London*, p. 103.
71 Gideon Harvey, *A Discourse of the Plague* (London, 1665), p. 16.
72 Skene, *Breve Descriptioun*, p. 18.

73 Patrick Wallis, "Plagues, morality and the place of medicine in early modern England", *English Historical Review* 121 (2006), pp. 1–24; Ole Peter Grell, "Conflicting duties: plague and the obligations of early modern physicians towards patients and Commonwealth in England and the Netherlands", in Andrew Wear, Johanna Geyer-Korsesch and Roger French (eds), *Doctors and Ethics: The Earlier Historical Settings of Professional Ethics* (Amsterdam: Rodopi, 1993), pp. 131–152.
74 Wallis, "Plagues, morality and the place of medicine", pp. 4–10.
75 Skene, *Breve Descriptioun*, p. 15.
76 Skene, *Breve Descriptioun*, pp. 3–4.
77 Päivi Pahta and Irma Taavitsainen, "Vernacularisation of scientific and medical writing in its sociohistorical context", in Päivi Pahta and Irma Taavitsainen (eds), *Medical and Scientific Writing in Late Medieval English* (Cambridge: Cambridge University Press, 2004), pp. 1–22, at p. 16.
78 John Caius, *A Boke, or Counseill against the Disease Commonly Called the Sweate, or Sweatyng Sicknesse* ([London], 1552), fol. 4v.
79 John Securis, *A detection and querimonie of the daily enormities and abuses committed in physick* ([London], 1566), fol. B.iir; '…if Englyshe Bookes could make men cunnying Physitions, then pouchemakers, threshers, ploughmen and coblers mought be Physitions as well'.
80 Thomas Phaer, *The preface to the boke of children*, in Jean Goeurot, *The Kegiment* [i.e., *Regiment*] *of life, wherunto is added a treatyse of the Pestilence, with the booke of children newly corrected and enlarged by T. Phayer* (London, 1546), p. 3; 'wolde [writers in Latin] haue no man to knowe but onely they?'
81 Skene, *Breve Descriptioun*, p. 3.
82 Thomas Moulton, *This is the Myrrour or Glasse of Helth* ([London, c. 1531]), Chapter 1.
83 Irma Taavitsainen and Päivi Pahta, "Corpus of early English medical writing 1375–1750", *ICAME Journal* 21 (1997), pp. 71–78, at p. 75.
84 Skene, *Breve Descriptioun*, p. 17.
85 Pope John XXI, *The Treasuri of Helth* [translated by Humfre Lloyd], introduction.
86 Wear, *Knowledge and Practice*, p. 45.
87 Pahta and Taavitsainen, "Vernacularisation of scientific and medical writing", p. 15; 'the question of readership is central to vernacularisation … [and] the basic facts of literacy provide the essential background for vernacularisation'.
88 Slack, "Mirrors of health", p. 258.
89 Slack, "Mirrors of health", p. 247.
90 Alastair J. Mann, *The Scottish Book Trade, 1500–1720: Print Commerce and Print Control in Early Modern Scotland* (East Linton: Tuckwell Press, 2000), pp. 205, 208.
91 Slack, "Mirrors of health", p. 273.
92 Gordon Donaldson (ed.), *Registrum Secreti Sigilli Regum Scotorum: Register of the Privy Seal of Scotland, vol. viii: 1581–1584* (Edinburgh: His Majesty's Stationery Office, 1982), pp. 58–59 (no. 354) [16 Jun 1581]; G.N. Clark, "Royal physicians in Scotland, 1568–1853", *Medical History* 11 (1967), pp. 402–406, at p. 403.
93 Andrew Maunsell, *The Seconde Parte of the Catalogue of English Printed Bookes: Eyther Written in Our Owne Tongue, or Translated Out of Any Other Language…* (London, 1595), pp. 21, 23. I am grateful to Dr Alastair Mann of the University of Stirling for alerting me to the inclusion of Skene's treatise in Maunsell's catalogue.
94 Kari Anne Rand, "A previously unnoticed fragment of John of Burgundy's plague tract and some connected pest regimens", *Notes and Queries* 53:3 (2006), pp. 295–297, at p. 295, where she describes this text as 'probably the best known medieval treatise in English on the subject'.
95 David Murray, *The Black Book of Paisley, and Other Manuscripts of the Scotichronicon; with a Note upon John de Burdeus or John de Burgundia, otherwise Sir John Mandeville,*

and the Pestilence (Paisley: Alexander Gardner, 1885); Walter Bower, *Scotichronicon*, vol. VII, book XIV [edited by A.B. Scott and D.E.R. Watt] (Aberdeen: Aberdeen University Press, 1996), pp. 272–273.

96 Murray, *The Black Book of Paisley*, pp. 43, 56–57. It eventually passed into private hands and might have ended up at the castle of the Roslin family by the time of Scotland's final outbreak in the 1640s.

97 Murray, *The Black Book of Paisley*, p. 46; Aberdeen was not apparently affected by this outbreak.

98 C. Innes (ed.), *Liber S. Marie de Calchou: Registrum Cartarum Abbacie Tironensis de Kelso, 1113–1567* (Edinburgh: Bannatyne Club, 1846), pp. 448–451.

99 Innes (ed.), *Liber S. Marie de Calchou*, p. 451.

100 For the standard bibliography of books printed in Scotland or outside Scotland for the Scottish market before 1701, see https://www.nls.uk/catalogues/scottish-books-1505-1640.

101 John Leyden (ed.), *The Complaynt of Scotland, Written in 1548. With a Preliminary Dissertation and Glossary* (Edinburgh: Archibald Constable, 1801), pp. 2, 87–89, 95, 269.

102 These included part of the fifth edition of Robert Burton's *Anatomy of Melancholy* (?1635) and a 1664 edition of the celebrated herbalist Nicholas Culpeper's classic work *Medicaments for the Poor, or, Physick for the Common People*, both printed at Edinburgh.

103 Including three works that were authored by the Aberdeen physician William Barclay: *Nepenthes, or The Vertues of tabacco* (Edinburgh, 1614); *Callirhoe, The Nymph of Aberdene* (Edinburgh, 1615); and *The Nature and Effects of the New-found Well at Kinghorne* (Edinburgh, 1618). Also published were texts by physician to Charles I, Patrick Anderson, *The Colde Spring of Kinghorne Craig* (Edinburgh, 1618) and several by John MakLuire: *Sanitatis Semita cum tractatu de febre pestilente praefixo* (Edinburgh, 1630); *The Buckler of bodilie health whereby health may bee defended, and sickesse repelled* (Edinburgh, 1630); *The Generall Practise of Medecine, by Philiatreus* (Edinburgh, 1634); see also James F. McHarg (with a historical introduction by Helen Dingwall), *In Search of Dr John MakLuire: Pioneer Edinburgh Physician Forgotten for Over 300 Years* (Glasgow: Wellcome Unit for the History of Medicine, University of Glasgow, 1997).

104 National Library of Scotland, Special Collections, Ferg.85: *Certain Necessary Directions, as well for the Cure of the Plague, as for preventing the Infection: with Many easy MEDICINES of small Charge, very profitable to His Majesty's Subjects. Set down by the College of Physicians. By the king's Majesty's special Command. London. Printed 1665* (Edinburgh, 1721).

105 William Mure (ed.), *Selections from the Family Papers Preserved at Caldwell: Part First. MCCCCXCVI-MDCCCLIII* (Glasgow: Maitland Club, 1854), p. 91 [12 Apr 1645].

106 NAS: GD345/978: Papers of the Grant family of Monymusk, Aberdeenshire, Enclosures in GD345/977, including 'directions against the plague', 1729–1742.

107 James Scott, *A History of the Life and Death of John, Earl of Gowrie, with Preliminary Dissertations* (Edinburgh: William Blackwood, 1818), pp. 310–312.

108 Wear, *Knowledge and Practice*, p. 315.

109 John Henderson, "Epidemics in Renaissance Florence: medical theory and government response", in Neithard Bulst and Robert Delort (eds), *Maladie et société (XIIe–XVIIIe siècles)* (Paris: Editions du CNRS, 1989), pp. 165–186, at p. 147.

110 Brian Pullan, "Plague and perceptions of the poor in early modern Italy", in Terence Ranger and Paul Slack (eds), *Epidemics and Ideas: Essays on the Historical Perception of Pestilence* (Cambridge: Cambridge University Press, 1992),

pp. 101–123, at p. 113; Henderson, "Epidemics in Renaissance Florence", p. 171.

111 Skene, *Breve Descriptioun*, pp. 4–5.

112 Sean P. Hier and Josh Greenberg, "Surveillance, the nation-state and social control: section introduction", in Sean P. Hier and Josh Greenberg (eds), *The Surveillance Studies Reader* (Maidenhead: Open University Press/McGraw-Hill, 2007), pp. 11–18, at p. 15.

113 'The plague-stricken town ... immobilised by the functioning of an extensive power that bears in a distinct way over all individual bodies – that is the utopia of the perfectly governed city'; Neil Leach (ed.), *Rethinking Architecture: A Reader in Cultural History* (London: Routledge, 1997), p. 359, quoting from Michel Foucault, *Discipline and Punish: The Birth of the Prison* (New York: Vintage, 1977).

114 Ann G. Carmichael, *Plague and the Poor in Renaissance Florence* (Cambridge: Cambridge University Press, 1986), p. 1.

115 Skene, *Breve Descriptioun*, p. 18.

116 H.C.M. Michielse, "Policing the poor: J.L. Vives and the sixteenth-century origins of modern social administration", *Social Service Review* 64 (1990), pp. 1–21, at p. 7; Paul Slack, *Poverty and Policy in Tudor and Stuart England* (London: Longman, 1988), p. 23.

117 Michielse, "Policing the poor", pp. 4, 7, 9, 10; Slack, *Poverty and Policy*, pp. 23, 69.

118 John McCallum, "'Fatheris and provisioners of the puir': Kirk Sessions and poor relief in post-Reformation Scotland", in John McCallum (ed.), *Scotland's Long Reformation: New Perspectives on Scottish Religion, c.1500–c.1660* (Leiden: Brill, 2016), pp. 69–86, at pp. 80–84.

119 McCallum, "'Fatheris and provisioners of the puir'", p. 85.

120 Useful examples of the extensive literature on this topic include: Thomas Max Safley (ed.), *The Reformation of Charity: The Secular and the Religious in Early Modern in Early Modern Poor Relief* (Leiden: Brill, 2003); Ole Peter Grell and Andrew Cunningham (eds), *Health Care and Poor Relief in Protestant Europe* (London: Routledge, 1997); Ole Peter Grell and Andrew Cunningham with Jon Arrizabalaga (eds), *Health Care and Poor Relief in Counter-Reformation Europe* (London: Routledge, 1999); Timothy G. Fehler, *Poor Relief and Protestantism: The Evolution of Social Welfare in Sixteenth-Century Emden* (Farnham: Ashgate, 1999); A.L. Beier, *Masterless Men: the Vagrancy Problem in England, 1560–1640* (London: Methuen, 1985); Brian Pullan, "Catholics, Protestants and the poor in early modern Europe", *Journal of Interdisciplinary History* 35:3 (2005), pp. 441–456; Brian Pullan, "Catholics and the poor in early modern Europe", *Transactions of the Royal Historical Society* 26 (1976), pp. 15–34.

121 McCallum, "'Fatheris and provisioners of the puir'", pp. 81–84. Additionally, for a very small minority, shelter and care would have been provided by a hospital or almshouse; John McCallum, "'Nurseries of the poore': hospitals and almshouses in early modern Scotland", *Journal of Social History* 48:2 (2014), pp. 427–449.

122 Robert Jütte, *Poverty and Deviance in Early Modern Europe* (Cambridge: Cambridge University Press, 1994), p. 22.

123 Morgan, "The representation and experience of English urban fire disasters", p. 270.

124 Slack, *The Impact of Plague*, pp. 201–202.

125 Slack, *The Impact of Plague*, p. 209.

126 Slack, *The Impact of Plague*, pp. 200–201.

127 John Booker, *Maritime Quarantine: The British Experience, c.1650–1900* (Aldershot: Ashgate, 2007), p. 17.

128 RPC.1/1.279 [Jul 1564], ACR.25.370 [10 Sep 1564]; RPC.1/12.62-63 [9 Aug 1619]; RPC.1/12.322-323 [14 Jul 1620]; RPC.2/1.111-113 [1 Aug 1625]; RPC.2/4.264-265 [5 Jul 1631]; RPC.2/6.246-247 [26 May 1636].
129 RPC.1/3.313-314 [20 Sep 1580]; RPC.1/5.94 [8 Aug 1593]; RPC.1/11.417 [28 Jul 1618]; RPC.1/13.622-623 [4 Nov 1624]; RPC.2/1.119 [20 Aug 1625]; RPC.2/1.199, 207 [28 Nov 1625]; RPC.2/3.386 [17 Dec 1629]; RPC.2/3.388-389 [22 Dec 1629].
130 W. Turnbull (ed.), *Extracta E Variis Cronicis Scocie from the Ancient Manuscript in the Advocates Library at Edinburgh* (Edinburgh: Abbotsford Club, 1842), p. 243.
131 John Ritchie, "The Rule of the Pestilence", *Medical History* 2:2 (1958), pp. 151–153, at p. 151.
132 RPS: 1456/7 [19 Oct 1456].
133 Ritchie, "The Rule of the Pestilence", p. 152; the twelfth-century law *De percussis lepra in burgo* had stipulated that native lepers were to receive twenty shillings for their support from local townsfolk in addition to spoilt food deemed unsuitable for sale at market.
134 Edinburgh Extracts, fols 204v–206v [17 Jan 1513]; James Balfour Paul (ed.), *Accounts of the Lord High Treasurer of Scotland, vol. IV: 1507–1513* (Edinburgh: General Register House, 1901), p. 404 [29 Jan 1513].
135 ACR.9.336 [24 Apr 1514]; ACR.9.367 [7 Aug 1514].
136 RPS: A1567/12/28 [after 15 Dec 1567].
137 RPS: 1649/1/117 [13 Feb 1649].
138 Pullan, "Plague and perceptions of the poor", p. 122.
139 For example, Samuel K. Cohn, Jr, *Cultures of Plague: Medical Thinking at the End of the Renaissance* (Oxford: Oxford University Press, 2010) provides an excellent study of the evolution of ideas about plague in late Renaissance Italy, which shows that medical thinking by no means remained entirely static even during earlier centuries.
140 J.D. Marwick (ed.), *Extracts from the Records of the Convention of the Royal Burghs of Scotland, vol. V: 1711–1738* (Edinburgh: Convention of Royal Burghs, 1885), pp. 268–270 [17 Nov 1720].
141 Victoria E. Clark, *The Port of Aberdeen: A History of its Trade and Shipping from the Twelfth Century to the Present Day* (Aberdeen: D. Wyllie and Son, 1921), pp. 94–95.

Bibliography

Agnew, L.R.C., "Scottish medical education", in C.D. O'Malley (ed.), *The History of Medical Education* (Los Angeles: University of California Press, 1970), pp. 251–261.

Balfour Paul, James (ed.), *Accounts of the Lord High Treasurer of Scotland, vol. IV: 1507–1513* (Edinburgh: General Register House, 1901).

Baratta, Luca, *A Marvellous and Strange Event: Racconti di nascite mostruose nell'Inghilterra della prima età moderna* (Florence: Firenze University Press, 2016).

Beier, A.L., *Masterless Men: The Vagrancy Problem in England, 1560–1640* (London: Methuen, 1985).

Black, R., "Manuscripts, medical", in Derick S. Thomson (ed.), *The Companion to Gaelic Scotland* (Glasgow: Gairm, 1994), pp. 195–196.

Bondeson, Jan, *The Two-Headed Boy and Other Medical Marvels* (Ithaca and London: Cornell University Press, 2000).

Booker, John, *Maritime Quarantine: The British Experience, c.1650–1900* (Aldershot: Ashgate, 2007).

Bower, Walter, *Scotichronicon*, vol. VII, book XIV [edited by A.B. Scott and D.E.R. Watt] (Aberdeen: Aberdeen University Press, 1996).

Bullough, Vern, "Medical study at medieval Oxford", *Speculum* 36 (1961), pp. 600–612.

Bullough, Vern, "The mediaeval medical school at Cambridge", *Mediaeval Studies* 24 (1962), pp. 161–168.

Calderwood, David, *The History of the Kirk of Scotland*, vol. V [edited by Thomas Thomson] (Edinburgh: Wodrow Society, 1844).

Cant, R.G., *The University of St Andrews: A Short History* (Edinburgh: Scottish Academic Press, 1970).

Carmichael, Ann G., *Plague and the Poor in Renaissance Florence* (Cambridge: Cambridge University Press, 1986).

Clark, G.N., "Royal physicians in Scotland, 1568–1853", *Medical History* 11 (1967), pp. 402–406.

Clark, Victoria E., *The Port of Aberdeen: A History of its Trade and Shipping from the Twelfth Century to the Present Day* (Aberdeen: D. Wyllie and Son, 1921).

Cocco, Sean, "Contesting Vesuvius and claiming Naples: disaster in print and pen, 1631–1649", in Michael J. Halvorson and Karen E. Spierling (eds), *Defining Community in Early Modern Europe* (Ashgate: Aldershot, 2008), pp. 307–326.

Cohn, Samuel K., Jr, *Cultures of Plague: Medical Thinking at the End of the Renaissance* (Oxford: Oxford University Press, 2010).

Cullen, Walter, "The Chronicle of Aberdeen, M.CCCC.XCI–M.D.XCV", in John Stuart (ed.), *Miscellany of the Spalding Club*, vol. II (Aberdeen: Spalding Club, 1842), pp. 29–70.

Donaldson, Gordon (ed.), *Registrum Secreti Sigilli Regum Scotorum: Register of the Privy Seal of Scotland, vol. viii: 1581–1584* (Edinburgh: His Majesty's Stationery Office, 1982).

Durkan, John and James Kirk, *The University of Glasgow, 1451–1577* (Glasgow: University of Glasgow Press, 1977).

Favier, René and Anne-Marie Granet-Abisset, "Society and natural risks in France, 1500–2000: changing historical perspectives", in Christof Mauch and Christian Pfister (eds), *Natural Disasters, Cultural Responses: Case Studies toward a Global Environmental History* (Lanham: Lexington Books, 2009), pp. 103–136.

Fehler, Timothy G., *Poor Relief and Protestantism: The Evolution of Social Welfare in Sixteenth-Century Emden* (Farnham: Ashgate, 1999).

French, Roger, "Medical teaching in Aberdeen: from the foundation of the university to the middle of the seventeenth century", *History of Universities* 3 (1983), pp. 127–157.

Grell, Ole Peter, "Conflicting duties: plague and the obligations of early modern physicians towards patients and Commonwealth in England and the Netherlands", in Andrew Wear, Johanna Geyer-Korsesch and Roger French (eds), *Doctors and Ethics: The Earlier Historical Settings of Professional Ethics* (Amsterdam: Rodopi, 1993), pp. 131–152.

Grell, Ole Peter and Andrew Cunningham (eds), *Health Care and Poor Relief in Protestant Europe* (London: Routledge, 1997).

Grell, Ole Peter and Andrew Cunningham with Jon Arrizabalaga (eds), *Health Care and Poor Relief in Counter-Reformation Europe* (London: Routledge, 1999).

Guthrie, Douglas, "Aberdeen's contribution to the progress of medicine", *Aberdeen University Review* 32 (1945), pp. 137–141.

Guthrie, Douglas, "King James the fourth of Scotland: his influence on medicine and science", *Bulletin of the History of Medicine* 21 (1947), pp. 173–192.

Heinrichs, E.A., "The live chicken treatment for buboes: trying a plague cure in medieval and early modern Europe", *Bulletin of the History of Medicine* 92:2 (2017), pp. 210–232.

Henderson, John, "Epidemics in Renaissance Florence: medical theory and government response", in Neithard Bulst and Robert Delort (eds), *Maladie et société (XIIe–XVIIIe siècles)* (Paris: Editions du CNRS, 1989), pp. 165–186.

Hier, Sean P. and Josh Greenberg, "Surveillance, the nation-state and social control: section introduction", in Sean P. Hier and Josh Greenberg (eds), *The Surveillance Studies Reader* (Maidenhead: Open University Press/McGraw-Hill, 2007), pp. 11–18.

Innes, C. (ed.), *Liber S. Marie de Calchou: Registrum Cartarum Abbacie Tironensis de Kelso, 1113–1567* (Edinburgh: Bannatyne Club, 1846).

Jillings, Karen, "Humanism and medicine in sixteenth-century Aberdeen", *Intellectual History Review* 18 (2008), pp. 31–40.

Jillings, Karen, "Monstrosity as spectacle: the *Two Inseparable Brothers*' European tour of the 1630s and 1640s", *Popular Entertainment Studies* 2:1 (2011), pp. 54–68.

Jones, E.L., S. Porter and M. Turner, *A Gazetteer of English Urban Fire Disasters, 1500–1900* (Norwich: Geo Books, 1984).

Jütte, Robert, *Poverty and Deviance in Early Modern Europe* (Cambridge: Cambridge University Press, 1994).

Kassell, Lauren, *Medicine and Magic in Elizabethan London. Simon Forman: Astrologer, Alchemist and Physician* (Oxford: Oxford University Press, 2005).

Keith, Alexander, *A Thousand Years of Aberdeen* (Aberdeen: Aberdeen University Press, 1972).

Kozák, Jan and Vladimír Čermák, *The Illustrated History of Natural Disasters* (Dordrecht: Springer, 2010).

Leach, Neil (ed.), *Rethinking Architecture: A Reader in Cultural History* (London: Routledge, 1997).

Leslie, John, *The Historie of Scotland*, vol. I [edited by E.G. Cody] (Edinburgh: Scottish Text Society, 1888).

Leyden, John (ed.), *The Complaynt of Scotland, Written in 1548. With a Preliminary Dissertation and Glossary* (Edinburgh: Archibald Constable, 1801).

Macfarlane, Leslie J., *William Elphinstone and the Kingdom of Scotland, 1431–1514: The Struggle for Order* (Aberdeen: Aberdeen University Press, 1985).

Macfarlane, Leslie J., "William Elphinstone's library revisited", in A.A. MacDonald, Michael Lynch and Ian B. Cowan (eds), *The Renaissance in Scotland: Studies in Literature, Religion, History and Culture offered to John Durkan* (Leiden: Brill, 1994), pp. 66–81.

Mann, Alastair J., *The Scottish Book Trade, 1500–1720: Print Commerce and Print Control in Early Modern Scotland* (East Linton: Tuckwell Press, 2000).

Marwick, J.D. (ed.), *Extracts from the Records of the Convention of the Royal Burghs of Scotland, vol. V: 1711–1738* (Edinburgh: Convention of Royal Burghs, 1885).

Mauelshagen, Franz, "Disaster and political culture in Germany since 1500", in Christof Mauch and Christian Pfister (eds), *Natural Disasters, Cultural Responses: Case Studies toward a Global Environmental History* (Lanham: Lexington Books, 2009), pp. 41–75.

McCallum, John, "'Nurseries of the poore': hospitals and almshouses in early modern Scotland", *Journal of Social History* 48:2 (2014), pp. 427–449.

McCallum, John, "'Fatheris and provisioners of the puir': Kirk Sessions and poor relief in post-Reformation Scotland", in John McCallum (ed.), *Scotland's Long Reformation: New Perspectives on Scottish Religion, c.1500–c.1660* (Leiden: Brill, 2016), pp. 69–86.

McHarg, James F. (with a historical introduction by Helen Dingwall), *In Search of Dr John MakLuire: Pioneer Edinburgh Physician Forgotten for Over 300 Years* (Glasgow: Wellcome Unit for the History of Medicine, University of Glasgow, 1997).

Michielse, H.C.M., "Policing the poor: J.L. Vives and the sixteenth-century origins of modern social administration", *Social Service Review* 64 (1990), pp. 1–21.

Mitchell, G.A.G., "The medical history of Aberdeen and its universities", *Aberdeen University Review* 37 (1958), pp. 225–238.

Morgan, John E., "The representation and experience of English urban fire disasters, c.1580–1640", *Historical Research* 89:244 (2016), pp. 268–293.

Mure, William (ed.), *Selections from the Family Papers Preserved at Caldwell: Part First. MCCCCXCVI–MDCCCLIII* (Glasgow: Maitland Club, 1854).

Murray, David, *The Black Book of Paisley, and Other Manuscripts of the Scotichronicon; with a Note upon John de Burdeus or John de Burgundia, otherwise Sir John Mandeville, and the Pestilence* (Paisley: Alexander Gardner, 1885).

Naphy, William G. and Penny Roberts (eds), *Fear in Early Modern Society* (Manchester: Manchester University Press, 1997).

Pahta, Päivi and Irma Taavitsainen, "Vernacularisation of scientific and medical writing in its sociohistorical context", in Päivi Pahta and Irma Taavitsainen (eds), *Medical and Scientific Writing in Late Medieval English* (Cambridge: Cambridge University Press, 2004), pp. 1–22.

Peckham, Robert (ed.), *Empires of Panic: Epidemics and Colonial Anxieties* (Hong Kong: Hong Kong University Press, 2015).

Proctor, Caroline, "Physician to the Bruce: Maino de Maineri in Scotland", *Scottish Historical Review* 86:1 (2007), pp. 16–26.

Pullan, Brian, "Catholics and the poor in early modern Europe", *Transactions of the Royal Historical Society* 26 (1976), pp. 15–34.

Pullan, Brian, "Plague and perceptions of the poor in early modern Italy", in Terence Ranger and Paul Slack (eds), *Epidemics and Ideas: Essays on the Historical Perception of Pestilence* (Cambridge: Cambridge University Press, 1992), pp. 101–123.

Pullan, Brian, "Catholics, Protestants and the poor in early modern Europe", *Journal of Interdisciplinary History* 35:3 (2005), pp. 441–456.

Raeburn, Gordon D., "Plague", in Susan Broomhall (ed.), *Early Modern Emotions: An Introduction* (Abingdon: Routledge, 2017), pp. 205–208.

Rand, Kari Anne, "A previously unnoticed fragment of John of Burgundy's plague tract and some connected pest regimens", *Notes and Queries* 53:3 (2006), pp. 295–297.

Ritchie, John, "The Rule of the Pestilence", *Medical History* 2:2 (1958), pp. 151–153.

Robb-Smith, A.H.T., "Medical education in Cambridge before 1600", in A. Rook (ed.), *Cambridge and its Contribution to Medicine* (London: Wellcome Institute of the History of Medicine, New Series, vol. XX, 1971), pp. 1–25.

Roberts, Penny, "Agencies human and divine: fire in French cities, 1520–1720", in William G. Naphy and Penny Roberts (eds), *Fear in Early Modern Society* (Manchester: Manchester University Press, 1997), pp. 9–27.

Roberts, R.S., "A note on Thomas Lodge's *A Treatise of the Plague* (1603)", *Medical History* 22:1 (1978), p. 89.

Safley, Thomas Max (ed.), *The Reformation of Charity: The Secular and the Religious in Early Modern in Early Modern Poor Relief* (Leiden: Brill, 2003).

Scott, James, *A History of the Life and Death of John, Earl of Gowrie, with Preliminary Dissertations* (Edinburgh: William Blackwood, 1818).

Scottish Books, 1505–1700 (Aldis updated catalogue): online at www.nls.uk/catalogues/scottish-books-1505-1640.

Short, A.I. and T.W.J. Lennard, *James IV of Scotland: Sovereign and Surgeon* (Durham: Thomas Harriot Seminar, Occasional Paper no. 7, 1992).

Shrewsbury, J.F.D., *A History of Bubonic Plague in the British Isles* (Cambridge: Cambridge University Press, 1970).

Slack, Paul, "Mirrors of health and treasures of poor men: the uses of the vernacular medical literature of Tudor England", in Charles Webster (ed.), *Health, Medicine and Mortality in the Sixteenth Century* (Cambridge: Cambridge University Press, 1979), pp. 237–273.

Slack, Paul, *The Impact of Plague in Tudor and Stuart England* (Oxford: Oxford University Press; 1985).

Slack, Paul, *Poverty and Policy in Tudor and Stuart England* (London: Longman, 1988).

Spinks, Jennifer and Charles Zika (eds), *Disaster, Death and the Emotions in the Shadow of the Apocalypse, 1400–1700* (London: Palgrave Macmillan, 2016).

Stephenson, W., "Four centuries of medicine in Aberdeen", in P.J. Anderson (ed.), *Studies in the History and Development of the University of Aberdeen* (Aberdeen: Aberdeen University Press, 1906), pp. 303–318.

Svensen, Henrik, *The End is Nigh: A History of Natural Disasters* (London: Reaktion Books, 2006).

Taavitsainen, Irma and Päivi Pahta, "Corpus of early English medical writing 1375–1750", *ICAME Journal* 21 (1997), pp. 71–78.

Turnbull, W. (ed.), *Extracta E Variis Cronicis Scocie from the Ancient Manuscript in the Advocates Library at Edinburgh* (Edinburgh: Abbotsford Club, 1842).

Wallis, Patrick, "Plagues, morality and the place of medicine in early modern England", *English Historical Review* 121 (2006), pp. 1–24.

Walsham, Alexandra, *Providence in Early Modern England* (Oxford: Oxford University Press, 1999).

Wear, Andrew, *Knowledge and Practice in English Medicine, 1550–1680* (Cambridge: Cambridge University Press, 2000).

Wightman, W.P.D., "The growth of medical education in Aberdeen", *Zodiac: A Journal of Aberdeen University Medical Society* 4 (1957), pp. 66–72.

Wylie, John A.H. and Leslie H. Collier, "The English Sweating Sickness (*Sudor Anglicus*): a reappraisal", *Journal of the History of Medicine and Allied Sciences* 36 (1981), pp. 425–445.

Wyness, Fenton, *City by the Grey North Sea: Aberdeen* (Aberdeen: Impulse Books, 1972).

3 Plague in Aberdeen before 1550

In his *Lives of the Bishops*, published in 1522, Hector Boece, the first principal of King's College, reflected on the recent turbulent events in his home city. He lamented that in 1514, 'a terrible pestilence broke out at Aberdeen… and lasted for two whole years. It carried off more victims than any similar plague within the memory of man…' Boece tied the outbreak to the death of Bishop William Elphinstone, writing that it 'added to the other troubles of the University, caused by the death of its founder'.[1] Boece was not at odds with his contemporaries in attributing the onset of plague to some other adverse event, such as enemy hostilities or a downturn in economic fortunes. Elphinstone's death meant the loss of one of the most influential men in the kingdom and Boece felt the scourge of plague to be a natural consequence. Writing so soon after the event, it is little wonder he felt it had such a disastrous impact on Aberdeen. After all, as the first epidemic to occur within the city he was correct to conclude that it was more devastating than any within living memory. As such, it presented an unprecedented challenge to the city's magistrates and community. The first half of the sixteenth century was a formative period for civic efforts to control disease, which were most likely formulated without professional medical input. Several years before plague first commanded the attention of local government, and even longer before its first physician was employed, the disease known as the Great Pox forced councillors to pass innovative legislation to check its spread which were founded on similar principles as those designed to tackle plague. Subsequent measures against that specific disease focused initially on preventing access to the city by both sea and land of all possible sources of infection. In the event that these did enter the burgh, efforts were extended to eliminating, segregating or cleansing these as required, particularly during the two occasions before 1550 when plague broke out.

1497: the Great Pox in Aberdeen

Even before plague itself threatened Aberdeen the government had to confront the threat to public health from what was recognised as an entirely different and hitherto unknown disease, which commentators across Europe acknowledged to have first broken out in Italy during the months after February 1495 among soldiers fighting for Charles VIII of France in his bid for the kingdom of Naples. Mercenaries who had fought in this short-lived campaign subsequently returned home, spreading the disease as they went. Commentators described it variously as the 'Great Pox' (in contrast to smallpox), the 'disease of Naples', and 'Morbus Gallicus' or the 'French disease'. Modern scholarly debate continues about the origins and clinical identification of this malady, particularly over whether it was a form of syphilis that already existed in Europe before the return of explorers from the New World, perhaps evolving as a result of favourable biological and ecological changes. Whatever its precise origins, contemporaries quickly acknowledged the venereal character, high contagiousness and low mortality of this new disease.[2] The extreme virulence of the Great Pox led to medical and municipal efforts to tackle the threat it posed, with magistrates in Aberdeen becoming the first civic authority in the British Isles to enact such legislation. On 21 April 1497 they decreed that, 'for the eschevin of the infirmitey cumm out of franche and strang partis, ... all licht wemen [are to] be chargit and ordanit to decist fra thar vicis and syne of venerie'. Such women were ordered to shut up shop and seek lawful employment, or face branding and banishment.[3]

While early continental commentators believed that the disease could also be spread through the air or via food and drink, descriptions of its clinical manifestations clearly showed it prevailed through sexual activity. Italian medical practitioners including the military surgeons Giovanni da Vigo and Marcello Cumano noted the appearance of a skin ulceration on the genitals coloured blue, black or white, followed by sores and pustules breaking out over the entire body. Secondary manifestations included painless regional lymphadenopathy, fever, mouth ulcers and a macular popular rash, which could give way to erosion of tissue in the extremities, painful tumours and eventual death.[4] The appearance of genital ulcers in the primary phase distinguished the Great Pox from the more familiar symptoms of plague, and these were most likely identifiable to the Aberdeen authorities and prompted them to respond accordingly. This was notwithstanding two hindrances: the non-existence of a resident physician and the absence for almost a century of the need to respond to what was recognised as the particular disease of plague. With sexual promiscuity deemed culpable in the spread of the Great Pox, attempts to minimise its damage focused on curtailing the professional activities of the city's prostitutes and rehabilitating them to undertake morally acceptable employment (thereby tackling both the assumed physical and moral origins of the disease). As a major port Aberdeen was the temporary home of many single (and married) men for whom prostitutes provided a popular service, and this might have influenced civic efforts to tackle prostitution through control rather than elimination as was the case, for example, in Zurich.[5]

The spread of the Great Pox subsequently prompted legislation by authorities in burghs further south, including Edinburgh, Glasgow, Stirling and Linlithgow.[6] The particular efficiency of the Aberdeen council's reaction and its recognition of the perceived origins of the Great Pox are remarkable. There are several possible routes by which information about the new disease (and, of course, the disease itself), reached Scotland and particularly Aberdeen. It is possible that Scots were among its first ever European victims, as the mercenaries fighting for Charles VIII in the Italian Wars included at least five hundred Scotsmen. One hundred Scots archers were recorded as participating in the battle of Fornovo near Parma on 6 July 1495, and it was the examination of infected soldiers from this battle that enabled the military surgeon Marcello Cumano to record his detailed description of the symptoms of the disease. Many participants would have returned home to Scotland, probably bringing with them the disease and reports of its existence.[7]

Not only did Scottish mercenaries participate in continental campaigns such as Charles VIII's attempted conquest of the kingdom of Naples, but also foreign soldiers joined forces which were involved in the ongoing Anglo-Scottish hostilities, and their participation could plausibly have been a factor in spreading the Great Pox to Scotland. Perkin Warbeck, a pretender to the English throne under the guise of the duke of York, was received at the court of Charles VIII of France and, having arrived at the Scottish king James IV's court in November 1495, subsequently launched a joint invasion of England from Scotland with the king's forces in September 1496. Warbeck's followers were reported to number 1,400 men 'of all manner of nations' and it has been suggested that infected participants spread the new disease into both Scotland and England during the failed invasion and subsequent skirmishes during the months that followed.[8] Although the burgesses of Aberdeen had been excused by the king from participating in the raid, at least eight members of Warbeck's retinue were funded to lodge in the city for a month and could have carried the disease with them.[9]

In addition to military links with the continent, Aberdeen maintained important contacts through diplomacy and education during the two years between the reported appearance of the disease in Italy and the council's proclamation. In early February 1495, barely a week after officially confirming Charles VIII's claim to the Neapolitan kingship and less than two weeks before the French king's forces entered Naples, Pope Alexander VI met with Bishop William Elphinstone and granted him a Bull of Foundation for what was to be King's College. On his journey home Elphinstone undertook other diplomatic work in various parts of Europe, reaching Bruges at Easter 1495.[10] The first mediciner at King's, James Cumming, studied at the medical faculty at Cologne and between 1493 and 1499 acted as Elphinstone's diplomat in the Low Countries, while Hector Boece studied and taught at Paris before his arrival in Aberdeen some time in 1497.[11] National diplomacy could also have enabled information about the Great Pox to be passed on, as royal couriers did occasionally visit the city on other matters, including in May 1496, while a Spanish embassy spent ten days at the royal court in Stirling in April 1497 and could have brought news of the disease which was subsequently conveyed to authorities in Aberdeen.[12] It is likely that information about the Great Pox, as well as the disease itself, was carried to Scotland – and to Aberdeen in particular – through one or more of these diplomatic, educational or military links with the continent. In any case, the Aberdeen council's distinction as the first government body in the British Isles to tackle the Great Pox indicates an early willingness to act on information received from foreign counterparts about disease and to legislate against carriers of it.

The chronology of plague to 1550

While some inhabitants of Aberdeen might have fallen victim to the Great Pox late in the fifteenth century, the city's residents fared significantly better than those in other parts of Scotland and further afield in their avoidance of plague. In 1401 magistrates had indicated their alarm at the prospect of pestilence by prohibiting strangers travelling from the plague-ridden south from entering the burgh.[13] Remarkably, that was to be the sole occasion on which the disease apparently troubled Aberdeen until almost the end of the fifteenth century, despite repeated outbreaks elsewhere in Scotland.[14] In February 1499 Edinburgh's council prohibited entry to people and goods from 'suspect places', and Aberdeen's officials followed suit thirteen days later and again in May by implementing regulations designed not only to prevent plague but also the 'strang seiknes abefore'.[15] Whether with the advice of medical or municipal authorities elsewhere, they clearly understood that the disease that now threatened was different from the 'strang seiknes' whose spread had required legislation 'abefore' – presumably a reference to the Great Pox. This endemic disease prompted further civic legislation to be enacted in 1507, when 'diligent inquisition', perhaps by James Cumming who was now in place as city physician, was to be made of all those suspected of suffering from the 'strange seiknes of nappillis'.[16]

However, aside from infrequent civic efforts to deal with the Great Pox or with individual cases of leprosy, plague was the disease that overwhelmingly threatened public health over the course of the subsequent decades. The disease lingered in the central belt and Fife into the first years of the sixteenth century, resulting in the recurrent implementation of local government legislation throughout the region. Aberdeen's council specifically responded to the threat of plague in 1499, 1501 (when the city's alderman ensured his family were provided for before embarking on a trip to Berwick, because 'the quyntray war dangerfull throw this plague of pestilence'[17]), 1506 and 1513. In addition to the ubiquitous 'southern parts', such threats were deemed to come from settlements as close as Pitfodels, Inverbervie, Monymusk and Strathbogie, as well as from as far away as the Baltic port of Danzig.[18] The breadth of places identified by the authorities indicates that already they were beginning to establish new (or exploit existing) networks of communication in order to gauge the extent of the spread of plague. In spite of the occasional flouting of civic legislation by residents, Aberdeen escaped each and every instance of plague to the north, west and south of the city before 1514.[19]

However, on 24 April of that year magistrates were forced to acknowledge that plague was by then 'ringand in ale partis about this burgh'.[20] This declaration marks the first occasion in recorded history that plague broke out within Aberdeen's boundaries. In the event it was to linger within the city for almost two years and continued to cause significant disruption in and around Edinburgh for a further two.[21] Thereafter, John Smyth, a Cistercian monk of Kinloss abbey near the Moray coast, recorded that in 1529 'plague prevailed this year in St Andrews, and at Edinburgh in the following one'.[22] The vehemence of the disease in Fife at the end of the 1520s seriously disrupted affairs at Scotland's oldest university, attacking it like a 'divine scourge' and preventing both classes and examinations from being held as well as a dean from being elected for the year.[23] The spread of plague to the capital in May 1530 was notwithstanding the typical efforts of the city's magistrates to prevent its inhabitants having contact with those living north of the Forth, particularly in St Andrews.[24] Aberdeen's officials also implemented measures designed to counter both this and subsequent outbreaks of 'a seyknes and smyttand plaig (callit the boiche)' in 1538 and 1539.[25] Thereafter, almost three decades were to pass before the city once more experienced plague first-hand. During the outbreak that began in 1545 government officials declared similar measures as those that had been implemented during the previous epidemic thirty years earlier. After all, ideas about transmission and prevention did not change significantly over the plague period and hence ways to tackle these aspects fundamentally altered little. Both of the epidemics that occurred in Aberdeen during the first half of the sixteenth century – those which broke out in 1514 and in 1545 – prompted intermittent civic responses that came to reflect attempts not only to prevent further cases of infection but also to deal with the myriad challenges arising from the need to identify, segregate, supervise and (in the event of presumed recovery) reintegrate those residents who fell victim to plague.

Prevention: monitoring entrance(s)

When plague threatened, the first response by officials charged with maintaining the common weal of any settlement was to ensure that potential sources of infection were prevented from entering its boundaries, first recorded as being undertaken in Scotland in 1468 when officials in Peebles shut their burgh's ports and prevented interaction with Edinburgh.[26] While evidence for other north-east settlements is scarce for the first half of the sixteenth century, officials in Elgin deprived George Crukshank of his trading privileges for 'the wrangus passing' to Aberdeen while it was labouring under its second outbreak and, when plague was feared to have broken out again several years later, baillies in Banff prohibited any visitor from being lodged in that burgh.[27] The need to guard against interlopers who might carry plague sometimes occurred simultaneously with the need to defend Aberdeen against the arrival (whether by sea or by land) of 'our auld Inimmeis of ingland', who threatened national and local security in the aftermath of the disastrous loss at Flodden in 1513 and again during the vulnerable minority years of Mary, Queen of Scots, both of which periods coincided with the two epidemics experienced in the burgh.[28] Throughout the entire plague period civic officials in Aberdeen were theoretically able to benefit from the city's coastal location and by the inhospitableness of its surrounding topography, discussed in Chapter 1. There were layers of defence regarding official means of arriving in the city: even after seaborne vessels had negotiated the harbour and its various checks on entry, once ashore at the settlement of Futty they could be subject to the discerning eyes of a temporary watch or turned away by residents threatened with punishment for lodging them.[29] They then reached the Futty port that gave entry to the city proper, which was placed under particularly heavy guard when plague threatened from the south, as was its most commonly perceived origin.[30] Because the majority of interactions took place between Aberdeen and areas to the south, the river Dee was a major access point. Magistrates were quick to make the most of the ease of monitoring visitors afforded by the completion of the stone bridge over the river in 1527, appointing a watch there during the hours of daylight on the first occasion when plague threatened from the south after its completion.[31] This task was sometimes expedited during outbreaks by the temporary construction of a timber port at the south end of the bridge, which could be locked at night by the watchers.[32] Regardless of which direction visitors came from, on reaching the bounds of the burgh they had to pass through one of six ports situated on the major thoroughfares, which formed a further barrier to entry.

In theory, therefore, monitoring the official entrances to the city was an apparently straightforward task. In practice, however, it could fail in two particular respects, both of which were ultimately attributable to human error. The first was that the watch was not always implemented in a timely manner and it can be conjectured that the tardy response of magistrates to plague in Edinburgh might have played a part in the disease breaking out in Aberdeen for the first time in recorded history, in 1514. Responses to the presence of plague had first been implemented by Edinburgh's government a whole year before Aberdeen's magistrates issued their own precautions.[33] This seems to be an extremely lackadaisical response, particularly considering that it was because of this epidemic that the Privy Council had decreed a set of plague statutes, written in the form of a letter in the name of James IV to magistrates in Edinburgh.[34] Less than a fortnight after it was issued on 17 January 1513 a messenger was dispatched to deliver a copy to every burgh north of the Forth and, although the Aberdeen authorities made no reference to it when they eventually issued their own plague legislation in October of the same year, it is highly likely that they would have received it, and by implication have known about the presence of plague in the capital city, long before then.[35] Having said that, other scenarios produced apparently random outcomes. On some occasions, Aberdeen's government was equally as lax in its response to plague, yet the city escaped infection. Conversely, magistrates responded swiftly to the threat of the disease in 1545, but still Aberdeen succumbed to its second epidemic. Moreover, the council might not always have been to blame in any apparent delay. It might have been the case that authorities elsewhere did not inform their Aberdeen counterparts in a timely manner about the existence of plague, or possibly messengers (who might usually have taken a matter of days to travel on horseback to the city from the central belt) became caught up in the general disruption to travel occasioned by the disease and failed to relay the news quickly. By and large, the council registers often referred to outbreaks elsewhere as having arisen 'of new', which, if not attributable to clerical convention, indicates a timely response on the part of the government.

The vetting of visitors to the city could also fail if those tasked with the job were in some way negligent. Magistrates tried to negate this possibility by stipulating that only 'honest, sufficient' men, who would not be susceptible to bribery or distraction, be hired at public expense.[36] The responsibility inherent in the task was emphasised by the requirement of the watcher to swear an oath upholding his diligence and reliability, and the threatened affray posed by new arrivals 'that wald mak ony demand' was countered by the stipulation that he was to be armed.[37] Depending on the perceived severity of the crisis, citizens were permitted to send a replacement (usually a servant), whose wages the head of the household was to pay and for whom he was to stand surety.[38] On no account were youths, whose irresponsibility was a given, to act as substitutes.[39] If the need was deemed particularly great, the responsibility to 'se, advyss ande provide for the kepin of the toune' was extended to every freeman, who was usually instructed to take his turn 'in proper person' to watch the port nearest the quarter in which he lived and to liaise with the relevant baillie in organising his shift.[40]

This stipulation was hampered by two additional challenges: instances of defiance and of flight. Though it was incumbent on every citizen to obey all statutes concerning the monitoring of the burgh during times of plague (whether by contributing financially or in terms of personnel, or by maintaining the external boundaries of their properties), their refusal to do so was apparently not uncommon, despite the council's repeated efforts at coercion.[41] This seems to have become a problem over time, perhaps as an initial willingness to partake in the safeguarding of the community gave way to resentment over the consequent burdens that this could entail in terms of both time and money. Furthermore, given instances of negligence in undertaking the watch, coupled with a dependence on inhabitants' diligent compliance in shoring up and monitoring the boundaries of their own properties, egress from the burgh was as difficult to control as entry to it. Residents with sufficient means and resources fled to the hinterland to escape infection, which proved to be a hindrance to the effective defence of the burgh against both harbourers of plague and English invaders.[42] It could also result in the abandonment of houses and the non-payment of rent, such as in January 1530 when John Tailor was ordered to pay Robert Culte 3*s* 4*d* for rent he owed on a house 'left by pest' (or the fear of it, in this case).[43] The council appears to have had little success with its insistence early in the second epidemic that those who had left were to return home to contribute to the watch 'as wther nychtboris dois that remaine', for two months later the need to support the city's infected inhabitants forced the authorities to burden those who had not fled with a special tax to compensate for financial losses incurred as a result of their absent neighbours, who 'war nocht present to grant the almes to the effortis forsaid'.[44]

Regardless of whether or not the keepers of official entrances were in practice sufficiently diligent in their task (and whether, indeed, they turned up at all), magistrates put in place various safeguards to test whether a visitor ought to be granted entry to the burgh during times of plague. They could insist on production of a testimonial from an official (whether a baillie, landlord or parish priest) in the would-be entrant's place of origin, certifying that they had come from a 'clean' place.[45] They could also require that the visitor have a local resident (usually his or her host, often a relative) stand surety for them.[46] In either case, the baillie of the relevant quarter, or occasionally an officer appointed specifically for the task (as Faukland Harrot was in 1530), was to be summoned to inspect all new arrivals personally and decide whether to grant entry; this was never to be decided by the keeper himself.[47] Although the reference to licensing an individual might sometimes have been a figurative turn of phrase, more commonly some kind of certificate was most likely issued which could be produced on demand to certify the legitimacy of the holder's presence within the burgh. A verbal promise from those seeking entry was unlikely to be enough to meet the demand for 'sufficient certification' that they had come from clean places.[48] His or her characteristics might also be described, presumably to ensure the legitimate identity of the holder. This was a common practice elsewhere; 'of ordinary stature with dark hair, head and face' was how a father and son were described in one bill of health from eighteenth-century Malta.[49] Besides which, officials also wrote testimonies of health for local residents embarking on their travels.[50] Not only was it their responsibility to help officials in other burghs to determine the health of a visitor, but also it was considered equally as important to prevent individuals from leaving Aberdeen to travel to infected places. This was the case in 1529, when magistrates refused to allow a merchant by the name of John Ferres to sail to his home town of St Andrews, where plague was then raging, 'ffor as thai wnderstuid the law wald compell na man to pas wnl[aw]fullie to his awin deid as thai belewit'.[51] The imposition by civic authorities of restrictions on social mobility during times of plague was a huge responsibility that could be literally a matter of life or death.

Each of these processes was concerned with monitoring visitors arriving at the ports, the bridges or the harbour which comprised Aberdeen's official entrances. While the city's location might have made this a relatively straightforward task in comparison to many other burghs, this could not counter the illicit entry to the town, often 'under silence of night', of those coming in via unguarded access points. In common with most of Scotland's towns at this time, Aberdeen was not walled, with fortified buildings (such as that which had stood on Aberdeen's Castle Hill) typically being deemed sufficient for defence against invaders. When plague first threatened in the late fifteenth century, the council came up with a scheme to build an outer wall connecting each of the burgh's ports, but this did not eventuate and, as a result, the security of the city against interlopers seeking entry at unmanned access points was largely dependent on the vigilance of those residents whose back walls and gates effectively delineated its external boundaries.[52] The vulnerability of these was exacerbated by the state of disrepair into which they could be allowed to fall, and during the first few decades of Aberdeen's plague era magistrates tried to compel both owners and landlords to rebuild and strengthen them.[53] The council increasingly dispensed with promulgating explicit orders for the upkeep of privately-owned outer boundaries. It is possible that these might have become incorporated into less specific proclamations for the maintenance of 'the town', though it could also be indicative of a recognition of the impossibility of preventing illicit access to the burgh, which as Chapter 4 will discuss led to an increased focus on targeting seaborne sources of infection. In any case, convictions for purchasing goods from the infected south, travelling to plague-ridden areas, scaling external walls and lodging outsiders show that residents could prioritise commercial interests and the provision of hospitality to family and friends over a concern for health and safety, whether their own or that of the wider community.[54]

Detection: notification and searching

Whether due to failings in the monitoring of official entrances or in the security of unofficial access points, magistrates recognised that, despite their best efforts, plague could be brought into the burgh from infected areas. If an outbreak within the community were to be curbed, it was essential that authorities were aware of each individual case so that appropriate action could be taken to remove the threat and so limit contagion (in the pre-modern sense of the concept). Ideally this would be a process supervised from within the official medical profession, members of which could diagnose cases and advise on appropriate action. However, there is no evidence from the first outbreak that the city's physician James Cumming played any part in this, and the same is true of Robert Gray, his successor as mediciner at King's College by the time of the second outbreak in the 1540s, who in any case was not employed officially by the council. Neither was necessarily present the entire time during their respective incumbencies; indeed, they might have acted in accordance with received medical wisdom and fled in the face of plague, as running a private practice carried no specific obligation to stay.[55] Instead, the responsibility for the detection and notification of cases fell on residents of the city themselves: indeed, it was a civic duty designed for the safeguarding of the health of the whole community. Though it was a necessary move, placing the burden of responsibility on inhabitants presented two challenges to the authorities in their efforts to implement the process effectively: the inability of the layperson to diagnose plague and an instinctive reluctance to do so, given the likely consequences.

The first problem for civic officials in calling for the notification of suspected cases of plague was the inherent difficulty in expecting residents to recognise the disease. The enormity of the task at hand, which could literally be a matter of life and death for those who had contact with the patient, was complicated by the significant dichotomy between signs (which were objective, if disputable) and symptoms (which were subjective). As Gilbert Skene had noted, plague was so dangerous precisely because it was invidious, able to take hold before the victim was aware and to be manifested in symptoms which could vary between individuals. How much more difficult it was, therefore, for an observer to act on their suspicions before infection could spread. Anyone accused of failing to notify the authorities of such a case could reasonably defend their actions on the grounds that they lacked the knowledge necessary for its recognition. To counter this difficulty, during outbreaks (whether within or outwith the burgh) the council required *all* forms of sickness to be declared, regardless of the age, status or gender of the suspected patient.[56] Notification, where specified, was to be made to the provost, a council member, the relevant quartermaster, or 'at the least' to his assistant.

While this information was expected to be given voluntarily by members of the household, it could also be ascertained through the appointment of searchers. As scholarship on the practice of notification has emphasised, the role of searcher was invested with a huge amount of symbolic and actual power, albeit transient, and was a task that in England was designated in statutory provision from 1572 to women (and 'ancient' ones at that).[57] The appointment of women (often widows) as searchers further marginalised a group already on the fringe of civic participation, by forcibly identifying each due to the dangerous nature of their work, yet at the same time invested them with significant control over others' lives. The threat their authority posed to the established social hierarchy embodied cultural anxieties that were also felt about other marginal females: like witches, their words had material consequences and, like prostitutes, their work associated them with the morally and physically corrupt body. Not least because of the inherent suspicion with which their initial motives and consequent testimonies were sometimes viewed, together with the challenges of making individual diagnoses, it has traditionally been assumed that many of those chosen were at best inept and at worst outright liars, motivated to identify cases by money or the opportunity to settle old scores. A reassessment of the evidence has shown that, in fact, searchers could be '"respectable" women, insofar as they adhered to communal forms of parish living', who were often accused of under-reporting the frequency of plague.[58] In Scotland no specific prescriptions were issued about what kind of people the searchers ought to be, and therefore both the examination and diagnosis of victims fell to whomever local governments chose to appoint for the tasks. During Aberdeen's two sixteenth-century outbreaks only men were recorded as being chosen, reflecting the standard practice of appointing males for governmental positions. In 1547 they were ordered to view the naked body of Alexander Scott's nephew in order to establish 'gif he hes or hed the pest', and they regularly assessed patients in quarantine.[59] It is not known how many officials were to carry out such an examination, but it is likely that several opinions would have been sought to validate the diagnosis. Whether through advice garnered from other governments or from medical personnel, or simply by using their own initiative when presented with unusual symptoms, the authorities knew which 'signs' they took to be indicative of plague – or at the least they knew who in the community they wished to pronounce infected.

Once a diagnosis of plague within a household was confirmed, the authorities could decide on remedial action. This segues into the second reason for the occasional contravention of the requirement to report suspected cases of plague. The consequences of the detection of infection within a household made its inhabitants reluctant to admit such occurrences. While it could have been argued that the identification of a case of plague meant that the sufferer could then be treated (and therefore, perhaps, cured), this did not appear to have been considered by those harbouring them and was not touted by authorities as a further reason to reveal sickness. Uppermost in the minds of those whose loved ones had fallen sick was the knowledge that reporting the case entailed the enclosure of the entire household or, at the very least, the removal of the victim to a segregated plague camp to undergo quarantine, neither of which was a welcome prospect. During the first outbreak several inhabitants took desperate measures to conceal the presence of plague by burying a man who had died from the disease in a midden in a close in the Gallowgate area of the city.[60] That those responsible were a married couple and their servant indicates that the death might well have occurred within their own house. Not only did their actions contravene the order to reveal all cases of sickness, but also it endangered the community by polluting the environment with a potent source of infection (though their very actions demonstrate that the prevailing urban conditions were hardly sanitary). The council banished the wrongdoers, though this was probably no more of a punishment than the enforced enclosure which would have been the alternative consequence once the death had been discovered. Several residents were also convicted during the second epidemic for concealing the sickness of their loved ones, despite the punishments that were threatened (and sometimes imposed) for contravention.[61]

Magistrates recognised the folly of relying on residents' honesty in revealing suspected instances of sickness within the burgh and accepted that it was necessary for them to be proactive in uncovering cases themselves. In addition to the monitoring of the city's ports when plague threatened, therefore, it became increasingly common for 'all parts and rows' of the burgh to be patrolled as well.[62] This was sometimes ordered to be undertaken at night as well as during the daytime, and was generally the job of the baillie of each quarter often with assistance from specially chosen 'certain honest neighbours'.[63] Sometimes their task was specified – such as to report any 'noyis of strangearis or seiknes'; more often, however, their duties were described obliquely as being 'to keep', 'to watch' or 'to walk' the burgh and to 'take inquisition' of whoever they came across.[64] This could also involve visiting individual households for various reasons including to uncover and destroy goods suspected of infection, and to impress upon each resident personally that contravening plague statutes imperilled the entire community.[65] House-to-house visits were also undertaken to search for strangers and cases of sickness, as well as to ascertain how many resided in each dwelling (and thereby discern whether or not the presence of each inhabitant was legitimate).[66] This was particularly important in determining the extent of certain categories of people who were considered to pose a special threat to the common weal, particularly during socio-economic crises such as outbreaks.

It had long been accepted that plague could be carried by people, animals and goods, and hence total bans on the entry or reception of all three of these categories were often imposed during times of outbreaks, particularly those deemed to have originated in plague-ridden areas. But the perceived threat posed by each of these broad categories was nuanced, and there existed certain elements within each that were considered to be particularly disposed to harbouring infection. As Gilbert Skene noted in his *Breve Descriptioun of the Pest*, foodstuffs such as onions and leeks were deemed particularly susceptible to plague, as were materials such as linen, flax and hemp, which were porous and better able to absorb plague poison. These goods were frequently targeted in legislation (a distinction which 'quite significantly' pre-dated equivalent measures adopted in England[67]), and hence these types of goods were ordered to be confiscated or banned.[68] While all animals were capable of transmitting plague, dogs, cats and pigs were identified as being especially dangerous during outbreaks. Not only could they harbour plague in their fur or skin, but also they were domesticated, given to indiscriminate wandering into and between dwellings, sharing living space with humans, and (as archaeological findings for Aberdeen have proved) foraging for scraps amongst the middens and offcuts that typically littered the streets.[69] When plague threatened it became lawful to slay without fear of reprisal any pigs, cats and stray dogs found wandering freely.[70]

More so than goods or animals, the most threatening carriers of plague were certain groups of people. Civic legislation calling for the monitoring of individuals variously targeted mendicants, beggars, 'gangrels', 'coddrochs' and chapmen in addition to general 'pur simpill folkis', and could further distinguish between incomers and those who were native to the burgh.[71] Given the importance of preventing the intrusion of interlopers who might be harbouring infection, officials were particularly determined to clamp down on those whose daily means of acquiring a living required them to travel from place to place and from house to house within those settlements. When plague threatened the burgh from the south in 1513, no 'gangerall' coming from the Mounth was to be permitted to enter the burgh without first having been vetted.[72] The targeting of 'gangrels' (a vagabond or, literally, a 'going-about person') shows that it was what might be termed the social promiscuity of these individuals which most concerned authorities: their unchecked meanderings increased the likelihood of their having picked up infection. Magistrates' concern might not have been entirely unfounded: by the time they were next targeted plague was raging within the city and officers were ordered to patrol the streets to round up any they came across who had arrived in the burgh 'of new'.[73] On the next few occasions when plague again threatened, no chapmen – itinerant salesmen – were permitted to 'set forth their packs' in the town, and no 'gangralis puirralis' were to be granted entry.[74] During times of plague, repeated efforts by successive councils to curb social promiscuity focused most particularly on those who survived by begging, including those resident mendicants of the burgh whose alms-seeking had a spiritual impetus.

As Chapter 2 outlined, beggars presented a particular threat to the health of the community in two ways: their social promiscuity and their perceived disposition to infection. They sought charitable donations by begging from house to house or from among the congregation at church, and hence came into contact with a substantial number of people on a regular basis. When plague first threatened at the end of the fifteenth century, magistrates ordered them to beg only at the doors of St Nicholas Kirk rather than enter the building and mix with the congregation.[75] This need to separate the healthy community from those who were particularly liable to infection became even more pressing during the city's first epidemic, when beggars who were 'decrepit or auld that may notht trawele' were again requested to sit by the walls or doors of the kirk away 'fra cumpany of pepill' to receive their alms.[76]

Secondly, beggars presented a particular threat during times of plague because contemporaries identified them as being especially disposed to infection as they were forced to exist in the dirty, malodorous environments in which it flourished. Gilbert Skene lived through Aberdeen's epidemic of the 1540s and it might have been this experience that led him to comment in the *Breve Descriptioun* that 'we see dalie the pure mair subiecte to sic calamitie [that is, plague] because they ar constrynit be pouertie to eit ewill and corrupte meittis'.[77] Furthermore, the poor could not afford to flee, which guaranteed their presence within the burgh and further threatened the health of others who remained. Plague exacerbated the situation by creating a category of pauper comprised of those from formerly self-sufficient lower income groups, able typically to eke out a precarious living, who became destitute as a result of the disruption to commercial life during outbreaks.[78] With their means of earning a living severely disrupted, the threat they posed increased and those who 'held opin houss' were to be expelled during the first epidemic.[79] They did at least have homes in which to live and their adverse circumstances were at least temporary. They stood in contrast to those paupers whose poverty resulted from unwillingness (rather than an inability) to work. These individuals, known as 'codderars' (from coddroch, 'idle, low class person'), were considered lazy and undeserving of charity, particularly when public resources were stretched during an economic crisis such as an epidemic. The immorality of their slothful natures also made them more susceptible to plague than those who had reluctantly been reduced to begging through adverse economic circumstances. The expulsion of those whose poverty resulted from persistent unscrupulous laziness enabled precious resources to be apportioned to those who deserved them and was, additionally, a method of divine appeasement, an 'act of propitiation and a gesture of public piety or charity on the part of the state itself'.[80] Coddrochs were banished during the first outbreak and again when the plague identified as the 'botch' threatened in 1539.[81] Licentious idleness made them depraved as well as deprived; getting rid of them eliminated a literal and figurative source of corruption from the community. Their removal was an act of charity towards the body politic that would find favour with God.[82]

Civic authorities had therefore to establish the whereabouts of the poor within the city, whether in order to determine their need or eligibility for charity, to assess whether their presence was legitimate, or simply to place checks on their mobility. Officers could be required to carry out the time-consuming task of making house-to-house enquiries to account for those with somewhere to live (or at least to lodge).[83] Auditing the numbers of poor with no fixed abode was less straightforward and could involve officials patrolling the streets and apprehending anyone they came across who aroused their suspicions.[84] Sometimes they convened the poor in one convenient location, by summoning them by the ringing of the hand bell throughout the town, or rounding them up directly by having baillies searching the streets or calling at residences. Individuals might on occasion have been physically frogmarched to the kirk yard, the appointed meeting place and a venue where many beggars routinely congregated in any case.[85]

Once gathered, each individual was assessed to determine whether or not they ought to be supported. This included establishing the resources each had to live on, with fire, fuel and ale considered basic necessities.[86] It also required officers to determine whether the claimant was native to the burgh (that is, born there or having resided there for at least seven years) and whether he or she was impoverished through circumstance or mere idleness. Prior to the establishment of Kirk Sessions after the Reformation to oversee poor relief in a more concerted and organised way, the sources of support for paupers within any given parish have been described as 'highly miscellaneous'.[87] Beggars received alms at church services (both the usual sermon and extraordinary gatherings such as anniversary masses) and by going door-to-door, while individual acts of pious benevolence in a variety of ways (such as doles, church offerings and bequests) helped both the beggar in their present life and the donor in the next. What might be termed state support under the control of the council supplemented these sources; while the government was ostensibly a secular organisation, it is important to recognise that its motives for providing charity stemmed from pious as well as practical considerations. Because plague was a sign of God's wrath, repentance through the distribution of charity was as important a step in bringing about the end of an epidemic as was ridding the community of immoral elements.

That being noted, governors were, above all, pragmatic and intended to prevent the social disorder that a starving and disenfranchised minority could instigate. This might help to explain why on the majority of occasions all native poor within the burgh were considered eligible to receive charity during both the threat and the presence of plague, apparently regardless of whether or not they were considered deserving of it.[88] In a further two instances, it was allocated on the condition that the recipients 'beand at hame & nocht seyk'. It is likely that the 'shamefaced' poor were here being referred to, too proud to beg but clearly in need of help. On both occasions the recipients were listed: forty-one residents on the first occasion and sixty on the second. Assuming Aberdeen's population at this point to have been around 5,500, this gives a proportion of 'extraordinary' poor similar to the 'ordinary' poor who received support in Dundee a century later.[89] Sources of funding for the support of the poor were not explicitly identified, but were almost certainly similar to those earmarked for the sustenance of those specifically undergoing quarantine in the nearby plague camp: the appropriation of collections gathered at St Nicholas Kirk, the imposition of a specific tax and, especially, the many fines accrued by residents for a wide variety of plague-related misdemeanours.

Those permitted to receive this charity were identified by having affixed to their clothing a token made of lead, 'bearing the towns arms' and imprinted with 'ABD'.[90] These were visible symbols of 'belonging, worthiness [and] entitlement'[91] that certified their status as a *bona fide* member of the community: 'that thai mai be knawin by wtheris', as the council termed it.[92] Ineligible claimants were routinely expelled, but this did not always rid the authorities of the financial or administrative burden of these individuals. Orders for banishment were not always easy to enforce, particularly when they were applied to multiple people, and when deficiencies in both the watch at official entrances and in the security of unmonitored access points meant that new arrivals could not always be prevented. Attempts to expel unlicensed beggars (that is, those not considered eligible according to the criteria then current) required time, money and manpower, all of which added to the administrative burden already caused by the monitoring of the burgh undertaken in order to detect paupers of all categories, interlopers and cases of sickness.

Isolation: enclosure and quarantine

In August 1500 magistrates in Aberdeen ordered twenty-one residences (some of which were situated in the Castlegate, the heart of civic life) to be shut up for fifteen days, with all the occupants of each consigned to remain within for the duration.[93] At least one member of each household had been suspected of having contact with people and goods recently arrived in a ship from the plague-stricken Baltic port of Danzig. The vessel had been transporting a chest that was ordered to be burnt and its crew were confined to unspecified remote buildings. This was the first occasion on which civic authorities feared that plague might actually have entered the burgh as a result of some failing in the *cordon sanitaire* they had imposed. Their ordinance was issued during an outbreak both in parts of Scotland and on the continent, of sufficient severity to be recalled in the communal civic memory fourteen years later as the time of 'the last deid' even though at least one further plague scare had occurred in the intervening period.[94] Subsequently, the following April the council ordered two named inhabitants (deemed 'infeckit folks') to be shut up within their houses for at least twenty days, with other residents to act as guarantors in the event that infection resulted. The order also prohibited goods from being brought into the town from Futty, typically the place of arrival for seaborne visitors, and this was extended to people two months later.[95]

The imposition of a *cordon sanitaire* around the city in response to the threat of plague was an attempt to prevent initial contact between healthy people and sources of infection, and this same principle was applied on a micro level within the bounds of the burgh itself. At the outset of the sixteenth century, on both of these early occasions when magistrates believed that plague might actually have entered Aberdeen, they recognised right away that it was necessary to prevent those within the community at large from coming into contact with potential sources of the disease, whether people or goods. They had to guide them in this a nominally nationwide legislative framework comprising the Rule of the Pestilence (1456) and the statutes contained in the letter of James IV, issued in January 1513 early in the epidemic under which much of Scotland then laboured. These two ordinances showed that the isolation of both suspected and confirmed cases of plague was a recognised practice, as was the confiscation of goods identified as arriving from infected places. As a major port Aberdeen was vulnerable to infection transmitted from overseas, and magistrates tried to counter this by refusing to let such goods be unloaded or by confiscating cargoes arriving from places where plague was then known or suspected. An outbreak in a number of Baltic ports in 1538 prompted the Privy Council to alert all eastern ports to be on their guard, resulting in Aberdeen's councillors ordering linen which had arrived on a vessel from Danzig to be 'put in loftis & sellaris & naie be handillit quhill the toun be forthir awysit'.[96] During the city's second outbreak officers sequestered the cargo (which included salt) of a returning vessel on which four of the crew had died from plague while in Flanders.[97] The consequent depreciation in value of certain goods and the spoilage of others with a limited shelf life meant that their confiscation was naturally resented by merchants, some of whom sought compensation.[98]

Before 1550 the vast majority of regulations surrounding the isolation of possible sources of plague related to people rather than goods. Initially this was implemented by shutting up potentially infected individuals within their own homes and enclosing these buildings to minimise interaction with the outside community. Enclosure within one's own residence could be undertaken for several purposes. As on both occasions in 1500, it could be imposed on ostensibly healthy people deemed to have come into contact with sources of infection (deliberately or otherwise), who could then be monitored over the duration of their confinement for the development of any symptoms.[99] It could also be used while arrangements were made for transferring a confirmed case to an isolation area outside the burgh, as well as for a further period on the return home of a recovered resident from this quarantine.[100] It could also be imposed to contain members of a household among whom a case of sickness had been detected.[101]

This final purpose of enclosure filled residents with particular dread. The forced confinement of an entire household as a precautionary measure meant the cessation for an indefinite period of normal day-to-day activities such as going to church and market, socialising and earning a living. In so doing, it fractured community relationships, and the associated stigma of suspicion 'transformed previously accepted individuals into enemies of the state ... a dangerous other'.[102] More ominously, it could effectively condemn all members of the household to infection and possible death (a scenario highlighted by critics of the practice).[103] Governments did not implement enclosure lightly. The dispersal throughout the city of infected inhabitants, or those suspected of being so, within numerous separate dwellings created an unwelcome administrative burden. Healthy residents had to be monitored regularly for symptoms, while the whole house had to be guarded to prevent any inhabitants escaping or having any unnecessary contact with others in the community. It was also necessary to provide for those in confinement, as it was unlikely that any but the wealthiest households would have sufficient resources to live on for more than a few days. Enclosure denied people the ability to support their ill loved ones by conventional means, for even the simple act of passing food and drink through a window required some contact with those inside the building and was therefore dangerous. While those on the outside were occasionally permitted to provide enclosed residents with necessities such as wine, this was usually the task of officers.[104]

Not surprisingly, the enforced curfew was sometimes contravened by individuals who managed to evade the guard in spite of the council's threats of execution, in accordance with James IV's regulations, of anyone who dared to 'cum furth of thair houssis ... be nicht or day'.[105] Though practiced widely in burghs throughout Scotland, the benefit of hindsight taught lawmakers that enclosure was, in practice, oppressive and inefficient. These were aspects that had long been criticised in English popular narratives, which cast it as 'punishment rather than aid'.[106] The contravention of plague orders, particularly in the concealment of a patient, could result in the lawbreaker being forcibly enclosed with that individual even though they themselves were not infected, a practice which risked their own physical health. In the eyes of officials the punishment therefore fitted the crime, as the initial concealment of infection had risked the health of the wider community, but the punitive aspect of enclosure contributed to its negative public perception as 'personal punishment rather than prudent policy'.[107] When plague threatened Scotland in 1720, the Convention of Royal Burghs ordered that

> howsoon any person falls sick of the plague in a house, that instead of shuting up the sound with the sick in such a house as has been the practise in too many places that sick persone be immediatly removed into the infirmary and be there duly attended and provided with food and medicines.[108]

This shift in policy, which in the event never needed to be implemented, promoted the other method of segregating sufferers that had long been used by urban governments both in Aberdeen and elsewhere.

The removal of sufferers from the town to one isolated, purpose-built area where they could be supervised, treated and provided for efficiently was intended to contain both infection and its victims separate from healthy society. It became termed quarantine (from *quaranta*, forty) due to the forty-day period typically imposed following its initial implementation in the port of Ragusa in 1377, both because Hippocratic theory taught that this was how long it took for an acute illness to be manifested and also because the length of time had religious and liturgical significance.[109] The practice spread throughout Europe and was supervised in many places by an overarching public health board (with early examples of their creation including Ragusa in the 1390s, Milan in 1450, Venice in 1486 and Florence in 1527) dedicated to administering each stage of the process, from promulgating and enforcing associated legislation to identifying and codifying patients.[110] In many Italian cities these became permanent administrative bodies, but tended to be temporary in towns north of the Alps.[111] In Scotland the relatively manageable size of each burgh and the satisfactory existing infrastructures of local government obviated the need for such an organisation. Neither did the governments of any of Scotland's towns see the need for the establishment of a designated pest-house in the mould of what became permanent *lazaretti* (as they were termed in Italian), which were founded in major urban centres for the dedicated isolation and care of victims. Italian and Spanish case studies have shown that this care could be extensive for those patients who could afford it, focused on optimising conditions in accordance with the Galenic six non-naturals including the purification of their surroundings, the provision of an optimum remedial diet, and attending to their spiritual needs.[112] Instead, civic authorities throughout Scotland found it sufficient to establish temporary camps with wooden lodges to which the infected (or those suspected of being so) were sent. Such segregated outdoor areas were used to absorb patients from overcrowded pest-houses in some English parishes, where they were termed pest-fields, and were intended as spaces where the infected could convalesce in the beneficial (relatively) fresh air. The Convention of Royal Burghs' proclamation of 1720 noted above, which stressed the preference for sufferers to be removed to 'the infirmary', was probably copied from contemporary (and controversial) regulations issued in London, which had a long tradition of sending the infected to pest-houses such as that located in the parish of St Martin in the Fields, which has been the subject of detailed study.[113] In 1504 the council in Edinburgh first designated an unspecified 'commoun place' where sufferers were enclosed, but evidence for the establishment of a temporary camp on the city's Burgh Muir comes only from 1530.[114]

Aberdeen might therefore have pre-dated the capital in establishing a camp for the quarantine of infected or suspected victims during its first epidemic, which was situated to the north-east beyond the boundaries of the burgh on the area known as the Gallow Hills towards the beach and was moved (or extended) to the Links closer to the coast in the 1540s.[115] Both were most likely *ad hoc* entities designed to cater for the needs of those affected by the particular outbreak. Given their temporary nature the camps, both in the 1510s and the 1540s, probably comprised a number of hastily erected wooden huts (known as 'lugis'), cheap and easy to build. Facilities at both were basic, perhaps with little more provided for bedding than straw, and conditions harsh. They may be contrasted with those in the sophisticated, permanent plague hospitals built in such cities as Genoa and Venice, wherein 'providing comfort was a priority embedded in care'.[116] Individuals removed from Aberdeen to its plague camp would at least have had their portable belongings with them, which would also have been presumed to be infected. Those with sufficient finances to pay for their own supplies fared better than poorer patients, some of whom benefited from donations from family members or from individual acts of charity. But responsibility for the upkeep of those residents sent to quarantine (or, for that matter, enclosed within their own houses) was that of the community, and ultimately of civic authorities. The Rule of the Pestilence of 1456 had made it clear that 'the towne suld find' for anyone sent to the camp with no possessions of their own, lest an infected individual might seek means of support elsewhere and in so doing 'fyle the cuntre about thame'. The subsequent financial burden that this imparted on urban governments weighed heavily on councillors in Aberdeen, who sought to offset it when plague threatened in 1549 by ordering heads of households to provide for any of their servants who were sent to the camp under suspicion of infection.[117]

During the outbreak of the 1540s, many of those in quarantine had been unable to fend for themselves and required state support. Analysis of the microeconomics of plague elsewhere has indicated that it tended to be the lower middle classes who were hit hardest. They could not afford to flee, but felt keenly the effects of commercial dislocation, which did not register with the very poor, who were used to relying on charity at the best of times.[118] In Aberdeen, the location of houses targeted to be enclosed was not identified except for the first time such an order was issued, when the majority were situated on the Castlegate. As the hub of administrative and commercial life, this area was where some of the city's wealthiest and most powerful residents owned houses (including the earls of Erroll, Mar and Buchan, whose houses were 'the finest in Aberdeen in their time') and therefore, in this specific example, those undergoing enclosure were likely to have the requisite resources to see them through their period of isolation.[119] The same would almost certainly have been true of three knighted individuals who underwent enclosure during the second outbreak.[120] The exponential practice of identifying those sent to the plague camp as 'the poor' may reflect the way in which economic dislocation caused by plague affected all but the extremely wealthy and it is probable that most individuals sent to the camp required public support. Throughout the epidemic of the 1540s, and during earlier outbreaks in burghs for which records survive, they were given firewood for warmth, and bread and ale for sustenance. In Dundee the construction and maintenance of the plague camp were funded by rentals owed to the parish church of St Clement, but Aberdeen's council had been forced to finance those in its huts by appropriating funds from the weekly collection at St Nicholas Kirk and the remainder of a heavy tax, and by dipping into its general coffers controlled by the dean of guild.[121] Most of the public money used for the support of the infected came from the many fines accrued by residents imposed for a wide variety of plague-related and other misdemeanours, from trading with 'intlanderis' to hiding infected clothes and being absent from the annual Head Court meeting.[122] Magistrates also commandeered victuals wherever they could, not least because the disruption to commerce caused by plague hindered the supply of goods and increased the problem of catering for those in the camp. During both outbreaks they sent confiscated foodstuffs, such as bread and ale deemed insufficient for sale, to the camp specifically or for the sustenance of the poor more generally, and in 1549 ordered any pigs found unrestrained in the market place to be slain and given to those in quarantine.[123]

Such support extended only as far as the provision of necessary consumables. Healthcare for those in the camp was practically non-existent, though a fortunate few residents might have brought with them a devoted relative or a nurse whom they had employed privately and whose duties would have been limited to personal rather than medical care. Having the financial means to afford a private companion or to purchase additional supplies would have done little to alleviate the uncomfortable conditions at the camp, which compounded the misery for patients of being forcibly separated from loved ones and of facing the uncertainty of when (or if) they would return home. It is perhaps surprising, therefore, that no convictions were recorded during this period of anyone trying to escape from quarantine and only one instance of violating home enclosure.[124] The authorities made this very difficult to do, by having the camp guarded and by forcing those sent there to be accompanied on their journey (which was a specific task of the official cleanser on his initial employment).[125]

Though healthcare at the plague camp was negligible, some form of medical examination was clearly necessary both in order to determine whether an individual ought to be sent to quarantine in the first place and, once there, to monitor the progress of his or her infection. The council registers sometimes framed the examination of patients in the passive, which obscured the mechanisms of the process; in May 1546, for example, two residents, their wives and households were allowed to leave the plague camp, 'it beand fundin that thai ar out of danger'.[126] It was most likely the case that an examination of an individual was limited to a cursory visual check for the manifestation of unusual symptoms, not least due to the probable absence of professional medical participation in the process. It would appear that, just as government officials were responsible for the identification of suspected cases of plague within individual households, so too were they charged with the task of monitoring sufferers sent to quarantine. In January 1546 the baillies were ordered to 'tak inquisitioun' of various persons in the camp who were now said to be 'clangit and clein', an indication that they had come into contact with infection but had not actually succumbed to it and so, having undergone the cleansing process, might now be judged safe.[127] The following August, a resident by the name of John Cruikshank was allowed to leave the camp, having been 'fundin clein' by the officers, and it might be supposed that other similar examinations went unrecorded.[128] It was usually the case that a number of residents were permitted to leave quarantine at any one time, often entire households together. This indicates that patients were examined in bulk, both for efficiency and to minimise risky visits by officials to the plague camp. The practice of quarantining whole households indicates that at the height of both of the epidemics the camp might have been relatively sizeable. The decline in recorded household sizes undergoing quarantine in some London parishes during the 1636–37 outbreak (from an average of 5.9 to 3.8) suggests that wealthier residents tended to flee, leaving behind their servants and apprentices to run the house.[129] In Aberdeen, conversely, the head of the household was often named specifically as being sent for quarantine, accompanied by a somewhat formulaic list comprised of wives, children and servants (a term which also included apprentices). In determining household sizes in the early modern burgh the most complete source is the poll conducted in 1695, which gave an average among Aberdeen's polled population of 4.3, the same as that indicated by a census of Old Aberdeen taken in 1636.[130] However, this figure masks a good deal of variance; the average household size within the semi-rural freedom lands was just over three people, while within the bounds of the burgh it was 4.6 and, due to a higher servant population than in other burghs, the wealthiest households averaged 7.3 people.[131] Notwithstanding the dangers of extrapolation for an earlier period, it is likely that the enclosure or removal to quarantine of an entire household would have affected several individuals across the spectrum of society.

For individuals presumed to be infected and sent to the plague camp, one of two outcomes awaited: recovery or death. Statistics do not exist to establish the mortality rates for Aberdeen's sixteenth-century outbreaks, and references to the practicalities of dealing with high fatalities (such as the personnel and financial outlay involved in digging graves and transporting bodies) are available only for the final epidemic in the 1640s. It can be surmised that, as with any substantial outbreak, the mortality rates – however high they actually were – added considerable grief and loss to the disruption and misery felt by the community in the throes of plague. As the examples cited above demonstrate, on the other hand, recovery from infection was by no means as unlikely an outcome as might be assumed. During the second of Aberdeen's epidemics in particular, the numbers of individuals returned to the burgh from quarantine in the camp is striking. This indicates strongly the belief that recovery from plague was eminently possible, which is consistent with the views of writers such as Gilbert Skene who discussed the treatment and cure of the disease with no hint that such efforts were fruitless. A modern interpretation of the apparent recovery of victims might infer that such individuals had been misdiagnosed in the first place, or that the authorities were mistaken in pronouncing them cured (which, in turn, might have perpetuated the cycle of infection). Indeed, in January 1515 magistrates declared that plague had recently been spread within the burgh by those who had 'bene infectit abefore and chapis' (that is, recovered), an indication that they lacked confidence in the ability of unqualified officials to recognise cases at such a relatively early stage in Aberdeen's experience of plague.[132] Officers might have attributed the recovery of certain residents from plague to a number of factors – the efficacy of cleansing, the success of remedies that had been administered, or (perhaps most likely) the result of sufficient contrition in the face of divine wrath.

Once an individual was fortunate enough to be considered to have recovered from plague, he or she no longer posed a threat to the health of the community and so could leave the camp and return to the burgh. Before this was allowed to happen, however, a number of safeguards were put in place to make absolutely sure of his or her good health. A further period of convalescence at the camp could be imposed, during which time the person was monitored for the reappearance of any symptoms of concern.[133] Some residents had their personal belongings cleansed again before they could leave (or had to carry out this task themselves), while others sought fellow residents to stand as guarantors for their clean status.[134] In addition, almost without exception those people now deemed 'safe' were licensed to validate their health and certify that they had permission to leave, creating a paper trail which the authorities would be able to consult if necessary.[135] Even with these various precautions in place it was not a straightforward case of being able simply to slot back into everyday life and resume normal activities within the community (or as normal as was possible during an epidemic). One (or both) of two additional safeguards was frequently put in place for those returned from the plague camp: a further period of home enclosure, or identification. It is difficult to fathom the rationale behind each individual scenario, though this is by no means to imply that such decisions were taken haphazardly. Further enclosure within one's own house was imposed on several occasions (either for eight or fifteen days[136]), perhaps when it was considered that an individual might somehow be irresponsible in their activities or whereabouts on their return to the city. This concern about unreliability may have underlain the restrictions imposed on Dauid Andersoune, who was permitted to make essential visits to hear mass in St Ninian's Chapel so long as he was accompanied at all times by an officer, who would escort him to and from his back gate.[137] A similar arrangement was put in place for Johnn Brabner, who was allowed to embark on supervised visits to his house from the plague camp to conduct business, while Jonat Mar was given permission to attend church daily on the condition that she talked to no-one and that she returned to her home enclosure as soon as the service had finished.[138] Conversely, Sir Johnn Wrycht was trusted entirely to ensure that he remained 'cautious' in his dealings with the community at large, 'as vderis nychtboris did that wer Inclusit', an indication that status might have played a part in the presumption of reliability.[139] During the threatened outbreak of 1549, when it appears that suspected individuals were removed straight away to the quarantine camp rather than being shut up in their houses, upwards of thirteen residents were subsequently permitted to return to the burgh so long as they then underwent a period of enclosure within their own homes and limited their public visits to church and market.[140]

In managing the return to the burgh of former sufferers, a far more common precaution imposed in Aberdeen was their forcible identification. As with their segregation, the visible distinguishing of victims of disease had biblical precedent and a long civic administrative pedigree, stretching back to legislation concerning lepers passed in the twelfth century under David I. The impetus to inform and protect healthy society from the infected continued with regard to plague, with both the Rule of the Pestilence and the letter of James IV ordering that the sick be marked out in order that 'the commond pepill may evaid thame as thai think expedient', as Aberdeen's council clerk termed it during the second outbreak.[141] During both epidemics magistrates invariably ordered recovered residents to carry a white stick rather than having them affix a white cloth to their clothing, the two alternative means of identification that the council acknowledged had been stipulated in James IV's letter.[142] The same legislation also decreed that the forestairs or doors of formerly infected dwellings were also to be adorned with a white cloth, though in Aberdeen they were never ordered to be distinguished in any manner.

Disinfection: cleansing of people, places and goods

Frequently, an additional condition of permitting recovered residents to return to the burgh was the stipulation that their goods, persons or dwellings be thoroughly cleansed. Cleansing was integral to the authorities' efforts to prevent or eliminate plague within their community despite its inherent disadvantages, including the damage to or destruction of belongings, and the administrative and financial outlay required for its undertaking. The necessity of cleansing as a means of eliminating infection stemmed from the same beliefs about plague causation and transmission that informed efforts to prevent, detect and isolate sources of the disease. Observation and experience taught magistrates that plague was generated by environmental corruption, the presence of which was indicated by bad odours and filthy conditions. It was regarded as a subtle poison which spread through the interchangeable notions of miasma (polluted air) and contagion (both direct and indirect contact). It was capable of being absorbed by porous materials, including not only the skin of both humans and animals but also inanimate objects like soft fruits and textiles such as linen and wool. Efforts to eliminate various sources of infection through cleansing were founded on these principles and might be supposed to act in several ways. The poison could be destroyed by extremes of temperature. Heat produced by fire could be applied either to infected objects or to the atmosphere more generally, though individual objects could also be subjected to boiling or scalding, or, conversely, exposure to extremely frosty conditions. These methods could be used in conjunction with strong smells such as the burning of heather or the washing of objects in vinegar to neutralise noxious odours. Thorough ventilation was also commonly applied to buildings and objects (particularly textiles) alike through exposure to fresh air which replaced the poisonous miasma. Items were subjected to any one or a combination of these methods repeatedly over a period of time whose length was naturally impossible to determine and, though entirely rationalised, was therefore somewhat arbitrary.

It is clear from each of these methods that the destruction of, or at least damage to, items was a common outcome of the cleansing process in spite of efforts to minimise spoilage. While coins and clothing tended to be boiled and generally survived this process, books and papers (unless made of vellum) would effectively be destroyed whichever method was employed. The risk to property through the cleansing process had been recognised in the Rule of the Pestilence, which had prohibited the burning of another's house to ward off infection unless this could be done without causing damage.[143] There are documented cases from other burghs of individual acts of destruction, such as in Peebles where William Frank's title deeds to nearby land were burnt during the outbreak of 1546.[144] Specific examples of cleansing methods used during Aberdeen's first two outbreaks refer only to the burning of goods: this was the destiny of 'certane tymber' that supposedly had been brought into the city from the plague camp, of merchandise belonging to pedlars from the south, of goods in the house of a woman convicted of receiving banished individuals, and of all belongings thought infected which were found within the houses of certain residents subsequently convicted for possessing them.[145] The destruction of items as a result of the process is evident from the dispute that arose in 1547, when Robert Atkin's one hundred sheep skins had been rendered worthless after being cleansed by Andro Losoun. Atkin sought compensation, while Losoun sought payment for carrying out the task; neither wanted the ruined skins.[146]

Cleansing necessitated contact with presumed sources of infection and was therefore an inherently risky business. The process itself was also a test of its efficacy and was therefore commonly referred to as 'trying' goods or subjecting them to 'assay' (that is, trial). If the individuals who had handled them subsequently developed plague it could be assumed that the goods remained infectious. Therefore, owners were often ordered to cleanse items themselves, the logic behind which being that if anyone were to catch plague from the goods then better it be those who owned them. This was applied both to individuals deemed to have had contact with infection, who were also subjected to home enclosure, and to former plague sufferers who had been returned to the burgh from quarantine.[147] As with searchers, it has been assumed that cleansers were 'generally of the lowest or roughest' social class, as Ritchie did with regard to Dumfries.[148] In Edinburgh, contrary to historiographical assumptions, those appointed as cleansers were not drawn from the lower ranks but rather were specifically ordered to be 'men of high substance'.[149] Likewise, in Aberdeen a military captain garrisoned in the city and the widow of a reader in the Kirk were both appointed cleansers during the final outbreak – both respectable individuals, and the latter female at that, and the same might also have been the case in earlier epidemics.[150] During the seventeenth century cleansers could be considered experts who were highly sought after and were procured from hundreds of miles away by a number of parishes and burghs in the north-east. During the pre-1550 period, however, there were no apparent issues with finding cleansers, perhaps because the relatively high wages on offer compensated for the inherently unpleasant nature of the task. During both of Aberdeen's outbreaks they were officially employed on an *ad hoc* basis by the council, paid from the public purse or occasionally by those who owned the goods to be cleansed. Additionally, while there is only one record of a cleanser employed privately by a wealthy household, this might not have been a unique occurrence given the existence of other references to individuals engaged in the process.[151] Certainly, the city's official cleansers were kept busy: Androw Mortymer, employed during the first epidemic, was subsequently granted the services of an assistant of his own choosing, while during the second outbreak Alexander Rattray had his initial contract renewed after only a month.[152]

As with the monitoring of unofficial entrances to the city, magistrates were recurrently hindered in their efforts to implement an effective cleansing process through their reliance on the diligence of individuals. During the first outbreak they were forced to reiterate the importance of carrying out the process carefully, due to a concern that plague was being spread by insufficiently cleansed goods, and had also to admonish their own official cleanser.[153] The perceived financial advantage to perpetuating infection often led to accusations of deliberate plague spreading, but in Aberdeen only one instance of this occurred: in 1547 a baker was accused by three other residents of travelling to Inverbervie deliberately in order to infect inhabitants there, as he was 'infeckit with this contagius seiknes & pest and it beand ryngand on his body'. It might have been the case that many such accusations were without foundation and entirely malicious, prompted by personal disputes. In this instance, the baker unsuccessfully sued for defamation, a verdict which hurt him 'bayt in body & mind', so perhaps upon inspection officers found the tell-tale signs of plague and felt the accusation had merit.[154] Cleansers also had privileged access to enter private dwellings and handle goods without being challenged, and were occasionally suspected of stealing belongings, leading to lingering disputes over ownership.[155] Such scenarios provided further impetus for entrusting disinfection to the owners of goods themselves. Since the cleansing process could result in items being stolen, damaged or destroyed, it was not surprising that convictions occurred of individuals who were either unwilling to surrender their belongings or who were prepared to handle infected goods themselves.[156] Despite these challenges, the task of disinfection at least served a psychological function, the importance of which Bowers stressed in her study of plague measures in Seville. Above all, the state had to be seen to be taking concerted action which reflected contemporary notions of plague causation and diffusion: consideration of the psychological usefulness of a particular measure adds a valuable dimension to traditional notions of the 'effectiveness' of such legislation.[157]

Plague in Aberdeen before 1550

As with their counterparts in other urban centres, the Aberdeen authorities' efforts to prevent the spread of plague during the first half of the sixteenth century were formulated in accordance with an understanding that the disease could be transmitted by both miasma and contagion. These interchangeable concepts held that it could be diffused by miasmic airborne vapours as well as through contact (which could be indirect) with myriad sources of infection, including not only people but also animals and inanimate objects. Initial attempts to prevent potential plague carriers from entering the burgh, through the monitoring of official entrances and associated safeguards to ensure the entrant's good health, were hampered by the negligence of the watchers and the challenge of relying on residents not to allow access via their back walls and gates. Accepting that interlopers might yet gain entry, officials were tasked to patrol the streets of each quarter, making home visitations if necessary, in order to root out illicit visitors and suspected cases of sickness which were also required to be notified to the authorities. The powers this gave for civic control over the movements of everyone within the city, under the guise of a concern for public health, entailed the targeting of those whose presence might be considered socially undesirable for ideological as well as practical reasons. This was evident in the civic approach to tackling both the Great Pox and plague: such diseases were the articulation of divine vengeance, and hence the removal or limiting of immoral elements within society was rational and justifiable on both medical and moral grounds. An associated concern to suppress disorder is revealed in certain specific civic regulations relating to plague, such as the requirement for officials to search houses both for cases of sickness and 'unlawchfull' folk, and the stipulation that those monitoring the ports ought to 'resist incomers and lurdans' (miscreants).[158]

A striking feature of the Aberdeen authorities' early approaches to tackling disease within the community is their innovativeness. It is widely acknowledged that the Italian city states led the way in the devising and implementing of plague legislation. Urban authorities in Scotland, and Aberdeen in particular, were remarkably far advanced of their English counterparts in promulgating legislation designed to tackle disease. To emphasise the speed with which the city's authorities responded to the Great Pox in particular, it is worth noting that during that same month a group of scholars gathered at the court of the Italian duke Ercole d'Este in Ferrara to discuss the new disease, a meeting which was 'the earliest major academic debate on mal francese'.[159] Although the Great Pox may have been spread to England by mercenaries fighting under Perkin Warbeck in September 1496, it was not until 1502 that the disease was specifically acknowledged there (on which occasion it was termed the 'French pox').[160]

It was similarly the case with plague. In England plague legislation was first implemented only in 1518, and then at the national rather than provincial level; it was not until the early seventeenth century that most major towns passed their own regulations. As the example of Aberdeen alone shows, it also lagged behind Scotland. There, the comparatively small size of the nation and the efficient co-operation between central government and local urban bodies helped to enable networks of communication to identify and restrict contact with infected areas, and to allow the dissemination and supervision of legislation at the national level which underpinned and co-ordinated subsequent local measures.

In Aberdeen, however, civic responses to plague may be characterised by their complete absence for almost an entire century after 1401. That local authorities within the city had no need to reimplement preventative legislation until 1499 – still almost twenty years before the first regulations were passed in England – suggests the success of urban measures that were implemented further south in Scotland to contain outbreaks. While legislation against plague was subsequently implemented on numerous occasions, only twice did the disease break out within the burgh – in 1514 and 1545 – and on both occasions might not have lingered as long as it did elsewhere. In addition, the council passed orders in 1500, 1506, 1529, 1538, 1539 and 1549 to prevent the entrance of plague which in each instance was believed to threaten the city. It is tempting – though possibly too simplistic – to infer that the avoidance of plague was a direct result of successful legislation and, conversely, that those few occasions when the city did succumb to an outbreak were a consequence of the failure of those regulations. In the task of implementing measures to prevent plague, it is likely that the city's location and surrounding topography played a role in easing the monitoring of access by both sea and land, which helped to check the spread of infection via people and goods (borne by rodent fleas, if one subscribed to that modern transmission model). This was augmented by the development of communication networks for the sharing of advice and information about plague, the genesis of which can be located in this era, with magistrates being proactive in efforts to locate infected areas and implementing certain orders 'until they be forder advisit'.

However, regulations passed by civic authorities required compliance in order to be successful, and there were instances when contravention or negligence apparently doomed them to failure. This could be the case with all efforts to control plague and its victims, including the granting of access to illicit visitors, the notification of sickness, the segregation of individuals through enclosure or quarantine, and the handling and cleansing of infected goods. The fines, branding, banishment, loss of freedom and execution that the council threatened for non-compliance were the same punishments as those imposed in other burghs and, therefore, do not seem to have been a sufficient deterrent to contravention. Indeed, there were occasions on which the council was lenient in the administering of punishment: it permitted Sande Trouip and his household to return to the burgh despite having been banished six weeks earlier for concealing infection, and the banishment for contravening plague statutes which was imposed on Hew Munro, master of the grammar school, was likewise rescinded.[161]

Finally, to contemporary minds there was one significant additional factor in the susceptibility of an individual or community to plague, and in the success of civic efforts to repel it: providence. Just as Edinburgh's magistrates acknowledged that the outbreak of 1530 would be overcome by both 'the grace of God and gud gouernans', it became a refrain of Aberdeen's councillors that their efforts to staunch plague were undertaken 'so far as the craft and ingine [that is, ability] of man may do, referrand the laif [that is, remainder] to the eternal god keipar of all'.[162] However, this example, recorded in 1546, is one of very few overt acknowledgements by the council of the role of divine omnipotence prior to the advent nationally of Protestantism in 1560. Before this time, recorded instances of the spiritual aspect of plague and its treatment are few and far between. There are glimpses, certainly, of the fundamental centrality of belief as it was reflected in inhabitants' lives. When plague threatened the burgh in 1506, the council prohibited the sick from being visited by anyone, with one notable exception – 'the curat'.[163] The care of the soul was clearly as crucial as the care of the body. Furthermore, when plague first broke out in Aberdeen in 1514, magistrates passed a raft of regulations to repel the attack under which the city then was from both plague and English forces. They prefaced their extensive legislation with an emphasis on the need to reform certain aspects of the Church, a clear acknowledgement that there was ample cause for the current manifestations of divine wrath. But there was no explicit response to plague in line with the processions, plays, donations and benefactions that notably increased during times of plague in continental towns. While responses to plague in Aberdeen may have been distinctly muted in this respect, the city did not necessarily differ to any great extent from other

Scottish burghs, among which Oram has detected 'little indication of an outpouring of patronage stimulated by the Great Mortality [that is, the Black Death] and subsequent epidemics'. Though he notes that this may partly be attributed to the lack of surviving evidence as a result of the destruction by Reformers of many ecclesiastical buildings,[164] it is possible that in Aberdeen other factors were at play.

One such factor may be the general trend toward insular piety in the north-east that resulted in a preference for the veneration of local saints. Roch and Sebastian, the two saints who were particularly associated with plague, had differing fortunes in the region. Sebastian was venerated in several places: altars devoted to him were founded in St Machar Cathedral in Old Aberdeen and in Aberdeen's St Nicholas Kirk, with a planned extension to the latter by the provost Gilbert Menzies approved by the council in July 1514 when the city's first epidemic was at its height.[165] Furthermore, that saint was depicted on one of six carved panels from the parish church of Fetteresso, situated ten miles south of Aberdeen to the west of Stonehaven near the major route south. In the roundel he is tied to a tree, flanked by archers whose arrows pierce him, reflecting the nature of his martyrdom and his subsequent role as protector from the arrows of plague.[166] The panels date from the first quarter of the sixteenth century, a time when plague was rife throughout Scotland. They may have been commissioned by King James IV, who had paid twenty shillings to the priests of St Nicholas Kirk in Aberdeen to say thirty masses of Sebastian for him in 1496 and several years later had confirmed a charter for a perpetual chaplain of that saint's altar in the church to pray for his soul and that of his father, James III.[167] Sebastian was also included in the Aberdeen Breviary and in the religious plays staged by the city's guilds, being represented by the fleshers.[168] By contrast there is no evidence of special devotion to Roch in the north-east; this might partly be explained by the fact that Sebastian was 'older and longer-established' than Roch.[169] Nevertheless, it is probable that the Edinburgh-based poet Sir David Lyndsay was describing a familiar practice when he wrote shortly before the Reformation of penitents venerating Roch 'with diligence, to saif thame from the pestilence'.[170] Turpie has observed that the cult of Roch existed in those burghs that 'maintained strong commercial ties with overseas partners', with foundations made in that saint's name in Edinburgh, Dundee, Perth, Glasgow and Stirling.[171] Aberdeen is a notable omission in this respect. Perhaps the relative absence of plague from Aberdeen conspired with wider spiritual introspection to prevent the cult of Roch from gaining local adherents. It can only be conjectured that the somewhat muted civic response to plague might also have been a manifestation of insular piety, by which expressions of profound Catholic belief were so taken for granted that there was simply no need to record them. As the next chapter will show, a recast and invigorated notion of providence was the sole explanation given by magistrates in 1603 for the city's remarkable ability to avoid plague for the remainder of the sixteenth century (and, in the event, for almost a further fifty years thereafter).[172] The slow acceptance of Protestantism across much of the north-east after 1560 may have underlain a desire by Aberdeen's council to emphasise outwardly its righteous adherence to the Reformed faith.

Notes

1 Hector Boece, *Murthlacensium et Aberdonensium Episcoporum Vitae* [edited and translated by James Moir] (Aberdeen: New Spalding Club, 1894), p. 112.
2 J. Arrizabalaga, J. Henderson and R. French, *The Great Pox: The French Disease in Renaissance Europe* (New Haven: Yale University Press, 1997); M.L. Powell and D.C. Cook (eds), *The Myth of Syphilis: The Natural History of Treponematosis in North America* (Gainsville: University of Florida, 2005); E. Tognotti, "The rise and fall of syphilis in Renaissance Europe", *Journal of Medical Humanities* 30 (2009), pp. 99–113; Ivana Anteric, Zeljana Basic, Katarina Vilovic, Kresimir Kolic and Simun Andjelinovic, "Which theory for the origin of syphilis is true?", *Journal of Sexual Medicine* 11:12 (2014), pp. 3112–3118; Bruce M. Rothschild, "History of syphilis", *Clinical Infectious Diseases* 41:10 (2005), pp. 1454–1463.
3 ACR.7.797 [21 Apr 1497].
4 Tognotti, "The rise and fall of syphilis", pp. 104, 101; R.S. Morton, "Some aspects of the early history of syphilis in Scotland", *British Journal of Venereal Diseases* 38:4 (1962), pp. 175–180, at p. 176.
5 Gabriella Eva Cristina Gall, Stephan Lautenschlager and Homayoun C. Bagheri, "Quarantine as a public health measure against an emerging infectious disease: syphilis in Zurich at the dawn of the modern era (1496–1585)", *GMS Hygiene and Infection Control* 11 (2016), pp. 1–10.
6 The disease was detected in Edinburgh by September 1497, when the government banished sufferers of 'this contagious seiknes callit the grandgore' to the offshore island of Inchkeith, ordering them to remain there 'quhill god provide for thair helth'; ECR Extracts, fol. 204r [22 Sep 1497]. This extreme form of segregation indicates a belief that the disease could be spread via the air as well as through sex. Treatment included the application of various ointments to the lesions; the ledger of Andrew Halyburton, Scots conservator in the Low Countries, shows that mercury and guaiacum, remedies commonly in use on the continent, were imported into Scotland before 1503; J.Y. Simpson, *Antiquarian Notices of Syphilis in Scotland in the Fifteenth and Sixteenth Centuries* (Edinburgh: Edmonston & Douglas, 1862), pp. 14–15, 10; Morton, "Some aspects of the early history of syphilis in Scotland", pp. 176–177.
7 Tognotti, "The rise and fall of syphilis", p. 101; P. Contamine, "Scottish soldiers in France in the second half of the fifteenth century: mercenaries, immigrants or Frenchmen in the making?", in G.G. Simpson (ed.), *The Scottish Soldier Abroad, 1247–1967* (Edinburgh: John Donald, 1992), pp. 16–30, at pp. 17–19, 24.
8 N. MacDougall, *James IV* (East Linton: Tuckwell Press, 1997), p. 128; Morton, "Some aspects of the early history of syphilis in Scotland", p. 176; J.M.S. Pearce, "A note on the origins of syphilis", *Journal of Neurology, Neurosurgery and Psychiatry* 64:4 (1998), pp. 542–547, at p. 542.
9 D. Dunlop, "The 'masked comedian': Perkin Warbeck's adventures in Scotland and England from 1495 to 1497", *Scottish Historical Review* 70 (1991), pp. 97–128, at p. 105; Morton, "Some aspects of the early history of syphilis in Scotland", pp. 175–176.
10 MacDougall, *James IV*, pp. 114–115.
11 Leslie J. Macfarlane, *William Elphinstone and the Kingdom of Scotland, 1431–1514: The Struggle for Order* (Aberdeen: Aberdeen University Press, 1985), pp. 322–323.
12 MacDougall, *James IV*, pp. 124, 136.
13 ACR.1.197 [2 Dec 1401].

14 1439 was a particularly bad year. What Robert Lindsay of Pitscottie termed 'ane horribill pest' coincided with severe famine, both subsequently described by Sir James Balfour as 'Gods tuo mightey rodes of indignatione', which together caused extensive mortality from Dumfries to Fife; Ae.J.G. Mackay (ed.), *The Historie and Cronicles of Scotland, from the Slauchter of King James the First to the Ane Thousande Fyve Hundreith Thrie Scoir Fyftein Zeir, by Robert Lindesay of Pittscottie,* vol. I (Edinburgh: William Blackwood and Sons, 1899), p. 30; James Haig (ed.), *The Historical Works of Sir James Balfour of Denmylne and Kinnaird, Knight and Baronet; Lord Lyon King at Arms to Charles the First, and Charles the Second. Published from the Original Manuscripts preserved in the Library of the Faculty of Advocates,* vol. I (Edinburgh: W. Aitchison, 1824), p. 169; Thomas Thomson, *The Auchinleck Chronicle: Ane Schort Memoriale of the Scottis Corniklis for Addicioun, with a Short Chronicle of the Reign of James the Second* (Edinburgh: printed for private circulation, 1819), p. 34; Annie I. Dunlop (ed.), *Acta Facultatis Artium Universitatis Sanctiandree, 1413–1588,* vol. I (Edinburgh: Scottish History Society, 1964), p. 51.

15 Edinburgh Extracts, fol. 208r–209v [6 Feb 1499]; ACR.7.934-936 [19 Feb 1499]; ACR.7.957 [17 May 1499].

16 ACR.8.753 [8 Oct 1507].

17 ACR.7.1073 [15 Mar 1501].

18 ACR.7.963 [21 Jun 1499]; ACR.9.468 [7 Jul 1515].

19 ACR.8.585 [20 Jun 1506]; ACR.8.591 [7 Jul 1506]; convictions were obtained for 'the Intaking of land mene' and for buying wool from 'suspect folkis and placis'.

20 ACR.9.336 [24 Apr 1514].

21 In addition to a concerted civic response it forced the removal of the young king James V from the city to nearby Craigmillar castle; Edinburgh Extracts, fols 183r–212v [14 Oct 1512–22 Sep 1518], *passim.*

22 John Stuart (ed.), "The chronicle of John Smyth, monk of Kinloss", in John Stuart (ed.), *Records of the Monastery of Kinloss with Illustrative Documents* (Edinburgh: Society of Antiquities of Scotland, 1872), pp. 3–13, at pp. lxvi [preface], 11: 'Item eodem anno [that is, 1529] grassabatur pestilencia in Sancto Andrea, et in sequenti anno [that is, 1530] in Edinburgo.'

23 Dunlop (ed.), *Acta Facultatis Artium Universitatis Sanctiandree,* vol. I, p. liii; Annie I. Dunlop (ed.), *Acta Facultatis Artium Universitatis Sanctiandree, 1413–1588,* vol. II (Edinburgh: Scottish History Society, 1964), pp. 362, 363n.

24 Edinburgh Extracts, fols 213v–214r [23 Nov 1529–Sep 1530], *passim.*

25 ACR.15.732 [20 Sep 1538]. These outbreaks caused serious disruption in those burghs it most severely affected including St Andrews, where the annual election of the faculty dean was once again cancelled, and Perth, which was brought to the 'poynt of uter distructioun' by the epidemic; Dunlop (ed.), *Acta Facultatis Artium Universitatis Sanctiandree,* vol. II, p. 387; R.K. Hannay (ed.), *Acts of the Lords of Council in Public Affairs, 1501–1554: Selections from the Acta Dominorum Concilii: Introductory to the Register of the Privy Council of Scotland* (Edinburgh: H.M. General Register House, 1932), p. 522.

26 W. Chambers (ed.), *Charters and Documents Relating to the Burgh of Peebles, with Extracts from the Records of the Burgh, AD 1165–1710* (Edinburgh: Scottish Burgh Records Society, 1872), pp. 157–158 [3 Oct 1468].

27 Elgin BCB.1.193 [21 Jan 1546]; William Cramond, *The Annals of Banff,* vol. I (Aberdeen: New Spalding Club, 1891), p. 25 [29 Oct 1549].

28 ACR.9.319 [17 Mar 1514]; ACR.9.322 [22 Mar 1514]; ACR.9.336–338 [24 Apr 1514]; ACR.9.341 [12 May 1514], ACR.9.353 [26 Jun 1514]; ACR.9.364 [7 Aug 1514]; ACR.9.427 [17 Apr 1515]; ACR.18.142 [1 Apr 1544]; ACR.18.166 [29 Apr 1544]; ACR.18.214 [14 Jul 1544]; ACR.18.513 [27 Jul 1545]; ACR.19.084 [12 Apr 1546]; ACR.19.388 [22 Aug 1547]; ACR.19.393 [9 Sep

1547]; ACR.20.61 [25 Jun 1548]; ACR.20.83 [13 Aug 1548]; ACR.20.85 [22 Aug 1548]; ACR.20.209–210 [5 Apr 1549]; ACR.20.242 [17 Jun 1549].

29 ACR.8.582 [8 Jun 1506]; ACR.8.513 [27 Jul 1545]; ACR.19.180 [6 Aug 1546]; ACR.19.190 [18 Aug 1546]; ACR.19.208–210 [13 Sep 1546]; ACR.19.224 [8 Oct 1546].

30 ACR.7.1085 [30 Apr 1501]; ACR.7.1105 [28 Jun 1501]; ACR.19.018 [5 Feb 1546]; ACR.19.209–210 [13 Sep 1546].

31 ACR.12/2.706 [22 Oct 1529].

32 ACR.15.732 [20 Sep 1538]; ACR.18.513 [27 Jul 1545]; ACR.18.557 [2 Nov 1545].

33 Edinburgh Extracts, fols 206v–207r [14 Oct 1512].

34 Edinburgh Extracts, fols 204v–206v [17 Jan 1513].

35 James Balfour Paul (ed.), *Accounts of the Lord High Treasurer of Scotland, vol. IV: 1507–1513* (Edinburgh: General Register House, 1901), p. 404 [29 Jan 1513]. Another messenger was dispatched to those burghs south of the Forth.

36 ACR.7.961 [14 Jun 1499]; ACR.7.993–994 [25 Oct 1499]; ACR.7.963–964 [21 Jun 1499]; ACR.8.576 [25 May 1506]; ACR.8.582 [8 Jun 1506]; ACR.9.338 [24 Apr 1514]; ACR.9.366 [7 Aug 1514]; ACR.9.468 [7 Jul 1515]; ACR.9.491 [2 Oct 1515]; ACR.12/2.706 [22 Oct 1529]; ACR.12/2.853 [27 Jul 1530]; ACR.15.732 [20 Sep 1538]; ACR.18.513 [27 Jul 1545]; ACR.18.524 [10 Sep 1545]; ACR.19.180 [6 Aug 1546]; ACR.19.209 [13 Sep 1546].

37 ACR.9.338 [24 Apr 1514]; ACR.12/2.853–854 [27 Jul 1530]; ACR.7.993 [25 Oct 1499].

38 ACR.8.594 [10 Jul 1506]; ACR.9.338 [24 Apr 1514]; ACR.9.365 [7 Aug 1514]; ACR.9.491 [2 Oct 1515]; ACR.12/2.706 [22 Oct 1529]; ACR.15.732 [20 Sep 1538]; ACR.18.524 [10 Sep 1545]; ACR.18.544 [12 Oct 1545]; ACR.19.209 [13 Sep 1546].

39 ACR.9.338 [24 Apr 1514].

40 ACR.7.958 [17 May 1499]; ACR.7.994 [25 Oct 1499]; ACR.9.365 [7 Aug 1514]; ACR.9.491 [2 Oct 1515].

41 ACR.9.491 [2 Oct 1515]; ACR.18.513 [27 Jul 1545]; ACR.18.524 [10 Sep 1545]; ACR.18.544 [12 Oct 1545]; ACR.19.209 [13 Sep 1546].

42 ACR.19.393 [9 Sep 1547].

43 ACR.12/2.748 [17 Jan 1530].

44 ACR.18.544 [12 Oct 1545]; ACR.18.578 [18 Dec 1545]. Absentee residents had been recalled in November, but clearly not all of them returned: ACR.18.557 [2 Nov 1545].

45 ACR.12/2.706 [22 Oct 1529]; ACR.18.524 [10 Sep 1545]; ACR.19.209 [13 Sep 1546].

46 ACR.7.934 [19 Feb 1499]; ACR.7.1105 [28 Jun 1501]; ACR.9.268 [7 Oct 1513]; ACR.9.305 [24 Jan 1514]; ACR.9.338 [24 Apr 1514]; ACR.9.518 [16 Nov 1515]; ACR.9.525 [3 Dec 1515]; ACR.9.533 [7 Jan 1516]; ACR.12/2.854 [27 Jul 1530]; ACR.16.346 [15 Sep 1539]; ACR.19.110 [18 May 1546]; ACR.19.179–180 [6 Aug 1546]; ACR.19.209 [13 Sep 1546]; ACR.19.224 [8 Oct 1546].

47 ACR.9.338 [24 Apr 1514]; ACR.12/2.876–877 [7 Sep 1530]; ACR.13.038 [7 Nov 1530]; ACR.18.524 [10 Sep 1545].

48 ACR.7.963 [21 Jun 1499].

49 Paul Cassar, "An eighteenth-century bill of health of the Order of St. John from Malta", *Medical History* 21 (1977), pp. 182–186, at p. 184.

50 ACR.19.276 [14 Jan 1547]; ACR.19.293 [14 Feb 1547].

51 ACR.12/2.689 [6 Oct 1529]. Despite the protestations of his fellow crew member William Symsonn, Ferres might have relented for he was still in

Aberdeen sixteen months later, when he was convicted of injuring a resident; ACR.12/2.690 [6 Oct 1529]; ACR.12/2.697–698 [15 Oct 1529]; ACR.12/2.699 [19 Oct 1529]; ACR.12/2.710 [29 Oct 1529]; ACR.13.094 [27 Feb 1531]; ACR.13.104 [7 Mar 1531].

52 ACR.7.935–936 [19 Feb 1499].

53 ACR.7.934 [19 Feb 1499]; ACR.7.1105 [28 Jun 1501]; ACR.8.582 [8 Jun 1506]; ACR.8.594 [10 Jul 1506]; ACR.9.339 [24 Apr 1514]; ACR.9.474 [30 Jul 1515]; ACR.12/2.853 [27 Jul 1530]; ACR.15.732 [20 Sep 1538]; ACR.18.524 [10 Sep 1545]; ACR.19.209 [13 Sep 1546].

54 ACR.9.403 [29 Jan 1515]; ACR.12/2.872 [29 Aug 1530]; ACR.16.036 [25 Oct 1538]; ACR.18.519 [6 Aug 1545]; ACR.19.206–207 [11 Sep 1546]; ACR.19.208 [13 Sep 1546]; ACR.19.212 [17 Sep 1546]; ACR.19.294 [19 Feb 1547]; ACR.19.294–295 [22 Feb 1547].

55 Patrick Wallis, "Plagues, morality and the place of medicine in early modern England", *English Historical Review* 121 (2006), pp. 1–24, at p. 9.

56 ACR.8.582 [8 Jun 1506]; ACR.9.365 [7 Aug 1514]; ACR.12/2.854 [27 Jul 1530]; ACR.19.265 [17 Dec 1546]; ACR.20.310 [16 Oct 1549].

57 Thomas R. Forbes, "The searchers", *Bulletin of the New York Academy of Medicine* 50:9 (1974), pp. 1031–1038; Richelle Munkhoff, "Reckoning death: women searchers and the bills of mortality in early modern London", in Jennifer C. Vaught (ed.), *Rhetorics of Bodily Disease and Health in Medieval and Early Modern England* (Farnham: Ashgate, 2010), pp. 119–134; Richelle Munkhoff, "Searchers of the dead: authority, marginality, and the interpretation of plague in England, 1574–1665", *Gender and History* 11:1 (1999), pp. 1–29.

58 Munkhoff, "Searchers of the dead", pp. 20–23, at pp. 20, 21.

59 ACR.19.312 [21 Mar 1547]; the boy was presumably judged to be infected as Scott subsequently admitted his wrongdoing: ACR.19.313 [28 Mar 1547].

60 ACR.9.518 [16 Nov 1515].

61 ACR.19.265 [17 Dec 1546]; ACR.19.330 [29 Apr 1547]; ACR.19.331 [30 Apr 1547].

62 ACR.19.179–180 [6 Aug 1546].

63 ACR.8.576 [25 May 1506]; ACR.8.582 [8 Jun 1506]; ACR.12/2.454 [20 Nov 1528]; ACR.12/2.853–854 [27 Jul 1530]; ACR.19.179–180 [6 Aug 1546]; ACR.19.394 [19 Sep 1547].

64 ACR.12/2.853 [27 Jul 1530].

65 ACR.9.444 [11 May 1515]; ACR.9.508 [19 Oct 1515].

66 ACR.9.364 [7 Aug 1514]; ACR.12/2.454 [20 Nov 1528].

67 John Booker, *Maritime Quarantine: The British Experience, c.1650–1900* (Aldershot: Ashgate, 2007), p. 17.

68 ACR.15.732 [20 Sep 1538]; ACR.19.212 [17 Sep 1546].

69 Catherine Smith, "Dogs, cats and horses in the Scottish medieval town", *Proceedings of the Society of Antiquaries of Scotland* 128 (1998), pp. 859–885, at p. 869.

70 ACR.16.036 [25 Oct 1538]; ACR.15.215 [2 Oct 1536]; ACR.15.230 [17 Oct 1536]; ACR.20.310 [16 Oct 1549]. For a study of the slaughter of dogs and cats as a specific attempt to combat plague, see Mark S.R. Jenner, "The great dog massacre", in William G. Naphy and Penny Roberts (eds), *Fear in Early Modern Society* (Manchester: Manchester University Press, 1997), pp. 44–61, while the nuisances posed by dogs more generally are discussed in Emily Cockayne, "Who did let the dogs out? Nuisance dogs in late medieval and early modern England", in Laura D. Gelfand (ed.), *Our Dogs, Our Selves: Dogs in Medieval and Early Modern Art, Literature, and Society* (Leiden: Brill, 2016), pp. 41–67.

71 ACR.9.366 [7 Aug 1514].

72 ACR.9.268 [7 Oct 1513].

73 ACR.9.444 [11 May 1515].

74 ACR.12/2.707 [22 Oct 1529]; ACR.12/2.853 [27 Jul 1530]; ACR.15.219 [6 Oct 1536].

75 ACR.7.936 [19 Feb 1499]; repeated when plague threatened fifty years later: ACR.20.310 [16 Oct 1549].

76 ACR.9.366 [7 Aug 1514].

77 Skene, *Breve Descriptioun*, pp. 6–7.

78 Robert Jütte, *Poverty and Deviance in Early Modern Europe* (Cambridge: Cambridge University Press, 1994), p. 22.

79 ACR.9.366 [7 Aug 1514].

80 Brian Pullan, "Plague and perceptions of the poor in early modern Italy", in Terence Ranger and Paul Slack (eds), *Epidemics and Ideas: Essays on the Historical Perception of Pestilence* (Cambridge: Cambridge University Press, 1992), pp. 101–123, at 102–104, especially p. 102.

81 ACR.9.366 [7 Aug 1514], ACR.16.346 [15 Sep 1539].

82 Brian Pullan, "Catholics, Protestants and the poor in early modern Europe", *Journal of Interdisciplinary History* 35:3 (2005), pp. 441–456.

83 ACR.9.364 [7 Aug 1514]; ACR.15.219 [6 Oct 1536].

84 ACR.19.179–180 [6 Aug 1546].

85 ACR.20.310 [16 Oct 1549].

86 ACR.9.366 [7 Aug 1514].

87 John McCallum, "'Fatheris and provisioners of the puir': Kirk Sessions and poor relief in post-Reformation Scotland", in John McCallum (ed.), *Scotland's Long Reformation: New Perspectives on Scottish Religion, c.1500–c.1660* (Leiden: Brill, 2016), pp. 69–86, at p. 82.

88 ACR.7.936 [19 Feb 1499]; ACR.9.444 [11 May 1515]; ACR.18.541 [9 Oct 1545]; ACR.19.110 [18 May 1546]; ACR.19.179–180 [6 Aug 1546]; ACR.20.310 [16 Oct 1549].

89 ACR.15.432 [12 Oct 1537]; ACR.16.622 [22 Oct 1540]. Up to 150 individuals were helped on a regular basis in the 1640s out of a population of 10–12,000; John McCallum, "Charity and conflict: poor relief in mid-seventeenth-century Dundee", *Scottish Historical Review* 95:1 (2016), pp. 30–56, at p. 51.

90 ACR.19.110 [18 May 1546]; ACR.20.310 [16 Oct 1549].

91 Gordon DesBrisay and Elizabeth Ewan with H. Lesley Diack, "Life in the two towns", in E. Patricia Dennison, David Ditchburn and Michael Lynch (eds), *Aberdeen Before 1800: A New History* (East Linton: Tuckwell Press, 2002), pp. 44–69, at p. 60.

92 ACR.15.219 [6 Oct 1536].

93 ACR.7.1067–1068 [21 Aug 1500].

94 ACR.9.367 [7 Aug 1514].

95 ACR.7.1085 [30 Apr 1501]; ACR.7.1105 [28 Jun 1501].

96 ACR.15.732 [20 Sep 1538].

97 ACR.18.575 [14 Dec 1545]; ACR.18.577 [18 Dec 1545]; ACR.19.002 [27 Jan 1546].

98 ACR.12/2.689 [6 Oct 1529]; ACR.18.577 [18 Dec 1545]; ACR.18.587 [15 Jan 1546].

99 ACR.19.312 [21 Mar 1547]; ACR.20.310 [16 Oct 1549]; ACR.18.524 [10 Sep 1545]; ACR.18.541 [9 Oct 1545]; ACR.19.212 [17 Sep 1546]; ACR.19.296 [25 Feb 1547].

100 ACR.19.394 [19 Sep 1547]; ACR.9.367 [7 Aug 1514]; ACR.18.582 [11 Jan 1546]; ACR.20.314 [28 Oct 1549]; ACR.20.316 [4 Nov 1549].

101 ACR.9.365 [7 Aug 1514]; ACR.19.296 [25 Feb 1547]; ACR.19.312 [21 Mar 1547]; ACR.20.310 [16 Oct 1549].

102 Kira L.S. Newman, "Shutt up: bubonic plague and quarantine in early modern England", *Journal of Social History* 45:3 (2012), pp. 809–834, at p. 825.
103 Newman, "Shutt up", p. 812.
104 ACR.20.310 [16 Oct 1549].
105 ACR.9.401 [25 Jan 1515]; ACR.19.331 [30 Apr 1547]; J.D. Marwick (ed.), *Extracts from the Records of the Burgh of Edinburgh*, vol. I (Edinburgh: Scottish Burgh Records Society, 1869), p. 140 [17 Jan 1513].
106 Newman, "Shutt up", p. 824. Furthermore, enclosure disproportionately affected the lower classes, who did not have sufficient resources to flee or to cushion the wider economic impact of the practice, or who were not homeowners and therefore vulnerable to being made homeless.
107 Newman, "Shutt up", pp. 810, 828.
108 RCRBS.5.299–301 [13 Dec 1721 reissue].
109 Gian Franco Gensini, Magdi H. Yacoub and Andrea A. Conti, "The concept of quarantine in history: from plague to SARS", *Journal of Infection* 49 (2004), pp. 257–261, at p. 258; Jane Stevens Crawshaw, "The places and spaces of early modern quarantine", in Alison Bashford (ed.), *Quarantine: Local and Global Histories* (London: Palgrave Macmillan, 2016), pp. 15–34, at p. 16; Jane Stevens Crawshaw, "The Renaissance invention of quarantine", in Linda Clark and Carole Rawcliffe (eds), *The Fifteenth Century XII: Society in an Age of Plague* (Woodbridge: Boydell, 2013), pp. 161–174.
110 See for example: Zlata Blažina Tomić and Vesna Blažina, *Expelling the Plague: The Health Office and the Implementation of Quarantine in Dubrovnik, 1377–1533* (Montreal and Kingston: McGill-Queen's University Press, 2015); Kristy Wilson Bowers, *Plague and Public Health in Early Modern Seville* (Rochester: University of Rochester Press, 2013); Alexandra Parma Cook and Noble David Cook, *The Plague Files: Crisis Management in Sixteenth-Century Seville* (Baton Rouge: Louisiana State University Press, 2009); Ann Carmichael, "Plague legislation in the Italian Renaissance", *Bulletin of the History of Medicine* 57 (1983), pp. 508–525; Ann G. Carmichael, *Plague and the Poor in Renaissance Florence* (Cambridge: Cambridge University Press, 1986); Ann Carmichael, "Contagion theory and contagion practice in fifteenth-century Milan", *Renaissance Quarterly* 44 (1991), pp. 213–256; Carlo M. Cipolla, *Public Health and the Medical Profession in the Renaissance* (Cambridge: Cambridge University Press, 1976); John Henderson, "Epidemics in Renaissance Florence: medical theory and government response", in Neithard Bulst and Robert Delort (eds), *Maladie et société (XIIe–XVIIIe siècles)* (Paris: Editions du CNRS, 1989), pp. 165–186.
111 Peter Christensen, "'In these perilous times': plague and plague policies in early modern Denmark", *Medical History* 47 (2003), pp. 413–450, at p. 432.
112 Jane Stevens Crawshaw, *Plague Hospitals: Public Health for the City in Early Modern Venice* (Farnham: Ashgate, 2012), especially p. 18, where she stresses the book's revision of the traditional view of *lazaretti* as 'prison-like' places where 'the sick poor were cruelly abandoned' to show instead that they could provide 'elaborate' care; Manuel Jesús García Martínez, "Nursing care given to the plague infected patients in the Hospital General of Madrid (Spain) in the seventeenth century", *Historia, Instituciones, Documentos* 43 (2016), pp. 219–241. John Henderson, "More feared than death itself? Isolation hospitals and plague in seventeenth-century Florence", in C. Bonfield, T. Huguet-Termes and J. Reinarz (eds), *Hospitals and Communities, 1100–1960* (London: Peter Lang, 2013), pp. 21–44, questions the extent to which *lazaretti* actually helped to mitigate plague.
113 Newman, "Shutt up", pp. 809–834.
114 Edinburgh Extracts, fols 213r [9 Oct 1504], 214r [15 Dec 1530]; Marwick (ed.), *Extracts from the Records of the Burgh of Edinburgh*, vol. I, p. 101 [9 Oct 1504];

J.D. Marwick (ed.), *Extracts from the Records of the Burgh of Edinburgh*, vol. II (Edinburgh: Scottish Burgh Records Society, 1871), p. 45 [15 Dec 1530].

115 ACR.9.367 [7 Aug 1514]; ACR.19.312 [21 Mar 1547]; ACR.20.310 [16 Oct 1549].

116 Crawshaw, "The places and spaces of early modern quarantine", p. 21.

117 ACR.20.310 [16 Oct 1549].

118 Newman, "Shutt up", pp. 816–819; Paul Slack, *The Impact of Plague in Tudor and Stuart England* (Oxford: Oxford University Press; 1985), p. 123.

119 D.H. Evans, J.C. Murray and J.A. Stones (eds), *A Tale of Two Burghs: The Archaeology of Old and New Aberdeen* (Aberdeen: Aberdeen Art Gallery and Museums, 1987), p. 12; Diane Morgan, *Lost Aberdeen: Aberdeen's Lost Architectural Heritage* (Edinburgh: Birlinn, 2004), p. 36. It would be wonderful were it possible to be able to undertake a comprehensive analysis of which sectors of Aberdeen's population were most affected by plague, such as that recently undertaken for the 1630–31 epidemic in Florence; John Henderson and Colin Rose, "Plague and the city: methodological considerations in mapping disease in early modern Florence", in Nicholas Terpstra and Colin Rose (eds), *Mapping Space, Sense, and Movement in Florence: Historical GIS and the Early Modern City* (Abingdon: Routledge, 2016), pp. 125–146.

120 ACR.19.305 [11 Mar 1547], when Sir Alexander Robertson, Sir Robert Spark and Sir William Walker were all licensed to leave their home enclosure.

121 William Hay, *Charters, Writs and Public Documents of the Royal Burgh of Dundee, the Hospital and Johnston's Bequest, 1292–1880* (Dundee: D.R. Clark and Son, 1880), pp. 30, 34 [30 Aug 1540]; ACR.18.524 [10 Sep 1545]; ACR.18.541 [9 Oct 1545]; ACR.18.582 [11 Jan 1546]; ACR.19.228 [11 Oct 1546].

122 ACR.18.527 [25 Sep 1545]; ACR.18.558 [5 Nov 1545]; ACR.18.565 [20 Nov 1545]; ACR.18.582 [11 Jan 1546]; ACR.19.056 [15 Mar 1546]; ACR.19.057 [19 Mar 1546]; ACR.19.079 [8 Apr 1546].

123 ACR.9.386 [20 Jan 1515]; ACR.9.508 [19 Oct 1515]; ACR.9.659 [20 Jan 1517]; ACR.19.150 [3 Jul 1546]; ACR.20.310 [16 Oct 1549].

124 ACR.9.401 [25 Jan 1515].

125 ACR.9.509 [19 Oct 1515].

126 ACR.19.101 [14 May 1546].

127 ACR.18.582 [11 Jan 1546].

128 ACR.19.385 [19 Aug 1547].

129 Newman, "Shutt up", pp. 820–821.

130 Grant G. Simpson, *Old Aberdeen in the Early Seventeenth Century: A Community Study* (Aberdeen: Friends of St Machar's Cathedral, 1975), p. 5.

131 Gordon DesBrisay, *Authority and Discipline in Aberdeen, 1650–1700* (University of St Andrews, unpublished PhD thesis, 1989), pp. 121–124; I.D. Whyte and K. Whyte, "The geographical mobility of women in early modern Scotland", in L. Leneman (ed.), *Perspectives in Scottish Social History: Essays in Honour of Rosalind Mitchison* (Aberdeen: Aberdeen University Press, 1988), pp. 83–106, at p. 97.

132 ACR.9.398 [22 Jan 1515].

133 ACR.9.367 [7 Aug 1514]; ACR.19.252 [19 Nov 1546].

134 Cleansing: ACR.9.367 [7 Aug 1514]; ACR.18.558 [5 Nov 1545]; ACR.18.582 [11 Jan 1546]; ACR.19.116 [24 May 1546]; ACR.19.147 [28 Jun 1546]; guarantors: ACR.9.525 [3 Dec 1515]; ACR.19.018 [5 Feb 1546]; ACR.19.034 [19 Feb 1546].

135 ACR.9.367 [7 Aug 1514]; ACR.18.541 [9 Oct 1545]; ACR.18.558 [5 Nov 1545]; ACR.18.566 [23 Nov 1545]; ACR.18.570 [4 Dec 1545]; ACR.18.582 [11 Jan 1546]; ACR.18.595 [22 Jan 1546]; ACR.19.038 [21 Feb 1546]; ACR.19.060 [19 Mar 1546]; ACR.19.097 [2 May 1546]; ACR.19.101 [14 May 1546]; ACR.19.116 [24 May 1546]; ACR.19.147 [28 Jun 1546]; ACR.19.212 [17 Sep 1546];

ACR.19.252 [19 Nov 1546]; ACR.19.296 [25 Feb 1547]; ACR.19.324 [22 Apr 1547]; ACR.19.353 [13 Jun 1547]; ACR.19.359 [24 Jun 1547]; ACR.19.385 [19 Aug 1547]; ACR.20.316 [4 Nov 1549]; ACR.20.318 [8 Nov 1549].

136 Eight days: ACR.18.570–571 [4 Dec 1545]; ACR.20.316 [4 Nov 1549]; ACR.20.314 [28 Oct 1549]; fifteen days: ACR.9.367 [7 Aug 1514]; ACR.18.582 [11 Jan 1546]; ACR.19.385 [19 Aug 1547].

137 ACR.19.097 [2 May 1546].

138 Johnn Brabner: ACR.19.256 [30 Nov 1546]; Jonat Mar: ACR.18.566 [23 Nov 1545].

139 ACR.19.116 [24 May 1546].

140 ACR.20.316 [4 Nov 1549]; ACR.20.318 [8 Nov 1549].

141 ACR.19.060 [19 Mar 1546].

142 ACR.18.566 [23 Nov 1545]; ACR.18.582 [11 Jan 1546]; ACR.18.595 [22 Jan 1546]; ACR.19.038 [21 Feb 1546]; ACR.19.060 [19 Mar 1546]; ACR.19.101 [14 May 1546]; ACR.19.147 [28 Jun 1546]; ACR.19.256 [30 Nov 1546]; ACR.19.385 [19 Aug 1547].

143 This was a fate that befell 'the hail housses, cornes, barnis, [and] barnyards' in Kelso in April 1645, which were 'brunt be fyre, causit be a clinging off ane of the houses thairoff quhilk wes infectit with the plaig'; Thomas Thomson (ed.), *A Diary of the Public Correspondence of Sir Thomas Hope of Craighall, Baronet, 1633–1645* (Edinburgh: Bannatyne Club, 1843), p. 215.

144 Robert Renwick, *Peebles During the Reign of Queen Mary* (Peebles: Neidpath Press, 1903), p. 129.

145 ACR.9.373 [20 Oct 1514]; ACR.9.398 [22 Jan 1515]; ACR.9.403 [29 Jan 1515]; ACR.9.444 [11 May 1515]; ACR.9.515 [5 Nov 1515].

146 ACR.19.373 [18 Jul 1547]; ACR.19.377 [29 Jul 1547].

147 ACR.9.367 [7 Aug 1514]; ACR.18.558 [5 Nov 1545]; ACR.19.030 [12 Feb 1546].

148 John Ritchie, "The plague in Dumfries", *Transactions of the Dumfriesshire and Galloway Natural History and Antiquarian Society*, third series, 21 (1939), pp. 90–105, at p. 94.

149 Edinburgh Extracts, fol. 204r [27 Nov 1499].

150 The woman, Janet Clerk, was paid fifty pounds, more than double the highest annual wage a woman could normally earn, and she was later awarded a pension, while Captain John Duff was paid 92*l* 6*d* 4*s*, almost twice what Janet received, and provided with a horse at an additional cost of 22*l*; ACR.53/1. [16 Feb 1648]; ATA [Michaelmas 1647–Michaelmas 1648]; E. Patricia Dennison, Gordon DesBrisay and H. Lesley Diack, "Health in the two towns", in Dennison *et al.* (eds), *Aberdeen Before 1800*, pp. 70–96, at pp. 84, 434 (endnote).

151 ACR.19.252 [19 Nov 1546], when Thom Branche, his wife and their cleanser were all licensed to return to the burgh from quarantine.

152 ACR.9.509 [19 Oct 1515]; ACR.19.293 [14 Feb 1547]; ACR.19.305 [11 Mar 1547].

153 ACR.9.584 [5 May 1516]; ACR.9.398 [22 Jan 1515]; ACR.9.444 [11 May 1515]; ACR.9.508 [19 Oct 1515].

154 ACR.19.308 [18 Mar 1547].

155 Accusations of stealing: Margaret Glen swore she had given Gyne Middillsoun her clothes to be cleansed, but the latter denied it; ACR.19.434 [9 Dec 1547]; disputes: George Listar unsuccessfully claimed expenses from a city officer, incurred through the confiscation of his goods 'in tyme of the last plag of pestilence'; ACR.9.618 [6 Oct 1516]; ACR.9.661 [26 Jan 1517]; ACR.9.668 [7 Feb 1517]; ACR.11.599 [21 Jul 1525], when a lingering dispute was recorded regarding the return of silver ring cleansed in 'the tyme of the daid'.

156 ACR.9.373 [20 Oct 1514]; ACR.9.515 [5 Nov 1515]; ACR.9.546 [17 Jan 1516]; ACR.18.558 [5 Nov 1545]. Despite her banishment, Canne Sueit was found in the burgh again seventeen years later, for which she was branded on the cheek and banished once more; ACR.13.461 [13 Jun 1532].

157 Bowers, *Plague and Public Health in Early Modern Seville*, p. 55.

158 ACR.7.934 [19 Feb 1499]; ACR.15.219 [6 Oct 1536].

159 Eamon, "Plagues, healers, and patients in early modern Europe", *Renaissance Quarterly* 52 (1999), pp. 474–486, at p. 481.

160 Simpson, *Antiquarian Notices of Syphilis in Scotland*, p. 17.

161 ACR.19.331 [30 Apr 1547]; ACR.19.353 [13 Jun 1547]; ACR.20.310 [16 Oct 1549]; ACR.20.314 [28 Oct 1549]. Other councils were also capable of leniency: notoriously, Edinburgh resident David Duly, convicted of concealing his wife's sickness, had his sentence for hanging commuted to banishment after the rope broke during his execution, with the council taking pity on him because he was 'ane pure man with small barnis'; Edinburgh Extracts, fol. 214r [2 Aug 1530]; Marwick (ed.), *Extracts from the Records of the Burgh of Edinburgh*, vol. II, p. 37 [2 Aug 1530].

162 Edinburgh Extracts, fol. 214r [25 May 1530]; first noted in ACR.19.209 [13 Sep 1546].

163 By contrast, inhabitants in Dundee during the 1544–45 epidemic were faithfully ministered to by the preacher George Wishart, who famously preached to a divided congregation at the east port of the Cowgate, the infected outside the town boundaries and the healthy within; John Spottiswoode, *History of the Church of Scotland*, vol. I [edited by M. Russell] (Edinburgh: Spottiswoode Society, 1847), pp. 151–152.

164 Richard D. Oram, "Lay religiosity, piety, and devotion in Scotland, c.1300 to c.1450", *Florilegium* 25 (2008), pp. 95–126, at p. 114; David McRoberts, "Material destruction caused by the Scottish Reformation", *Innes Review* 10:1 (1959), pp. 126–172.

165 Jane Geddes, "Piping pigs and mermaid groping: six carved panels from Fetteresso", in Jane Geddes (ed.), *Medieval Art, Architecture and Archaeology in the Dioceses of Aberdeen and Moray* (Abingdon: Routledge, 2016), pp. 158–182, at p. 168; James Cooper (ed.), *Cartularium Ecclesiae Sancti Nicholai Aberdonensis*, vol. II (Aberdeen: New Spalding Club, 1892), p. lv [founded in 1452]; ACR.9.363 [28 Jul 1514].

166 Geddes, "Piping pigs and mermaid groping", pp. 166–167.

167 Geddes, "Piping pigs and mermaid groping", p. 177.

168 Mairi Cowan, *Death, Life, and Religious Change in Scottish Towns, c.1350–1560* (Manchester: Manchester University Press, 2012), pp. 69, 71; Geddes, "Piping pigs and mermaid groping", p. 168.

169 Tom Turpie, *Kind Neighbours: Scottish Saints and Society in the Later Middle Ages* (Leiden: Brill, 2015), p. 88.

170 David Laing (ed.), *The Poetical Works of Sir David Lyndsay of the Mount*, vol. I (Edinburgh: W. Paterson, 1871), p. 313 [from "Ane Dialog betuix Experience and ane Courteour" (c.1554) [lines 2363–2364]].

171 Turpie, *Kind Neighbours*, p. 154; dedications to Roch are detailed in the *Survey of Dedications to Saints in Medieval Scotland* compiled by members of Edinburgh University's School of History, Classics and Archaeology, available online: www.shca.ed.ac.uk/Research/saints/.

172 ACR.41.408 [11 Oct 1603].

Bibliography

Anteric, Ivana, Zeljana Basic, Katarina Vilovic, Kresimir Kolic and Simun Andjelinovic, "Which theory for the origin of syphilis is true?", *Journal of Sexual Medicine* 11:12 (2014), pp.3112–3118.

Arrizabalaga, J., J. Henderson and R. French, *The Great Pox: The French Disease in Renaissance Europe* (New Haven: Yale University Press, 1997).

Balfour Paul, James (ed.), *Accounts of the Lord High Treasurer of Scotland, vol. IV: 1507–1513* (Edinburgh: General Register House, 1901).

Blažina Tomić, Zlata and Vesna Blažina, *Expelling the Plague: The Health Office and the Implementation of Quarantine in Dubrovnik, 1377–1533* (Montreal and Kingston: McGill-Queen's University Press, 2015).

Boece, Hector, *Murthlacensium et Aberdonensium Episcoporum Vitae* [edited and translated by James Moir] (Aberdeen: New Spalding Club, 1894).

Booker, John, *Maritime Quarantine: The British Experience, c.1650–1900* (Aldershot: Ashgate, 2007).

Bowers, Kristy Wilson, *Plague and Public Health in Early Modern Seville* (Rochester: University of Rochester Press, 2013).

Carmichael, Ann, "Plague legislation in the Italian Renaissance", *Bulletin of the History of Medicine* 57 (1983), pp. 508–525.

Carmichael, Ann G., *Plague and the Poor in Renaissance Florence* (Cambridge: Cambridge University Press, 1986).

Carmichael, Ann, "Contagion theory and contagion practice in fifteenth-century Milan", *Renaissance Quarterly* 44 (1991), pp. 213–256.

Cassar, Paul, "An eighteenth-century bill of health of the Order of St. John from Malta", *Medical History* 21 (1977), pp. 182–186.

Chambers, W. (ed.), *Charters and Documents Relating to the Burgh of Peebles, with Extracts from the Records of the Burgh, AD 1165–1710* (Edinburgh: Scottish Burgh Records Society, 1872).

Christensen, Peter, "'In these perilous times': plague and plague policies in early modern Denmark", *Medical History* 47 (2003), pp. 413–450.

Cipolla, Carlo M., *Public Health and the Medical Profession in the Renaissance* (Cambridge: Cambridge University Press, 1976).

Cockayne, Emily, "Who did let the dogs out? Nuisance dogs in late medieval and early modern England", in Laura D. Gelfand (ed.), *Our Dogs, Our Selves: Dogs in Medieval and Early Modern Art, Literature, and Society* (Leiden: Brill, 2016), pp. 41–67.

Contamine, P., "Scottish soldiers in France in the second half of the fifteenth century: mercenaries, immigrants or Frenchmen in the making?", in G.G. Simpson (ed.), *The Scottish Soldier Abroad, 1247–1967* (Edinburgh: John Donald, 1992), pp. 16–30.

Cook, Alexandra Parma and Noble David Cook, *The Plague Files: Crisis Management in Sixteenth-Century Seville* (Baton Rouge: Louisiana State University Press, 2009).

Cooper, James (ed.), *Cartularium Ecclesiae Sancti Nicholai Aberdonensis*, vol. II (Aberdeen: New Spalding Club, 1892).

Cowan, Mairi, *Death, Life, and Religious Change in Scottish Towns, c.1350–1560* (Manchester: Manchester University Press, 2012).

Cramond, William, *The Annals of Banff*, vol. I (Aberdeen: New Spalding Club, 1891).

Crawshaw, Jane L. Stevens, *Plague Hospitals: Public Health for the City in Early Modern Venice* (Farnham: Ashgate, 2012).

Crawshaw, Jane Stevens, "The Renaissance invention of quarantine", in Linda Clark and Carole Rawcliffe (eds), *The Fifteenth Century XII: Society in an Age of Plague* (Woodbridge: Boydell, 2013), pp. 161–174.

Crawshaw, Jane Stevens, "The places and spaces of early modern quarantine", in Alison Bashford (ed.), *Quarantine: Local and Global Histories* (London: Palgrave Macmillan, 2016), pp. 15–34.

Dennison, E. Patricia, Gordon DesBrisay and H. Lesley Diack, "Health in the two towns", in E. Patricia Dennison, David Ditchburn and Michael Lynch (eds), *Aberdeen Before 1800: A New History* (East Linton: Tuckwell Press, 2002), pp. 70–96.

DesBrisay, Gordon, *Authority and Discipline in Aberdeen, 1650–1700* (University of St Andrews, unpublished PhD thesis, 1989).

DesBrisay, Gordon and Elizabeth Ewan with H. Lesley Diack, "Life in the two towns", in E. Patricia Dennison, David Ditchburn and Michael Lynch (eds), *Aberdeen Before 1800: A New History* (East Linton: Tuckwell Press, 2002), pp. 44–69.

Dunlop, Annie I. (ed.), *Acta Facultatis Artium Universitatis Sanctiandree, 1413–1588*, vol. I (Edinburgh: Scottish History Society, 1964).

Dunlop, Annie I. (ed.), *Acta Facultatis Artium Universitatis Sanctiandree, 1413–1588*, vol. II (Edinburgh: Scottish History Society, 1964).

Dunlop, D., "The 'masked comedian': Perkin Warbeck's adventures in Scotland and England from 1495 to 1497", *Scottish Historical Review* 70 (1991), pp. 97–128.

Eamon, William, "Plagues, healers, and patients in early modern Europe", *Renaissance Quarterly* 52 (1999), pp. 474–486.

Evans, D.H., J.C. Murray and J.A. Stones (eds), *A Tale of Two Burghs: The Archaeology of Old and New Aberdeen* (Aberdeen: Aberdeen Art Gallery and Museums, 1987).

Forbes, Thomas R., "The searchers", *Bulletin of the New York Academy of Medicine* 50:9 (1974), pp. 1031–1038.

Gall, Gabriella Eva Cristina, Stephan Lautenschlager and Homayoun C. Bagheri, "Quarantine as a public health measure against an emerging infectious disease: syphilis in Zurich at the dawn of the modern era (1496–1585)", *GMS Hygiene and Infection Control* 11 (2016), pp. 1–10.

Geddes, Jane, "Piping pigs and mermaid groping: six carved panels from Fetteresso", in Jane Geddes (ed.), *Medieval Art, Architecture and Archaeology in the Dioceses of Aberdeen and Moray* (Abingdon: Routledge, 2016), pp. 158–182.

Gensini, Gian Franco, Magdi H. Yacoub and Andrea A. Conti, "The concept of quarantine in history: from plague to SARS", *Journal of Infection* 49 (2004), pp. 257–261.

Haig, James (ed.), *The Historical Works of Sir James Balfour of Denmylne and Kinnaird, Knight and Baronet; Lord Lyon King at Arms to Charles the First, and Charles the Second. Published from the Original Manuscripts preserved in the Library of the Faculty of Advocates*, vol. I (Edinburgh: W. Aitchison, 1824).

Hannay, R.K. (ed.), *Acts of the Lords of Council in Public Affairs, 1501–1554: Selections from the Acta Dominorum Concilii: Introductory to the Register of the Privy Council of Scotland* (Edinburgh: H.M. General Register House, 1932).

Hay, William, *Charters, Writs and Public Documents of the Royal Burgh of Dundee, the Hospital and Johnston's Bequest, 1292–1880* (Dundee: D.R. Clark and Son, 1880).

Henderson, John, "Epidemics in Renaissance Florence: medical theory and government response", in Neithard Bulst and Robert Delort (eds), *Maladie et société (XIIe–XVIIIe siècles)* (Paris: Editions du CNRS, 1989), pp. 165–186.

Henderson, John, "More feared than death itself? Isolation hospitals and plague in seventeenth-century Florence", in C. Bonfield, T. Huguet-Termes and J. Reinarz (eds), *Hospitals and Communities, 1100–1960* (London: Peter Lang, 2013), pp. 21–44.

Henderson, John and Colin Rose, "Plague and the city: methodological considerations in mapping disease in early modern Florence", in Nicholas Terpstra and Colin Rose (eds), *Mapping Space, Sense, and Movement in Florence: Historical GIS and the Early Modern City* (Abingdon: Routledge, 2016), pp. 125–146.

Jenner, Mark S.R., "The great dog massacre", in William G. Naphy and Penny Roberts (eds), *Fear in Early Modern Society* (Manchester: Manchester University Press, 1997), pp. 44–61.

Jütte, Robert, *Poverty and Deviance in Early Modern Europe* (Cambridge: Cambridge University Press, 1994).

Laing, David (ed.), *The Poetical Works of Sir David Lyndsay of the Mount*, vol. I (Edinburgh: W. Paterson, 1871).

MacDougall, N., *James IV* (East Linton: Tuckwell Press, 1997).

Macfarlane, Leslie J., *William Elphinstone and the Kingdom of Scotland, 1431–1514: The Struggle for Order* (Aberdeen: Aberdeen University Press, 1985).

Mackay, Ae.J.G. (ed.), *The Historie and Cronicles of Scotland, from the Slauchter of King James the First to the Ane Thousande Fyve Hundreith Thrie Scoir Fyftein Zeir, by Robert Lindesay of Pittscottie*, vol. I (Edinburgh: William Blackwood and Sons, 1899).

Martínez, Manuel Jesús García, "Nursing care given to the plague infected patients in the Hospital General of Madrid (Spain) in the seventeenth century", *Historia, Instituciones, Documentos* 43 (2016), pp.219–241.

Marwick, J.D. (ed.), *Extracts from the Records of the Burgh of Edinburgh*, vol. I (Edinburgh: Scottish Burgh Records Society, 1869).

Marwick, J.D. (ed.), *Extracts from the Records of the Burgh of Edinburgh*, vol. II (Edinburgh: Scottish Burgh Records Society, 1871).

McCallum, John, "Charity and conflict: poor relief in mid-seventeenth-century Dundee", *Scottish Historical Review* 95:1 (2016), pp. 30–56.

McCallum, John, "'Fatheris and provisioners of the puir': Kirk Sessions and poor relief in post-Reformation Scotland", in John McCallum (ed.), *Scotland's Long Reformation: New Perspectives on Scottish Religion, c.1500–c.1660* (Leiden: Brill, 2016), pp. 69–86.

McRoberts, David, "Material destruction caused by the Scottish Reformation", *Innes Review* 10:1 (1959), pp.126–172.

Morgan, Diane, *Lost Aberdeen: Aberdeen's Lost Architectural Heritage* (Edinburgh: Birlinn, 2004).

Morton, R.S., "Some aspects of the early history of syphilis in Scotland", *British Journal of Venereal Diseases* 38:4 (1962), pp. 175–180.

Munkhoff, Richelle, "Searchers of the dead: authority, marginality, and the interpretation of plague in England, 1574–1665", *Gender and History* 11:1 (1999), pp. 1–29.

Munkhoff, Richelle, "Reckoning death: women searchers and the bills of mortality in early modern London", in Jennifer C. Vaught (ed.), *Rhetorics of Bodily Disease and Health in Medieval and Early Modern England* (Farnham: Ashgate, 2010), pp. 119–134.

Newman, Kira L.S., "Shutt up: bubonic plague and quarantine in early modern England", *Journal of Social History* 45:3 (2012), pp. 809–834.

Oram, Richard D., "Lay religiosity, piety, and devotion in Scotland, c.1300 to c.1450", *Florilegium* 25 (2008), pp. 95–126.

Pearce, J.M.S., "A note on the origins of syphilis", *Journal of Neurology, Neurosurgery and Psychiatry* 64:4 (1998), pp. 542–547.

Powell, M.L. and D.C. Cook (eds), *The Myth of Syphilis: The Natural History of Treponematosis in North America* (Gainsville: University of Florida, 2005).

Pullan, Brian, "Plague and perceptions of the poor in early modern Italy", in Terence Ranger and Paul Slack (eds), *Epidemics and Ideas: Essays on the Historical Perception of Pestilence* (Cambridge: Cambridge University Press, 1992), pp. 101–123.

Pullan, Brian, "Catholics, Protestants and the poor in early modern Europe", *Journal of Interdisciplinary History* 35:3 (2005), pp. 441–456.

Renwick, Robert, *Peebles During the Reign of Queen Mary* (Peebles: Neidpath Press, 1903).

Ritchie, John, "The plague in Dumfries", *Transactions of the Dumfriesshire and Galloway Natural History and Antiquarian Society*, third series, 21 (1939), pp. 90–105.

Rothschild, Bruce M., "History of syphilis", *Clinical Infectious Diseases* 41:10 (2005), pp. 1454–1463.

Simpson, Grant G., *Old Aberdeen in the Early Seventeenth Century: A Community Study* (Aberdeen: Friends of St Machar's Cathedral, 1975).

Simpson, J.Y., *Antiquarian Notices of Syphilis in Scotland in the Fifteenth and Sixteenth Centuries* (Edinburgh: Edmonston & Douglas, 1862).

Slack, Paul, *The Impact of Plague in Tudor and Stuart England* (Oxford: Oxford University Press, 1985).

Smith, Catherine, "Dogs, cats and horses in the Scottish medieval town", *Proceedings of the Society of Antiquaries of Scotland* 128 (1998), pp. 859–885.

Spottiswoode, John, *History of the Church of Scotland*, vol. I [edited by M. Russell] (Edinburgh: Spottiswoode Society, 1847).

Stuart, John (ed.), "The chronicle of John Smyth, monk of Kinloss", in *Records of the Monastery of Kinloss with Illustrative Documents* (Edinburgh: Society of Antiquities of Scotland, 1872), pp. 3–13.

Thomson, Thomas, *The Auchinleck Chronicle: Ane Schort Memoriale of the Scottis Corniklis for Addicioun, with a Short Chronicle of the Reign of James the Second* (Edinburgh: printed for private circulation, 1819).

Thomson, Thomas (ed.), *A Diary of the Public Correspondence of Sir Thomas Hope of Craighall, Baronet, 1633–1645* (Edinburgh: Bannatyne Club, 1843).

Tognotti, E., "The rise and fall of syphilis in Renaissance Europe", *Journal of Medical Humanities* 30 (2009), pp. 99–113.

Turpie, Tom, *Kind Neighbours: Scottish Saints and Society in the Later Middle Ages* (Leiden: Brill, 2015).

University of Edinburgh, School of History, Classics and Archaeology, *Survey of Dedications to Saints in Medieval Scotland*: www.shca.ed.ac.uk/Research/saints/.

Wallis, Patrick, "Plagues, morality and the place of medicine in early modern England", *English Historical Review* 121 (2006), pp. 1–24.

Whyte, I.D. and Whyte, K., "The geographical mobility of women in early modern Scotland", in L. Leneman (ed.), *Perspectives in Scottish Social History: Essays in Honour of Rosalind Mitchison* (Aberdeen: Aberdeen University Press, 1988), pp. 83–106.

4 Plague in Aberdeen after 1550

The second half of the sixteenth century was a tumultuous time for many people, not only across the north-east but throughout the whole of Scotland. In addition to the unprecedented social, political and spiritual repercussions resulting from the uneven spread of the Reformed faith, much of the nation was subjected to regular famine and dearth which caused economic depression and a steep decline in real wages. In addition to the challenge of increased poverty, Aberdeen's civic tensions were heightened by struggles between merchants and craftsmen, and by the decline in power of the Menzies family who had dominated local politics for so long. Social order and stability became further threatened by the perceived rise in witchcraft, which resulted in systematic persecutions that reached their height under James VI.

On top of this came plague, with intermittent outbreaks throughout much of Scotland, including severe episodes in the 1560s, the 1580s and early years of the 1600s. On these occasions, the civic measures taken in Aberdeen to prevent it were essentially the same as those which had been put into place since at least the late fifteenth century. Those passed by the council in April 1607, by which point Aberdeen had been plague-free for almost an unprecedented sixty years, demonstrate how legislative and administrative continuity may have been factors that were perceived to be significant in the success of the city's plague orders. On this occasion the council recalled preventative legislation that had been passed on specific occasions during the previous decade, in 1596, 1597 and 1603.[1] The significant role that memory could play in the reimplementation of plague legislation was cemented in Aberdeen by continuity in civic personnel during this ten-year period.[2] Not only did the make-up of the council remain fairly static, but also for much of this time the position of city provost had alternated between Alexander Rutherford of Rubislaw and Alexander Cullen, two equally formidable men who both possessed an established pedigree of municipal leadership. Cullen was occupying his third (non-consecutive) term as provost when the April 1607 regulations were passed and had sat on the council during the intervening years. Rutherford was likewise well acquainted with past plague legislation, having served as provost when the measures of 1597 and 1603 were issued and with his election for the former term having followed shortly after the implementation of the 1596 regulations.[3] None of this is to imply that recourse to previous measures was always made in light of meticulous evaluation of their effectiveness: reference to specific pieces of legislation may simply have been seen as an efficient way of reimplementing them without the necessity of detailing each one. On the other hand, it is reasonable to infer that in 1607 council personnel might have recalled these previous plague orders not least because of their assumed success.

This success gave plague legislation passed in Aberdeen during the nine decades after 1550 a peculiar characteristic, as it meant the total absence of any regulations concerning most of the practicalities arising from the consequences of having to deal with an epidemic, such as the disposal of a large number of corpses or the management of the return of recovered individuals from an external quarantine camp. The relatively few measures taken to control suspected infection – home enclosure and the cleansing of goods and people – were emphatically proactive rather than reactive. Moreover, responses to plague in this period became significantly influenced by the nominal spread of Protestantism throughout the north-east, by recasting – and, in so doing, vitalising – spiritual efforts to assuage infection, which gave believers a significant sense of agency. This chapter will analyse responses to epidemics in the completely plague-free ninety-eight years after c.1550 and consider factors that might have had a bearing on this remarkable immunity. It will show that magistrates put into place established methods for the monitoring of arrivals to Aberdeen both by land and by sea, and that there were several aspects which might have influenced the success of these legislative efforts and helped to mitigate the ongoing challenges of compliance. Chief among these was a discernible effort to maintain and grow networks of information about the incidence of plague and how best to tackle it, involving not only civic bodies but also individual lairds on whose lands settlements large and small were located, and elders of the Reformed Kirk, who further aided (and often directed) the enforcement of plague measures in the parishes.

Arrivals by land

As had been the case before 1550, the council was most concerned when plague threatened to monitor comings and goings to and from the bounds of the burgh, to which end typical civic measures continued to be put in place. Necessary repairs were made to the six ports that comprised the official entrances and watches installed at those that remained open.[4] Despite the consequent inconvenience others could be kept closed, particularly the Netherkirkgate and Shiprow (Trinity) ports, which tended to be considered the most likely entry points for people and goods coming by land from the plague-stricken south.[5] The same reasoning lay behind concerted efforts to watch the Bridge of Dee.[6] The costly inefficiency of installing temporary timber ports at its southern end was finally remedied in 1604, after which time approaching travellers were met by watchers from their relatively comfortable and sheltered vantage point of a porch situated above a sturdy stone archway.[7]

As had been the case before 1550, these watchers were typically residents fulfilling their civic duty, 'every neighbour his day about', either 'in proper person' or occasionally by a paid substitute, each tasked with assessing all arrivals.[8] Certain individuals continued to arouse particular concern, such as itinerant salesmen whose job took them through a number of settlements *en route* to the city and all those who could not produce an 'authentic testimonial' validated by a civic official such as a clerk, or a minister of the holder's parish of origin.[9] Possession of one of these was a condition of entry to any watched settlement: it certified not only the bearer's cleanness from plague, but also their good character and, by extension, their legitimacy and worthiness of being admitted among the civic body. While a testimonial did not grant the holder the contiguous rights of a citizen, it could be a necessary passport enabling him or her to conduct business, to visit family, even to return home. However, it was not a guarantee of entry, as particular caution was still exercised towards individuals who had come from a plague-stricken area even if they and their goods had been declared free of infection. The acknowledgement that plague might yet develop in an apparently healthy person or 'clean' commodity underpinned the notion of enclosure and lay behind the decision taken to isolate William Hunter, an Edinburgh burgess who sought entry at the Bridge of Dee during a severe epidemic in the south in 1585. Hunter had admittedly arrived from plague-stricken Dundee, whereupon he was temporarily enclosed in a lodge beside the bridge (which had most likely been purpose-built) and allowed to be attended to only by his servant and a relative while he underwent 'sufficient tryall'.[10] Guards at Aberdeen's ports were also charged with assessing those wishing to leave the city as well as enter it, with the former forbidden from travelling to places where plague was suspected or confirmed.[11] Aberdeen's council continued to face the ongoing challenge of depending on residents to shore up their back walls and gates to prevent unlawful entry.[12] Strangers required permission to be lodged, but on only one occasion was a patrol of the streets implemented, perhaps because the Kirk Session's regular 'searches' in the enforcement of godly discipline (discussed below) were considered a sufficient substitute.[13]

Commerce was also severely curtailed during outbreaks, particularly the trading of goods which might 'breid suspectioun of the plague' such as hops, hards (coarse flax or hemp), fruit, wool and timber.[14] Traders were often forbidden from visiting not only the regular, local markets held throughout the region, but also major annual events such as the Martinmas fair on 11 November and the St Bartholomew's fair held in Kincardine O'Neil over three days from 24 August.[15] Bans were also put on engaging trade with infected areas, whether the nebulous 'south' or specific areas such as Moray, Dundee and Perth.[16] While the majority of surviving civic plague policy implemented in the north-east is for the city of Aberdeen, we know that officials in the smaller burghs of Elgin, Banff, Inverurie, Ellon and Old

Aberdeen also took steps to strengthen external walls, to remove middens, to implement watches to prevent 'suspect geir' and arrivals without testimonials, to patrol the town to prohibit the unauthorised lodging of strangers and beggars, and to restrict the brewing of ale when plague threatened.[17]

By and large the regulations surrounding the monitoring of people's movements survive from the perspective of those who implemented and enforced them. There is, however, at least one interesting exception which gives some insight into the effects of such legislation on travellers themselves, in this case highlighting the difficulty of journeying through the north-east during a widespread outbreak. At the end of 1624, a merchant named John Mean was one of five burgesses from Edinburgh exiled to Elgin having been caught up in a factional dispute. On 15 December of that year he successfully petitioned the Privy Council to be allowed to return to the capital, where plague had recently broken out, in order to attend to his family affairs. Though plague had not yet reached the north-east, officials in settlements throughout the region had taken the precaution of restricting access to outsiders and Mean found it difficult to obtain lodging as he made his way south. After his eventual arrival in Edinburgh, he came before the Privy Council to request an extension to his stay, partly because he wished to remain with his heavily pregnant wife and 'numerous familie', but also because 'the feare of the contagioun quhairwith the whole cuntrey is possessed' would make it practically impossible that he would be given lodging or sustenance on his return north. In the event, his stay in Edinburgh was extended until the end of March 1625 and, while his desire to remain at home with his family probably made him exaggerate the hardships of his travels, it is plausible to assume that such difficulties during outbreaks were not uncommon.[18]

Arrivals by sea

Civic efforts to prevent the arrival of plague to Aberdeen specifically via inland routes were regarded by magistrates themselves as a primary factor in the city's avoidance of outbreaks after the 1540s. So successful were these in staving off plague that in 1597 the council confidently believed that now 'the gryter perrell that may cum to this burght, is fearit to be the frequent cumming of boittis craris and vther weschillis fra the south pairtis',[19] where plague was raging. Over the course of the following decade, a period in which the disease encroached on the city to an unprecedented extent, the 'imminent danger ... that may ensew to this burgh is fearit to cum be sey with merchandice cuming fra suspect places'.[20] As both a cause and a consequence of such statements, quarantine on shipping was a much stronger feature of Aberdeen's plague policy during the years after 1550 as it had been before that time. Measures concerning the monitoring, evaluation and 'trying' of seaborne arrivals were part of a wider commercial policy adopted during plague that also included bans on trade and the issuing of health certificates, and which was necessarily influenced by economic as well as medical considerations.[21] In Europe's larger ports, such as Seville and Ragusa, authorities came under extreme pressure when plague threatened due to the constant interaction between its traders and those from a host of nations, who not only maintained extensive and ongoing commercial contacts but who also settled in sufficient numbers to warrant the establishment of foreign enclaves in the town.[22] As Chapter 1 discussed, though Aberdeen was one of Scotland's major ports, its overseas contacts were comparatively limited and it did not have the same challenge of monitoring constant arrivals of foreign traders or mariners. All those who did make it to Aberdeen's harbour, however, needed to be vetted before landing. The harbour and shoreline were monitored, often from the vantage point of the Blockhouse from where the watchers could be on the lookout not only for vessels from faraway ports but also from destinations much closer to home.[23] Given the possibility that plague could be transported from the immediate south to Aberdeen not only by land but also by sea, the ferry which transported passengers the short distance across the Dee between Torry and Futty was permitted to operate only during daylight hours; outside of these the ferryman was to dock on the city side of the river where his movements could be supervised.[24]

Most of the council's energies were directed towards vessels arriving from suspect ports located in 'the south' or otherwise further away than Torry. Whether designed independently or instigated at the behest of the Privy Council, regulations for dealing with the arrival of potentially infected vessels typically followed a set pattern, judged by the maritime historian Booker (perhaps with some understatement) to have been a 'relatively sophisticated system'.[25] When a vessel first arrived in the anchorage, small boats would sometimes row out to intercept it and speak to the crew: given the danger in interacting with potential sources of infection, this was only to be undertaken with council permission and usually with monetary compensation for the task.[26] On these occasions, officers wanted to know certain pertinent facts about the vessel and its occupants: the port(s) of embarkation, the nature of the cargo being carried, the total number of those on board, whether any of them displayed symptoms of sickness and whether there had been any deaths during the voyage. If it could be established that a vessel had arrived from a suspect port it was likely to be 'instantly repelled' from the harbour, though the council could seek the opinion of the burgh community in individual cases, as happened in 1602 when the citizens voted not to receive a boat of Bo'ness which had sailed from plague-stricken Glasgow.[27] In Aberdeen, as with the medical evaluation of individuals within houses, the inspection of crews and passengers for signs of sickness was almost certainly undertaken by untrained government officials.[28] Bodily examinations to confirm the absence of symptoms would ideally be substantiated by the production of an authentic testimonial certifying that neither occupants nor cargo posed any health risk. While none survive for Aberdeen, a testimonial presented in 1564 by Edward Johnston to the magistrates of Dumfries contains what was most likely a formulaic assurance from their counterparts in Edinburgh that his goods were 'cleine [and] void of all danger' (in this case, following a precautionary twenty-day cleanse).[29] If officers were satisfied, then all passengers were allowed to come ashore and to land their goods.[30]

If, on the other hand, the delegation of officials sent to ascertain the circumstances of a particular vessel discovered sick or dead occupants, the infection needed to be contained. The gibbets that were on one occasion erected at the harbour to execute plague-stricken crew members immediately were apparently never used.[31] Instead, magistrates subjected suspect crews and their cargoes to quarantine and cleansing. In doing so, they were hindered by the city's immediate surrounds. Following a precedent set around the Mediterranean, wherein numerous islets became quarantine stations and lazaretto sites,[32] governors in Edinburgh had at their disposal a number of offshore islands situated in the Firth of Forth to which suspected sources of infection could be sent, securely marooned from the mainland. Inchcolm seems to have been the most frequently used, in addition to Inchkeith, Inchgarvie and the Isle of May.[33] Though Aberdeen did not have in its vicinity any offshore islands of any size, its harbour did contain a number of inches (small islands), which were so often a hindrance to smooth navigation up the inlet. These tidal islands were occasionally used for the temporary grounding of suspect vessels – as in 1602 when the *Gift of God* commanded by William Mason arrived from Danzig – but were probably too impermanent to be seriously considered for quarantine.[34] With little alternative, therefore, officials in Aberdeen generally had to allow the craft to dock in the harbour before a decision was made about how to proceed. This meant that the danger of infection was much closer to the community, and particular diligence was required to prevent interaction between inhabitants and the people and goods on board the suspect vessel.

Because of this, more often than not the decision was taken to have the crew and passengers disembark and be enclosed in the immediate vicinity of the harbour, often in the Blockhouse which was consequently given up as a vantage point. Here they were held until the state of their health became evident, during which time they were subjected to a ban on visitors and other such restrictions typically imposed on those undergoing home enclosure within the city. The length of the duration of quarantine varied, but in Aberdeen was never as long as the particularly protracted period of 115 days endured by the crew of the *William* which arrived in the Forth from Flanders in 1580.[35] The crew of the *Gift of God* was quarantined in Aberdeen for only sixteen days in September 1602, while those on board the *James* were held for twenty-nine days that October and those of the *Johne* for a fortnight in November 1603.[36] Echoing contemporary objections voiced since the early sixteenth century, Booker has commented that the unusual length of quarantine that could be imposed on suspect crews represents 'the cruellest aspect' of Scottish maritime plague measures.[37] Crews probably detested being forced to undergo quarantine for the same reasons that ordinary residents resented home enclosure, from minor irritants such as the interruption to normal routines it caused right up to the major fear of death as a result of being shut up with those who might be infected. Moreover, being confined to the cold, bare and harsh conditions of a building such as the Blockhouse, without the familiarity of one's own belongings or other home comforts, most likely made it an even more unpleasant experience.

The suspect cargoes and vessels themselves had also to be 'tryed' by a period of cleansing, using a method deemed most efficacious for the type of object. Iron and pitch could be heated to an extreme temperature, while clothing and other textiles were often washed in seawater at the shoreline, boiled, or 'cast to the wind'.[38] There was no safe option other than to burn goods considered 'maist infective and dangerous', such as soft fruits and bedding.[39] The vessels themselves could be cleansed by being scuttled in tidal water, sometimes with small holes being bored in the hull to enable the constant movement of the sea to rinse away any infection.[40] Booker finds the cleansing of cargoes the 'most interesting' aspect of Scottish maritime plague policy, noting that in this respect Scotland was more closely aligned with continental practice than with that in England, where the focus was on the quarantine of crews due not least to the lack of suitable airing ground in the Thames estuary which was the focus of the English Privy Council's concerns.[41] The cleansing and frequent spoiling of belongings was understandably lamented by all those who owned them; the destruction of entire cargoes through disinfection was particularly devastating to crews, not least since it entailed severe financial loss, whether as a result of being unable to sell goods on as intended or because of the need to compensate their owners.

A suspect vessel could also be commanded to return to its port of registration even if those on board were from Aberdeen. This was the case in 1602 when the *James* arrived from plague-ridden Danzig, crewed by three local mariners, and was ordered to sail to its home port of Montrose to undergo quarantine there.[42] This order was ignored but was reinstated with greater urgency three days later after the skipper, David Fullartowne, confessed that while the ship was still in Danzig one of their crew had died of plague and another had been left behind after falling sick. Despite this, he had allowed on board a number of passengers, one of whom was also infected.[43] The council's order was again ignored and the next day the crew were fined for their disobedience, yet garnered sufficient support from local burgesses who acted as their guarantors so long as they remained in Aberdeen's anchorage.[44] Faced with the crew's continued refusal to leave, the council became frustrated that they had risked not only the 'perrell and indangering of this burt and inhabitants thairof bot also of the hail countrie' in sailing back from Danzig fully aware that several among their company had fallen victim to plague. Payment of the subsequent fine became the responsibility of their guarantors. The crew claimed that their vessel had sprung a leak and therefore leaving the haven of Aberdeen would be to their 'peril and hazard'. This was found to be false, but they had, however, fallen foul of the harbour's notorious shallow waters. The tide was by now such that the *James* was too heavily laden to be able to leave and magistrates had no choice but to carry out the cleansing and quarantine process in Aberdeen's harbour after all. They provided the crew with keel boats so that they could transport the clapboard, pitch and iron on board to the Raik islet in the tidal basin and there submerge them in the river to be cleansed. The contents of the chests on board, including papers, were to be burnt, while all coinage was to be boiled. The crew members were to strip naked and boil or burn their clothes as directed, before receiving clean clothes and being placed under lock and key in the Blockhouse, where they were subjected to the usual restrictions occasioned by quarantine.[45] A strict round-the-clock watch stationed on both sides of the river was implemented to ensure that no one could board the *James* for as long as it remained docked.[46] The harsh confinement of the Blockhouse was lessened somewhat for the crew sixteen days later, when the door of the building was replaced by a latticed iron gate, perhaps to give the occupants some degree of fresh air.[47] Their ordeal finally came to an end on 23 October, twenty-nine days after their initial arrival in Aberdeen's harbour, when they were found to be 'frie and clene [of plague] god be praisit' and so released from quarantine.[48]

The need to contain seaborne sources of infection applied equally the opposite way, that is, when mariners from Aberdeen were sailing to a suspect destination. Among the standard prohibitions on the transportation of goods by sea out of Aberdeen to suspect ports, one instance stands out.[49] In September 1603, when plague was reported to be raging across Flanders, the council took issue with a bark called the *Johne* which was ready to set sail from its home port of Aberdeen to travel to that region. Magistrates convened a meeting with the nineteen-strong crew, skippered by Alexander Ramsay, and forbade them from disembarking or landing their cargo at any suspect port. They also reduced the crew size to eleven, partly because this was judged a more suitable number for the size of the vessel and partly because fewer passengers made it more probable that they would 'cairfullie and diligentlie await unscatterit or dispersit' in potentially infected areas. Upon arrival at any port, only the skipper and two merchants of his choosing were to disembark and get 'sure intelligence' from the conservator or magistrates that the area was plague-free. On the crew's return to Aberdeen, a testimonial was to be presented certifying the clean status of both the port they had sailed from and the cargo they were bringing back.[50] Guarantors were found that each crew member would obey this ordinance, and it was announced that their bodies and goods were to be tried on their return from Flanders.[51] Despite these precautions, plague was contracted by the skippers of both the *Johne* and of another bark, registered in Dysart and captained by William Williamson, which arrived in Aberdeen's harbour on the same day. Rudimentary wooden lean-tos were immediately erected in the vicinity of the Blockhouse wherein the crews of both vessels were quarantined along with their goods.[52] These included onions that one merchant, William Forsyth, admitted to having brought back in defiance of magistrates' prohibition on the import of such 'infective and dangerous' goods. Forsyth further confessed that while abroad he had cohabited with his son James, who had recently sailed to Burntisland on a vessel containing several passengers who displayed symptoms of plague, leading to their subsequent enclosure on arrival in Leith. The crews of both vessels remained in quarantine by the Blockhouse for the next fortnight and the captain of the *Johne* was additionally convicted of disembarking from his vessel without permission.[53] To this example may be added the only recorded testimonial that was sent to Aberdeen from abroad. An informer called Patrick Drummond wrote from Veere to the magistrates of the city in 1637, letting them know that he had warned a crew who had arrived in the port from Aberdeen not to 'meddle with' goods from suspect places while they were in the area, upon which they had assured him that they had indeed been 'verie cairfull' not to do so. He was therefore able to certify that there was 'no dangere to be feared' from the goods they were bringing back with them.[54] Reports such as these might have helped the council identify suspect places and evaluate how to deal with such crews and cargoes on their arrival at (or return to) Aberdeen.

Challenges in the implementation of civic legislation

Efforts to implement plague legislation were hindered in many urban centres by the flight, sickness or death of civic personnel and by the precautionary postponement or relocation of routine meetings, which also disrupted national as well as local administrative and judicial business. The disruption to governments occasioned by the severe outbreak of 1584–85 throughout Fife and the central belt illustrates this. Much of Scotland was considered to be in 'lang want of the administration of civile justice' because plague made the Lords of Session unable to meet; neither could the Exchequer.[55] Edinburgh's burgh council became so overwhelmed with the task of 'supressing seiknes' that from May it began to convene on a daily basis and the common clerk was seconded to validate testimonials, though as plague spread individuals had to be co-opted to serve in place of members who were sick or enclosed, and royal intervention was subsequently required to force the appointment of the new council.[56] Linlithgow was deprived of its provost during this epidemic and became sorely in need of a replacement,[57] while by the end of the year St Andrews had 'becum altogidder without cair, reull or governament' through the flight of leading citizens and the unscrupulous usurpation of council by a faction in the guise of a royal commission intended to impose good order on the burgh, who had taken advantage of plague's devastation by misappropriating the belongings of the dead through impeding their lawful redistribution by notaries under the threat of imprisonment or death. The 'pretendit baillies' were only deposed through the intervention of the Privy Council and their lawful replacements were forced to impose an extraordinary tax to pay the cleansers' wages, and to support the poor and infected who had been left 'destitute of all conforte and provisioun'.[58] The extensive spread of plague in the south prompted Aberdeen's council to appoint assistants to each quartermaster, because 'the burding will be grit and the charge intollerabill to the four baillies by themselves without help and assistance' as a result of the extra duties required to ward off the disease.[59] Appointments were made for the same reason during renewed threats of plague in 1602 and 1603.[60] As with the decision by Old Aberdeen's council in 1606 to ease administration by quartering the burgh 'for allaying of the said plaige', these appointments in Aberdeen were made despite the fact that plague did not actually strike the city on any of these occasions.[61] The increased administrative burden was considered to be bad enough even without the unpleasant and dangerous duties associated with the consequences of actual infection, such as the 'veray paynfull and chairgeabill' task of distributing supplies to those in quarantine for which William Logan was compensated for undertaking in Edinburgh.[62]

The inherent stress under which civic officials of various burghs in the north-east were placed during plague was exacerbated by aggression and selfishness on the part of residents. Patrik Dunbar was convicted in February 1601 for menacing Elgin's porter, insulting council member Alexander Boynd and tricking James Jamesone, keeper of the town's Nether port, by bringing in two outsiders.[63] In Inverness, Robert Waus and Johne Clerk were convicted of taking away a wall built specifically 'for awoding of the pest' and using the materials for their own ends.[64] These challenges notwithstanding, those tasked with plague-related duties appear to have been comparatively diligent in carrying them out. Although in 1585 the council complained that both the harbour mouth and the Bridge of Dee had been 'negligentlie observit',[65] forcing them to appoint water baillies at both locations, such a claim cannot be substantiated; certainly it was not preceded by a flurry of convictions for dereliction of duty or for unlawful entry to the burgh. By contrast, for example, specific instances were recorded in Prestonpans and elsewhere of officials failing to prevent infected crew members from coming ashore.[66] Additionally, there were several instances of the Privy Council interrogating civic officials in a number of ports to answer for their apparent neglect in enforcing maritime quarantine: in 1625 the baillies of Inverkeithing used 'force and violence' to prevent a suspect ship from Leith being quarantined in their harbour, while several years later officials from eight ports in Fife were charged with having been 'most remise and negligent in the execution and careful advertance to that whiche was given thame in charge'.[67] While individuals in Aberdeen were occasionally fined by the council for evading plague-related tasks, none was ever called before the Privy Council to answer for neglect of duties.

The conscientious performance of civic duty extended to the top of local government. Perhaps because plague never became an actuality during the nine decades before the 1640s, Aberdeen's councillors appear not to have fled and might therefore have provided the city with some much-needed administrative stability, in line with the historiographical revision of the assumption that the evasion of civic office during plague was widespread and undermined local governance and order.[68] The absence of infection might also have accounted for magistrates not explicitly hiring the services of professional medical practitioners, in contrast to Edinburgh where the council employed the surgeon James Henrysoun to assess the sick and 'give his trew jugement to the magistrats in decerning the said seiknes fra all vther seiknes'. He was to 'cure, heal and relieve' those he identified as plague sufferers, using medicines provided at the council's expense.[69] There existed a fairly consistent (though small) presence of qualified physicians in the vicinity of Aberdeen from at least the early 1560s, when Gilbert Skene was installed as third mediciner at King's College, augmented by the foundation of Marischal College in the city proper in 1593, whose first principal Patrick Dun concurrently held the post of mediciner at King's from 1619. However, none was employed in an official capacity by the council until the final outbreak in the 1640s and any advice they might have given regarding plague prevention before this time went unrecorded.

The role of Kirk Sessions during plague

While medical practitioners might or might not have played a role in Aberdeen's plague policy, the council certainly gained input from an entirely new source of personnel thanks to the process of Church reform. In the aftermath of the Reformation parishes became administered by Kirk Sessions, each comprising perhaps a dozen to twenty-five lay elders presided over by at least one minister.[70] Though in theory each Session was fairly representative of the social spectrum, the farmers and craftsmen who became elders were likely dominated by the landowners and businessmen among their number. Nevertheless, the Sessions enabled a substantial proportion of citizens to participate in parish affairs; in Aberdeen this amounted to 40% of all guildsmen and a third of craftsmen during the latter half of the seventeenth century. The Kirk Session occupied a 'carefully delineated niche in the structure of local authority', beholden both to the Church hierarchy of presbytery, synod and General Assembly, and also to civic authorities who maintained kirk buildings, paid ministers' stipends, and decreed when and where they would preach.[71]

Often members of the Kirk Session also sat on the civic council where these existed (invariably in each royal burgh, but with a fluctuating presence and power in burghs of barony and of regality), with 80% of all Aberdeen's elders between c.1650 and 1700 serving on the council at some point in their public careers.[72] This overlap in personnel meant that, while Kirk Sessions and civic officials were not immune from disputes occasioned by the vagaries of loyalty to self and kin or from divergent interests in prioritising their respective institutional concerns, they tended to co-operate and produce co-ordinated responses to social crises such as famine and plague which have been described as 'classic examples of secular and ecclesiastical bodies working in harmony'.[73] They effectively formed 'what amounted to a single seamless ruling elite',[74] who maintained similar priorities, interests and concerns particularly regarding godly discipline and poor relief which converged in the matter of social order. In common with the majority of burghs Aberdeen consisted of only one parish, that of St Nicholas, whose Kirk Session supported the implementation and enforcement of the council's plague policy.

In rural parishes, wherein settlements were scattered and the population less able to be checked, Kirk Sessions took greater responsibility for both the implementation of measures to tackle plague and the support of those affected by it. An insight into this is provided by the example of the parish of Elgin when plague broke out late in 1600 and caused such high mortality that elders were forced to forbid further burials in the burgh of Elgin's kirk yard.[75] James Fraser, minister of the parish of Kirkhill west of Inverness, later relayed the suspicion that this outbreak 'had its rise uppon the Buchan Coast out of a Dutch cask with onyons and hops cast ashoare',[76] perhaps at Findhorn, which was the commercial hub of and principal harbour for the area. Its spread throughout the parish north and west of Elgin (from Duffus, Burghead and Spynie through Mosstowie, Miltonduff and Pluscarden towards Nairn[77]) prompted elders, sometimes explicitly in consultation with the burgh's officials, to implement measures typically put in place by urban governments, many of which they reinstated when plague subsequently threatened. These included the instigating of watches both in Elgin and throughout its immediate hinterland, the appointment of a guard to compile a meticulous written record of each person entering or leaving Elgin's ports, and the strengthening of back walls and yard heads at their owners' expense.[78] The minister found himself responsible for ascertaining cases of sickness and for granting or receiving testimonials required to travel, on one occasion even when he himself was subjected to home enclosure.[79] These were routinely issued for matters of ecclesiastical concern such as a new parishioner's 'godly and honest behaviour where they were before'[80] and were stipulated during plague for strangers before they would be lodged, with residents to swear oaths not to receive any individual without one.[81] Elgin's Kirk Session also took responsibility for 'trying' the quarters of the burgh and for hiring cleansers who had perhaps been sourced through word of mouth, as on the first occasion one was acquired from Dundee (with his payment to be met by a tax imposed by burgh officials on residents of Elgin) and on the second from Edinburgh, 'for clenging of the infected parts, together with the bodies of the persons infected'.[82]

Plague, punishment and godly discipline

As the Scots Confession, the first Reformation parliament and the *First Book of Discipline* had each articulated, one important function of each Kirk Session was its enforcement of godly discipline, 'whereby vice is repressed, and vertew nurished'.[83] The providentialist interpretation of plague and other disasters made it clear to believers that 'God held all accountable for the sins of a few' and so the ramifications of sinful behaviour were felt not only by the immoral individual but by a multiplicity of concentric circles comprised of those associated with (and by extension responsible for) him or her in some way. This is typified by the burgh court of Inverness's threatened banishment in 1578 of those who would spread the Great Pox, as their 'commoun harlottrie, huirdome, fornication and adultre' was 'to the greit sclander' not only of the congregation but to the entire Kirk, as well as to the 'reproche, schame, and dishonour of this burcht and magistratis thairof'.[84] Each parishioner therefore had a vested interest in the prevention of sin and the upholding of godliness, which Todd notes might explain why Kirk Sessions' intrusion into parishioners' everyday affairs was so tolerated.[85] The elders' authority was effective and accepted as legitimate because they were local figures who personally knew those they governed.[86] The eminent seventeenth-century Presbyterian pastor Samuel Rutherford described them as 'the eyes, ears and hands' of the Kirk, and their methods for monitoring discipline included loitering in the vicinity of suspicious behaviour and eavesdropping on local gossip.[87] Such tactics, which exemplified 'the extension of early modern state authority into the field of moral regulation',[88] also included carrying out house-to-house visits throughout the parish, referred to as the practice of 'searching' and often undertaken on Sundays with a view to preventing absence from church.[89] Those searches carried out to enforce discipline should not be confused with those undertaken during plague with the specific aim of detecting cases of sickness and other individuals whose presence risked infection, such as illicit lodgers, people who had previously been banished and beggars, though clearly searching – whether by elders or baillies – could uncover these regardless of its purported purpose.[90] In their efforts to enforce attendance at the weekly sermon, elders accepted that there were exceptional circumstances which could excuse this. Langley has shown that the care of family members, particularly if this was palliative or required excessive travel, was one such circumstance.[91] So too was the presence of plague, which could complicate the practicalities of getting to church even if one were not reluctant to attend through fear of infection. In addition to exercising discretionary leniency during such times, elders could also permit parishioners from actions that would normally attract censure, such as one Sunday in 1603 when Helen Andersoun was not punished for travelling 'landward' from Elgin because 'hir motiue wes to visie the seik'.[92] Plague could equally be used as an excuse for avoiding attendance by feigning infection, as Jone Cokburne and his wife attempted to do in February 1604.[93]

In cases of inexcusable moral or criminal behaviour, Kirk Session elders and civic authorities alike were concerned to punish miscreants, though the former naturally emphasised spiritual over temporal consequences. This was not a new development with the advent of Protestantism; public repentance had been a common punishment imposed by pre-Reformation clergy, typically through compelling individuals to provide candlewax, wear sackcloth and seek forgiveness on bended knee in front of the congregation.[94] Elders continued to favour public humiliation and admonishment for various crimes, including specific immoral actions, which were punished in a range of ways from a rebuke from the pulpit during the weekly service to making the offender conspicuously sit on a purpose-built stool or stand in sackcloth.[95] Punishments designed to express repentance publicly 'helped to create a community that was involved in both the successes and the failures of its members'.[96] At the heart of the Kirk's disciplinary actions was the importance of sincere contrition and remorse, as these alone would lead to absolution and reconciliation both with the Christian community and with God Himself. This differentiated Kirk discipline from punishments imposed by civic officials or the later seventeenth-century justices of the peace, 'for whom punishment was an end in itself and it mattered little whether or not the offender accepted his or her sentence'.[97]

Kirk Sessions also imposed temporal punishments on parishioners who contravened plague statutes that were in line with those meted out by the courts not only in royal burghs but also in smaller burghs of barony and regality, which together with the justice ayres in the sheriffdoms formed a complex, interrelated network of public and private courts. Closer inspection of the punitive aspect of Aberdeen's plague policy throws into question the assertion by the medical historian Creighton that though the city 'may have owed its immunity to various causes ... there can be no question of the Draconian rigour of its decrees against the plague'.[98] Comparison with other burgh councils as well as Kirk Sessions reveals that Aberdeen's officials were no more stringent than their counterparts in their punishment of lawbreakers during plague – in fact, as with their policy before 1550, they may actually have been more lenient. There were no statutory criteria attaching specific punishments to particular crimes, so it was not unusual for the same crime (such as harbouring strangers) to be punished with differing severity, which was perhaps dictated by the perceived level of risk at that time. The Aberdeen council's specific treatment of plague-related misdemeanours must be contextualised by considering its punishment of other crimes. In the second half of the sixteenth century, the majority of offences brought before the burgh court were statute breaking and regrating the market (that is, buying up commodities with a view to reselling them for profit), both of which offended the common weal and tended to attract fines.[99] The council also fined those committing various plague-related misdemeanours ranging from illicit attendance at rural fairs and travelling to or importing goods from infected areas, to providing food and lodging to outsiders, banished residents, those from suspect places, or crew members who had arrived from a suspect port, and for being negligent in watching the entrances, the harbour mouth or the Bridge of Dee.[100] Fines were also meted out in Old Aberdeen for plague-related offences including not strengthening back walls, and receiving visitors and purchasing wool originating in plague-stricken areas, while in Edinburgh landing suspect goods, allowing privies to overflow, middens to accumulate and swine to roam freely were all misdemeanours which would result in a fine.[101] The council in Dundee fined quartermasters found neglecting their duties and residents absent from the watch, as well as those who travelled to rural fairs or who resisted removal to the quarantine camp following suspected contact with infection, while during the outbreak of 1600–01 in the parish of Elgin fines were meted out by the Kirk Session on Margrat Innes for trying to conceal her visitors and on Johne Mow for consorting with individuals from the plague-stricken hinterland.[102]

Banishment was 'the harshest punishment under burgh law ... for this meant loss of all personal rights and privileges'.[103] It had to be imposed carefully during times of plague, as the 1456 Rule of the Pestilence had decreed that infected individuals were the responsibility of urban authorities and ought not to be ejected, lest they might 'file the cuntry about thame'. However, it was a punishment that was rarely enforced in Aberdeen regardless of the nature of the crime.[104] Nevertheless, as was the case elsewhere, the burgh's governors prioritised the health of its citizens over that of the hinterland and occasionally banished those convicted of plague-related misdemeanours including harbouring outsiders and scaling back walls, as well as for consorting with or carrying letters on behalf of suspect individuals.[105] Banishment was also imposed by authorities in Dundee on a man who brought in cloth from plague-stricken St Andrews, though his punishment was partly for 'abusing' the minister of Leuchars by inventing a testimonial from him.[106] As Kirk Sessions were not subject to the Rule of the Pestilence, the elders of Elgin were particularly wont to rid the community of immoral elements and had few qualms about banishing miscreants, including strangers and those found consorting with or visiting individuals from suspect places.[107]

Execution (typically by hanging) was reserved for the most severe of plague-related crimes, those which endangered lives 'to the infectioun of sum and hasart [that is, risk] of mony' as Edinburgh's council put it.[108] In Aberdeen, as in Dundee and in Edinburgh, execution was threatened for the crimes of escaping enclosure, avoiding the cleansing process, bringing into the city goods from infected areas, attending rural markets, harbouring strangers without permission, failing to secure back walls, and negligence in participating in the watch.[109] Accordingly, gibbets were erected in Aberdeen on two occasions when plague was considered a significant threat: in 1585 at the harbour mouth, the Bridge of Dee and the market cross, and in 1608 at the meal market and in Futty.[110] There is, however, no evidence that they were ever put to use. This contrasts with the situation in Edinburgh, whose council employed an executioner when it built gibbets in 1585, and which was forced during the epidemic of 1566 to strengthen the walls surrounding the gallows it had built by the quarantine area on the Burgh Muir, in order to prevent dogs from dragging away the corpses of those executed for trying to escape.[111] In part, at least, this was a likely consequence of the presence of actual infection. It might also partly have resulted from the leniency the Aberdeen authorities were capable of showing in their dealings with individuals who contravened statutes, which Falconer interprets as 'further indication of the burgh magistrates being more flexible with the law's prescriptions'.[112] During the epidemic of 1585, as a result of the intervention of two landed gentry, two women convicted of secretly hosting outsiders had their sentence of execution commuted to banishment, the same punishment meted out to their visitors who had entered the city over a back wall.[113] Several months later James Conoy, a messenger, was found to have carried letters from Abarok Bissat, a burgess of Aberdeen then resident in Edinburgh, to his compatriot who had been enclosed in a lodge beside the Bridge of Dee on his arrival from plague-stricken Dundee. Bissat ought to have been banished for his attempted correspondence, but instead was let off with a warning that any future misdemeanour would not be met with such leniency.[114] On one occasion, magistrates reduced the fine imposed on several crew members sailing from Danzig who attempted to land plague-stricken passengers in Aberdeen, and in so doing even explained that they 'inclyn[ed] rather to clemencie nor [that is, than] rigor'.[115]

Notwithstanding magistrates' lenient treatment of individuals who contravened plague statutes, in the early seventeenth century they considered the threat posed by non-compliance with legislation to have reached its zenith. By October 1603, Aberdeen had been without plague for an unparalleled fifty-five years. The council could have been forgiven for regarding this state of affairs as evidence of the success of its plague policy, but the burgh's immunity was instead wholly (and entirely rationally) attributed to divine benevolence; the council registers proclaimed that 'it hes pleasit the gudnes of God of his infinit mercie to with hauld the said plaig fra this burght thir fyftie fyue yeris bygane'. Paradoxically, the fact that barely any residents by then had any lived experience of plague was seen as imperilling the current favourable circumstances, because it bred in them 'ane sluggische cairlesnes and littill fear to obey the ordinances sett doun be thair magistrattis thairanent'.[116] This perception contrasts with contemporary feeling in Genoa, another port city which was comparatively spared from plague, wherein one commentator blamed the fifty-one year gap between the outbreaks of 1528 and 1579 for the subsequent increase in fear of the disease.[117] In Aberdeen the council was compelled to petition the Privy Council for a commission of justiciary to enforce compliance with plague legislation and to cement its authority to punish all those who contravened such orders.[118] Such commissions could be issued to underpin the legality of responses to various crises including witchcraft, which under James VI became an especial moral threat to social stability and which in Aberdeen led to the issuing of two commissions to legitimise the identification and condemnation in 1597 of at least eighty individuals, following extensive pre-trial investigations by Kirk Sessions throughout the shire.[119] In shoring up its efforts to tackle plague, Aberdeen was by no means alone in its request: commissions were also granted to Stirling, Edinburgh, St Andrews, Inverleith and Dysart which confirmed the authority of burgh officials to take action to control plague in the matters of enforcing enclosure, quarantine and cleansing.[120]

Requests for such a commission from the Privy Council cast an interesting light on the relationship between central government authority and various burghs in an age when the notion of 'nationwide' legislation was somewhat anachronistic. Aberdeen's request might have been made to emphasise to parliament in Edinburgh as well as to the local population their success to date in repelling plague and their determination to ensure that this would continue. After all, the city was 'as yit clene fra the said seiknes'.[121] In its response three weeks later, the Privy Council emphasised its keenness to ensure that those areas which had so far escaped plague were to be protected in order that they may remain free from infection. Their affirmation was perhaps surprising, as by this time the lack of accountability had led to the privileges of a commission being abused in the pursuit of unjust convictions and the Privy Council proved unwilling to allow their continuation (a feeling aided by the departure to London of James VI on his accession to the English throne).[122] Perhaps as an acknowledgement of the success the council in Aberdeen was so far having in implementing its plague legislation, the Privy Council endorsed officers' efforts to date and granted them ongoing powers 'to mak prescryve and publeis actis and constitutiouns for watcheing, warding and keiping of the said toun cleine', with contingencies in the event of infection for quarantine and enclosure, for taxing inhabitants to fund necessary measures and to support the poor, for the employment of additional officers to ensure the implementation of measures, and for the execution of those who knowingly spread the disease.[123] The council took the endorsement as a green light to appoint additional men in each quarter of the city to assist the officers in enforcing plague legislation.[124]

At the Head Court meeting the following May, the provost Alexander Rutherford took the opportunity to emphasise to all citizens in attendance that the council's plague measures had full royal authorisation and therefore could not reasonably be ignored or challenged.[125] These included the harshest possible punishments for contravention – death and dismemberment, or at the least imprisonment and 'pecunial pains' for lesser associated misdemeanours.[126] The Privy Council's endorsement was explicitly used on subsequent occasions to justify threats of execution for crimes that risked the spread of plague to the city.[127] The commissary powers granted to magistrates of Edinburgh highlighted the necessity of relieving the poor and protecting residences in the city from 'reiff, stouth [that is, plunder, theft] and violence of disordourit personis', but no such specifics were mentioned with regard to Aberdeen.[128] Although the Aberdeen council continued to report that plague measures (at least those issued prior to the Privy Council's intervention) had been 'no wayes observit and kepit', such pronouncements seem to have been rhetorical, perhaps to emphasise the possible devastating consequences if negligence were to continue, to justify the threat (if not the use) of execution for contravention, and to ensure that the city upheld its remarkable immunity from plague.[129]

Plague and the poor in the parishes

Perhaps the greatest contribution that Kirk Sessions made in terms of social welfare concerned the poor, for whom Christian duty compelled elders to care and pragmatic considerations of social order and cost compelled them to regulate. During plague the poor continued to be viewed as particularly susceptible to infection and as a threat to both moral and physical wellbeing. Burgh councils in Aberdeen, Old Aberdeen and Elgin explicitly identified their removal as one method of lessening the likelihood of plague.[130] While magistrates had a duty to provide 'a tender care over, and a cordiall Charity towards the Poor', as Baillie Alexander Skene stated in 1685, it has been claimed that a genuine governmental concern for poverty 'arrived late, if at all' and that Kirk Sessions were the only established bodies 'regularly interested' in charitable provision.[131] Despite the apparent failure of legislative efforts to implement compulsory contributions to poor relief, civic systems of providing for the poor ought not to be regarded as 'weak and ineffective'.[132] Burgh councils 'were active in supporting the poor', particularly since they worked in close co-operation with the local Kirk Session, for whom caring for the needy was a 'key concern' and an important part of the Kirk's mission of reformation.[133] The Sessions were the 'ideal institution to provide poor relief in early modern Scotland' through their control of collections at services and accrual of fines for moral misdemeanours.[134] McCallum's investigations have concluded that from the early years of its inception Aberdeen's Kirk Session was one that 'took poor relief seriously', though he also detected an 'intriguing' perception that it was seen to lag behind its counterparts in the provision of relief to the native poor of the parish, which may have resulted from the need to concentrate in its early years on enforcing religious conformity.[135]

In Aberdeen the main sources of support for the poor were: fines for immoral behaviour, the importance of which as supplementary revenue throughout Scotland's parishes ought not to be understated; mortifications; rents; the hiring out of mortcloths and other funerary paraphernalia; and almsgiving, donated either in kind (usually meal) or money.[136] Alms were amassed either on attendance at sermons or through door-to-door collections undertaken regularly by elders, often accompanied by a council official.[137] These donations were given directly in person and were therefore the most reliable source of support, unencumbered by the challenges faced in the accumulation of other sources, such as chasing monies owing or the unpredictability of legacies.[138] Though theoretically the provision of charity was a voluntary act of Christian duty, an element of compulsion appears to have crept in, with the Kirk Session ordaining in 1618 that two officials were to be stationed daily at the door of St Nicholas Kirk in order to receive contributions towards both the poor and the upkeep of the church fabric. Indeed, social problems resulting from epidemics could be the catalyst for the imposition of compulsory contributions which alleviated pressure in subsequent crises, as Laura Stewart found was the case in the aftermath of the outbreak of the 1580s in Edinburgh.[139]

Plague also affected the accrual and dispersal of poor relief in other ways, as during such times the clamour for charity was exacerbated by its diminishing availability. This required traditional forms of support to be supplemented, including through the appropriation of funds intended for the upkeep of church fabric or the imposition of a special tax under the authority of a Privy Council directive.[140] Regional outbreaks precipitated an influx to the larger settlements of desperate (and possibly infected) rural migrants displaced from their usual cottage industries – this was a particular issue in Aberdeen as the dominant urban centre of the north-east. Parliamentary Acts were passed in 1579 and 1617 prohibiting individuals from begging in a different parish from that in which they were born, but renewed outbreaks and scarcity of victual exacerbated the difficulties of enforcing these measures across the region.[141] Plague also continued to create 'extraordinary' poor within the burgh who found themselves no longer able to subsist on their meagre, if generally sufficient, resources and instead fighting for a share of support alongside 'ordinary' paupers who were on the standard Roll kept by the Kirk.[142]

During times of plague, deciding the eligibility of individuals for support was fairly straightforward within the burghs of Aberdeen and Old Aberdeen, where all poor were convened in the kirkyards of St Nicholas and St Machar respectively in order to be assessed.[143] Beyond the burghs, parishes such as Elgin covered a considerable area and it could take several days to carry out censuses to determine eligibility in scattered settlements and subsequently just as long to distribute the charity required.[144] In any case, if the rural and dispersed parishes of the north-east were anything like their equivalents in Fife, it was likely that 'traditional forms of charity and hospitality', perhaps by benevolent landowners, continued to be important.[145] As had been the case before the Reformation, these were equally valued within the burgh, such as the philanthropic actions of Aberdeen's William Guild, who founded a hospital in 1631 and bequeathed a sizeable sum in his will for the care of the city's orphans.[146] The size of parishes could also present problems to paupers with mobility issues and some found themselves able to seek alms only by being carried from door to door on wooden stretchers, though a fortunate few were permitted to have a proxy collect support on their behalf.[147] Efforts were made to regulate the movements of poor throughout parishes, so that no particular district ever found itself overwhelmed by alms-seekers; in 1631 Banff was divided into quarters, with each only to receive a fixed number of poor at any one time, while in 1636 the Kirk Session of Old Aberdeen decreed certain days on which the poor could visit the different districts.[148]

As with pre-Reformation practice, tokens were issued to eligible recipients, which were made of lead, wood or mixed metal.[149] These badges made it obvious to which town the individual belonged (however that may have been defined): the burgh's coat of arms was often portrayed, while tokens for the town's poor in Old Aberdeen were adorned with 'ane floure de luce' and those signifying the landward poor displaying a star.[150] Those granted such tokens were expected to attend weekly sermons in person, though the difficulty in enforcing this was evident in the Aberdeen Kirk Session's ordinances of 1604 and 1621 reiterating the stipulation and threatening the cessation of alms for those who failed to do so.[151] As was the case in English parishes, over time badges for the poor may have evolved from 'tokens of approval' to 'symbols of humiliation', with municipal authorities deliberately exploiting the shame of poverty to ease the financial burden of public relief by discouraging its conspicuous receipt.[152] Paupers deemed ineligible were apprehended, shamed and expelled by both civic officials and Kirk elders in Aberdeen, Elgin, Old Aberdeen, Belhelvie and Banff (wherein a special tax was imposed to fund the administrative cost of doing so).[153]

Though support tended to be reserved for those who 'belonged' to the burgh or the parish, non-native poor could also receive it so long as they had a 'lawfull calling and industrie', or even if they were proven to be 'honest decant personis', emphasising the concern with moral rectitude.[154] Parish elders considered the idle poor a nuisance and formulated measures to punish and banish them, but they remained a persistent irritant. During the first decades of the seventeenth century, there were intermittent attempts by Kirk Sessions throughout the north-east, including Elgin, Aberdour, Fraserburgh, Lonmay and Old Deer, during the first decades of the seventeenth century to appoint individuals whose responsibility it was to round up and eject such beggars.[155] Elders and magistrates alike most wanted to avoid charity being diverted to this category of pauper, as their idleness made them both a moral and literal burden on the community particularly during outbreaks. McCallum has observed that in times of real crisis, Kirk Sessions simply 'could not cope with the massive increase in human need and suffering'.[156] This is probably true, though the efforts of Elgin's Kirk Session elders during the outbreak of 1600–01 (for which extensive records survive) indicate that they went to great lengths to uphold the *First Book of Discipline*'s call for the Kirk to care for the needy.

Spreading the word: networks of communication

After 1550 there was an increase in the use of communication networks that helped the council to identify, and thereby limit contact with, infected areas. This ought to be contextualised by recognising the efforts of Aberdeen's council to foster more efficient communications with its neighbours about all matters of concern, being in the sixteenth century among the first to appoint a dedicated messenger, perhaps in recognition of the relative distance of the burgh from the central belt in particular.[157] The identifiable increase in the exchange of information specifically regarding plague is unlikely to be attributable solely to the exponential rise in extant sources, with the extensive survival of the Aberdeen council registers alone making it possible to identify an increase, particularly from about 1600, not only in proactive efforts to share information about where plague was and how best to prevent it, but also in the breadth of places across the north-east involved in this exchange. These ranged from major burghs such as Peterhead, Fraserburgh, Banff, Inverurie and Kintore to scattered parochial settlements and landed estates including Boddam, Collieston, Slains, Cruden, Foveran, Monymusk, Pitfodels, Drum, Leys, Lumphanan, Sluie Hill, Hillhead and Whitehaugh.

Sometimes it was recorded that the council 'understands' or had been 'credibilie informit' of the 'certified' existence of plague, through 'credible report and informatioun'.[158] Drawing attention to the credibility of such reports emphasised to residents the scale of the threat and the importance of complying with consequent preventative measures. While there were many instances in official civic and ecclesiastical administrative records noting the exchange of information about infection, these tell an incomplete story. Oftentimes, the first official notification of plague in the registers provides no clue about how an awareness of it had first been acquired. In any case, recorded exchanges, detailed or not, were likely supplemented substantially by rumours of plague garnered unofficially through contacts maintained across the region for the everyday purposes of business, market trading and visiting relatives and friends. This ought to be borne in mind when considering the recorded evidence we have for the ways in which the Aberdeen council shared such information.

News could be conveyed as fast as it took a messenger to travel between two given locations, which meant that *prima facie* Aberdeen was disadvantaged by its relatively isolated location from the central belt, where the population was concentrated and where the seat of national government was located. Although central government clearly had a vested interest in ensuring that national directives regarding plague were communicated far and wide, in practice these were often aimed only at governors in the vicinity of Edinburgh and in Fife, and Aberdeen and other northern burghs subsequently learnt of them indirectly through contact with civic counterparts. The exchange of information between urban governments was a primary mechanism for the co-ordinated implementation of civic measures to tackle sources of plague, and the Aberdeen council received news from burghs including Culross, Peterhead and Dundee alerting it to the presence of plague in locations as far apart as Orkney and the parishes of Ruthven and Tealing in modern Angus.[159] Notably, magistrates sometimes implemented a watch of the city – the standard first line of defence against plague – specifically in light of news that other 'clene' burghs had already begun to do so, and likewise stood it down for the same reason.[160] They became increasingly proactive in writing to southern burghs including Brechin and Edinburgh to gauge the extent of infection, and in passing on news they received to their counterparts elsewhere in the north-east.[161]

As burgh councils were often comprised of landed gentry, the networks of intermarriage, kinship, and bonds of manrent and of friendship which bound noble families could be used to great advantage in the dissemination of information about plague. Key north-east families included the Menzies of Pitfodels, who had dominated Aberdeen's council in the sixteenth century, and the Gordon earls of Huntly, whose power stretched across the north-east at least as far as Elgin and whose role as agents of the Crown had enabled them to become 'regional lords of national significance', until this became countered as the seventeenth century progressed by a reassertion of royal influence in law and order.[162] Other important families included the Hays of Erroll, whose ancestral home was Slains on the Buchan coast, and the hereditary earls Marischal the Keiths, whose seats included Dunnottar Castle.[163] Rumours of infection in Aberdeen's hinterland were sufficiently serious – and comparatively rare – to ensure that such information would be circulated amongst aristocratic families and so reach the ears of burgh councillors. In October 1603, George Keith, the fifth earl Marischal and the founder of Marischal College, wrote to both Peterhead and Fraserburgh about plague measures, while William Forbes, whose ancestral home of Tolquhon Castle was situated near the river Ythan, wrote in 1605 to warn the Aberdeen council that plague was in Banff.[164]

Many of those landowners involved in exchanges about plague owned lands in vulnerable spots situated on the coast or either side of the major regional rivers of the Dee, Don and Ythan. At small coastal locations, goods were routinely unloaded at simple, unguarded wooden jetties, while rivers provided an alternative route to inland areas in addition to the inefficient road system. During the severe epidemic in London of 1625, the Privy Council expressed its concern about 'the daylie and frequent arryvall' of vessels whose crews, pleading ignorance or oversight, either docked at unmanned bays and ports or did so at 'obscure pairtis and burnis along the coast' under cover of darkness, from where those on board could 'publictlie and avowedlie travellis athort that is, across the cuntrey' to be received by family and friends.[165] On several occasions the Aberdeen council sought to prevent such possibilities. It sent letters instructing their counterparts in Newburgh, Peterhead and Fraserburgh not to 'suffir the boit suspect of the pest to entir in thair herberis', and likewise told the heads of the estates of Monymusk, Drum, Pitfodels and Leys, all of which bordered the Dee, to instigate watches of their 'watteris and fuirdis' and to make sure their tenants 'resett na personis cuming frome the Forthe, for feir of the pest'.[166] Two officials convened at Foveran with landowners along the Ythan, while the earl of Erroll, then in Perth, was sent advice on how best to guard his 'ports' of Slains and Cruden.[167] These examples demonstrate the way in which links between landed families and the council expedited the co-ordinated dissemination of news about plague and the implementation of measures: Thomas Menzies, provost in 1602–03, owned the estate of Pitfodels, while Leys was the seat of the Burnett family, whose head Alexander had been made an honorary burgess of Aberdeen in 1598.[168] The likely value of marital ties is also apparent in this instance, with the families of Menzies and Irvine linked at this point through the marriage of former provost George Menzies to Margaret, daughter of the laird of Drum Alexander Irvine, himself a generous benefactor who endowed several bursaries at Marischal College in 1629.[169]

Aristocratic networks also helped spread information at the parochial level; for example, Patrick Forbes, who became bishop of Aberdeen in 1618, was a member of a house which had been active in north-east life for centuries and which controlled lands stretching from Strathdon to the Lowlands of Buchan.[170] Kirk personnel were vital sources of knowledge about events in the parish, and the Aberdeen council actively sought information about the existence of plague from the parsons of Kincardine O'Neil and Turriff, as well as from William Forbes, the minister of Alford who subsequently was appointed principal of Marischal College.[171] The overlap in personnel between the Kirk and local councils helped to ensure co-ordinated responses to plague particularly in smaller, rural settlements, most notably regarding the severe epidemics in the parishes of Elgin (in 1600–01) and Strachan (in 1606).[172] Furthermore, information about plague (as with myriad other issues) was disseminated among parishes through the 'interdependent web' of Kirk Sessions, or informally by members of individual congregations.[173] The weekly church sermon was the forum by which most parishioners were told of an outbreak, usually through admonitions for fasts and additional acts of repentance to appease the divine wrath which had precipitated it. Officials in Aberdeen and across the north-east were not recorded as going to such lengths to elicit information as was the case in Seville, where councillors opened private correspondence during plague to establish the movements of suspected individuals.[174] Nevertheless, it is highly likely that, through a host of official and informal contacts, they became better able to understand where plague existed and consequently better prepared to prevent its spread.

The spiritual dimension

Kirk Sessions not only provided a vital administrative layer to the imposition and supervision of plague measures, but also their close co-operation with Aberdeen's council gave civic legislation a spiritual dimension which had been surprisingly muted prior to the Reformation. The unequivocal interpretation of plague as the manifestation of divine wrath, though clearly articulated in earlier decades, became infused with Protestant zeal as plague became a weapon in the struggle to impose godly discipline on errant congregations. Notwithstanding the relatively reluctant acceptance of the Reformed faith among civic personnel, it would appear that publicly they presented at least a rhetorical Protestant front. In 1568, when Aberdeen's magistrates implemented plague measures for the first time since the national implementation of the Reformation, they acknowledged that

> we suld not contempt nor tempt the maiestie off god but wse sick devotioun prayar and ordinar menis as god willis ws to do for eschewing of his plaig and punischment quhilk justly we desserue for our iniquitie and offenssis.

Not only were the ports to be closed and a watch to be implemented, but also 'spirituall repentence and incalling of the name of god' were to be undertaken, 'for auerting of his said plaig frome ws'.[175] Just as God inflicted plague through secondary causes, so likewise did He spare individuals and demonstrate His benevolence through the success of temporal measures: writing in *Ane Breve*

Descriptioun of the Pest, Gilbert Skene believed the successful administering of preservative medicines to be the 'support [that] it hes plesit his Godlie will to schaw vs'.[176] Likewise, governments recognised that it was positively 'guid & godlie' to implement earthly measures.[177] They were simply 'menis instrumentall meanis' that unequivocally would only meet with success when coupled with 'the guid plesor of god', 'but [that is, without] quhois keiping all is in vaine'.[178] The council's pronouncement of 1568 contained the essential elements repeated in almost every subsequent plague regulation passed in the Reformed city.

God alone dictated where and when plague would strike, whom it would afflict and spare, and when it would end. Hence, when magistrates noted the prospect of infection, this was often followed up with the term 'God forbid', while the phrase 'God be praised' tended to supplement notifications of the cessation of a nearby outbreak or the discovery that suspect items were in fact clean.[179] The Privy Council warned Aberdeen's council in 1603 that the severe epidemic then raging might spread even further, 'gif god of his mercy put not to his helping hand'.[180] In turn, the council echoed this almost exactly and further attributed the city's extraordinary immunity at that time to divine benevolence.[181] Individuals also expressed these sentiments in their personal correspondence: Patrick Drummond wrote home to Aberdeen's council from Veere, praising God that plague in the region had recently ceased.[182] Writing to John, Earl of Mar, the Viscount of Fenton (later Earl of Kellie) lamented the deaths of several of his associates during an epidemic then raging in London, but was comforted by the fact that 'god [would] remove it if it be his good pleasor'.[183]

God's pleasure would be heightened by suitable responses on the part of believers, which ideally took a two-pronged approach. One was to cease the sinful actions that provoked His anger, while the other was to seek His appeasement through suitably deferential repentance. The various iniquities that angered Him were extensive and Reformed ministers took great pains to decry to their cowering flocks the particular moral failings that were the cause of current divine wrath in order to convey their own political, social or confessional messages. Congregations throughout the north-east were told that the cause of the plague outbreak then current was 'the manifauld sinnis of the people', which included 'the gryt contempt of the gospell', blasphemy, Sabbath-breaking, 'harlotrie', 'the desolation in the cuntrey in religion and policie', and 'prophaine pastymes' such as riding the marches.[184] In 1608 even the custom of salmon fishing on Sundays was punished by elders: though it had been

> forbidden by the light of God's word . . . yet the possessors of the waters, preferring, as it appears, their greed and avarice to the glory and worship of God, have continued and persisted hitherto in working and fishing of their waters on the Sabbath day, to the high dishonour of God, the manifest contempt of his law, and slander of the gospel.[185]

'[G]ryt and manifold abuses' could arise at wakes, so elders limited attendance at them to six people; while this reduced the risk of contagion it also ensured that those present could be 'occupeit in praysing God be singing of psalmes and reding sum pairtis of scripture', which was in all probability of greater concern.[186] Through ungodly pursuits the faithful had lost their way, and plague ought justly to serve as a call to repentance, so that they 'may be the bettir movit to draw neir to god'.[187]

Following the Reformation one of the most popular forms of repentance was the biblically-endorsed act of fasting, a liturgical phenomenon which, in Alec Ryrie's words, 'provided significant lubrication for the process of religious change'.[188] Under the charge of John Knox, the architect of Scotland's Reformation of 1560, the earlier function of calendrical fasting as a strictly regulated, private act of contrition was shunned as smacking of 'works righteousness' and superstition, and became reinvented by the Protestant Kirk largely as an occasional public event of penitence ordered in response to a specific crisis that warranted divine appeasement.[189] Fasts were, therefore, inherently *ad hoc*, and their dissociation with Catholic practices was further articulated in orders for them to take place on two successive Sundays rather than on Fridays as had been traditional. The first and last days, from 8pm on the Saturday until 5pm on the Sunday, were days of actual fasting and the intervening week comprised a period of 'humiliation', that is, an outward sign of inner humility before God, reflecting a true sorrow for sin.[190] It was intended as a time of austerity in all areas of life. A 'temperate diet' was to be favoured, modest dress was to be worn, with so-called 'gorgeous apparel' specifically frowned upon, and all forms of frivolity, from card games to wedding celebrations, were forbidden.[191] Of most importance to the consequent success of the whole enterprise, however, was the requirement that during this period each participant had the right spiritual intent. Fasting was seen to 'give wings to prayer', to quote the oft-cited phrase, and was to be undertaken with genuine and sincere contrition.[192] It was to be accompanied by long periods of individual contemplation, 'every family apart'.[193] This time was to be spent reading pertinent biblical passages and reflecting on one's own relationship with God. On the actual fast days, this spiritual contemplation was structured around a programme of set prayers, silent meditations and at least one sermon (routinely two in Aberdeen[194]) which functioned as the forum that enabled the preacher to impress upon his congregation the urgency and rationale for all acts of penitence during such times of national fasting.

Unlike in England, the complex political machinations of the century following the Reformation meant that in Scotland fasts were not regularly under the control of the Crown until the Restoration period, though in 1625 the archbishop of St Andrews acted with direct royal assent in ordering the bishops of Aberdeen and Moray to instigate a fast both to 'destroy the malaise' of plague and to request a bountiful harvest.[195] Fasts were usually ordered in the parishes of Aberdeen and Elgin by Kirk Session elders (and occasionally also by civic officials), and were promulgated in response to plague outbreaks both near and far, including not only in major burghs such as Edinburgh and Dundee, but also throughout the parishes of Elgin and of Strachan only twelve miles from Aberdeen, as well as in the burgh of Torry, separated from the city only by the narrow stretch of the river Dee.[196] The minister's recitation from the pulpit of the official order for the fast exemplifies an important way in which ordinary parishioners received news of nationally significant events – albeit filtered through the sieve of official Kirk or government censure. Through such orders landlocked parishioners learned of coastal storms, urban dwellers received early notification of failed harvests, and those living in the north of the kingdom were made aware of a plague outbreak in the south. Orders for fasts in response to epidemics tended to be relatively short on detail, though congregations would have been suitably affected by reports during the Dundee epidemic of 1607 that 'sindrie ar deid', as well as by the way in which imminent plague was described as God 'drawin narrir ... be his correcting hand'.[197]

In the eyes of the Reformers repentance ought not to be confined to individuals but could be more effective as a corporate activity, though the Scottish Kirk was unique among Reformed Churches in devising a special order of service – the 'Order of the General Fast', first published in 1566 – to articulate this form of communal repentance.[198] But practical considerations could challenge spiritual responses. Crises such as plague made communal worship and contrition all the more important, but this was hampered by the very real fear of contagion in situations where people gathered together. The first fast ordered for plague in England (in 1563) specially requested that 'prudent' measures be taken to segregate infected people from the healthy, while later amendments limited fast day sermons to an hour ostensibly due to the possibility of infection (though this was in all probability bound up with a concern to repress the puritan enthusiasm for preaching).[199] The Aberdeen Kirk Session on occasion substituted the usual sermon with a short exhortation when plague threatened and ensured their church doors were kept locked outside such times,[200] but the fact that sermons were not regularly cancelled before the 1640s is most likely due to the absence of actual outbreaks during these decades.

The fear of contagion could challenge the ideal of public fasting as a united and simultaneous effort. The idea underpinning the concept of special orders for national fasts was that all members of the realm should worship together on the same dates, using the same texts, and doing so for the same purpose. The aim was to present a united front of repentance to the Almighty, 'the nation conceived as a single spiritual and moral body', as Natalie Mears has put it, seeking forgiveness for their collective sins.[201] The need for synchronicity in temporal responses to plague was mirrored in spiritual responses: just as burgh councils often implemented watches in light of reports that other burghs had instigated them, Kirk Sessions could order fasts because other parishes had done so.[202] It is important to note that contemporaries unequivocally believed that fasting could achieve its intended purpose. The subsequent cessation of an outbreak (or a storm or drought) could often be interpreted as a direct result of communal acts of repentance, while their continuation might be taken as a sign that penitents had been insufficiently contrite, or that not enough parishioners had participated. The practice of fasting in response to natural events exemplifies what Thomas has called the 'self-confirming quality' of the doctrine of providence.[203] Such acts were an important psychological tool to cope with plague. In fact, it could be argued that the greatest historical significance of fasts and other penitential acts undertaken in response to disasters was the sense of agency and involvement they gave to individuals. Not only did the providential framework help them to make sense of these crises, it enabled each individual to play his or her own small part in averting them, in feeling that their actions had a tangible, positive effect on the course of events. This should not be underestimated, particularly within the context of a time in which the majority of people were disenfranchised, with few if any alternative means of influencing the course of situations which nevertheless fundamentally affected them, including not only political events but also natural phenomena. The liturgical act of fasting, underpinned by a belief in providentialism, offered one solution to the crisis of plague to which each believer throughout the north-east and further afield could contribute.

Plague in Aberdeen after 1550

Though plague never broke out in the city of Aberdeen itself, it swept through neighbouring Torry in 1608, with fifty-one confirmed deaths according to the council's estimate in November and still others 'presently sick and decased'. Magistrates procured from St Andrews a dyer called Walter Findlayson to begin the following morning cleansing infected houses, goods and individuals until the bounds of Torry had been 'perfytlie clengit'. He was also to burn the corpses of those who had succumbed to infection, with the help of a couple of assistants of his own choosing. He was to be provided with food and drink during his residency and paid a fee of one hundred pounds, with his wife to receive an initial payment on his behalf after eight days on the job.[204] Since plague was then just a short distance away from Aberdeen on the other side of the Dee, the council had gibbets erected in Futty and at Aberdeen's meal market to act as deterrents to the contravention of plague orders and also made provisions in case it did spread to the city.[205] It organised sufficient victual and funds to be accrued: this would enable the poor to be fed and the cleansers to be paid in the event that the imposition of a *cordon sanitaire* should leave most inhabitants in a 'wonderfull great strait' for want of sustenance. Those citizens present at the meeting consented to paying whatever tax the council felt was required to maintain order and reduce the possibility of goods being acquired illicitly.[206]

Cleansers were shared between Torry, Cowie and Stonehaven that winter, as during that time infection had also swept through the latter two settlements situated several miles to the south.[207] There is a lasting reminder in Stonehaven of the epidemic's devastating effects in the form of a grave stone recording the death of a seaman by the name of Magnus Tailiour, 'qvha depairtit in November, (in the time of) pest, 1608'.[208] The disease was also feared to have been present to the north of Aberdeen in Belhelvie, where a suspect house was apparently burnt down as a result of fumigation, with the fortunate owner – 'ane puir boy' – unusually receiving compensation.[209] It was also thought to have spread to Kintore and Inverurie, to where officers were sent to 'try' suspect goods.[210] However, there is no evidence that the disease ever spread within the bounds of Aberdeen itself. Indeed, aside from organising affairs in Torry during that outbreak, there were remarkably few occasions on which the city's governors had to counter what they feared was the presence of plague, which they did through cleansing and enclosure with apparent success. Each of these instances took place during the 1605–06 financial year at a time when plague swept through many parts of the north-east, coming within twelve miles of Aberdeen. In addition to a discernible drive on the part of the council to communicate with rural landowners about the extent of plague during this fraught period, magistrates provided sustenance to an enclosed resident of Torry, who was forbidden from coming to Aberdeen 'for feir he had the plaig'. They also dispatched officials to Stonehaven, where they were to 'try' some chests 'suspectit of the plaig' which had arrived by sea from Leith. Other officers were to ride to nearby Sheddocksley to inspect the body of Margreit Burnett, who was suspected to have died from the disease, and subsequently purchased three bundles of heather which were to be burned to fumigate her house situated in the Green quarter of the burgh.[211]

These instances represent the sum total of all measures taken by the Aberdeen council to identify, to prevent or to eliminate presumed sources of infection on the fringes of its city. This was as close as plague came to Aberdeen itself during this period. To what may this remarkable immunity be attributed? As this chapter has shown, magistrates did not implement any different measures from those put in place in earlier decades or by their counterparts elsewhere, nor did they punish lawbreakers with any more severity – in fact, they were demonstrably capable of being lenient. It can be conjectured that increased networks of communication helped to identify quickly areas where plague had broken out, and that the restrictive narrowness of the harbour and the surrounding topography of the hinterland facilitated the subsequent monitoring of arrivals to the city both by sea and by land. Contemporaries identified an equally valid reason for why the city of Aberdeen had avoided each and every outbreak that had occurred since the advent of Protestantism in Scotland. The council had noted in 1603 that the burgh had avoided plague for the previous fifty-five years specifically because God had chosen to spare it; the same might have been deemed to be true in the subsequent four decades. To the current incumbents of a civic body that had embraced the Protestant faith some time before it was widely accepted throughout the north-east as a whole, the reason was clear: the Reformed island in a sea of idolatry was spared by providence.

Notes

1 ACR.43.073 [22 Apr 1607].

2 Ann G. Carmichael, "The last past plague: the uses of memory in Renaissance epidemics", *Journal of the History of Medicine and Allied Sciences* 53:2 (1998), pp. 132–160.

3 Alexander M. Munro, *Memorials of the Aldermen, Provosts, and Lord Provosts of Aberdeen, 1272–1895* (Aberdeen: privately printed, 1897), pp. 112–128.

4 Repairs: ACR.31.488 [28 Sep 1584]; ACR.40.305 [2 Dec 1601]; ACR.41.683 [16 May 1604]; watches: ACR.31.612 [21 May 1585]; ACR.40.414 [10 Feb 1602]; ACR.42.315 [14 Aug 1605]; ACR.42.362 [18 Sep 1605]; ACR.42.792 [24 Jun 1606]; ACR.42.857 [24 Jul 1606]; ACR.43.073 [22 Apr 1607].

5 ACR.26.637 [2 Oct 1568]; ACR.31.488 [28 Sep 1584]; ACR.31.612 [21 May 1585]; ACR.40.305 [2 Dec 1601]; ACR.42.843 [18 Jul 1606]; ACR.42.857 [24 Jul 1606].

6 ACR.26.209 [2 Sep 1566]; ACR.31.489 [28 Sep 1584]; ACR.31.612–613 [21 May 1585]; ACR.41.671–672 [8 May 1604]; ACR.42.315 [14 Aug 1605]; ACR.43.071 [20 Apr 1607]. On one occasion the council implemented a watch at each ford of the river Dee between the bridge and the haven mouth, but the manpower required for this meant that it was apparently not repeated; ACR.31.488 [28 Sep 1584].

7 ACR.31.489 [28 Sep 1584]; AGA [1601–1602]; ACR.40.414 [10 Feb 1602]; ACR.41.675 [9 May 1604]; ACR.41.683 [16 May 1604]; ACR.41.999 [8 Dec 1604].

8 ACR.26.637 [2 Oct 1568]; ACR.31.489 [28 Sep 1584]; ACR.39.690 [5 Nov 1600]; ACR.40.816 [28 Sep 1602]; ACR.41.409 [11 Oct 1603]; ACR.41.715 [4 Jun 1604]; ACR.41.999 [8 Dec 1604]; ACR.42.100 [22 Mar 1605]; ACR.42.315 [14 Aug 1605]; ACR.42.792 [24 Jun 1606].

9 Itinerant salesmen: ACR.31.490 [28 Sep 1584]; ACR.42.100–101 [22 Mar 1605]; ACR.42.315 [14 Aug 1605]. By the same rationale magistrates in Edinburgh sought to limit the activities of pawnbrokers, presumably since these involved goods changing hands multiple times; Edinburgh CMB.4.445–446 [15 Oct 1568]; Edinburgh CMB.5.35r [26 Oct 1574]; testimonials: ACR.31.489 [28 Sep 1584]; ACR.31.612 [21 May 1585]; ACR.40.414 [10 Feb 1602]; ACR.41.671–672 [8 May 1604]; ACR.43.071 [20 Apr 1607].

10 ACR.31.666 [4 Sep 1585].

11 ACR.31.488 [28 Sep 1584]; ACR.39.690 [5 Nov 1600]; ACR.40.305 [2 Dec 1601]; ACR.40.414 [10 Feb 1602]; ACR.41.403 [7 Oct 1603]; ACR.41.672 [8 May 1604]; ACR.41.999 [8 Dec 1604]; ACR.42.100 [22 Mar 1605]; ACR.42.315 [14 Aug 1605]; ACR.42.792 [24 Jun 1606]; ACR.43.071 [20 Apr 1607].

12 ACR.31.490 [28 Sep 1584]; ACR.31.613 [21 May 1585]; AGA [1601–1602]; ACR.40.305 [2 Dec 1601]; ACR.40.464 [17 Mar 1602]; ACR.41.715 [4 Jun 1604]; ACR.42.315 [14 Aug 1605]; ACR.42.792 [24 Jun 1606]; ACR.43.077 [24 Apr 1607].

13 Permission to lodge: ACR.26.209 [2 Sep 1566]; ACR.26.226 [23 Sep 1566]; ACR.31.488 [28 Sep 1584]; ACR.31.613 [21 May 1585]; ACR.39.690 [5 Nov 1600]; ACR.41.715 [4 Jun 1604]; ACR.41.999 [8 Dec 1604]; ACR.42.315 [14

Aug 1605]; ACR.42.792 [24 Jun 1606]; ACR.43.077 [24 Apr 1607]; patrol: ACR.40.414 [10 Feb 1602].

14 Quote: ACR.52/1.265 [28 Apr 1636]; fruit: ACR.31.488 [28 Sep 1584]; wool: ACR.42.826 [8 Jul 1606]; timber: ACR.42.849 [19 Jul 1606]. On only one occasion were (unspecified) goods ordered to be burned: AGA [1601–1602].

15 Regional markets: ACR.31.488 [28 Sep 1584]; ACR.31.613 [21 May 1585]; ACR.41.680 [15 May 1604]; ACR.42.314–315 [14 Aug 1605]; ACR.42.826 [8 Jul 1606]; fairs in Turriff and Old Rayne: AGA [1605–06]; Martinmas fair: ACR.39.690 [5 Nov 1600]; St Bartholomew's fair: ACR.42.314–315 [14 Aug 1605].

16 South: ACR.40.305 [2 Dec 1601]; ACR.41.403 [7 Oct 1603]; ACR.43.077 [24 Apr 1607]; Moray: ACR.39.690 [5 Nov 1600]; Dundee and Perth: ACR.42.857 [24 Jul 1606].

17 Walls: Elgin BCB.3.274 [22 Nov 1574]; Old Ab CMB.1.5 [8 Jul 1603]; Old Ab CMB.1.42 [3 March 1606]; Old Ab CMB.1.68 [11 Oct 1608]; middens: Old Ab CMB.1.68 [11 Oct 1608]; suspect gear: William Cramond, *The Annals of Banff*, vol. I (Aberdeen: New Spalding Club, 1891), p. 53 [13 Dec 1624]; arrivals with no testimonial: Elgin BCB.3.1001 [28 Oct 1584]; Thomas Mair, *Records of the Parish of Ellon* (Aberdeen: A. Brown and Co., 1876), p. 58 [7 Jun 1604]; Old Ab CMB.2.15–16 [16 May 1635]; Old Ab CMB.2.27 [5 Dec 1636]; Old Ab CMB.2.39 [28 Oct 1640]; strangers and beggars: Elgin BCB.3.1032 [15 Mar 1585]; Old Ab CMB.1.18 [12 Aug 1604]; Old Ab CMB.1.27 [14 Jan 1605]; Old Ab CMB.1.68 [11 Oct 1608]; NAS: B36/6: Inverurie Burgh Court Book, vol. I, fol. 39v [12 Oct 1608]; brewing: NAS: B36/6: Inverurie Burgh Court Book, vol. I, fol. 39v [12 Oct 1608].

18 RPC.1/13.664 [15 Dec 1624], 666 [11 Jan 1625], 677–678 [14 Jan 1625], 690 [1 Feb 1625], 700 [4 Feb 1625], 708–709 [9 Mar 1625].

19 ACR.36.754 [7 Sep 1597].

20 'Speciallie fra incumming of schippis crearis and boittes fra the south pairtis': ACR.41.408 [11 Oct 1603]; ACR.42.100 [22 Mar 1605].

21 Bashford has drawn attention to the historiographical trend for analysing quarantine measures in terms also of political and military agendas, which during conflict could effectively turn sequestered crews into 'prisoners of war'; Alison Bashford, "Maritime quarantine: linking old world and new world histories", in Alison Bashford (ed.), *Quarantine: Local and Global Histories* (London: Palgrave Macmillan, 2016), pp. 1–12, at p. 4. For example, the Privy Council's embargo on trade with London in 1665 may be seen as being predicated partly in retaliation for the conditions imposed by the 1662 Navigation Act, which disadvantaged Scotland to the same extent as other foreign nations; John Booker, *Maritime Quarantine: The British Experience, c.1650–1900* (Aldershot: Ashgate, 2007), p. 23. For a nineteenth-century case study, see Birsen Bulmuş, *Plague, Quarantines and Geopolitics in the Ottoman Empire* (Edinburgh: Edinburgh University Press, 2012).

22 Kristy Wilson Bowers, *Plague and Public Health in Early Modern Seville* (Rochester: University of Rochester Press, 2013), p. 61; the notorious reputation ships had for bringing in diseases was the motivation for the development of the first quarantine efforts at Ragusa; Zlata Blažina Tomič and Vesna Blažina, *Expelling the Plague: The Health Office and the Implementation of Quarantine in Dubrovnik, 1377–1533* (Montreal: McGill-Queens' University Press, 2015).

23 ACR.31.488 [28 Sep 1584]; ACR.31.613 [21 May 1585]; ACR.41.408–409 [11 Oct 1603]; ACR.42.100 [22 Mar 1605]; ACR.52.297 [28 Sep 1636]; ACR.52:1.299 [5 Oct 1636].

24 ACR.31.488 [28 Sep 1584]; ACR.31.613 [21 May 1585]. During plague Edinburgh and Dundee also attempted to restrict the passage of ferries over the much

wider rivers Forth and Tay respectively; Edinburgh: RPC.1/3.696 [4 Nov 1584]; Edinburgh CMB.7.127r [6 Nov 1584], 141r [11 Dec 1584], 153v [27 Jan 1585], 182r [5 May 1585]; RPC.1/3.713–714 [18 Dec 1584], 728 [9 Mar 1585], 737 [17 Apr 1585]; Dundee: Dundee CMB.3, fol. 22v [29 May 1604], fols 38v–39r [6 Aug 1605], fols 57r–v [15 Aug 1606].

25 Booker, *Maritime Quarantine*, p. 18.

26 ACR.31.489 [28 Sep 1584]; ACR.40.305 [2 Dec 1601]; AGA [1601–02]; AGA [22 Oct 1603]; ATA, p. 758 [1636–37].

27 ACR.36.754 [7 Sep 1597]; ACR.40.464 [17 Mar 1602].

28 An exception to this nationwide practice was recorded in 1627, when the misnamed *Good Fortune* arrived at Leith from London with sick and dead crew members on board. The living were subsequently quarantined at Alloa under the supervision of Lawrence Cokeburn, 'chirurgion in Edinburgh', who reported examining 'one of the companie that had a byle upon him, whom he found sound and weele'; John Ritchie, "Quarantine for plague in Scotland during the sixteenth and seventeenth centuries", *Edinburgh Medical Journal* 55 (1948), pp. 691–701, at p. 697.

29 John Ritchie, "A plague "testimonial" of the sixteenth century", *Caledonian Medical Journal*, new series 15 (1932), pp. 94–98, at p. 95.

30 ACR.31.488 [28 Sep 1584]; ACR.31.613 [21 May 1585]; ACR.40.415 [10 Feb 1602]; ACR.40.767 [8 Sep 1602]; ACR.41.408–409 [11 Oct 1603]; ACR.42.100 [22 Mar 1605]; ACR.52:1.299 [5 Oct 1636].

31 ACR.31.613 [21 May 1585].

32 Bashford, "Maritime quarantine", p. 2.

33 Inchcolm: Edinburgh CMB.4.216 [1 Sep 1564], 492 [21 Sep 1569]; RPC.1/1.280–282 [23 Sep 1564]; C.T. McInnes (ed.), *Accounts of the Treasurer of Scotland, vol. XII: 1566–1574* (Edinburgh: Scottish Record Office, 1970), p. 282 [Sep 1571]; RPC.1/3.313 [20 Sep 1580], 330–331 [22 Nov 1580]; RPC.1/5.94 [8 Aug 1593]; RPC.2/1.199, 207 [28 Nov 1625]; Inchkeith: Edinburgh CMB.4.492 [21 Sep 1569]; RPC.1/3.330–331 [22 Nov 1580]; Inchgarvie: RPC.1/3.330–331 [22 Nov 1580]; Isle of May: RPC.1/3.330 [22 Nov 1580]; Hamish Haswell-Smith, *The Scottish Islands: A Comprehensive Guide to Every Scottish Island* (Edinburgh: Canongate, 2004), pp. 488–494 gives the description and history of each island, including their various uses as sites of a monastery, a fort and Scotland's first lighthouse.

34 ACR.40.739 [23 Aug 1602].

35 Ritchie, "Quarantine for plague in Scotland", pp. 695–696.

36 They were released after no sign of infection 'god be praysit hes bene fund during the tyme of thair tryell ather in their bodyes or guids'; ACR.40.767 [8 Sep 1602]; ACR.40.842 [20 Oct 1602]; ACR.41.472–474 [21 Nov 1603]; ACR.41.488 [25 Nov 1603]; ACR.41.496 [30 Nov 1603].

37 Booker, *Maritime Quarantine*, p. 18.

38 ACR.25.370 [10 Sep 1564]; ACR.40.739 [23 Aug 1602]; cast to the wind: RPC.1/1.280–282 [23 Sep 1564].

39 ACR.41.357 [13 Sep 1603].

40 RPC.2/1.215 [26 Dec 1625]; Ritchie, "A plague "testimonial" of the sixteenth century", p. 96.

41 Booker, *Maritime Quarantine*, pp. 24–25.

42 ACR.40.808 [24 Sep 1602].

43 ACR.40.809 [27 Sep 1602].

44 ACR.40.811–812 [28 Sep 1602].

45 A new lock and key were ordered the next day for the 'mair seuir keping of the nichtboris merchandis of this burgh'; ACR.40.817 [29 Sep 1602].

46 ACR.40.811–816 [28 Sep 1602].
47 ACR.40.833 [13 Oct 1602].
48 ACR.40.842 [20 Oct 1602].
49 ACR.26.209 [2 Sep 1566]; ACR.43.077 [24 Apr 1607].
50 ACR.41.356–358 [13 Sep 1603], at ACR.41.357.
51 ACR.41.380 [18 Sep 1603].
52 ACR.41.465 [17 Nov 1603].
53 ACR.41.472–474 [21 Nov 1603]; ACR.41.488 [25 Nov 1603]; ACR.41.496 [30 Nov 1603]. The *Johne*, with Ramsay as captain, was still travelling between Aberdeen and Flanders six years later; Louise B. Taylor (ed.), *Aberdeen Shore Works Accounts, 1596–1670* (Aberdeen: Aberdeen University Press, 1972), p. 57 [9 Nov 1609].
54 ACL.1.067 [4 Mar 1637].
55 RPC.1/4.039 [14 Dec 1585].
56 Daily basis: Edinburgh CMB.7.184v [19 May 1585]; clerk: Edinburgh CMB.7.186v [24 May 1585]; replacements: Edinburgh CMB.7.203r [25 Aug 1585], 207r–v [5 Oct 1585], when magistrates received a letter from James VI reminding them of the importance of choosing councillors for the coming year because 'ane greitt pairt of the inhabitants of our said burgh' was infected.
57 Edinburgh CMB.7.212v [24 Nov 1585].
58 RPC.1/4.42–44 [13 Jan 1586], 47–48 [15 Feb 1586], 53 [9 Mar 1586].
59 ACR.31.614 [21 May 1585].
60 ACR.40.414–415 [10 Feb 1602]; ACR.41.437–438 [26 Oct 1603].
61 Old Ab CMB.1.41 [3 Mar 1606].
62 Edinburgh CMB.7.192r [16 Jun 1585].
63 Elgin KS.2.63v [21 Feb 1601].
64 Highland Archive Centre, Inverness: BI/1/1: Inverness Burgh Court Books, vol. II, fol. 305v [26 Mar 1575].
65 ACR.31.614 [21 May 1585].
66 Booker, *Maritime Quarantine*, pp. 19–20.
67 Inverkeithing: Ritchie, "Quarantine for plague in Scotland"; Fife: Booker, *Maritime Quarantine*, p. 19.
68 Shona Kelly Wray, *Communities and Crisis: Bologna During the Black Death* (Leiden: Brill, 2009), especially pp. 121–128; Jennifer I. Kermode, "Urban decline? The flight from office in late medieval York", *Economic History Review*, new series 35:2 (1982), pp. 179–198; Trevor Dean, "Plague and crime: Bologna, 1348–1351", *Continuity and Change* 30:3 (2015), pp. 367–393.
69 Edinburgh CMB.7.187r–v [26 May 1585]. Before plague had spread to Edinburgh he had been employed to 'try' suspected cases in West Wemyss and, in the event that these were indeed plague, to advise on the best course of action; Edinburgh CMB.7.097r [22 Jul 1584]. He was later exempted in perpetuity from further taxation in recognition of his services, which had resulted in he and his wife contracting plague, from which his wife died; Edinburgh CMB.7.206r [22 Sep 1585]. He was also employed by Perth's council during the outbreak of 1606; John Ritchie, "James Henrysoun, 'chirurgian to the poore'", *Medical History* 4:1 (1960), pp. 70–79, at p. 77.
70 Margo Todd, *The Culture of Protestantism in Early Modern Scotland* (New Haven: Yale University Press, 2002), pp. 8–9.
71 Gordon DesBrisay, *Authority and Discipline in Aberdeen, 1650–1700* (University of St Andrews, unpublished PhD thesis, 1989), pp. 309–310.
72 DesBrisay, *Authority and Discipline in Aberdeen*, p. 311.
73 Laura A.M. Stewart, *Urban Politics and the British Civil Wars: Edinburgh, 1617–53* (Leiden: Brill, 2006), p. 71.

74 DesBrisay, *Authority and Discipline in Aberdeen*, pp. 310–311.
75 Elgin KS.2.83v [16 Dec 1601].
76 William MacKay (ed.), *Chronicles of the Frasers, The Wardlaw Manuscript ... by James Fraser, 916–1674* (Edinburgh: Scottish History Society, 1905), p. 236. He also noted that, although plague raged in the district as far away as Glenelg, 'non dyed there nor in our farr Highlands and north isles' because they escaped to 'the purer aire' in the hills.
77 Bruce B. Bishop, *The Lands and People of Moray: Part 1: Inverlochty, Mosstowie, Pittendreich, Manbeen, Auchtertyre, Miltonduff and Pluscarden Prior to 1850: in the Parish of Elgin* (Elgin: J. and B. Bishop, 2000), pp. 6, 28; Bruce B. Bishop, *The Lands and People of Moray: Part 2: Westfield, Quarrywood, Findrassie, Myreside and Spynie, prior to 1850: in the Parish of Spynie* (Elgin: J. and B. Bishop, 2001), p. 3.
78 Watches: Elgin KS.2.55v [29 Aug 1600]; Elgin KS.2.57v [8 Oct 1600]; Elgin KS.2.60v [28 Dec 1600]; guard: Elgin KS.2.57v [24 Oct 1600]; walls: Elgin KS.2.57v [8 Oct 1600].
79 Ascertaining sickness: Elgin KS.2.149v [14 Feb 1604]; testimonials: Elgin KS.2.147v [27 Jan 1604].
80 Todd, *The Culture of Protestantism*, p. 12: 'so great was the value of a testimonial that there was an active trade in counterfeits'.
81 Testimonials: Elgin KS.2.143r [18 Dec 1603]; oaths: Elgin KS.2.57v [8 Oct 1600]; Elgin KS.2.75r [22 Jul 1601].
82 'Trying' quarters: Elgin KS.2.149v [14 Feb 1604]; Elgin KS.2.147v [27 Jan 1604]; Elgin KS.2.45 [25 April 1600]; hiring cleansers: Elgin KS.2.59r [26 Nov 1600]. This 'Bell ane cleinger out of Dundey' was most likely the cleanser John Bell, who was accused by relatives of Thomas Duncane of having caused the death of that baker and other residents of Dundee through 'sleuth [sloth] and negligence ... in cleansing of infected gear' during that city's severe epidemic in 1607. He was banished as punishment but readmitted six months later; Dundee CMB.3 fol. 67v–68r [17 Sep 1607]; fol. 73r [15 Mar 1608].
83 Bruce Lenman, "The limits of godly discipline in the early modern period with particular reference to England and Scotland", in Kaspar von Greyerz (ed.), *Religion and Society in Early Modern Europe, 1500–1800* (London: Allen and Unwin, 1984), pp. 124–145, at p. 124; Michael Graham, *The Uses of Reform: 'Godly Discipline' and Popular Behaviour in Scotland and Beyond, 1560–1610* (Leiden: Brill, 1996).
84 Highland Archive Centre, Inverness: BI/1/1: Inverness Burgh Court Books, vol. II, fol. 359v [29 Nov 1578].
85 Todd, *The Culture of Protestantism*, pp. 174–175.
86 Julian Goodare, *The Government of Scotland, 1560–1625* (Oxford: Oxford University Press, 2004), p. 193.
87 Bruce Lenman and Geoffrey Parker, "Crime and control in Scotland, 1500–1800", *History Today* 30:1 (1980), pp. 13–17, at p. 16.
88 Goodare, *The Government of Scotland*, p. 192. The 'first major effort to control public behaviour' through a focus on moral conduct pre-dated the Reformation, having been made by the national government during James VI's minority in the 1550s; A. Mann, "Introduction: a brief history of an ancient institution: the Scottish parliament", *Scottish Parliamentary Review* 1:1 (2013), pp. 1–27, at p. 24; A.J. Mann, "The law of the person: parliament and social control", in K.M. Brown and A.R. MacDonald (eds), *The History of the Scottish Parliament, vol. 3: Parliament in Context: 1235–1707* (Edinburgh: Edinburgh University Press, 2010), pp. 186–215.
89 Todd, *The Culture of Protestantism*, pp. 31–34; searching could be particularly useful on those occasions when such searches were extended from Sunday to be

undertaken on Wednesdays as well; e.g., Elgin KS.2.64v [4 Mar 1601]; Elgin KS.2.81v [29 Nov 1601].

90 Punishments: Elgin KS.2.50v [18 Jun 1600]; Elgin KS.2.59v [5 Dec 1600]; Elgin KS.2.59v [10 Dec 1600]; Elgin KS.2.63r [10 Feb 1601]; beggars: Elgin KS.2.45 [25 Apr 1600]; Elgin KS.2.81v [29 Nov 1601]; Elgin KS.2.128v [12 Jun 1603]; baillies: Elgin KS.2.45 [25 April 1600]; removal of banished persons: Elgin KS.2.52 [29 Jun 1600].

91 Chris R. Langley, "Lying sick to die: informal care and authority in Scotland, ca.1600–1660", *Sixteenth Century Journal* 48:1 (2017), pp. 27–46, at pp. 38–44.

92 Elgin KS.2.134v [2 Sep 1603].

93 Elgin KS.2.149v [14 Feb 1604].

94 This was the punishment imposed on two individuals convicted in Aberdeen in 1544 of a breach of the peace; Denis McKay, "Parish life in Scotland, 1500–1560", *Innes Review* 10:2 (1959), pp. 237–267, at p. 265.

95 Lenman and Parker, "Crime and control in Scotland", p. 16; Todd, *The Culture of Protestantism*, Chapter 3: "Performing repentance", pp. 127–182.

96 Kristen Post Walton, "Scotland's 'City on a Hill': The godly and the political community in early Reformation Scotland", in Michael J. Halvorson and Karen E. Spierling (eds), *Defining Community in Early Modern Europe* (Ashgate: Aldershot, 2008), pp. 247–265, at p. 258.

97 DesBrisay, *Authority and Discipline in Aberdeen*, p. 324.

98 Charles Creighton, *A History of Epidemics in Britain, vol. I: From A.D. 664 to the Great Plague* [1891] (New York: Barnes and Noble, second edition, 1965), p. 371.

99 J.R.D. Falconer, *Crime and Community in Reformation Scotland: Negotiating Power in a Burgh Society* (London: P and C, 2013), p. 80.

100 Attending fairs: ACR.42.314–315 [14 Aug 1605]; travelling to infected areas: ACR.41.403 [7 Oct 1603]; AGA [22 Oct 1603]; ACR.42.792 [24 Jun 1606]; importing goods from infected areas: ACR.52:1.265–266 [28 Apr 1636]; food and lodging to strangers: ACR.26.226 [23 Sep 1566]; ACR.31.662 [23 Aug 1585]; lodging banished residents: ACR.42.826–827 [8 Jul 1606]; lodging those from suspect places: ACR.42.830 [11 Jul 1606]; lodging suspected crew members: ACR.31.662 [23 Aug 1585]; ACR.40.811–816 [28 Sep 1602]; visiting suspected crew members: ACR.40.842–843 [20 Oct 1602]; disembarking at suspected ports: ACR.41.356–358 [13 Sep 1603]; neglecting the watch: ACR.26.209 [2 Sep 1566]; ACR.26.226 [23 Sep 1566]; ACR.39.690 [5 Nov 1600]; ACR.40.816 [28 Sep 1602]; ACR.41.409 [11 Oct 1603]; ACR.52:1.299 [5 Oct 1636].

101 Not strengthening walls: Old Ab CMB.1.42 [3 Mar 1606]; receiving visitors, especially beggars: Old Ab CMB 1.18 [12 Aug 1604]; Old Ab CMB.1.69 [28 Oct 1608]; buying suspect wool from 'ane banist theiif': Old Ab CMB.1.43 [11 Jul 1606]; landing suspect goods: Edinburgh CMB.14.379r–v [30 Apr 1636], fol. 407r [25 Nov 1636]; privies, middens, swine: Edinburgh CMB.7.180v–181r [30 Apr 1585].

102 Neglect of duties: Dundee CMB.3 fol. 39r [6 Aug 1605]; attending rural fairs: Dundee CMB.3 fols 57v–r [15 Aug 1606]; resisting quarantine: Dundee CMB.3 fol. 74v [28 Jun 1608]; concealing visitors: Elgin KS.2.42 [2 Apr 1600]; consorting with suspect individuals: Elgin KS.2.45 [23 Apr 1600].

103 E. Patricia Dennison, "Power to the people? The myth of the medieval burgh community", in Sally M. Foster, Allan I. Macinnes and Ranald MacInnes (eds), *Scottish Power Centres: from the Early Middle Ages to the Twentieth Century* (Glasgow: Cruithne, 1998), pp. 100–131, at p. 101.

104 Falconer, *Crime and Community*, p. 80.

105 Harbouring outsiders: ACR.31.616 [27 May 1585]; ACR.42.826–827 [8 Jul 1606]; scaling walls: ACR.31.616 [27 May 1585]; consorting with suspect individuals: ACR.31.666 [8 Sep 1585]; ACR.31.668 [18 Sep 1585]; carrying letters on behalf of suspect individuals: ACR.31.668 [18 Sep 1585].
106 Dundee CMB.3 fol. 36v [27 May 1605].
107 McKay, "Parish life in Scotland", pp. 266–267; consorting with suspect individuals: Elgin KS.2.45 [25 Apr 1600]; visiting suspect individuals: Elgin KS.2.59v [5 Dec 1600].
108 Edinburgh CMB.7.185v [21 May 1585].
109 Avoiding enclosure or cleansing: ACR.40.811–816 [28 Sep 1602]; ACR.40.833 [13 Oct 1602]; Dundee CMB.3 fol. 74v [28 Jun 1608]; Edinburgh CMB.7.185v [21 May 1585]; bringing in infected goods: ACR.42.849 [19 Jul 1606]; Edinburgh CMB.5.34v [26 Oct 1574]; Edinburgh CMB.7.110v [24 Sep 1584]; Edinburgh CMB.7.189r [1 Jun 1585]; attending rural markets: ACR.42.315 [14 Aug 1605]; ACR.31.613–614 [21 May 1585]; negligence on the watch: ACR.40.415 [10 Feb 1602]; harbouring strangers or not securing back walls: ACR.31.613 [21 May 1585]; Dundee CMB.3 fol. 22v [29 May 1604]; resulting in plague: ACR.42.315 [14 Aug 1605]; ACR.31.613–614 [21 May 1585]; Edinburgh CMB.7.189r [1 Jun 1585].
110 ACR.31.612–613 [21 May 1585]; AGA [22 Nov 1608].
111 Edinburgh CMB.4.313 [9 Oct 1566]; Edinburgh CMB.7.183r [10 May 1585]; Edinburgh CMB.7.185v [21 May 1585]; Edinburgh CMB.7.186v [26 May 1585]; Edinburgh CMB.7.200v [23 Jul 1585].
112 Falconer, *Crime and Community*, p. 80.
113 ACR.31.616 [27 May 1585].
114 ACR.31.668 [20 Sep 1585].
115 ACR.40.817 [29 Sep 1602].
116 ACR.41.408 [11 Oct 1603].
117 Jane Stevens Crawshaw, "The places and spaces of early modern quarantine", in Bashford (ed.), *Quarantine: Local and Global Histories*, pp. 15–34, at p. 19.
118 AGA [22 Oct 1603]: the affirmative correspondence brought back from Edinburgh authorising the commission was referred to as the letter 'of lyiff and deathe'.
119 Though these trials took place in the context of regional plague outbreaks, no specific accusations of plague-spreading were levelled against any individual, though conversely curing various ailments (though not plague) was a common charge; Julian Goodare, "The Aberdeenshire witchcraft panic of 1597", *Northern Scotland* 21:1 (2001), pp. 17–37; P.G. Maxwell-Stuart, "Witchcraft and the Kirk in Aberdeenshire, 1596–97", *Northern Scotland* 18:1 (1998), pp. 1–14. William G. Naphy, *Plagues, Poisons and Potions: Plague-Spreading Conspiracies in the Western Alps, c. 1530–1640* (Manchester: Manchester University Press, 2002) explores these accusations primarily in Geneva and convincingly refutes the historical construct that witchcraft and plague-spreading were linked. Todd, *The Culture of Protestantism*, pp. 355–359 discusses the surviving pre-Christian culture of healing through fairies and charms, the early modern belief in which has been read as the failure of Protestantism 'to meet the propitiatory needs of congregations' (p. 357).
120 Stirling: RPC.1/4.008 [27 Aug 1585]; Edinburgh: RPC.1/5.411 [18 Aug 1587]; St Andrews: RPC.1/7.34 [4 Apr 1605]; Inverleith: RPC.1/7.151–152 [5 Dec 1605]; Dysart: RPC.2/8.165–166 [c.1646]; powers for the enforcement of maritime legislation by commission were granted to ports on the northern shore of the Forth, and to Dundee, St Andrews and Montrose following reports of plague in France, Orkney and Shetland; Booker, *Maritime Quarantine*, p. 19; RPC.1/6.496–497 [8 Dec 1602].

121 ACR.41.672–673 [8 May 1604].
122 Goodare, *The Government of Scotland*, p. 200.
123 ACL.1.94–95 [4 Nov 1603, dated at Perth].
124 ACR.41.437–438 [26 Oct 1603].
125 ACR.41.671–673 [8 May 1604].
126 ACR.41.408 [11 Oct 1603].
127 ACR.42.315 [14 Aug 1605]; ACR.42.849 [19 Jul 1606]; ACR.43.903–905 [22 Mar 1609].
128 RPC.1/5.411 [18 Aug 1587].
129 ACR.41.715 [4 Jun 1604].
130 Elgin BCB.3.1032 [15 Mar 1585]; ACR.39.690 [5 Nov 1600]; Old Ab CMB.1.41 [3 Mar 1606].
131 Philopoliteious, (or) a lover of the Publick well-fare [Alexander Skene], *Memorialls for the Government of the Royal-Burghs in Scotland. With some Overtures laid before the Nobility and Gentry of several shyres in this Kingdom. As Also, a Survey of the City of Aberdeen with the Epigrams of Arthur Johnstoun, Doctor of Medicin, upon some of our chief Burghs translated into English by I.B.* (Aberdeen: John Forbes, 1685), p. 120; Rosalind Mitchison, "Poor relief and health care in Scotland, 1575–1710", in Ole Peter Grell and Andrew Cunningham (eds), *Health Care and Poor Relief in Protestant Europe, 1500–1700* (London: Routledge, 1997), pp. 220–233, at pp. 221–222; Goodare, *The Government of Scotland*, p. 195.
132 John McCallum, "Charity and conflict: poor relief in mid-seventeenth-century Dundee", *Scottish Historical Review* 95:1 (2016), pp. 30–56, at p. 31; John McCallum, "'Fatheris and provisioners of the puir': Kirk Sessions and poor relief in post-Reformation Scotland", in John McCallum (ed.), *Scotland's Long Reformation: New Perspectives on Scottish Religion, c.1500–c.1660* (Leiden: Brill, 2016), pp. 69–86, at p. 70.
133 McCallum, "'Fatheris and provisioners of the puir'", pp. 80, 74, 70.
134 McCallum, "'Fatheris and provisioners of the puir'", p. 85.
135 McCallum, "'Fatheris and provisioners of the puir'", p. 75.
136 J.M. McPherson, *The Kirk's Care of the Poor, with Special Reference to the North East of Scotland* (Aberdeen: John Avery and Co., 1941), pp. 38–39, 52, 68, McCallum, "'Fatheris and provisioners of the puir'", pp. 72–75; ACR.28.292 [8 Oct 1574]; ACR.28.323 [15 Nov 1574]; Aberdeen KS.1.68 [18 Aug 1575].
137 McPherson, *The Kirk's Care of the Poor*, p. 37.
138 McCallum, "Charity and conflict", pp. 40, 41.
139 McCallum, "'Fatheris and provisioners of the puir'", p. 80; Laura Stewart, "Poor relief in Edinburgh and the famine of 1621–24", *International Review of Scottish Studies* 30 (2005), pp. 5–41, at p. 8.
140 Church fabric: ACR.28.292 [8 Oct 1574]; tax: ACR.43.765–766 [8 Nov 1608]; ACR.51/1.31 [22 Jan 1623]; ACR.51/2.169 [26 Apr 1625]; Privy Council: ACL.1.94–95 [4 Nov 1603, dated at Perth]; ACR.41.671–673 [8 May 1604].
141 RPC.1/4.302 [27 Jul 1588]; ACR.39.690 [5 Nov 1600]; James Godsman (ed.), *A History of the Burgh and Parish of Ellon, Aberdeenshire* (Aberdeen: W. and W. Lindsay, 1958), p. 345.
142 McPherson, *The Kirk's Care of the Poor*, pp. 175–176.
143 Aberdeen KS.1.27 [24 Sep 1568]; Aberdeen KS.1.64 [21 Dec 1574]; ACR.40.414 [10 Feb 1602]; Aberdeen KS.2.30 [10 Jun 1603]; Old Ab CMB.1.41 [3 Mar 1606].
144 Elgin KS.2.34 [3 Feb 1600]; Elgin KS.2.57v [8 Oct 1600]; Elgin KS.2.56v [12 Oct 1600]; Elgin KS.2.57v [22 Oct 1600]; Elgin KS.2.58r [29 Oct 1600]; Elgin KS.2.61r [7 Jan 1601]; Elgin KS.2.64r–v [27 Feb 1601].
145 McCallum, "'Fatheris and provisioners of the puir'", p. 79.

146 McCallum, "'Fatheris and provisioners of the puir'", p. 82.
147 McPherson, *The Kirk's Care of the Poor*, pp. 196–198; John McCallum, "Charity doesn't begin at home: ecclesiastical poor relief beyond the parish, 1560–1650", *Journal of Scottish Historical Studies* 32:2 (2012), pp. 107–126, at p. 124.
148 McPherson, *The Kirk's Care of the Poor*, p. 203.
149 ACR.28.323 [15 Nov 1574]; ACR.31.488 [28 Sep 1584]; Elgin KS.2.72r [14 Jun 1601]; Elgin KS.2.74r [12 Jul 1601]; ACR.40.414 [10 Feb 1602].
150 McPherson, *The Kirk's Care of the Poor*, p. 204.
151 McPherson, *The Kirk's Care of the Poor*, p. 201.
152 Steve Hindle, "Dependency, shame and belonging: badging the deserving poor, c.1550–1750", *Cultural and Social History* 1 (2004), pp. 6–35, at p. 8.
153 ACR.26.209 [2 Sep 1566]; Aberdeen KS.1.27 [24 Sep 1568]; ACR.28.323 [15 Nov 1574]; ACR.31.490 [28 Sep 1584]; ACR.31.613 [21 May 1585]; Elgin KS.2.48r [1 Jun 1600]; Elgin KS.2.57v [8 Oct 1600]; Elgin KS.2.68v [10 May 1601]; Elgin KS.2.72v [21 Jun 1601]; Elgin KS.2.75r [22 Jul 1601]; Elgin KS.2.81v [29 Nov 1601]; ACR.40.305 [2 Dec 1601]; ACR.40.414 [10 Feb 1602]; Elgin KS.2.91r [21 Feb 1602]; Aberdeen KS.2.6 [10 Oct 1602]; Elgin KS.2.28v [12 Jun 1603]; Elgin KS.2.143r [18 Dec 1603]; Elgin KS.2.149v [14 Feb 1604]; Old Ab CMB.1.27 [14 Jan 1605]; Aberdeen KS.2.192 [13 Apr 1606]; Aberdeen KS.2.205 [13 Jul 1606]; Aberdeen KS.2.299 [19 Jun 1608]; CH2/32/1: Belhelvie KS [31 Jul 1636]; Cramond, *The Annals of Banff*, vol. I, p. 53 [13 Dec 1624].
154 ACR.40.414 [10 Feb 1602]; Aberdeen KS.1.66 [26 Jan 1575].
155 McPherson, *The Kirk's Care of the Poor*, p. 184.
156 McCallum, "'Fatheris and provisioners of the puir'", p. 86.
157 In September 1595 the council ordered him a uniform of blue cloth with the city's arms emblazoned on the left sleeve, an indication that he had been in regular employment before this time. It was not until 1667 that the increasing transmission of letters between Aberdeen and Edinburgh became a formal twice-weekly service, extended two years later to Inverness; ACR.54.725–728 [2 Jan 1667]; ACR.54.733–734 [2 Jan 1667]; A.R.B. Haldane, *Three Centuries of Scottish Posts: an Historical Survey to 1836* (Edinburgh: Edinburgh University Press, 1971), pp. 6, 16–18; William Lewins, *Her Majesty's Mails: A History of the Post-Office, and an Industrial Account of its Present Condition* (London: Sampson Low, Son, and Marston, 1865), pp. 62–64.
158 ACR.31.666 [4 Sep 1585]; ACR.40.305 [2 Dec 1601]; ACR.40.413 [10 Feb 1602]; ACR.41.356 [13 Sep 1603]; ACR.41.402 [7 Oct 1603]; ACR.41.408 [11 Oct 1603]; ACR.42.314 [14 Aug 1605]; ACR.42.792 [24 Jun 1606]; ACR.43.071 [20 Apr 1607]; ACR.43.073 [22 Apr 1607]; ACR.43.077 [24 Apr 1607]; ACR.52/1.265 [28 Apr 1636]; ACR.52/1.299 [5 Oct 1636].
159 AGA [1601–02]; ACR.40.767 [8 Sep 1602]; AGA [1604–05]; ACR.42.314 [14 Aug 1605]; ATA, p. 560 [1629–30].
160 ACR.40.413 [10 Feb 1602]; ACR.41.999 [8 Dec 1604]; ACR.43.073 [22 Apr 1607]; ACR.43.077 [24 Apr 1607].
161 Brechin: AGA [18 Aug 1597]; AGA [1604–05]; Edinburgh: ACR.41.714–715 [4 Jun 1604]; ATA, p. 758 [1636–37].
162 They were successful in their installation on two occasions of their nominees for bishop of Aberdeen; Barry Robertson, *Lordship and Power in the North of Scotland: The Noble House of Huntly, 1603–1690* (Edinburgh: John Donald, 2011), pp. 22–23, 26–27, 183–184.
163 Robertson, *Lordship and Power*, pp. 18, 21.
164 AGA [2 Oct 1603]; AGA [1604–1605]; Alistair Tayler and Henrietta Tayler, *The House of Forbes* (Aberdeen: Third Spalding Club, 1937); William Forbes (ed.),

Genealogy of the Family of Forbes, from the Account of Mr Mathew Lumsden of Tulliekerne, written in 1580 (Inverness: Printed at the Journal Office, 1819).

165 RPC.2/1.112 [1 Aug 1625].

166 AGA [1601–02]. This might have been prompted by a decree from the Privy Council prohibiting crewmen arriving by sea from docking at any Scottish port without first having received a licence from resident officials; RPC.1/6.289 [26 Sep 1601]; AGA [2 Oct 1603].

167 ACR.41.408 [11 Oct 1603]; AGA [22 Oct 1603].

168 Munro, *Memorials of the Aldermen, Provosts, and Lord Provosts of Aberdeen*, p. 126; George Burnett, *The Family of Burnett of Leys: With Collateral Branches* [edited by James Allardyce] (Aberdeen: New Spalding Club, 1901), p. 32.

169 John Mackintosh, *History of the Valley of the Dee, from the Earliest Times to the Present Day* (Aberdeen: Taylor and Henderson, 1895), pp. 28, 72.

170 Robertson, *Lordship and Power*, p. 19.

171 Turriff and Kincardine: AGA [1604–05]; Forbes: AGA [1611–12].

172 Elgin KS.2.61r [7 Jan 1601]; Elgin KS.2.64r–64v [27 Feb 1601]; ACR.42.792 [24 Jun 1606]; Aberdeen KS.2.206 [13 Jul 1606].

173 Todd, *The Culture of Protestantism*, p. 11.

174 Alexandra Parma Cook and Noble David Cook, *The Plague Files: Crisis Management in Sixteenth-Century Seville* (Baton Rouge: Louisiana State University Press, 2009).

175 ACR.26.637 [2 Oct 1568].

176 Gilbert Skene, *Ane Breve Descriptioun of the Pest, quhair in the causis, signis and sum speciall preseruatioun and cure thairof ar contenit* (Edinburgh, 1568), p. 17.

177 ACR.31.612 [21 May 1585].

178 ACR.31.488 [28 Sep 1584]; ACR.31.612 [21 May 1585]; ACR.41.408 [11 Oct 1603]; ACR.41.715 [4 Jun 1604]; ACR.42.315 [14 Aug 1605]; ACR.43.077 [24 Apr 1607]; ACR.43.073 [22 Apr 1607].

179 'God forbid': ACR.41.673 [8 May 1604]; ACR.42.314 [14 Aug 1605]; ACR.43.071 [20 Apr 1607]; ACR.43.765 [8 Nov 1608]; RPC.2/1.77 [19 Jul 1625]; God be praised': ACR.40.767 [8 Sep 1602]; ACR.40.842 [20 Oct 1602]; ACR.41.999 [8 Dec 1604]; ACR.42.1080 [26 Dec 1606].

180 ACL.1.094 [4 Nov 1603].

181 ACR.41.408 [11 Oct 1603].

182 ACL.1.067 [4 Mar 1637].

183 NAS: GD124/15/27/231: Correspondence and Personal Papers of the Erskine Family, Earls of Mar and Kellie: Letter to John, Earl of Mar, from Thomas, Viscount of Fentoun [Fenton], later Earl of Kellie. Deaths from the Plague [29 Jul 1625].

184 'Manifauld sinnis': Aberdeen KS.2.324 [9 Nov 1608]; 'contempt of the gospell': Aberdeen KS.2.203 [22 Jun 1606]; Sabbath-breaking and 'harlotrie': Aberdeen KS.2.318 [9 Oct 1608]; 'desolation': Elgin KS.2.72r [12 Jun 1601]; 'prophaine pastymes': Elgin KS.2.157v [25 May 1604].

185 Aberdeen KS.2.324 [13 Nov 1608].

186 Aberdeen KS.2.206 [20 July 1606]. Wakes had also been banned by the council during an earlier epidemic; ACR.31.489 [28 Sep 1584]. Raeburn points out that frivolous behaviour would also have appeared unseemly during what ought to have been a sombre occasion; Gordon D. Raeburn, "Death, superstition, and common society following the Scottish Reformation", *Mortality* 21:1 (2016), pp. 36–51, at p. 41; Todd, *The Culture of Protestantism*, pp. 212–213, notes the particular concern to repress the practical jokes associated with the ritual.

187 Aberdeen KS.2.206 [13 Jul 1606].

188 Alec Ryrie, "The fall and rise of fasting in the British Reformations", in Natalie Mears and Alec Ryrie (eds), *Worship and the Parish Church in Early Modern Britain* (London: Ashgate, 2013), pp. 89–108, at p. 90.

189 Ryrie, "The fall and rise of fasting in the British Reformations", pp. 89–90. Alexandra Walsham, *Providence in Early Modern England* (Oxford: Oxford University Press, 1999), pp. 148–149 points out that

> there was far less difference in practice than Protestants so energetically alleged ... Reformed liturgies for fasting and prayer look like direct substitutes for the corporate acts of contrition by which medieval and continental communities sought to induce God to suspend hostilities against them – albeit without the aid of intermediary sacred beings.

190 Ryrie, "The fall and rise of fasting in the British Reformations", p. 95.

191 *The Order and Doctrine of the General Fast, appointed by the General Assembly of the Church of Scotland, Edinburgh, 15 December 1565* (London, 1603), p. 69; Todd, *The Culture of Protestantism*, p. 346.

192 Ryrie, "The fall and rise of fasting in the British Reformations", pp. 102, 108; Natalie Mears, "Public worship and political participation in Elizabethan England", *Journal of British Studies* 51:1 (2012), pp. 4–25, at p. 20.

193 *The Order and Doctrine of the General Fast*, p. 70.

194 Todd, *The Culture of Protestantism*, p. 348.

195 Natalie Mears, Alasdair Raffe, Stephen Taylor and Philip Williamson (with Lucy Bates) (eds), *National Prayers: Special Worship Since the Reformation, vol. I: Special Prayers, Fasts and Thanksgivings in the British Isles, 1533–1688* (Woodbridge: Boydell, 2013), p. lviii; GD188/20/9/5: Records of the Guthrie family of Guthrie, Angus, Royal and Privy Council correspondence, mostly to the Bishop of Murray [13 Jul 1625].

196 Plague in Edinburgh: Aberdeen KS.2.204 [6 Jul 1606]; Aberdeen KS.2.206 [13 Jul 1606]; Aberdeen KS.2.206 [20 Jul 1606]; Aberdeen KS.2.215 [7 Sep 1606]; Aberdeen KS.2.215 [21 Sep 1606]; Aberdeen KS.2.216 [28 Sep 1606]; Aberdeen KS.2.210 [10 Aug 1606]; plague in Dundee: Aberdeen KS.2.248 [26 Apr 1606]; Aberdeen KS.2.255 [14 Jun 1607]; plague in Elgin: Elgin KS.2.45 [25 Apr 1600]; Elgin KS.2.48v [6 Jun 1600]; Elgin KS.2.55v [29 Aug 1600]; Elgin KS.2.59r [26 Nov 1600]; Elgin KS.2.59v [5 Dec 1600]; Elgin KS.2.62v [30 Jan 1601]; Elgin KS.2.72r [12 Jun 1601]; ACR.39.767 [3 Dec 1600]; Elgin KS.2.147v [27 Jan 1604]; plague in Strachan: Aberdeen KS.2.203 [22 Jun 1606]; Aberdeen KS.2.204 [29 Jun 1606]; Aberdeen KS.2.318 [9 Oct 1608]; plague in Torry: Aberdeen KS.2.320 [16 Oct 1608]; Aberdeen KS.2.322 [23 Oct 1608]; Aberdeen KS.2.323 [30 Oct 1608]; Aberdeen KS.2.327 [20 Nov 1608]; Aberdeen KS.2.328 [27 Nov 1608]; Aberdeen KS.2.329 [4 Dec 1608]; Aberdeen KS.2.333 [12 Dec 1608]; Aberdeen KS.2.324 [9 Nov 1608].

197 Dundee: Aberdeen KS.2.248 [26 Apr 1607]; 'God drawin narrir': Aberdeen KS.2.206 [13 Jul 1606]; Aberdeen KS.2.323 [30 Oct 1608]; echoed precisely in ACR.43.765 [8 Nov 1608].

198 Jane Dawson, "Discipline and the making of Protestant Scotland", in Duncan B. Forrester and Doug Gay (eds), *Worship and Liturgy in Context: Studies and Case Studies in Theology and Practice* (London: SCM Press, 2009), pp. 123–136, at p. 134.

199 Mears *et al.* (eds), *National Prayers: Special Worship since the Reformation*, pp. 57, 204.

200 Aberdeen KS.2.206 [13 Jul 1606].

201 Mears *et al.* (eds), *National Prayers: Special Worship since the Reformation*, p. lx.

202 Aberdeen KS.2.73 [6 May 1604]; Aberdeen KS.2.75 [10 Jun 1604]; AGA [1605–06].

203 Quoted in Alasdair Raffe, "Nature's scourges: the natural world and special prayers, fasts and thanksgivings, 1541–1866", in Peter Clarke and Tony Claydon (eds), *God's Bounty? The Churches and the Natural World* (Woodbridge: Studies in Church History 46, 2010), pp. 237–247, at p. 242. Clerical commentators implied that 'moral regeneration and earnest invocation were an almost infallible means of diverting plagues ... [that] could have near mechanical efficacy', 'a foolproof method of staving off the fatal consequences of sin'; Walsham, *Providence in Early Modern England*, pp. 150–151.
204 ACR.43.765–766 [8 Nov 1608]; ACR.43.903–907 [22 Mar 1609] (though his employment had started on 15 November 1608). Findlayson received subsequent payments of 1*l* and 3*l* 6*s* 8*d*; AGA [1613]; ATA [1617].
205 AGA [22 Nov 1608]. Despite the epidemic on the south side of the Dee, it appears as though the ferry between Futty and Torry continued to make frequent journeys 'during the plaig' as the ferryman was paid to have his boat mended, probably as a result of it having been cleansed; AGA [6 Apr 1609].
206 ACR.43.765–766 [8 Nov 1608].
207 AGA [26 Dec 1608; 20 Jan 1609].
208 This can now be seen set into a wall on an uphill public footpath at the corner of Victoria Street, located beside another grave stone dating from the 1648 epidemic; Historic Environment Scotland website: https://canmore.org.uk/site/36909/stonehaven-plague-burials.
209 AGA [9 Dec 1608].
210 ATA, p. 236 [1608–09].
211 AGA [1605–06].

Bibliography

Bashford, Alison, "Maritime quarantine: linking old world and new world histories", in Alison Bashford (ed.), *Quarantine: Local and Global Histories* (London: Palgrave Macmillan, 2016), pp. 1–12.

Bishop, Bruce B., *The Lands and People of Moray: Part 1: Inverlochty, Mosstowie, Pittendreich, Manbeen, Auchtertyre, Miltonduff and Pluscarden Prior to 1850: In the Parish of Elgin* (Elgin: J. and B. Bishop, 2000).

Bishop, Bruce B., *The Lands and People of Moray: Part 2: Westfield, Quarrywood, Findrassie, Myreside and Spynie, Prior to 1850: In the Parish of Spynie* (Elgin: J. and B. Bishop, 2001).

Blažina Tomič, Zlata and Vesna Blažina, *Expelling the Plague: The Health Office and the Implementation of Quarantine in Dubrovnik, 1377–1533* (Montreal: McGill-Queens' University Press, 2015).

Booker, John, *Maritime Quarantine: The British Experience, c.1650–1900* (Aldershot: Ashgate, 2007).

Bowers, Kristy Wilson, *Plague and Public Health in Early Modern Seville* (Rochester: University of Rochester Press, 2013).

Bulmuş, Birsen, *Plague, Quarantines and Geopolitics in the Ottoman Empire* (Edinburgh: Edinburgh University Press, 2012).

Burnett, George, *The Family of Burnett of Leys: With Collateral Branches* [edited by James Allardyce] (Aberdeen: New Spalding Club, 1901).

Carmichael, Ann G., "The last past plague: the uses of memory in Renaissance epidemics", *Journal of the History of Medicine and Allied Sciences* 53:2 (1998), pp. 132–160.

Cook, Alexandra Parma and Noble David Cook, *The Plague Files: Crisis Management in Sixteenth-Century Seville* (Baton Rouge: Louisiana State University Press, 2009).

Cramond, William, *The Annals of Banff*, vol. I (Aberdeen: New Spalding Club, 1891).

Crawshaw, Jane Stevens, "The places and spaces of early modern quarantine", in Alison Bashford (ed.), *Quarantine: Local and Global Histories* (London: Palgrave Macmillan, 2016), pp. 15–34.

Creighton, Charles, *A History of Epidemics in Britain, vol. I: From A.D. 664 to the Great Plague* [1891] (New York: Barnes and Noble, second edition, 1965).

Dawson, Jane, "Discipline and the making of Protestant Scotland", in Duncan B. Forrester and Doug Gay (eds), *Worship and Liturgy in Context: Studies and Case Studies in Theology and Practice* (London: SCM Press, 2009), pp. 123–136.

Dean, Trevor, "Plague and crime: Bologna, 1348–1351", *Continuity and Change* 30:3 (2015), pp. 367–393.

Dennison, E. Patricia, "Power to the people? The myth of the medieval burgh community", in Sally M. Foster, Allan I. Macinnes and Ranald MacInnes (eds), *Scottish Power Centres: From the Early Middle Ages to the Twentieth Century* (Glasgow: Cruithne, 1998), pp. 100–131.

DesBrisay, Gordon, *Authority and Discipline in Aberdeen, 1650–1700* (University of St Andrews, unpublished PhD thesis, 1989).

Falconer, J.R.D., *Crime and Community in Reformation Scotland: Negotiating Power in a Burgh Society* (London: P and C, 2013).

Forbes, William (ed.), *Genealogy of the Family of Forbes, from the Account of Mr Mathew Lumsden of Tulliekerne, Written in 1580* (Inverness: Printed at the Journal Office, 1819).

Godsman, James (ed.), *A History of the Burgh and Parish of Ellon, Aberdeenshire* (Aberdeen: W. and W. Lindsay, 1958).

Goodare, Julian, "The Aberdeenshire witchcraft panic of 1597", *Northern Scotland* 21:1 (2001), pp. 17–37.

Goodare, Julian, *The Government of Scotland, 1560–1625* (Oxford: Oxford University Press, 2004).

Graham, Michael, *The Uses of Reform: 'Godly Discipline' and Popular Behaviour in Scotland and Beyond, 1560–1610* (Leiden: Brill, 1996).

Haldane, A.R.B., *Three Centuries of Scottish Posts: An Historical Survey to 1836* (Edinburgh: Edinburgh University Press, 1971).

Haswell-Smith, Hamish, *The Scottish Islands: A Comprehensive Guide to Every Scottish Island* (Edinburgh: Canongate, 2004).

Hindle, Steve, "Dependency, shame and belonging: badging the deserving poor, c.1550–1750", *Cultural and Social History* 1 (2004), pp. 6–35.

Historic Environment Scotland: https://canmore.org.uk/site/36909/stonehaven-plague-burials.

Kermode, Jennifer I., "Urban decline? The flight from office in late medieval York", *Economic History Review*, new series 35:2 (1982), pp. 179–198.

Langley, Chris R., "Lying sick to die: informal care and authority in Scotland, ca.1600–1660", *Sixteenth Century Journal* 48:1 (2017), pp.27–46.

Lenman, Bruce and Geoffrey Parker, "Crime and control in Scotland, 1500–1800", *History Today* 30:1 (1980), pp. 13–17.

Lenman, Bruce, "The limits of godly discipline in the early modern period with particular reference to England and Scotland", in Kaspar von Greyerz (ed.), *Religion and Society in Early Modern Europe, 1500–1800* (London: Allen and Unwin, 1984), pp. 124–145.

Lewins, William, *Her Majesty's Mails: A History of the Post-Office, and an Industrial Account of its Present Condition* (London: Sampson Low, Son, and Marston, 1865).

MacKay, William (ed.), *Chronicles of the Frasers, The Wardlaw Manuscript ... by James Fraser, 916–1674* (Edinburgh: Scottish History Society, 1905).

Mackintosh, John, *History of the Valley of the Dee, from the Earliest Times to the Present Day* (Aberdeen: Taylor and Henderson, 1895).

Mair, Thomas, *Records of the Parish of Ellon* (Aberdeen: A. Brown and Co., 1876).

Mann, A.J., "The law of the person: parliament and social control", in K.M. Brown and A.R. MacDonald (eds), *The History of the Scottish Parliament, vol. 3: Parliament in Context: 1235–1707* (Edinburgh: Edinburgh University Press, 2010), pp. 186–215.

Mann, A., "Introduction: a brief history of an ancient institution: the Scottish parliament", *Scottish Parliamentary Review* 1:1 (2013), pp. 1–27.

Maxwell-Stuart, P.G., "Witchcraft and the Kirk in Aberdeenshire, 1596–97", *Northern Scotland* 18:1 (1998), pp. 1–14.

McCallum, John, "Charity doesn't begin at home: ecclesiastical poor relief beyond the parish, 1560–1650", *Journal of Scottish Historical Studies* 32:2 (2012), pp. 107–126.

McCallum, John, "Charity and conflict: poor relief in mid-seventeenth-century Dundee", *Scottish Historical Review* 95:1 (2016), pp. 30–56.

McCallum, John, "'Fatheris and provisioners of the puir': Kirk Sessions and poor relief in post-Reformation Scotland", in John McCallum (ed.), *Scotland's Long Reformation: New Perspectives on Scottish Religion, c.1500–c.1660* (Leiden: Brill, 2016), pp. 69–86.

McInnes, C.T. (ed.), *Accounts of the Treasurer of Scotland, vol. XII: 1566–1574* (Edinburgh: Scottish Record Office, 1970).

McKay, Denis, "Parish life in Scotland, 1500–1560", *Innes Review* 10:2 (1959), pp. 237–267.

McPherson, J.M., *The Kirk's Care of the Poor, with Special Reference to the North East of Scotland* (Aberdeen: John Avery and Co., 1941).

Mears, Natalie, "Public worship and political participation in Elizabethan England", *Journal of British Studies* 51:1 (2012), pp. 4–25.

Mears, Natalie, Alasdair Raffe, Stephen Taylor and Philip Williamson (with Lucy Bates) (eds), *National Prayers: Special Worship Since the Reformation, vol. I: Special Prayers, Fasts and Thanksgivings in the British Isles, 1533–1688* (Woodbridge: Boydell, 2013).

Mitchison, Rosalind, "Poor relief and health care in Scotland, 1575–1710", in Ole Peter Grell and Andrew Cunningham (eds), *Health Care and Poor Relief in Protestant Europe, 1500–1700* (London: Routledge, 1997), pp. 220–233.

Munro, Alexander M., *Memorials of the Aldermen, Provosts, and Lord Provosts of Aberdeen, 1272–1895* (Aberdeen: privately printed, 1897).

Naphy, William G., *Plagues, Poisons and Potions: Plague-Spreading Conspiracies in the Western Alps, c. 1530–1640* (Manchester: Manchester University Press, 2002).

Raeburn, Gordon D., "Death, superstition, and common society following the Scottish Reformation", *Mortality* 21:1 (2016), pp. 36–51.

Raffe, Alasdair, "Nature's scourges: the natural world and special prayers, fasts and thanksgivings, 1541–1866", in Peter Clarke and Tony Claydon (eds), *God's Bounty? The Churches and the Natural World* (Woodbridge: Studies in Church History 46, 2010), pp. 237–247.

Ritchie, John, "A plague 'testimonial' of the sixteenth century", *Caledonian Medical Journal*, new series 15 (1932), pp. 94–98.

Ritchie, John, "Quarantine for plague in Scotland during the sixteenth and seventeenth centuries", *Edinburgh Medical Journal* 55 (1948), pp. 691–701.

Ritchie, John, "James Henrysoun, 'chirurgian to the poore'", *Medical History* 4:1 (1960), pp. 70–79.

Robertson, Barry, *Lordship and Power in the North of Scotland: The Noble House of Huntly, 1603–1690* (Edinburgh: John Donald, 2011).

Ryrie, Alec, "The fall and rise of fasting in the British Reformations", in Natalie Mears and Alec Ryrie (eds), *Worship and the Parish Church in Early Modern Britain* (London: Ashgate, 2013), pp. 89–108.

Stewart, Laura, "Poor relief in Edinburgh and the famine of 1621–24", *International Review of Scottish Studies* 30 (2005), pp. 5–41.

Stewart, Laura A.M., *Urban Politics and the British Civil Wars: Edinburgh, 1617–53* (Leiden: Brill, 2006).

Tayler, Alistair and Henrietta Tayler, *The House of Forbes* (Aberdeen: Third Spalding Club, 1937).

Taylor, Louise B. (ed.), *Aberdeen Shore Works Accounts, 1596–1670* (Aberdeen: Aberdeen University Press, 1972).

Todd, Margo, *The Culture of Protestantism in Early Modern Scotland* (New Haven: Yale University Press, 2002).

Walsham, Alexandra, *Providence in Early Modern England* (Oxford: Oxford University Press, 1999).

Walton, Kristen Post, "Scotland's 'City on a Hill': The godly and the political community in early Reformation Scotland", in Michael J. Halvorson and Karen E. Spierling (eds), *Defining Community in Early Modern Europe* (Ashgate: Aldershot, 2008), pp. 247–265.

Wray, Shona Kelly, *Communities and Crisis: Bologna During the Black Death* (Leiden: Brill, 2009).

5 Aberdeen's final plague

The outbreak of 1647–48

In a sermon given in Edinburgh towards the end of 1644, the blind preacher Archibald Skeldie explained to his congregation how God's wrath against Scotland was then being manifested: 'by the devouring sword that hath killed many of our brethren in the North, and by the plague of pestilence that for certaine months hath continued in the South, wherewith now this Citie and the places about are fearfully threatned'.[1] During the preceding months plague had spread from the north of England into parts of the Borders and, in the event, was to reach the capital by April 1645. While the Reverend Skeldie was advising his listeners in Edinburgh how best to behave in the event of plague striking their city, residents of Aberdeen were being besieged by the hand of man rather than of God. The 'sword' in the north to which Skeldie referred belonged to the marquis of Montrose, who had defeated a Covenanting army at Tippermuir near Perth on 1 September, and stormed and sacked Aberdeen a fortnight later as part of an ongoing campaign of civil hostilities. An important factor both for contemporaries and for modern observers analysing the incidence and effects of plague in the 1640s is the complete entanglement of outbreaks and the concurrent civil wars of the Three Kingdoms in these considerations. Commentators were quick to note this, with regard not only to its progression but also to its initial causation. The contemporary Aberdeen-based Royalist John Spalding reckoned that 'riving the King's prerogative frae him' was the 'mother-sin' that had caused 'this misery, God's wrath, pest and sword',[2] while James Fraser, author of the Wardlaw Manuscript, implied that the outbreak at Aberdeen was attributable to divine vengeance for the earlier purging of King's College by a visitation from the Covenanting General Assembly.[3] Patrick Gordon of Ruthven, whose family was one of the major powers in the north of Scotland at this time, noted in his own Royalist account of the wars that 'from Edinburgh, Lithgoe, Striwilling, and all other places, the plague ... both chessed and followed' the Covenanting troops and attributed this to God punishing their 'wicked intensiones and vnlawefull designes'.[4] We must be mindful of the havoc wreaked by the wars when analysing the effects on Aberdeen of its final epidemic. The widespread economic and social dislocation caused both by the sacking of the city and by the prolonged quartering of troops there meant that its infrastructure was already severely weakened, and its long-suffering residents embattled and wearied, years before plague arose within the city for the first time in almost a century.

An altered Aberdeen

This book has so far suggested that an efficient communications network to warn of nearby infection and compliance with the preventative legislation imposed by civic authorities might have helped to ensure that, after the mid-sixteenth century, Aberdeen completely escaped the bouts of plague that repeatedly hit surrounding areas. Almost a century had passed by the time the disease struck again, so the civil wars of the preceding several years were only one factor which had altered the social, political, religious and economic make-up of the city during the intervening plague-free decades. The Aberdeen of the 1640s was significantly different from that of the 1550s. To begin with, the population of the city had changed markedly, both in terms of size and in likely attitude towards plague. The frequency with which the affliction struck other parts of Scotland (as well as further afield) and threatened Aberdeen's neighbours and environs would never have allowed the town to forget the danger that plague posed. Nevertheless, it could be assumed that with the passage of time local residents might have been tempted to become complacent about the disease. After all, in terms of experience (for which there was no real substitute) none had personally lived through plague: by the 1640s two generations would have come and gone without experiencing an outbreak first-hand. Barely any surviving resident would even have heard tales from older relatives of their own youthful experience of such a devastating event. Moreover, local authorities would have lost the valuable insights that personal experience could have afforded them in any subsequent outbreak. In short, by 1647 the overwhelming majority of the population and, especially, those in power had neither personal nor second-hand experience of plague in Aberdeen. Experience was, after all, one of the greatest factors in deciding the course of action undertaken within an urban environment actively beset by plague. City governments typically instigated standard regulations and would then adapt or add to them as time and circumstances required and allowed, as had been the case when Aberdeen was struck by prolonged outbreaks during the 1510s and the 1540s. Since the population and magistracy in these previous epidemics were to a significant extent comprised of the same individuals, it is possible to assume a certain degree of continuity in experience both at the leadership and popular levels. By 1647 this chain of civic experience had been broken in the city. Its magistrates could not count on a body of medical workers or officials, let alone a population, who had had experience with plague and the regulations necessary to control its spread. This situation might give rise to naivety at best, apathy at worst. This was a concern which the council had bemoaned as early as 1603, when it noted that, given that the burgh had then been free from plague for fifty-five years, residents were beginning to regard plague statutes with 'ane sluggische cairlesnes' and had 'littill fear' in disobeying them.[5] In the event, this was only halfway through its plague-free period. How much more lethargic and careless might residents be after nearly an entire century without direct experience of the disease?

Other, equally significant changes had taken place within Aberdeen in the plague-free period between the 1550s and the 1640s. Not only was the population now composed of an entirely different, inexperienced, generation and the inherent disadvantages this entailed, it had also increased dramatically in size. Throughout the first half of the sixteenth century, intermittent outbreaks and subsequent migration from the hinterland ensured that Aberdeen's population levels remained broadly unchanged, at around 5,000. From the 1570s there was an upward trend which continued well into the seventeenth century, during which years plague was absent. By 1640–44, the period immediately before the disease hit, the city's population averaged 8,300. This was approaching twice the number of inhabitants there had been in 1550: thus, through immigration and natural increase (a not unimportant factor in a city not regularly culled by plague), Aberdeen's population had significantly increased, if not quite doubled, within the space of a century.

This affected the city's physical size and, hence, its physical boundaries and defences, which were never completely secure at the best of times. It also placed additional pressure on available resources: for example, the actual amount of arable land in the immediate environs of the city did not 'grow' along with the urban population, which would come to be particularly troublesome during crises such as an epidemic when the number of poor, both transient and those native to the city, markedly increased. The trade embargoes occasioned by nearby outbreaks complicated the necessity of relying on this immediate hinterland at a time when there was an increase in the actual number of mouths to feed. The consequent rise in the number of unemployed, and thus poor, made the authorities' commitment to the common weal (both in terms of sustenance and maintaining social order) all the more difficult. Their concern about 'the daylie incres of pepill' had occasioned a short-lived proposal in 1595 to divide the town into four parishes for the 'edifeing of euerie inhabitant', 'comfort of the seik' and 'releiff of the puire', and it is possible that they also felt an increasing administrative burden in dealing with the rising population.[6]

While the population doubled over the century as a whole, there were obvious intermittent fluctuations in levels. Although Aberdeen avoided the outbreaks of plague which struck its neighbouring settlements during the ninety-eight years after 1549, it did fall victim periodically to other mortality crises. One such crisis that has yet to be explained took place across the north-east in 1616 and 1617, during which time burial numbers far exceeded their yearly average.[7] It may have been more than coincidence, therefore, that more skilled medical practitioners than usual were made burgesses around this time, with a physician, a surgeon and an apothecary admitted by the council in 1617, followed by Patrick Dun, the fourth mediciner at King's College, in

May 1618.[8] Smallpox outbreaks occurred in 1635 and 1641 throughout Aberdeenshire, prompting Spalding to write of

> ane great death, both in burgh and land, of young bairness in the pox, so that nyne or ten children would be buried in New Aberdein in one day, and continowed a long time; all for our sins, and yet not taken to heart.[9]

Aside from these diseases, famines helped to dictate population fluctuations. There was an increase in the frequency of periodic dearth, with five such instances recorded during the second half of the sixteenth century.[10] The early seventeenth century fared only slightly better. Harvest failures in two consecutive years caused severe famine in 1623 and typhus probably followed as a secondary cause of catastrophe, with disease, starvation and vagrancy combining to produce mortality at least twice that of previous years.[11] In February 1624 the council took action over the numbers of poor within the town, forbidding excessive banqueting at christenings because it was still considered to be a time of 'darth and famyne, [with] mony poor anes dieing and starving at dyikkes and undir staires for cauld and hunger'.[12] In spite of this concern, no apparent action was taken to provide the support they acknowledged was desperately required, especially as continued bad weather and food shortages further hindered the population's recovery.[13] The arrival of plague in Aberdeen in 1647, therefore, struck a population weakened by a number of mortality crises.

Aberdeen and the Covenanting wars

Furthermore, the city was then caught up in the cataclysmic civil wars of the Three Kingdoms and had particularly suffered due to its centrality to the hostilities over the preceding years.[14] The National Covenant proclaimed in 1638 had been adhered to by Scots opposed to Charles I's intended 'anglicanisation' of the Kirk in his northern kingdom, with its hierarchy of Episcopalian-style bishops with the monarch assuming primacy. Political and ideological concerns as much as liturgical issues underpinned the Bishops' War of 1639 and subsequent hostilities, which were played out on both sides of the border as well as across the Irish Sea. Though early in 1644 Charles's Scottish supporters 'were rather thin on the ground',[15] the north-east was one area where Royalist sympathies were relatively strong, and the king's cause was given a boost in April when the powerful earl of Huntly launched a short-lived rebellion and seized Aberdeen. Though his efforts were quickly suppressed by forces under the marquis of Argyll, Huntly's support was to prove crucial in the course of the war in the north-east, particularly the important role the city of Aberdeen was to play. This culminated in the 'Battle for Aberdeen' on 13 September 1644 when Royalist forces under the marquis of Montrose, numbering some 1,500 infantry and seventy cavalry, stormed the city.[16] The fighting gave way to a destructive spree of violence and robbery as the visiting troops sought material rewards for their efforts. Vivid descriptions survive of the destruction caused: men were killed indiscriminately and their corpses left to rot openly, while their wives were raped or forced into servitude, the city jail was stormed and widescale looting occurred for some days after the battle itself had ended. The mercenaries went on the rampage, 'hewing and cutting down all maner of man they could overtak within the toune, vpone the streites, or in thair houssis ... but mercy or remeid', lamented Spalding. These men killed, robbed and plundered the town 'at thair plesour', so that all that could be heard was 'pitifull hovling, crying, weiping, mvrning, throw all the streittis'.[17]

The existing garrison had been mustered from Fife in April 1644 and so had been stationed in Aberdeen for five months before it saw action. During this time the troops had placed extreme pressure on the resources of the city even though their numbers had fallen, due to desertion, from 700 in May to 400 by September, particularly as the regiment still claimed quartering for 1,000 men.[18] Their ongoing presence resulted in myriad grievances for the inhabitants. Not least of these was the severe financial burden which the soldiers' presence occasioned. By January 1646 it had become necessary to request victuals, as the citizens were so badly troubled by the town's hardship that their 'groans and cryes [were] intollerable and wold pearce the hardest heart'. The lucrative plaiding trade had all but ground to a halt by this time,[19] while the trade in victuals had also been disrupted as the soldiers 'hes stoppit the bringing in of meill, malt, fewall for fyre and all other provisions necessar for maintenance'. Residents were 'not able to enterteine thamselffis and thair famelies, ffar less to enterteine two regimentis thair officers and sojors upon frie quarteris'.[20] By October of that year the town had suffered greatly at the hands of the troops, who had plundered houses, killing and looting as they went, and exacting money without repayments. Even its wealthier inhabitants had been reduced to begging and the council had become forced to request that the city be freed from its substantial debts. The once brave town had become a 'dieing and decaying member of the comonwealthe'.[21] Residents could no longer earn their living, had been forced to live hand to mouth and could not even buy peat in order to bake their own bread.[22]

It is quite clear that many other burghs in the north-east suffered greatly from the ravages of the civil wars, particularly as a result of the garrisoning of and plundering by troops from both sides. Banff was plundered at least twice, in April 1644 and again in March 1645, when Montrose visited.[23] The Elgin Kirk Session lamented in 1645 that 'the Irisches with Montrose and Col. cam in to Elgin and spoyled it...', while the subsequent garrisoning of troops further strained the burgh's resources.[24] The Inverness council appealed to parliament in 1646 for 300 merks due to the 'great lossis ... and sufferinges [of the] nytbouris and inhabitantis of the towne ... dureing the tyme of the troubles'.[25] Other burghs such as Forres and Nairn were 'in a constant state of turmoil' during the wars, with the depletion by 1648 of the former's funds due to the quartering of troops, forcing their relocation to the west of the river

Findhorn.[26] Closer to Aberdeen, inhabitants of Inverurie were also severely put upon by being required to supply staples including oats, malt, beer, mutton, butter and candles to the soldiers billeted there.[27]

Parson James Gordon of Rothiemay's lamentation in 1660 that 'the civill warrs did overrun all' starkly summarises the domination that the hostilities had over life in many of the north-east's burghs throughout the decade of the 1640s and beyond.[28] In March 1647, weeks before plague was identified as having broken out in Aberdeen, parliament agreed to discharge the quartering of troops in the city 'in respect off their heauie burdens', following an impassioned plea by its representative at the Commission of Estates conveying 'the lamentable estait of this toun, and great sufferings thairof'.[29] Plague's arrival severely exacerbated an already unstable, disrupted and fearful community. Had the city not already been so weakened economically, psychologically, demographically and socially by the hostilities, the subsequent epidemic might not have wrought so much damage.

Plague returns to Scotland

The transmission of infection was known to occur when many bodies existed in close confinement and, with the movement of troops engaged in the civil wars of the Three Kingdoms, so plague spread from England into Scotland. On 12 October 1644, Covenanting forces under the Scottish general Alexander Leslie had taken the city of Newcastle, leading Spalding to note that 'the pest follouit Newcastell to Edinbrughe and divers uther pairtis, to oure gryte lois'.[30] Several local mariners identified goods from that city as a potential source of infection and quickly warned magistrates in Aberdeen about the 'English catche that came from Newcastell, being suspect of the plague'. Taking advantage of the presence in the town of troops, the council commandeered several of them 'to hold aff the men that came in [that] Inglish catche', and rewarded Johne Andersone's wife in Torry for summoning them as well as the mariners who had initially warned of their arrival. The suspect merchandise was most likely disinfected, to judge from the payment of six shillings to 'ane cleanger', though this could also have been a precautionary retainer in the event of infection being detected within the city.[31] While Aberdeen continued to escape plague at this time, by the end of the year it had taken hold in parts of the Borders and the south-west of Scotland, including the settlements of Langholm and Largs, where huts were erected to house victims undergoing quarantine.[32] Magistrates in Glasgow became alarmed at plague's proximity and on 9 November ordered all residents to strengthen their back walls and prohibited them from receiving unlicensed strangers.[33] Over in the east, authorities in Edinburgh had granted clean bills of health to a number of ships bound for the Spanish port of Cadiz and tried to ensure that the city remained plague-free by imposing quarantine on all vessels and people arriving from suspect places, with Newcastle singled out.[34]

But in the event, these measures could only hold off plague for so long. Maritime links may have been responsible for the appearance of the disease in Bo'ness early in the new year, prompting parliament on 16 January 1645 to appoint a commission to segregate the infected and to order guards to shoot dead any who would escape to the surrounding populous areas.[35] Despite this, plague swept through much of the central belt as well as the Borders, with infection reported in Berwickshire, Kelso and Govan before breaking out in the capital by April, resulting in steep expenditure for the construction of a quarantine camp and for the payment of watchers, cleansers and gravediggers.[36] Edinburgh's magistrates also ordered its physician Dr Jon Paulitius (to whom they had first paid a retainer in December) to visit 'all such persones [that] sall happen to deceis', and had subsequently to employ George Rae as an additional (or possibly replacement) physician.[37] The high school and College shut and additionally, as Spalding recorded, 'divers houssis [were] cloissit wp, many fleing the toune; and thair Committee, courtis of kirk and Parliament . . . removed out of Edinbrughe'.[38] On 4 May the former bishop of Moray, John Guthrie, by then retired to his Angus estate, lamented in his diary that due to the present turmoil believers 'suld seairch and try our selffis and turne againe to the lord . . . and mak confessioun of our sinnes'.[39] Accordingly, the spread of the 'fearful consuming plague of pestilence' prompted the General Assembly to proclaim a fast to be held due to 'the encrease of weight and bitternes of the Lord's rodde vpon us for sinne'.[40] Sir Ewan Cameron of Locheil recounted that when defeated Covenanting forces stopped at Stirling the following month on their journey south, Archibald Campbell, the marquis of Argyll 'durst not venture out of his coach for the pestilence, which had already almost desolated that town, and raged with excessive furry through all Brittain'.[41]

Meanwhile, plague was spreading north and moving closer to Aberdeen. Towards the end of June the city's provost, Robert Farquhar, reported to the council the worrying news that the disease

> is rageing abroad in this kingdome, and dyverse of our nichtbours burges infected thairwith: lykeas the same wes come neirer to our selues, being in the schirrefdome of Angus, quharin the touns of Drumkilbo and Kirktoun of Megle wer infected with the said plague, as we ar informed.[42]

The precise reporting of infection on these landed estates suggests that first-hand accounts continued to be conveyed and indicates the efficacy of the networks of communication that might very well have helped Aberdeen to stave off plague during the previous century. Magistrates responded by instigating a 'strict watch' to be maintained round the clock at each entrance to the burgh, all of which were to be locked overnight. Notwithstanding the present council's lack of experience of outbreaks, the instinct to monitor the city's points of entry had a clear rationale, given the reports of approaching plague.

A watch entailed the monitoring of all those wishing to enter the city via its official entrances and, as it functioned in theory both as the first and last line of defence, it continued to be important to ensure the calibre of those posted to it. Council orders frequently refer to the need for 'sufficient' and 'honest' people to be engaged as watchers. In this first piece of civic legislation concerned with impending plague to be issued in almost a decade (with the last regulation before that being decreed to combat the outbreak of 1608–09 and therefore hardly within living memory for many), magistrates probably hand-picked the sixteen men appointed to the task and ordered them to present themselves 'in proper persone', that is, to prevent their evasion of duty by sending along a less reliable substitute. But in the event, this is most likely what happened. It seems as though the lack of experience of plague did indeed make those appointed to the watch less inclined to appreciate its threat and take their duties seriously, in spite of the punishments threatened by the council for negligence. On 6 August the watch was reimposed and extended to all inhabitants, who were to take their turn 'in thair awne personnes' (with the exception of widows and elderly men, who were permitted to find a suitable representative to take their place).[43] Clearly residents saw this duty as an unwelcome imposition by the council, for a fortnight later magistrates gathered the citizens together to impress upon them the necessity of watching the town. By this time the authorities had 'receavit certane intelligence' contained in a number of letters that plague had also broken out in the relatively major port of Peterhead to the north.[44] This outbreak proved to be the most severe the inhabitants of Peterhead had experienced; it forced local authorities to burn down the tollbooth, site of its first known victims, and subsequently to build eight timber huts for the isolation of the sick and to dig deep trenches in which to bury its estimated three hundred fatalities.[45] The correspondence received by the council was read out to those present and feedback sought about what ought to be done. By this consultation process the council was able to persuade residents that the watch was the best course of action to prevent plague spreading to the town and probably also made them less grudging about doing their duty. Entry was to be prohibited for those coming from Peterhead or from southern locations suspected of plague, unless they could produce a sufficient testimonial signed by the minister of the parish whence they had come, affirming 'upon his conscience' that they were free from infection. The fact that those travelling from infected places were not automatically barred is interesting and indicates a certain naivety on the part of magistrates, perhaps attributable to their lack of direct experience of outbreaks.

It might be surmised that this lack of experience would make the authorities more wary of implementing any regulation to curb plague that might damage local commercial life, but this was not the case. Despite the inevitable disruption to regional trade, they also banned residents from buying cloth (a material deemed particularly susceptible to harbouring infection) from 'cuntre people' or attending one of Aberdeenshire's major commercial events, the three-day long St Bartholomew's Fair.[46] Despite this particular prohibition on travel, the council did permit three inhabitants to journey 'towards Ross' a fortnight later, being satisfied that they had not had contact with any suspect place.[47] As part of the ideological commitment to the common weal, it was important for magistrates to protect the health not only of those living under their immediate jurisdiction but also of those outside it. To this end, the need for reliable testimonials was applied to those wishing to leave the burgh as well as enter it. By this time, reports of the earlier carelessness of the watch, perhaps even first-hand accounts, had filtered through to those living in neighbouring settlements, a number of whom wrote to Aberdeen's magistrates expressing their concerns. The council quickly wrote back to reassure them that the watch was being adhered to with due diligence. This would have come as a relief not only to their correspondents but also to residents within the city, as plague had by then spread not only to the north and south of the city but also to the west; knowledge of the existence of infection at Licklyhead near Insch and Raemoir near Banchory, both of which were the seats of country estates, again points to first-hand reports being imparted.[48]

The initial diligence of the watch could only be sustained for so long. On 10 October it was again deemed necessary for the provost to remind the assembled citizens that plague was by now 'both be-south and be-north' of the city and to obtain their consent for the watch to be (re)implemented.[49] It is perhaps not so surprising that the watch was being neglected: after all, barely anyone involved in it had any experience of plague and therefore no proper appreciation of the enormity of the threat. Moreover, participation was a considerable burden, whether in terms of responsibility, time or finance. The council now ordered those able to, to stand guard for a full twenty-four hours beginning at three o'clock in the afternoon. Any resident unable to perform this duty, including the elderly and widows, had to find a reliable replacement at a cost of ten shillings or six shillings plus the provision of meals for the duration of their service on guard. This was a significant imposition, particularly when combined with the financial outlay magistrates additionally demanded of residents obliged to strengthen their back walls and gates against unwarranted entry. In fact, the not infrequent need to reimplement the watch in other burghs indicates that compliance was a problem for magistrates even in places whose residents were personally aware of the damage plague could do. In Dumfries, for example, a burgh which had so far escaped the current epidemic but which had succumbed regularly to plague on previous occasions (the last being in 1623[50]), the council found it necessary to (re)order the watch four separate times in 1645; on the final occasion that December, it was because of 'the slackness of keiping the watche in yis burghe now in such dangerous tymes' that magistrates arranged to co-operate with quartermasters in compelling the watch to report at the proper time and obey orders conscientiously.[51] The imposition of a constant watch was irritating even for residents who were likely to have had experience of plague: how much more of a burden might it have seemed for those who had no such experience?

Notwithstanding (or perhaps because of) the necessity of twice having to reimpose the watch after its initial implementation in June 1645, Aberdeen avoided plague breaking out within its boundaries despite the increasing encroachment of the disease. By the autumn, infection had arisen within Stirling and its vicinity, forcing the council to hold its annual election in a nearby park,[52] and had spread into Fife, most notably affecting Culross and Dunfermline, whose Kirk Session elders recorded the 'distress thair flocks are vnder, because of the plague of pestilence'.[53] Sir James Balfour recorded in November that the ongoing parliamentary infighting had 'prouoked Gods tuo grate seriants aganist [the country], the suord and plauge of pestilence, quho had ploughed vpe the land with deipe furrowes'.[54] Over the course of 1646 plague swept through Edinburgh, Leith, Peebles, Glasgow, Lanark, Perth, Dundee, and many other places, including in Aberdeenshire. Despite this, what is remarkable is that no preventative legislation concerning plague was imposed by the council in Aberdeen during the eighteen months between October 1645 and April 1647, until such occasion when it became necessary to respond to the specific threat of its proximity. It might possibly have been the case that in terms of staving off plague, the concurrent civil war actually helped in this respect. War as much as plague continued to wreak havoc throughout much of Scotland: troops spread infection (with David Leslie's Covenanting army being held responsible for '[leaving] the Pestilence in the country' on their rampage through Argyll in 1647) and also caused fatal secondary infections such as 'war typhus'.[55] The course of hostilities was affected by the outbreak as plague weakened the ability to repel attack, as was the case in Edinburgh, when mortality from infection 'scarce left thrie scoir fensible persones to defend the Town' against the Covenanting forces of the marquis of Montrose, who in the event were prevented from entering anyway by the fear of infection.[56] But in terms of administration the dual threats of plague and war arguably eased the handling of each, both in terms of the tasks undertaken and the personnel required for these. Many of the policies implemented that were ostensibly concerned with the ongoing hostilities – holding emergency council meetings, searching quarters, commissioning reports of the state of nearby settlements, implementing watches, and so on – were all actions that were useful in tackling the threat of infection as well as dissidence. The last of these, in particular, had already been proven to be the most obvious way of preventing plague and in all probability continued to be sufficient. In any case, Aberdeen successfully held off infection until the spring of 1647, by which time plague encircled the city.

Plague reaches Aberdeen

As we have seen, by the end of 1646 the civil wars had caused residents of Aberdeen intolerable hardships – and plague had not even arrived yet. As had been the case in 1603, magistrates held providence responsible for the city being so far spared from the outbreak, expressing their hope in a letter written in November that God would 'hold off us your poore servantis this last & most terrible plague that yit for a little space [our] lives may be preserved for a little while longer'.[57] Weeks later, the captain of one Argyll regiment abandoned his planned visit to Aberdeen 'in respect of his sicknes lyeing in the cuntrie [which] is not as yet cum to this town'.[58] But this state of affairs was not to last. On 12 April 1647 the citizens were summoned to the town house, where the provost Patrick Leslie reported the ominous news of 'certaine intelligence' that the disease had broken out in Inverbervie to the south of the city.[59] Despite the consequent prohibition on receiving strangers from the south and the implementation of a round-the-clock watch, fifteen days later came the even more alarming discovery that infection 'wes werilie instantlie expected to be neir our doore', having broken out in Pitmuckston to the immediate south-west of the city. It was thought to have been brought by a woman arriving from Brechin, where plague had recently killed two members of her family. The most worrying aspect of this news was the possibility that 'the infection wes enterit in this brugh alreadie', since one of the plague victims in Pitmuckston had been a child who had attended school in Aberdeen and had therefore 'had conversation with the children of many of the inhabitants within this burghe'.[60] This disastrous situation was judged to have arisen due to failings in the watch, either through certain citizens simply not participating or else having irresponsibly sent 'some weak nauchtie persone' in their place. Once again the safety of the city had been compromised by the failure of its fundamental defence mechanism. All the authorities could do was to instigate as secure a watch as possible – it was to be on guard both night and day, and to be comprised of one hundred and twenty people, with all 'vigorous and fencible' inhabitants to participate under threat of a substantial fine of one hundred pounds for non-compliance.

Magistrates now also implemented legislation to address the likely presence of plague within the city. For the most part these were typical responses that sought to eliminate (or at least repress) sources of infection within the local environment, as well as to limit interactions between residents of Aberdeen and those in the vicinity, even to the inevitable detriment of regional commercial life. No one was to attend the forthcoming Rood fair in Ellon (which took place annually in early May) or purchase any cloth sourced from it. No interactions, commercial or otherwise, were to take place with the inhabitants of the parish of Nigg which bordered the south bank of the Dee, particularly those in the settlement of Torry. A warrant was to be obtained from a baillie or watcher there before entering Aberdeen from the parish. Within the city itself, dogs and cats (believed to harbour infection in their fur) were to be killed, and poison laid 'for destroying myce and ratons', the first such regulation of its kind. No explanation was provided for this measure and it most likely arose from empirical observation: rodents were naturally drawn to the everyday detritus of the burgh – rotting foodstuffs and the like – and it was precisely these types of conditions that were believed to generate plague. Residents were therefore ordered to remove all middens and filth from the main thoroughfares, particularly before any ploughs or harrows were drawn through the burgh on the way to the fields. The usual proscriptions were also placed on receiving strangers into lodgings and selling clothing. In case infection should break out, the names of the sick were immediately to be given to the baillies of the quarter, though the consequence of forced enclosure for the whole household might have made residents reluctant to comply with this.[61] In recognition of the financial and moral crises that constituted a plague outbreak, all 'ydle and stranger beggars' were ordered to leave. This would allow scarce resources to be directed towards those native poor who actually deserved them, both in order to lessen the threat of social disorder which might arise from the demands of the desperately starving and to appease God through the dispensing of charity to those less fortunate brethren. The banishment of undeserving undesirables also removed from the town one social element who would defile the city 'with all kynd of vyce', as magistrates in Edinburgh had articulated it the previous year.[62] It was to be hoped that doing so would reduce the hardships caused by what the former prelate John Guthrie then termed in his diary the 'desolationes the lord hath made in this land', including the 'plagues of pestilence and famine in many partis'.[63]

In spite of these measures plague swept through the city, bringing with it a sense of panic and uncertainty. In such circumstances magistrates were very aware of the need to maintain social order, but this was a task severely complicated by the disruption to everyday affairs which the epidemic caused. The fear of infection forced the council to suspend its regular meetings from 26 May, 'in respect of the seiknes that wes in this toun'.[64] Debates about the ethics of abandoning one's duties could wait: for now, self-preservation was what mattered. The councillor (and later provost) Alexander Jaffray offered no excuse for fleeing the city at this time, stating in his diary simply that he was 'every day among the sick people, being a magistrate' and so during the 'five or six months' in which plague raged, he 'removed to Kingswells' to the immediate west of the city with his family.[65] Other members of local government probably also sought refuge outside Aberdeen during this time. When magistrates did meet again, on 11 August, they did so on the margins of the city at the Woolmanhill.[66] The town was by this time desperately 'distrest' due not least to the financial burden under which it had laboured 'this long time bygane', no doubt a reference to the damage done not only by plague but also by the continued garrisoning of troops. Magistrates acknowledged 'the great extremitie quhairin the toun stands for the present' and expressed their concern that unless remedy was soon found it would be 'castin loose, and no ordour keipit at all', a most fearful scenario. With no council meetings having taken place, it is probable that *ad hoc* efforts had been made to address the destitution caused by the disruption to trade and likely instances of enclosure following detection of sickness, which went unrecorded. Funds were clearly desperately required and the council's meeting of 11 August was probably an emergency summit to address the worsening crisis. At this meeting the city's baillies were authorised to take any necessary steps to accumulate sufficient funds from possible sources either within the burgh or in the hinterland, with any debts incurred from this to be written off. All their efforts were for the 'weill and saiftie of the distrest toun', so any contribution 'ocht and sould be thankfullie payit'.[67] Having issued this plea, magistrates once again dispersed.

By this time plague had taken hold across much of Scotland. Robert Baillie, Principal of Glasgow University, summed up the dreadful situation in a letter written at Edinburgh on 1 September. 'The pestilence, for the time, vexes us', he lamented to his correspondent William Spang. 'Aberdeen, Brechin, and other parts of the north, are miserably wasted. St Andrews and Glasgow, without great mortality, are so threatened, that the schools and colleges now in all Scotland, except Edinburgh, are scattered'.[68] Tradition has it that most of the staff and students of King's College relocated from Old Aberdeen to Fraserburgh, where classes were held in the former building of the short-lived university, though while such a move was planned, no concrete evidence survives to confirm that it took place.[69] The exception to this was the Divinity class, which the Synod of Aberdeen permitted to meet in Kintore because of the prohibitive cost to the professor Mr William Douglas of moving his numerous family members to Fraserburgh.[70] Marischal College moved from the city of Aberdeen north to Peterhead, which was presumably judged free from plague by then. Commenting some years later James Fraser, who studied at King's in the 1650s and was a boy of around thirteen when the colleges dispersed, noted that during the exodus of its personnel 'the gates and windowes of the University [were] shut up all that time'.[71] Fraser also penned a most evocative description of the disruption to everyday life that plague caused in Aberdeen. Comparing the city with Oxford, whose college life had then also been brought to a standstill by an epidemic, he invited his readers to remember 'Gods visitation uppon these two townes thir last two yeares; the pestilence raged in them, so that the grass was in the streetes, and not a smoake in both townes, but one in old Doctor Duns Chamber'. His description, while alluding to the continuation of Patrick Dun in his post as principal of Marischal College, evokes a scenario of streets devoid of footfall and precious few other signs of habitation, and echoes Baillie's comment that much of the north of Scotland had been 'miserably wasted' by plague.

Six weeks after its last meeting the council convened again to hold its annual election. In order to lessen the possibility of infection this took place in the open air (at Gilcomston), the only recorded instance when a local government election was held outwith the burgh boundaries.[72] The new council held a further crisis meeting that December, at which its only agendum was to make two appointments, those of a cleanser and someone to distribute confiscated items 'to the richt awniris' following the cleansing process.[73] The following week magistrates met once more, whereupon they ordered that new cases of sickness were to be reported to the quartermasters and that unlicensed strangers were to be refused lodgings. Suspect goods were to be forfeited and cleansed through exposure to the wintry 'frost air'.[74] The ongoing plight of the city weighed heavily on councillors' minds, forcing them to take the decision to appeal to parliament to be relieved of the burden of garrisoning soldiers and of paying excise, particularly since they had just reimbursed Sir William Forbes of

Craigievar £1,500 for the meal he had provided to inhabitants at the height of the outbreak.[75]

But by this time it was apparent that the epidemic was at last waning in Aberdeen. Cases began to be heard again by the sheriff court for the first time since the previous April, when plague had entered the city.[76] The council made a series of payments to individuals for the 'help and supplie' they had given the town during 'the tyme of the lait visitatioun', including a cleanser named George Watt.[77] Furthermore, the city's tacksman was given a substantial reprieve on the duty payable on the mills and on the weigh and pack houses by the harbour, due to the 'great losses' sustained due to plague.[78] On 2 March, a letter was received by the Presbytery of Garioch from their counterparts in Aberdeen, calling for a day of thanksgiving to be observed for the deliverance of the city from 'the flying arrow of pestilence'.[79]

This may have been a premature expression of gratitude. As a precautionary measure, magistrates appointed additional cleansers who were to station themselves 'constantlie' at 'the kills' [that is, the kilns] and cleanse any person or goods 'as happens to be infectit', for which a quantity of vinegar was purchased at a cost of twenty pounds.[80] James Graham, who had been acquired from Leith some months previously, was designated 'ane of the principal and chief cleangeris' of the burgh and racked up significant personal expenses including wine, tobacco pipes and the use of a horse.[81] Individuals in Aberdeen continued to be enclosed or quarantined, with elders in Old Aberdeen being forced in July to postpone the trial of an adulterous couple as the male was then lodging with a resident in Aberdeen who was 'suspect of the infectione'.[82] The following month all those enclosed were each given four pounds to live on.[83] By this time, there was a real fear that plague was once more spreading throughout the city. Elders in Old Aberdeen held their scheduled sermon at seven o'clock in the morning on 6 August to dissuade attendance by residents of the new town, wherein they believed 'the infectione is broken out agayne'.[84] That October the Aberdeen council expressed its alarm at 'the dangerous conditioun of the toun be the infectioun daylie increasing' and, in the aftermath of a contested election in which no member would accept the role of magistrate, each agreed to do his best to help take charge of the situation 'in respect of the necessitie the toun was in'.[85] With no further measures taken by city councillors, this fear of renewed plague appears to have been misplaced. There is, however, an interesting footnote to Aberdeen's final epidemic. In the only recorded instance of plague being spread from Aberdeen, the Dundee council was forced to take action following the death there of a footman who had recently arrived from the city and, 'being visite be the phicitianes is found to be suspected to be dead in the plague'. Consequently, Andro Nicol, the stabler in whose house he had died, was ordered with his family to undergo quarantine and cleansing in a specially constructed lodge 'in the feildis'.[86] Four days later a member of Nicol's household also died, as a consequence of which quartermasters were appointed to search all houses for further cases.[87] The 'spotting of the plague' soon engulfed Dundee, prompting the imposition over the subsequent months of typical civic measures to tackle the outbreak.[88]

Plague elsewhere in the north-east

Kirk Sessions continued to be at the vanguard of plague measures implemented in parishes throughout the north-east, in ways which reveal the tension between the duty of caring for the poor and the pragmatic and propitious desire to curtail their presence. The fear of infection meant that sermons were sometimes postponed and collections therefore not taken. These impediments to both the spiritual and charitable duties of the Kirk were compounded by occasions when it was deemed prudent to prohibit beggars from attending the weekly service. Often the charitable donations that were accumulated were dispensed only to the needy of the parish (as was the statutory requirement),[89] though when their own parishes were plague-free the elders of Belhelvie and Dyce orchestrated collections for 'distressed' Aberdonians labouring under plague,[90] and even for peripatetic beggars who 'in such a suspicious tyme … durst not travel any wher abroad',[91] examples which accord with McCallum's findings that ecclesiastical poor relief was by no means always restricted to resident parishioners.[92] Elders in Elgin also continued to order their parishioners not to receive servants without a testimonial and to report cases of sickness to the minister, who was to visit them, while any stranger then within the burgh was warned not to expect re-entry if they attempted to journey over the river Spey.[93] They also forbade Patrik Garden from allowing his daughter Katreine into his house, while she was to be banished for being in the company of a man suspected of having plague after she had been forbidden from doing so.[94] Even closer to Inverness, elders in the parish of Croy and Dalcross prohibited anyone from Dundee from entering the burgh (perhaps in anticipation of them arriving by boat),[95] while the minister of the adjacent parish of Petty reported that he had visited William McGillichallun 'and some other seik persones' in Brackley, and asked the elders to let him know of any other suspected cases in the parish. Twelve shillings was given by the Kirk Session to one of those sick individuals, and all those living on that estate were required to be inspected.[96]

Old Aberdeen provides a good example of the continued co-operation between Kirk and civic authorities in the implementation of plague measures. Shortly after infection had been acknowledged to be present in Aberdeen, elders in Old Aberdeen had attempted to prevent its spread by requiring those wishing to enter the burgh or parish to present a certificate of health signed by their local minister.[97] This attempt to filter out those who were sick had clearly failed, as on 11 June 1647 local magistrates elected to divide the burgh into quarters in order to facilitate the necessary task of ascertaining the extent of infection, with one 'honest' man chosen to visit each house in his own quarter to 'tak wp the naimes of everie familie within thair divisioune' and identify sick inhabitants.[98] The collection at St Machar Cathedral was to be received in a basin under the supervision of an elder,[99] so that the coins would not have to be touched and could then undergo disinfection. When John Farquhar oversaw the weekly collection on 8 July 1647, he ensured that the twelve shillings received came not from any non-parishioners but only from those 'that ware within the toune' despite the inevitable consequence of collecting less money.[100] By this time the epidemic had spread to such an extent throughout Old Aberdeen that the council was forced to implement a concerted series of typical measures 'in respect of the plaige'. This included a ban on frequenting taverns (including the specific prohibition on purchasing beer or wine, which points to a desire to rein in unruly behaviour) and on any craftsman receiving textiles from outwith the town. All public markets were cancelled and a twenty-four hour watch was imposed, to commence each afternoon at four o'clock. Women and children were forbidden from travelling to the city of Aberdeen; men were permitted to go there as long as they had been granted 'ane speciall varrand' from the baillies, but this made it difficult to discern 'who is foule or cleine of the Infectione' and the usual Sunday sermon was cancelled as a result.[101] The primary cause of plague was also addressed, with the Kirk Session repeatedly punishing the 'delation of filthiness' and other immoral actions of its parishioners, including sleeping through the sermon, excessive drinking and possible illegitimacy.[102] In December elders went so far as to take an inventory of 'the wholl falts fallen forth throughout the parish since the beginning of the infection', in order to admonish those responsible and thereby gain divine approval.[103]

Such measures could not prevent the continued spread of plague, forcing Kirk officials to cancel the regular sermons at St Machar Cathedral from 18 July until just after Christmas 'for feare of the Infectione'. In their place special services (often referred to as 'lectors', indicating that they consisted only of a simple Bible reading) were held on an *ad hoc* basis, 'sumetymes in the morning and at night on the lords day', throughout estates in the parish including Grandholm, Sclaty, Carngully and Persley.[104] Due to the 'vehemencie of the infectione' such a service was given on 15 August on the Corse Hill at six o'clock (most likely in the morning rather than evening, in order to lessen the chance of too large an audience gathering), while a fortnight later a reading was given there at three in the afternoon.[105] Services were also held 'at the huts' (on Scotstown moor) in recognition of the need to continue to minister to the sick despite the danger this entailed for the reader. No collection was taken on such occasions, an attempt to limit the spread of infection through tainted coins, but probably also an acknowledgement of the financial straits faced by most of the victims lodged within.[106] By the end of 1647 there were signs that plague was on the wane in Old Aberdeen, as it was in the new city. Beginning on 26 December services were once again held in their usual location, the parish cathedral of St Machar, and were attended by the tithe collector Mr John Lundie, the Boxing Day sermon 'being his entrie efter the infection'.[107] In late February 1648, the Old Machar Kirk Session was able to proclaim several days of thanksgiving 'for deliverance from the plague',[108] though elders continued to crack down on sinful behaviour and were required to absolve one parishioner from performing repentance due to his suspected sickness.[109]

The chronology of the recorded incidence of plague elsewhere in the region is interesting and reveals that attempting to trace the spread of a past epidemic based necessarily on written accounts is an inexact task. Despite the pitfalls inherent in trying to reconstruct the spread of plague from scattered and incomplete evidence, it might be suggested that the pattern of the 1640s epidemic throughout Aberdeen's vast hinterland casts aspersions on the notion that plague always reached the city from the more heavily populated south (often an apparent default position for contemporaries) and indicates that regional communications throughout the north-east were sufficiently enduring to spread the disease, perhaps even initially from overseas. Notwithstanding the identification of Brechin as the origin of Aberdeen's outbreak and the council's understanding in April 1647 that Inverbervie was infected, Aberdeen and Old Aberdeen were hardest hit between May and December of that year, which was apparently some months before the area to the immediate south of the city was affected. Indeed, as we have already seen, Aberdeen itself was identified as the origin of Dundee's outbreak in August 1648, though it is perhaps more likely that, while the footman deemed responsible started his journey in the city, he caught plague on his travels south before he reached Dundee. We have hard evidence (literally) that Stonehaven was afflicted during 1648: a gravestone survives in the burgh that records the deaths, attributed to plague, of two brothers aged nine and twelve in June of that year.[110] Subsequently, it was not until near the end of that year that the local clerk in Montrose recorded his alarm about the 'fearfull persewing pestilence [which has] entered into the Citie Inlarging and spredding itself daylie'.[111] The specific presence of plague in both Montrose and Dundee prompted the Kirk Session of the parish of Kinneff and Catterline, situated south of Stonehaven and north of Inverbervie, to order a fast, though its only other plague-related action had occurred some sixteen months previously, when no collection had been taken for three weeks over the summer 'for fear of the infection'.[112]

Mentions of plague to the north and west of Aberdeen similarly reveal an uneven pattern. Peterhead had been severely infected by August 1645, almost two years before Aberdeen was struck. To the west of Peterhead, the Kirk Session of Longside forbade beggars from participating in the weekly sermon 'be reason of the pregnancie of the plague of pestilence in abr [that is, Aberdeen] and other places adjacent', with no hint that the disease had broken out within its own parish.[113] Likewise, the congregation of Boharm to the west of Keith held a thanksgiving in September 1647 'for the stay of the plague of pestilence qlk was all this summer in aberdene' and its elders subsequently ordered a fast the following month; even though this was due to 'the continewing of the pestilence qhuair it hath beine of a long tyme and the spreading of it [in] thess partes qr the sword did formellie chast and destroy', it was also in recognition that 'the lord hath bene graciouslie pleased to keepe the pestilence from spreading across the face of all the land', including, perhaps, their parish.[114] Closer to Aberdeen, in September 1647 the Belhelvie Kirk Session had taken a special collection for 'the distressed peopl of abd [that is, Aberdeen], being now under the plague'[115] (and presumably therefore was not then in similar dire straits) and the following month ordered another fast and public contrition for the sins of the congregation, 'which are the causes of gods jugementis now come to our dorres after long and mornfull forbairance'.[116] In the event, it was to be another twelve months before several extraordinary appointments to its Session were made, due to the deaths or desertion of a substantial number of elders.[117] Meetings were subsequently disrupted due to the fear of plague, and on 29 October the trial of a parishioner called David Simpson was deferred due to the death from 'the infectioun' of a man on the nearby Hill of Keir estate.[118] The Kirk Session of Dyce to the immediate north-west fared rather better; though a sermon was cancelled at the beginning of August 1647 'because of suspicion of infection in sindrie places of the parochin', it proved to be a false alarm and the service scheduled for the following Sunday was held, albeit outside in the kirkyard.[119] Elders made contingency plans to ensure the spiritual needs of their parishioners were met despite the ongoing fear of infection, by stipulating that anyone who became suspected of plague was to remain at home 'and the minister should goe and lecture to them . . . upon the lords dayes afternoon, or at uther occasions as he should think fit'. Further north-west, beyond Dyce, the court in Inverurie prohibited residents from leaving the burgh without permission from the baillies or minister and ordered any sickness to be reported to those same authorities. Alexander Porter was fined ten pounds for attending a 'suspectit' burial outwith the town, while his accomplice James Taylor was fined forty shillings.[120] Officials there also instigated watches and prohibited strangers from being lodged unless they possessed a testimonial and were accompanied to the property.[121] Elsewhere, a 'strong guard of armed men' was stationed where ramparts most likely existed at the confluence of the Leuchar and Gormack burns slightly to the west of Peterculter, indicating local attempts to monitor those coming and going to the immediate north of the river Dee.[122]

Though plague affected many parts of the north-east, it would appear that Highland settlements further west escaped. James Fraser described plague's devastation of Aberdeen with no hint that Inverness, from where he was writing, had been similarly affected. While he attributed the town's earlier avoidance of an epidemic in 1601 to the 'pure air' of the area,[123] it is apparent that magistrates in Elgin made good use of the natural barrier presented by the river Spey to monitor comings and goings between the burgh and areas to the east, particularly Aberdeen. Once news of plague in settlements to the south and east reached local authorities, the Elgin Kirk Session ordered a fast to be held in gratitude for the burgh being spared, while the council implemented a watch, ordered back walls to be strengthened and threatened punishment for anyone travelling south of the river Spey.[124] It followed this up a week later with particular measures instigated 'in respect of the plague in Aberdeen'. Two residents of Elgin who had come from there, a merchant named Adam Gordoun and another merchant's servant Patrick Ros, were forbidden from any socialising without first obtaining a licence from the burgh's magistrates, with confiscation of their goods and expulsion threatened for contravention. That day the council also ordered six burgesses of Elgin not to travel beyond the river Spey or buy any merchandise originating from that area. Finally, no resident was to eat, drink or receive money from those being held at the port, an indication that certain unnamed merchants had been detained on arrival by sea.[125] Within the week the Kirk Session also threatened its own punishment for those who would receive strangers, particularly servants, without testimonials.[126] This order was followed up two days later by a further decree advising any stranger within the town that they would not be granted re-entry if they travelled beyond the Spey.[127] Several convictions were secured for the contravention of these regulations.[128] Synodal representatives led by example and chose not to attend a meeting scheduled to take place in Aberdeen and it was likely that Elgin escaped plague.[129] In February 1648 Bessie Douglas wrote from the burgh to her son Mr John Innes of Leuchars, who was then lodged at an inn in Leith. Having dispensed with the business at hand (concerning a meeting with her late husband's creditors), she confided to John that she was worried about him being so far from home. 'I wish you heastie returne', she wrote, 'for it puts me in great affrightment to heare that the Pest is broken up both in Leith and Edinbrugh'.[130] Bessie herself was clearly not writing from a town that had itself been infected. In the event, she need not have worried, for the reports she had received were already out of date and Edinburgh was by then free from plague.

Counting the cost

It had been a devastating sixteen months or so, during which the outbreak of plague had compounded the misery of already battle-weary and put-upon communities throughout the north-east. Contemporaries could have been forgiven for the desolation they might have felt. Those who had lived through the epidemic had experienced the severe limitation of commercial life and of everyday social interaction, to say nothing of the grief and horror in the face of relatively extreme mortality and the uncertainty over who might be afflicted next. Most would have asked pragmatic and philosophical questions when contemplating their plight. How will I cope with the death of five of my extended family? How will I get my business off the ground again? How am I going to feed my children? Why has this happened to me, to us? As with earlier outbreaks, this plague was patently divine wrath as a result of sin. James Fraser attributed the epidemic in Aberdeen to God's punishment of 'a vitious, lascivious, dissloyall people', a reference to the purging of King's College personnel by Covenanting forces some years previously. The devastation plague had caused was clearly a call to repentance. 'The way to Zion mourn', Fraser lamented,

> because non come to the solemn feasts, all her gates ar desolat, her priests sigh, her virgins are afflicted, and she is in bitterness. O vain, wanton Aberdeen, art thou awakened by this visitation? Art thou reformd? Pure and penitent, say with Job, what shall I doe quhen he riseth up, and quhen God shall visit, what shall I answeir him?[131]

This question would have been on the minds of many Aberdonians as they struggled to rebuild their lives and livelihoods in the wake of plague, their uncertainty that it really had receded from their community compounded by the pressures of continued military occupation. The civil wars that dominated the decade either side of the epidemic make it impossible completely to distinguish the particular demographic and economic impact of plague, and parliamentary records and personal accounts more often than not stressed the losses caused by both 'burning sword plunderings and the plague of pestilence'.[132]

Mirroring the nationwide trend, inhabitants of Aberdeen and its environs buried significantly more family, friends and neighbours than usual during the 1640s. While a considerable proportion of these deaths would have been a result of the civil wars (whether due to active combat or to atrocities inflicted on civilians by rampaging soldiers), plague must also have been responsible for many more fatalities than those specifically attributed to it in parish registers. Although the annual burial register for the parish of Old Machar (encompassing Old Aberdeen) recorded only two deaths as a result of the 'infection', it is probable that most victims were buried outside the churchyard as an expedient to the effects of large-scale mortality. This was certainly the case in Aberdeen itself, where the number of dead far exceeded the seventy-one recorded plague victims buried in St Nicholas kirkyard in the latter half of 1647, during which time the epidemic was gathering pace by the day.[133] The city treasurer's accounts detail the substantial expenditure required in digging, liming and covering a mass grave for plague victims near the harbour mouth, the remains of which were disturbed during building work in the late nineteenth century to the east of modern-day York Street.[134] By 1640 the city's population may have numbered around 8,300 (plus another 900 or so in Old Aberdeen), falling to between 7,000 and 7,500 in the post-plague period.[135] Taking into account natural population fluxes – including losses caused by war and additions due to rural immigration and recovering birth rates – this indicates that the contemporary estimate of 1,600 fatalities from plague within Aberdeen (with a further 140 in Futty and Torry) was fairly accurate.[136] Some areas of Scotland were hit far worse: the six hundred people recorded on a tombstone as having been killed by plague in Brechin amounted to two-thirds of the population,[137] while Edinburgh and its vicinity lost at least a quarter of its inhabitants with Leith and Canongate each losing at least half.[138] It has been suggested that one in five urban dwellers in Scotland overall died as a result of this epidemic, so the inference is that Aberdeen's mortality rate of about 18% was fairly average. Population levels across Scotland recovered with the passage of time, due in part to the absence of further epidemics, and the 1660s at last saw a return (for the time being, at least) to relative demographic stability.[139]

The human cost of plague and war in much of the country was recognised by parliament, which in May 1648 granted dispensation to a number of burghs from levying the full complement of inhabitants to fight in future hostilities. By this time plague had largely ceased in many populated areas in the southern half of Scotland, so it is not surprising that it was mainly from settlements in Fife and further north, including Aberdeen, that parliament was prepared to levy a lesser proportion of men and horses. Perth and Culross had their levies reduced due specifically to the effects of plague, while all other settlements in Perthshire were granted these due either 'to the same or by the warr'. Further north, Brechin in Angus was permitted to contribute thirty fewer men than usual. While no dispensation was granted to the sheriffdoms of Kincardine and of Aberdeen to the west, the rest of the sheriffdom was permitted to levy 1,600 men, with the city of Aberdeen itself to contribute sixty fewer men than would otherwise be expected 'inregaird of thair vastatioune be the pestilence'. Dispensation was also granted to the sheriffdom of Banff to the north-west of the city of Aberdeen, with the burgh of Banff itself obliged to levy seven fewer men than usual and that of Cullen six. Similar leniency was displayed in designating the levies to be raised by the other sheriffdoms along the coast east of the river Ness: six fewer men were to be sent by the burgh of Forres and, in levying only a third of the usual number of men from the burgh of Nairn, parliament specifically recommended to that shire's committee of war that they should 'have consideratioun of the vastatioune'. The same consideration was to be given to the neighbouring burgh of Inverness 'inrespect of its great and extraordinarie conditioune', and only three-quarters of the usual levy was to be raised both from that burgh and from nearby Elgin.[140] As argued above, plague did not affect these latter two burghs to a great extent and it is probable that their hardships arose from war rather than plague. In particular, consideration must have been given to the extensive terrorisation and looting suffered by the people of Elgin through its successive occupation by both Parliamentary and Royalist forces in 1645–46.[141]

Many of those who had been killed in Aberdeen's epidemic were craftsmen, the lifeblood of urban commercial life. Due to the infrequency of council meetings 'in respect of the plague of pestilence that wes within this burghe', no new burgesses had been admitted between June and December 1647.[142] When magistrates did meet again they set about replenishing craft membership, depleted due to the severe mortality of the previous eight months or so, and in mid-January 1648 allowed each craft to take on any apprentice of its members' choosing at a greatly reduced fee.[143] Subsequently there was a notable rise in the numbers admitted to the city's guilds in 1648 and 1649, a number of whom came from outwith the burgh. For some individuals – such as the servant to the provost Patrick Leslie – this was in recognition of exceptional service provided during the outbreak. Various craftsmen became honorary or trade burgesses for the same reason, including a saddler, a dyer, four weavers and two butchers.[144] Others were admitted to help the recovery of local manufacturing: four smiths (including one from Clinterty), two weavers, a carpenter, a cutler (from Kilmarnock), a heel maker (from Old Aberdeen), a stocking maker and an apothecary, each due to the 'paucitie of craftismen of that trad within the burt' . . . '[because] sindrie of the said trade ar dead of the plague of pestilence'.[145]

In their efforts to boost the recovery of local industry, magistrates faced other challenges besides the depletion of craft personnel. Extensive military occupation, together with the indiscriminate sacking and looting that had taken place, had left residents financially as well as psychologically devastated by the wars, and the outbreak of plague compounded an already desperate situation. The council's earlier efforts to prevent the spread of infection to the city had required significant financial outlay, but these expenses paled in comparison with those incurred once these efforts failed. A significant proportion of funds went on creating and maintaining the quarantine area on the Links and sustaining those residents who were sent there, and the accounts for this reveal much about the conditions that prevailed at the camp. A large quantity of timber was bought and transported to the quarantine site where five huts were constructed. Making the most of ongoing military occupation, the council paid Captain John Duff and his retinue 820*l* to guard the camp, as well as constructing another hut at which they were stationed.[146] Lit candles were purchased for the guards at a cost of 4*l* 16*s* to facilitate the round-the-clock nature of their task.[147] It is likely that a makeshift chapel of some sort was erected to serve the spiritual needs of those in quarantine, with 12*s* being spent on buying rosin to burn in the chapel and the same amount paid to two men to burn it, their relatively high wage a reflection of the danger of infection inherent in this task.[148] Workers were employed at a total cost of 2*l* 15*s* to build, carry and erect gibbets beside the hut where the soldiers stood guard as a constant reminder of the punishment for those who would attempt to escape from their enforced quarantine. The gibbets were to be constructed from two trees, and were only removed from the quarantine area to the market cross on 12 January 1648, by which time the worst of the epidemic had passed.[149] Additionally, several men were paid to build a scaffold, attached to which were jougs (an iron collar on a chain), and the city's first printer Edward Raban was paid 16*s* for 'printing the papers that is printed on the brists of those that stand on the scaffold', in order to heap further shame on any lawbreakers through heightened public visibility of their crimes.[150] There is no record of the scaffold or the gibbets being used during the epidemic itself, an indication either that they served as effective deterrents or of the council's tendency towards judicial leniency. The scaffold was however subsequently used when Patrik Watsone, a dyer, was imprisoned, fined and pilloried for 'conceilling ane seik persone within his hous'.[151] This would have been a deliberate humiliation, as Watsone was also a constable and, as one who held the duty of recording cases of infection, therefore ought to have known better.

Those living in quarantine in the huts required sustenance, having been denied the ability to earn their livelihood, though there are few recorded instances of authorised payments for this, and it might have been the case that unofficial donations through charitable and familial obligations helped to boost support garnered from official bodies despite the burgh's dire financial circumstances. One unfortunate victim left forty pounds 'for [the] supplie of poor people that ar in the huts', perhaps never expecting that he himself was to end his own life 'there' in September 1647.[152] Civic funds were used to purchase large quantities of meal with which to bake bread 'for the poor people', with additional meal obtained from prominent Aberdeenshire landowners.[153] The Old Machar Kirk Session occasionally diverted money donated at their makeshift services to sustain those in the Aberdeen huts as well as in Old Aberdeen's own quarantine camps at Ferryhill and on Scotstown moor, and to cover other expenses associated with the epidemic (including the purchase of whisky to sustain patients and the support of a 'stranger' with a 'famous testimoniall' of his house being burnt down, which might possibly have been as a result of fumigation).[154] As in previous epidemics magistrates did not officially employ a physician when plague broke out, but may have taken informal advice from trained medical practitioners in the vicinity, such as the principal of Marischal College Patrick Dun, who had studied medicine abroad under the celebrated Aberdeen physician Duncan Liddel and maintained an active interest in the subject, or Andrew Muir (More), who was then mediciner at King's College. Additionally, they were able to secure the services of the peripatetic 'doctor of phisick' James Leslie, who undertook the 'visiting and curing [of] the poor people during the tyme of the visitatioun'. Leslie provided his expertise 'frielie wpone his awn charges without ony payment', and was later granted exemption from paying any taxes in return for settling in Aberdeen and continuing the arrangement.[155] He subsequently became an ordinary physician in the city.[156] Unspecified medicines were purchased by the council for his use during the epidemic and, as he was described as curing the infected, he was presumably highly regarded whatever his success rate.[157] Notwithstanding the physician's efforts, the burial of a vast number of inhabitants killed by plague incurred substantial expenditure. Robert Walker was paid the substantial sum of 55*l* 10*s* for cutting the 37,000 squares of peat it took to 'cover the graves of thame that died in the infectione and var buried among the sandis'; the same amount was given to Alexander Cruikschank and George Blaik for carrying the turfs to their destination, and Alexander Deanes received twenty merks for laying them.[158] Lime had to be purchased and carried to the gravesite, and sand was also required to cover up the pits.[159] Other plague-related expenses incurred by the council included the purchase of two massive locks to secure the Bridge of Dee, as well as ammunition and stocks as additional deterrents to unlawful entry or exit over it. The further purchase of a tree for timber 'to be a baer' points to preparations for transporting corpses from the area. Additionally, a merchant was compensated for others' debts and letters were sent at a cost of 12*s* to Lord Fraser 'and uther barons on Die syd', instructing them to be on the lookout for infected people or goods.[160]

The dire financial circumstances in which Aberdeen found itself due to the expenditure required to deal with the practical effects of plague, compounded by the backdrop of military occupation, were further exacerbated by the severe restrictions placed on commerce regionally, nationally and internationally as a result of the epidemic. Activity at Aberdeen's port dropped dramatically during the outbreak: there were ninety-eight active cargoes registered in 1645–46 (an increase of ten from the previous year), with ninety vessels entering and eight departing, but between March and December 1647 when plague was at its height this fell to a low of thirty-seven, with thirty-four arriving and a mere three departing. In 1648–49 the port had sufficiently recovered to register a total of ninety-five active cargoes, though only four of these were departing vessels.[161] The resultant scarcity of victuals in Aberdeenshire made a number of craftsmen redundant[162] and temporarily pushed prices up. A measure of wheatmeal fetched 6*l* 10*s* in 1632–33, 8*l* in 1649–50 and 7*l* 13*s* 4*d* in 1650–51; for the same years great oats without fodder fetched 4*l* 10*s*, 7*l* and 6*l* 6*s* 8*d* respectively.[163] Compounded by the ruinous burden of the wars, the city remained in deep economic trouble. In May 1648 parliament suspended or reduced contributions to the ongoing war effort to be taken from various shires due to their having been 'brunt and waisted' by soldiers. Most of these were in the Highlands or north-east, with particular leniency being shown to Inverness and Nairn. The sheriffdom of Aberdeen had its contribution reduced from £6,543 to £1,333 6*s* 8*d*, while that of the city itself was almost halved, from £1,260 to £666 13*s* 4*d*.[164] Six weeks later the citizens consented to a tax of 7,000 merks to raise money 'in respect of the distrest and mean estait of the toun'.[165] But this was not enough to lessen the financial pressure on magistrates who calculated that reparations due to the town for the losses occasioned by the wars by the end of that year stood at at £1,582,910.[166] The estimated £30,000 cost to the city specifically as a result of the plague epidemic[167] seems comparatively insignificant, but it was certainly an unwelcome additional burden which in financial terms alone compounded an already dreadful situation. The extreme pressures under which the city had been placed by the combined effects of plague and war were starkly summarised in a petition to parliament in February 1649, in which its council sought a reprieve from excises it owed in consideration of money it had lent to the war effort in more affluent times. By this time the wars had been a financial drain on the city for over five years and, coupled with the epidemic, the situation was proving intolerable, with loans secured from local landowners to help meet the burden of plague unable to be repaid even though over a year had passed.[168] Magistrates claimed that through the 'losses wee have had that way by pestilence, plundering, fyre or sword, which is knowne to have bein verie greivous and sad', their 'poore toun is now brought to such a sad and pitifull condition', more so than any other burgh, and a reprieve from its debts would ensure that 'a poore city will be saved from ruine'.[169] The council also continued to feel losses in terms of men as well as money and were forced to petition parliament in May 1649 to reduce the number of inhabitants to be levied in the event of future hostilities, because of 'the great losses of men this toune hes haid be the warre and pestilence'.[170]

Aberdeen's final plague: the outbreak of 1647–48

While the epidemic had been felt most severely in Aberdeen from May 1647 until early the following year, contingency measures regarding plague were put in place during the summer of 1648 and individual cases might have lingered on a smaller scale into 1649. By this time the disease had all but disappeared from Scotland, with the Kirk Session of Montrose, the last major burgh to be affected, pleased to record in March 1649 that no new cases had been identified for several weeks.[171] The epidemic had devastated life across much of the country, with comparative assessments by the Convention of Royal Burghs made that year finding at least six of the nine wealthiest towns had been seriously affected by plague.[172] As was the case in other burghs, government authorities in Aberdeen had responded to reports of plague by implementing well-worn, rational preventative measures: monitoring official entrances, issuing and requiring trustworthy bills of health, prohibiting commercial interaction both locally and regionally, and cleansing the urban environment of sources of infection such as roaming animals and rotting middens. When these measures failed, the presence of plague was tackled by segregating victims and their households, disinfecting suspect goods, and arranging for the disposal of a massive number of bodies. As with communities elsewhere, these measures were implemented and sustained against the disruptive backdrop of civil war. Unlike communities elsewhere, however, those living in Aberdeen had no direct experience of plague and hence were comparatively unable to benefit from any confidence or knowledge that memory (whether individual or collective) or consistency of personnel might bring. Nevertheless, the epidemic in Aberdeen was not without precedent, so the council would have been able to implement regulations which 'conforme[d] to the laudable custome observed of before therintill in ilk exigencie', as magistrates in Glasgow described their own efforts to tackle the outbreak of plague in November 1646.[173] In addition, the authorities in Aberdeen might have taken advice, formally or otherwise, through the consultation or employment of experienced personnel elsewhere. As in earlier outbreaks, they implemented regulations in response to what they understood about how infection spread. Limiting external contact, eliminating sources of potential infection within the immediate environment, closing the colleges, church and markets, and segregating suspected victims were all rational measures, regardless of the inevitable damage caused to the social, commercial and spiritual lives of the community. Lastly, throughout the north-east, as in Aberdeen itself, nearly all those parishes for which records survive had undertaken regular fasts to implore God to end plague through collective propitiation, and thanksgivings when their contrition had been recognised.[174] Aberdeen's final epidemic had taken 1,600 lives – about a fifth of the population – and required upwards of £30,000 in expenses, but those who lived through it might at least have taken comfort in knowing that, for the time being, they had been spared by providence.

Notes

1 Edinburgh Central Library, Edinburgh and Scottish Collection: Archibald Skeldie, *The Only Sure Preservative Against the Plague of Pestilence. Described in a Sermon upon the Fifth and Sixth Verses of the Ninetie One Psalme* (Edinburgh, 1645), p. 1; John Ritchie, "A seventeenth-century sermon anent the pestilence", *Medical History* 2:2 (1958), pp. 149–151, at p. 149.

2 John Spalding, *The History of the Troubles and Memorable Transactions in Scotland, from the Year 1624 to 1645*, vol. II [*fl.*1650] (Aberdeen: A. Angus and Son, 1792), p. 290.

3 James Fraser, *Chronicles of the Frasers, The Wardlaw Manuscript, Entitled 'Polichronicon Seu Policratica Temporum, or, the True Genealogy of the Frasers, 916–1674'* [edited by William MacKay] (Edinburgh: Scottish History Society, 1905), p. 350.

4 Patrick Gordon of Ruthven, *A Short Abridgement of Britane's Distemper from the Yeare of God 1639 to 1649* [edited by John Dunn] (Aberdeen: Spalding Club, 1844), p. 55.

5 ACR.41.408 [11 Oct 1603].

6 ACR.36.380 [17 Nov 1595].

7 M. Flinn (ed.), *Scottish Population History from the Seventeenth Century to the 1930s* (Cambridge: Cambridge University Press, 1977), Appendix A.

8 A.M. Munro (ed.), "Register of burgesses of guild and trade of the burgh of Aberdeen, 1399–1631", in *Miscellany of the New Spalding Club*, vol. I (Aberdeen: Spalding Club, 1890), pp. 1–162, at pp. 118–120 [28 May 1617–20 May 1618].

9 John Spalding, *The History of the Troubles and Memorable Transactions in Scotland, from the Year 1624 to 1645*, vol. I [*fl.*1650] (Aberdeen: A. Angus and Son, 1792), p. 338; Flinn (ed.), *Scottish Population History*, pp. 131–132.

10 Ian D. Whyte, *Scotland Before the Industrial Revolution: An Economic and Social History* (London: Longman, 1995), p. 122. Famines occurred throughout Scotland in the early 1550s, 1562–63, 1571–73, 1585–87 and 1594–98, mirroring those in England where the death rate as a result of the latter famine may have averaged 6%; Paul Slack, *Poverty and Policy in Tudor and Stuart England* (London: Longman, 1988), p. 49.

11 Forty burials were recorded in St. Nicholas kirkyard in 1621, rising to ninety-one in 1622 and eighty in 1623. Levels fell in subsequent years, to thirty-five in 1624 and thirty-eight in 1625; Archibald Strath Maxwell, *Register of Burials: St. Nicholas Churchyard, Aberdeen, Scotland, 1571–1647* vol. I (Aberdeen: A.S. Maxwell, 1969), pp. 38–47. During this period of increased mortality, two physicians and a surgeon were admitted as burgesses '*ex gratia*'; Munro (ed.), "Register of burgesses of guild and trade", pp. 131–133 [5 Aug 1622; 2 Jul 1623; 23 Jul 1623].

12 Flinn (ed.), *Scottish Population History*, p. 125.

13 Spalding noted that the winter of 1642/43 was particularly cold and frosty, with great rains and storms producing harvest failures, ensuring that victuals were 'monstrous dear' and 'scarce gettable' in the city. Furthermore there were 'few fish gotten, to the great grief of the people'; Spalding, *The History of the Troubles*, vol. II, pp. 64, 82.

14 DesBrisay has commented that 'more than any other burgh, Aberdeen lay on the contested frontier between the Covenanting south and the royalist north' and has elsewhere pointed out that pragmatism dictated that the city 'was essentially caught in the crossfire and co-operated with both sides (which unfortunately meant it could be trusted by neither)'; Gordon DesBrisay, "'The civill warrs did overrun all'; Aberdeen, 1630–1690", in E. Patricia Dennison, David Ditchburn and Michael Lynch (eds), *Aberdeen Before 1800: A New History* (East Linton: Tuckwell Press, 2002), pp. 238–266, at p. 247; Gordon DesBrisay, *Authority and Discipline in Aberdeen, 1650–1700* (University of St Andrews, unpublished PhD thesis, 1989), p. 10.
15 Chris Brown, *The Battle for Aberdeen, 1644* (Stroud: Tempus, 2002), p. 25.
16 Brown, *The Battle for Aberdeen*, p. 65.
17 Spalding, *The History of the Troubles*, vol. II, p. 237.
18 Brown, *The Battle for Aberdeen*, p. 63.
19 DesBrisay, *Authority and Discipline in Aberdeen*, p. 7.
20 ACL.3.024 [24 Jan 1646].
21 ACL.3.059–062 [Oct 1646]. Another request was made shortly before Christmas for grain to be given to the town's poor rather than the visiting regiments; ACL.3.072 [21 Dec 1646].
22 ACL.3.066 [Nov 1646].
23 Robert Gourlay and Anne Turner, *Historic Banff: The Archaeological Implications of Development* (Glasgow: Scottish Burgh Survey, 1977), p. 2.
24 Bruce B. Bishop, *The Lands and People of Moray: Part 1: Inverlochty, Mosstowie, Pittendreich, Manbeen, Auchtertyre, Miltonduff and Pluscarden Prior to 1850: In the Parish of Elgin* (Elgin: J. and B. Bishop, 2000), p. 7.
25 Inverness CMB.4.37r [24 Jun 1646].
26 Bruce B. Bishop, *Lost Moray and Nairn* (Edinburgh: Birlinn, 2010), pp. 81–82.
27 NAS: GD1/503/1: Inverurie Burgh Court Book fragments, 1646–71 [6 Feb 1646].
28 Quoted in DesBrisay, "'The civill warrs did overrun all'", p. 239.
29 CA/8/2/1: Aberdeen Letters: Correspondence Received by the Burgh, Supplementary I: 1615–1759 [5 Mar 1647]; ACR.53/1.123 [14 Apr 1647].
30 Spalding, *The History of the Troubles*, vol. II, p. 282.
31 ATA [1644–45].
32 John Hyslop and Robert Hyslop, *Langholm as it Was: A History of Langholm and Eskdale from the Earliest Times* (Sunderland: Hills and Company, 1912), p. 417; John Marius Wilson, *The Imperial Gazetteer of Scotland: Or Dictionary of Scottish Topography*, vol. II (London and Edinburgh: Fullerton and Co., 1868), p. 300.
33 Special Collections, Mitchell Library, Glasgow: C1/1/11: Glasgow Council Minute Book, 3 Oct 1642–27 May 1648 [9 Nov 1644].
34 Edinburgh CMB.16.2r [28 Aug 1644], 5v [13 Sep 1644], 6r [18 Sep 1644], 9r [9 Oct 1644], 14r [25 Oct 1644], 15r [1 Nov 1644], 27r–27v [23 Dec 1644, 25 Dec 1644].
35 RPS: 1645/1/22 [16 Jan 1645].
36 Edinburgh Town Treasurer Accounts, 1636–50, pp. 20–28 [Nov 1644–Jul 1645]; Edinburgh CMB.16.44v–79r [30 Apr 1645–11 Mar 1646].
37 Edinburgh CMB.16.27v [25 Dec 1644], 43r [10 Apr 1645], 54r [13 Jun 1645].
38 Edinburgh CMB.16.42v [10 Apr 1645]; Spalding, *The History of the Troubles*, vol. II, p. 322.
39 NAS: GD188/25/1/6/1: Diary Entry of John Guthrie, former Bishop of Moray [4 May 1645].

40 John Robertson (ed.), *Ecclesiastical Records: Selections from the Registers of the Presbytery of Lanark, 1623–1709* (Edinburgh: Abbotsford Club, 1839), p. 44 [12 Jun 1645].
41 John Drummond, *Memoirs of Sir Ewen Cameron of Locheill, Chief of the Clan Cameron, with an Introductory Account of the History and Antiquities of that Family and of the Neighbouring Clans* [edited by James Macknight] (Edinburgh: Maitland Club, 1842), p. 72 [Jul 1645].
42 ACR.53/2.1324 [28 Jun 1645].
43 ACR.53/1.047 [6 Aug 1645].
44 ACR.53/2.1338 [22 Aug 1645].
45 The ruins of these huts remained in 1774 when a proposal to remove them in order to use the land aroused local opposition, which was not appeased until 'the principal physicians of Edinburgh' had been consulted due to superstition about the prospect of disturbing previously plague-infused land; Peter Buchan, *Annals of Peterhead, from its Foundation to the Present Time* (Peterhead: Peter Buchan, 1819), p. 102; R. Neish, *Old Peterhead: An Authentic Account of the Origin and Development of the Burgh of Barony of Peterhead* (Peterhead: P. Scrogie, 1950), pp. 154–156; Anne Turner Simpson and Sylvia Stevenson, *Historic Peterhead: The Archaeological Implications of Development* (Glasgow: Scottish Burgh Survey, 1982), pp. 29–31, which fixed the location of the graves to the Gadle Braes along the coast.
46 ACR.53/2.1338 [22 Aug 1645].
47 ACL.3.014 [3 Sep 1645].
48 ACL.3.014 [4 Sep 1645].
49 ACR.53/2.1347 [10 Oct 1645].
50 William McDowall, *History of the Burgh of Dumfries* (Edinburgh: Adam and Charles Black, 1867), p. 438.
51 John Ritchie, "The plague in Dumfries", *Transactions of the Dumfriesshire and Galloway Natural History and Antiquarian Society*, third series, 21 (1939), pp. 90–105, at pp. 101–102 [6 Dec 1645].
52 Plague was abating in Stirling just as Aberdeen became infected; Robert Renwick (ed.), *Extracts from the Records of the Royal Burgh of Stirling, A.D. 1519–1666* (Glasgow: Printed for the Glasgow, Stirlingshire and Sons of the Rock Society, 1887), pp. 187–188, 191–193 [28 Jul 1645–26 Jul 1647], *passim*.
53 A hidden gravestone on Culross Moor records a death from plague on 14 Sept 1645; Historic Environment Scotland: https://canmore.org.uk/site/48019/culross-moor; Charles Baxter (ed.), *Ecclesiastical Records: Selections from the Minutes of the Synod of Fife, 1640–1687* (Edinburgh: Abbotford Club, 1837), pp. 144–145 [7 Oct 1645].
54 James Haig (ed.), *The Historical Works of Sir James Balfour of Denmylne and Kinnaird, Knight and Baronet; Lord Lyon King at Arms to Charles the First, and Charles the Second. Published from the Original Manuscripts preserved in the Library of the Faculty of Advocates*, vol. III (Edinburgh: W. Aitchison, 1825), p. 311.
55 Robert Wodrow, *The History of the Sufferings of the Church of Scotland, from the Restauration to the Revolution*, vol. I (Edinburgh: James Watson, 1721), p. 49; Flinn (ed.), *Scottish Population History*, p. 143.
56 Flinn (ed.), *Scottish Population History*, p. 139.
57 ACL.3.067 [Nov 1646].
58 ACL.3.69–70 [11 Dec 1646].
59 ACR.53/2.1456 [12 Apr 1647].
60 ACR.53/2.1457 [27 Apr 1647]. Pitmuckston/Pitmuxton (from the Gaelic meaning 'place of the pigs') was the site of a mill at Pitmuckston Burn and the woman may have approached Aberdeen via a small adjacent bridge over the Dee, both of which appear on James Gordon's map of 1661.

61 ACR.53/2.1457–1459 [27 Apr 1647].
62 Edinburgh CMB.16.68v [4 Feb 1646].
63 NAS: GD188/25/1/6/2: Lengthy Diary Entry of John Guthrie, Former Bishop of Moray [4 May 1647].
64 ACR.53/1.130 [26 May 1647].
65 John Barclay (ed.), *Diary of Alexander Jaffray, Provost of Aberdeen* (London: Darton & Harvey, second edition, 1834), p. 32.
66 ACR.53/1.130–131 [11 Aug 1647].
67 ACR.53/1.131 [11 Aug 1647].
68 Robert Aitken, *Letters and Journals Written by the Deceased Mr Robert Baillie, Principal of the University of Glasgow, with an Account of the Author's Life Prefixed*, vol. II (Edinburgh: W. Gray, 1775), p. 260 [1 Sep 1647].
69 Robert S. Rait, *The Universities of Aberdeen: A History* (Aberdeen: James Gordon Bisset, 1895), p. 264; John Cranna, *Fraserburgh: Past and Present* (Aberdeen: Rosemount Press, 1914), p. 206.
70 John Davidson, *Inverurie and the Earldom of the Garioch* (Edinburgh: David Douglas, 1878), p. 295.
71 Fraser, *Chronicles of the Frasers*, pp. 350–351.
72 ACR.53/1.133 [22 Sep 1647]; ACR.53/1.138 [22 Sep 1647]; Barclay (ed.), *Diary of Alexander Jaffray*, pp. 181–182; Alexander M. Munro, *Memorials of the Aldermen, Provosts, and Lord Provosts of Aberdeen, 1272–1895* (Aberdeen: privately printed, 1897), p. 156.
73 ACR.53/1.138 [15 Dec 1647].
74 ACR.53/2.1474 [23 Dec 1647].
75 ACR.53/1.139 [15 Dec 1647].
76 10/11/13: Aberdeen County Sheriff Court: Judicial Enactments (Copy Excerpts from Court Books), 1633–52; on 2 February 1648 Alexander Lesk, the minister at Maryculter brought the first case to be heard since 7 April 1647.
77 CA/7/1/1: Court Book of the Guildry of Aberdeen, vol. I, 7 Sep 1637–23 Dec 1697, p. 48 [20 Jan 1648]; ACR.53/1.148 [16 Feb 1648]; ACR.53/1.152 [1 Mar 1648]; ACR.53/1.154 [15 Mar 1648].
78 ACR.53/1.180–181 [20 Sep 1648]; ATA [1647–48].
79 J.M. McPherson, *The Kirk's Care of the Poor, with Special Reference to the North East of Scotland* (Aberdeen: John Avery and Co., 1941), p. 23.
80 ATA [9 Dec 1647]; ACR.53/1.158 [29 Mar 1648]; ACR.53/1.175 [23 Aug 1648].
81 AGA [9 Oct 1647]; Aberdeen City and Aberdeenshire Archives: CA7/4/1: Aberdeen Register of Burgesses of Guild, vol. I, 1632–94, p. 153 [8 Dec 1647]; ACR.53/1.152 [10 Mar 1648]; ACR.53/1.157 [22 Mar 1648]. Graham does not appear to have been employed as a cleanser either in Leith or in Edinburgh.
82 Old Machar KS.2.317 [30 Jul 1648].
83 ACR.53/1.175 [23 Aug 1648].
84 Old Machar KS.2.317 [6 Aug 1648].
85 ACR.53/1.188 [11 Oct 1648].
86 Dundee CMB.4.211v [22 Aug 1648].
87 Dundee CMB.4.211v [26 Aug 1648].
88 Dundee CMB.4.211v–214v [26 Aug 1648–2 Nov 1648].
89 Longside KS.2.117 [22 Jan 1646]; Petty KS.1.23 [29 Jun 1645], 53 [10 Oct 1647].
90 Belhelvie KS.2.64 [5 Sep 1647]; Dyce KS.1.3 [9 Nov 1645, 16 Nov 1645], 4 [30 Nov 1645], 13 [17 Jan 1647], 15 [21 Mar 1647], 18 [8 Aug 1647, 15 Aug 1647, 22 Aug 1647, 29 Aug 1647], 21 [5 Mar 1648, 12 Mar 1648], 22 [19 Mar 1648, 26 Mar 1648].
91 Dyce KS.1.18 [6 Aug 1647].

92 John McCallum, "Charity doesn't begin at home: ecclesiastical poor relief beyond the parish, 1560–1650", *Journal of Scottish Historical Studies* 32:2 (2012), pp. 107–126.
93 No servants: Elgin KS.6.153A [18 Jul 1647]; report to minister: Elgin KS.6.119 [25 Nov 1645]; no stranger from over the Spey: Elgin KS.6.153A [20 Jul 1647].
94 Elgin KS.6.168A [14 Jan 1648].
95 Croy and Dalcross KS.1.22 [27 Jun 1647].
96 Petty KS.1.46 [20 Jun 1647].
97 Old Machar KS.2.283 [23 May 1647].
98 *Records of Old Aberdeen* I, p. 78 [11 Jun 1647].
99 *Records of Old Aberdeen* II, p. 143 [27 Jun 1647].
100 *Records of Old Aberdeen* II, p. 143 [8 Jul 1647].
101 *Records of Old Aberdeen* I, pp. 78–79 [3 Jul 1647]; Old Machar KS.2.287 [7 Jul 1647].
102 Old Machar KS.2.286 [7 Jul 1647]; 287 [7 Jul 1647]; 287 [9 Jul 1647]; 289 [26 Dec 1647].
103 Old Machar KS.2.288 [26 Dec 1647].
104 Old Machar KS.2.288 [18 Jul 1647]; *Records of Old Aberdeen* II, p. 144 [4 Nov 1647].
105 *Records of Old Aberdeen* II, p. 144 [15 Aug 1647, 29 Aug 1647].
106 *Records of Old Aberdeen* II, p. 144 [31 Oct 1647].
107 *Records of Old Aberdeen* II, p. 144 [26 Dec 1647].
108 Old Machar KS.2.297 [20 Feb 1648]; 299 [27 Feb 1648].
109 Old Machar KS.2.300 [5 Mar 1648]; 303 [19 Mar 1648]; 317 [30 Jul 1648].
110 This can now be seen set into a wall on an uphill public footpath at the corner of Victoria Street, located beside another grave stone dating from the 1608 epidemic; that relating to the 1640s outbreak is inscribed: 'Heir lyes ane Honest mans bairns Alexander and William Brokie, sones lawful to Alexander Brokie, who departet the 12 of Jwnie, of the age tvalf and nyn yeirs old, in ano 1648'; Historic Environment Scotland: https://canmore.org.uk/site/36909/stonehaven-plague-burials.
111 Duncan Fraser, *Montrose (Before 1700)* (Montrose: Standard Press, 1967), pp. 132–136, at p. 135.
112 Kinneff and Catterline KS.1.26 [29 Oct 1648], 74 [8 Jun–18 Jul 1647].
113 Longside KS.2.125 [16 Jun 1647].
114 Boharm KS.1.79 [25 Sep 1647], 80 [30 Oct 1647].
115 Belhelvie KS.2.64 [5 Sep 1647].
116 Belhelvie KS.2.65 [24 Oct 1647].
117 Belhelvie KS.2.75 [1 Oct 1648].
118 Belhelvie KS.2.76 [22 Oct 1648], 77 [29 Oct 1648].
119 Dyce KS.1.18 [30 Jul 1647, 6 Aug 1647].
120 NAS: B36/6: Inverurie Burgh Court Book, vol. III [3 Dec 1647].
121 NAS: B36/6: Inverurie Burgh Court Book, vol. III [10 May 1647, 14 Jul 1647, 30 Nov 1647].
122 John A. Henderson, *Annals of Lower Deeside, Being a Topographical, Proprietary, Ecclesiastical and Antiquarian History of Durris, Drumoak and Culter* (Aberdeen: D. Wyllie and Son, 1892), p. 110.
123 Flinn (ed.), *Scottish Population History*, p. 145.
124 Elgin KS.6.150A [18 Jun 1647]; Local Heritage Services, Moray Council, Elgin: A2/7: Elgin Council Minute Book, 1636–59 [5 Jul 1647].
125 Local Heritage Services, Moray Council, Elgin: A2/7: Elgin Council Minute Book, 1636–59 [12 Jul 1647].
126 Elgin KS.6.153A [18 Jul 1647].

127 Elgin KS.6.153A [20 Jul 1647].
128 Patrik Garden was ordered not to receive his daughter Katreine into his house under pain of twenty pounds, while Andrew Dik was also cautioned under the same pain. Katreine herself was to be banished 'for accompanieing a man suspect of the plague efter scho was forbidden'; Elgin KS.6.168A [14 Jan 1648]. A woman was subsequently ordered to perform public repentance for going over the Spey; Elgin KS.6.174A [26 Mar 1648].
129 Elgin KS.6.175A [4 Apr 1648].
130 C. Innes (ed.), *Ane Account of the Familie of Innes, Compiled by Duncan Forbes of Culloden, 1698* (Aberdeen: Spalding Club, 1864), p. 238 [12 Feb 1648].
131 Fraser, *Chronicles of the Frasers*, pp. 350–351 [referencing Job 31 v.14].
132 ACL.3.070 [15 Dec 1648].
133 Archibald Strath Maxwell, *Register of Burials: St. Nicholas Churchyard, Aberdeen, Scotland, 1647–1670*, vol. II (Aberdeen: A.S. Maxwell, 1969), pp. 2–11.
134 AGA [28 Jan 1648]; J.A. Stones and J. Cross, "York Place, disturbed burials", in Edwina V.W. Proudfoot (ed., assisted by B.E. Proudfoot), *Discovery and Excavation in Scotland* (Edinburgh: Council for British Archaeology, 1987), pp. 17–18; Historic Environment Scotland: https://canmore.org.uk/site/19987/aberdeen-york-street-plague-burials.
135 Ian Blanchard, Elizabeth Gemmill, Nicholas Mayhew and Ian D. Whyte, "The economy: town and country", in Dennison *et al.* (eds), *Aberdeen Before 1800*, pp. 129–158, at p. 147.
136 Flinn (ed.), *Scottish Population History*, p. 136; Joseph Robertson, *The Book of Bon Accord, or, a Guide to the City of Aberdeen* (Aberdeen: Lewis Smith, 1839), p. 326; Barclay (ed.), *Diary of Alexander Jaffray*, pp. 181–182; Munro, *Memorials of the Aldermen*, pp. 156–157.
137 Charles Rogers, *Monuments and Monumental Inscriptions in Scotland*, vol. II (London: Grampian Club, 1872), p. 202; RPS: 1649/5/219 [21 Jun 1649].
138 Edinburgh itself lost about 5,000 people, bringing the total number of fatalities in the area to 9–12,000, at least a quarter of the overall population. Leith was estimated to have lost 2,736 inhabitants in 1646; a contemporary account put the burgh's pre-plague population at around 4,000, entailing a death toll of well over half. The similarly-sized adjacent parish of Canongate was reckoned to have lost 2,000 inhabitants; Flinn (ed.), *Scottish Population History*, pp. 138–140, 147.
139 Baptism figures recovered relatively quickly and within five years surpassed the level at which they had been in 1635–49; Flinn (ed.), *Scottish Population History*, pp. 147, 155–156.
140 RPS: 1648/3/104 [4 May 1648].
141 John Barrett and Alistair Mitchell, *Elgin's Love-Gift: Civil War in Scotland and the Depositions of 1646* (Elgin: Phillimore, 2007).
142 Aberdeen City and Aberdeenshire Archives: CA7/4/1: Aberdeen Register of Burgesses of Guild, vol. I, 1632–94, p. 152 [26 May 1647].
143 ACR.53/1.144–145 [19 Jan 1648]; AGA [1647–48]: payments were subsequently received from deans of crafts for apprentices who were made freemen.
144 Aberdeen City and Aberdeenshire Archives: CA7/4/1: Aberdeen Register of Burgesses of Guild, vol. I, 1632–94, pp. 153–196 [8 Dec 1647–26 Dec 1649].
145 Aberdeen City and Aberdeenshire Archives: CA7/4/1: Aberdeen Register of Burgesses of Guild, vol. I, 1632–94, pp. 154–186 [22 Dec 1647–30 May 1649], at p. 172 [7 Jun 1648], p. 154 [22 Dec 1647].
146 ATA [1647–48]; in mid-1647 Jon Donald was paid 11*l* 11*s* for carrying more timber to the huts.
147 AGA [29 Oct 1647].
148 AGA [9 Dec 1647].

149 AGA [12 Jan 1648].
150 AGA [28 Jan 1648].
151 ACR.53/2.1496 [15 Mar 1648].
152 AGA [13 Sep 1647].
153 ATA [1646–47].
154 *Records of Old Aberdeen* II, pp. 144–145 [15 Aug 1647, 29 Aug 1647, 17 Nov 1647, 4 Dec 1647, 10 Feb 1648, 6 Mar 1648, 15 Mar 1648, 18 Jun 1648, 13 Aug 1648].
155 ACR.53/1.304–305 [26 Mar 1651].
156 ACR.54.235 [21 Nov 1660].
157 William Kennedy, *Annals of Aberdeen, from the Reign of King William the Lion, to the End of the Year 1818* (London: Brown, 1818), p. 272.
158 AGA [28 Jan 1648].
159 AGA [1647–48].
160 ACR.53/1.154 [15 Mar 1648]; AGA [1647–48].
161 Aberdeen City and Aberdeenshire Archives: CA/6/4/1 (1): Accounts of the Master of Shore Works, 1596–1656, fols 280r–290v [1645–46], 293r–295v [1647], 304r–315r [1648–49].
162 ACL.3.143 [May 1649]; a decrease in the number of brewers was noted due to 'the dearth and skersitie of malt'.
163 David Littlejohn, "Fiars prices of Aberdeenshire", in P.J. Anderson (ed.), *Miscellany of the New Spalding Club*, vol. II (Aberdeen: New Spalding Club, 1908), p. 19.
164 RPS: 1648/3/13 [9 May 1648].
165 Aberdeen City and Aberdeenshire Archives, CA/5/1/7: Aberdeen Baillie Court Book, Jun 1648–Nov 1652 [4 Jul 1648].
166 ACL.3.111 [10 Aug 1648], 117–124 [Dec 1648].
167 ACL.3.227–228 [19 Apr 1654].
168 RPS: 1649/1/176 [24 Feb 1649]; Robert Faquharson of Invercauld found it necessary to petition parliament in order to recover the 3,700 merks he had lent the city 'the tyme Aberdene was visited with the pestilence'.
169 RPS: 1649/1/65 [1 Feb 1649, remitted 12 Mar 1649]; just under half the requested amount was reimbursed: DesBrisay, *Authority and Discipline*, p. 7.
170 ACL.3.142–143 [May 1649].
171 Fraser, *Montrose (Before 1700)* p. 136 [29 Mar 1649].
172 Flinn (ed.), *Scottish Population History*, p. 147.
173 Special Collections, Mitchell Library, Glasgow: C1/1/11: Glasgow Council Minute Book, 3 Oct 1642–27 May 1648 [5 Nov 1646].
174 Belhelvie KS.2.44 [29 Jun 1645, 3 Jul 1645], 45 [7 Sep 1645, 14 Sep 1645], 56 [25 Oct 1645], 60 [28 Mar 1647], 61 [Apr 1647, May 1647], 63 [6 Jun 1647, 13 Jun 1647, 20 Jun 1647, 4 Jul 1647], 65 [24 Oct 1647, 31 Oct 1647], 74 [3 Sep 1648], 75 [10 Sep 1648]; Dyce KS.1.15 [25 Apr 1647], 16 [2 May 1647], 17 [6 Jun 1647], 19 [24 Oct 1647, 31 Oct 1647]; Botriphnie West KS.1.7 [21 May 1648]; Boharm KS.1.79 [25 Sep 1647], 80 [30 Oct 1647], 94 [20 Sep 1648]; Elgin KS.6.150A [18 Jun 1647]; Petty KS.1.24 [3 Aug 1645], 31 [16 Jul 1646]; Kinneff and Catterline KS.1.26 [29 Oct 1648].

Bibliography

Aitken, Robert, *Letters and Journals Written by the Deceased Mr Robert Baillie, Principal of the University of Glasgow, with an Account of the Author's Life Prefixed*, vol. II (Edinburgh: W. Gray, 1775).

Barclay, John (ed.), *Diary of Alexander Jaffray, Provost of Aberdeen* (London: Darton & Harvey, second edition, 1834).

Barrett, John and Alistair Mitchell, *Elgin's Love-Gift: Civil War in Scotland and the Depositions of 1646* (Elgin: Phillimore, 2007).

Baxter, Charles (ed.), *Ecclesiastical Records: Selections from the Minutes of the Synod of Fife, 1640–1687* (Edinburgh: Abbotford Club, 1837).

Bishop, Bruce B., *The Lands and People of Moray: Part 1: Inverlochty, Mosstowie, Pittendreich, Manbeen, Auchtertyre, Miltonduff and Pluscarden Prior to 1850: In the Parish of Elgin* (Elgin: J. and B. Bishop, 2000).

Bishop, Bruce B., *Lost Moray and Nairn* (Edinburgh: Birlinn, 2010).

Blanchard, Ian, Elizabeth Gemmill, Nicholas Mayhew and Ian D. Whyte, "The economy: town and country", in E. Patricia Dennison, David Ditchburn and Michael Lynch (eds), *Aberdeen Before 1800: A New History* (East Linton: Tuckwell Press, 2002), pp. 129–158.

Brown, Chris, *The Battle for Aberdeen, 1644* (Stroud: Tempus, 2002).

Buchan, Peter, *Annals of Peterhead, from its Foundation to the Present Time* (Peterhead: Peter Buchan, 1819).

Cranna, John, *Fraserburgh: Past and Present* (Aberdeen: Rosemount Press, 1914).

Davidson, John, *Inverurie and the Earldom of the Garioch* (Edinburgh: David Douglas, 1878).

DesBrisay, Gordon, *Authority and Discipline in Aberdeen, 1650–1700* (University of St Andrews, unpublished PhD thesis, 1989).

DesBrisay, Gordon, "'The civill warrs did overrun all'; Aberdeen, 1630–1690", in E. Patricia Dennison, David Ditchburn and Michael Lynch (eds), *Aberdeen Before 1800: A New History* (East Linton: Tuckwell Press, 2002), pp. 238–266.

Drummond, John, *Memoirs of Sir Ewen Cameron of Locheill, Chief of the Clan Cameron, with an Introductory Account of the History and Antiquities of that Family and of the Neighbouring Clans* [edited by James Macknight] (Edinburgh: Maitland Club, 1842).

Flinn, M. (ed.), *Scottish Population History from the Seventeenth Century to the 1930s* (Cambridge: Cambridge University Press, 1977).

Fraser, Duncan, *Montrose (Before 1700)* (Montrose: Standard Press, 1967).

Fraser, James, *Chronicles of the Frasers, The Wardlaw Manuscript, Entitled 'Polichronicon Seu Policratica Temporum, or, the True Genealogy of the Frasers, 916–1674'* [edited by William MacKay] (Edinburgh: Scottish History Society, 1905).

Gordon, Patrick of Ruthven, *A Short Abridgement of Britane's Distemper from the Yeare of God 1639 to 1649* [edited by John Dunn] (Aberdeen: Spalding Club, 1844).

Gourlay, Robert and Anne Turner, *Historic Banff: The Archaeological Implications of Development* (Glasgow: Scottish Burgh Survey, 1977).

Haig, James (ed.), *The Historical Works of Sir James Balfour of Denmylne and Kinnaird, Knight and Baronet; Lord Lyon King at Arms to Charles the First, and Charles the Second. Published from the Original Manuscripts preserved in the Library of the Faculty of Advocates*, vol. I (Edinburgh: W. Aitchison, 1824).

Haig, James (ed.), *The Historical Works of Sir James Balfour of Denmylne and Kinnaird, Knight and Baronet; Lord Lyon King at Arms to Charles the First, and Charles the Second. Published from the Original Manuscripts preserved in the Library of the Faculty of Advocates*, vol. III (Edinburgh: W. Aitchison, 1825).

Henderson, John A., *Annals of Lower Deeside, Being a Topographical, Proprietary, Ecclesiastical and Antiquarian History of Durris, Drumoak and Culter* (Aberdeen: D. Wyllie and Son, 1892).

Historic Environment Scotland: https://canmore.org.uk/site/19987/aberdeen-york-street-plague-burials.

Historic Environment Scotland: https://canmore.org.uk/site/36909/stonehaven-plague-burials.

Historic Environment Scotland: https://canmore.org.uk/site/48019/culross-moor.

Hyslop, John and Robert Hyslop, *Langholm as it Was: A History of Langholm and Eskdale from the Earliest Times* (Sunderland: Hills and Company, 1912).

Innes, C. (ed.), *Ane Account of the Familie of Innes, Compiled by Duncan Forbes of Culloden, 1698* (Aberdeen: Spalding Club, 1864).

Kennedy, William, *Annals of Aberdeen, from the Reign of King William the Lion, to the End of the Year 1818* (London: Brown, 1818).

Littlejohn, David, "Fiars prices of Aberdeenshire", in P.J. Anderson (ed.), *Miscellany of the New Spalding Club*, vol. II (Aberdeen: New Spalding Club, 1908).

Marius Wilson, John, *The Imperial Gazetteer of Scotland: Or Dictionary of Scottish Topography*, vol. II (London and Edinburgh: Fullerton and Co., 1868).

Maxwell, Archibald Strath, *Register of Burials: St. Nicholas Churchyard, Aberdeen, Scotland, 1571–1647*, vol. I (Aberdeen: A.S. Maxwell, 1969).

Maxwell, Archibald Strath, *Register of Burials: St. Nicholas Churchyard, Aberdeen, Scotland, 1647–1670*, vol. II (Aberdeen: A.S. Maxwell, 1969).

McCallum, John, "Charity doesn't begin at home: ecclesiastical poor relief beyond the parish, 1560–1650", *Journal of Scottish Historical Studies* 32:2 (2012), pp. 107–126.

McDowall, William, *History of the Burgh of Dumfries* (Edinburgh: Adam and Charles Black, 1867).

McPherson, J.M., *The Kirk's Care of the Poor, with Special Reference to the North East of Scotland* (Aberdeen: John Avery and Co., 1941).

Munro, A.M. (ed.), "Register of burgesses of guild and trade of the burgh of Aberdeen, 1399–1631", in A.M. Munro (ed.), *Miscellany of the New Spalding Club*, vol. I (Aberdeen: Spalding Club, 1890), pp. 1–162.

Munro, Alexander M., *Memorials of the Aldermen, Provosts, and Lord Provosts of Aberdeen, 1272–1895* (Aberdeen: privately printed, 1897).

Munro, A.M. (ed.), *Records of Old Aberdeen MCLVII–MDCCCXCI*, vol. I (Aberdeen: New Spalding Club, 1899).

Munro, A.M. (ed.), *Records of Old Aberdeen MCCCCXCVIII–MCMIII*, vol. II (Aberdeen: New Spalding Club, 1899).

Neish, R., *Old Peterhead: An Authentic Account of the Origin and Development of the Burgh of Barony of Peterhead* (Peterhead: P. Scrogie, 1950).

Rait, Robert S., *The Universities of Aberdeen: A History* (Aberdeen: James Gordon Bisset, 1895).

Renwick, Robert (ed.), *Extracts from the Records of the Royal Burgh of Stirling, A.D. 1519–1666* (Glasgow: Printed for the Glasgow, Stirlingshire and Sons of the Rock Society, 1887).

Ritchie, John, "The plague in Dumfries", *Transactions of the Dumfriesshire and Galloway Natural History and Antiquarian Society*, third series, 21 (1939), pp. 90–105.

Ritchie, John, "A seventeenth-century sermon anent the pestilence", *Medical History* 2:2 (1958), pp. 149–151.

Robertson, John (ed.), *Ecclesiastical Records: Selections from the Registers of the Presbytery of Lanark, 1623–1709* (Edinburgh: Abbotsford Club, 1839).

Robertson, Joseph, *The Book of Bon Accord, or, a Guide to the City of Aberdeen* (Aberdeen: Lewis Smith, 1839).

Rogers, Charles, *Monuments and Monumental Inscriptions in Scotland*, vol. II (London: Grampian Club, 1872).

Simpson, Anne Turner and Sylvia Stevenson, *Historic Peterhead: The Archaeological Implications of Development* (Glasgow: Scottish Burgh Survey, 1982).

Slack, Paul, *Poverty and Policy in Tudor and Stuart England* (London: Longman, 1988).

Spalding, John, *The History of the Troubles and Memorable Transactions in Scotland, from the Year 1624 to 1645*, vol. I [*fl.*1650] (Aberdeen: A. Angus and Son, 1792).

Spalding, John, *The History of the Troubles and Memorable Transactions in Scotland, from the Year 1624 to 1645*, vol. II [*fl.*1650] (Aberdeen: A. Angus and Son, 1792).

Stones, J.A. and J. Cross, "York Place, disturbed burials", in Edwina V.W. Proudfoot (ed., assisted by B.E. Proudfoot), *Discovery and Excavation in Scotland* (Edinburgh: Council for British Archaeology, 1987), pp. 17–18.

Whyte, Ian D., *Scotland Before the Industrial Revolution: An Economic and Social History* (London: Longman, 1995).

Wodrow, Robert, *The History of the Sufferings of the Church of Scotland, from the Restauration to the Revolution*, vol. I (Edinburgh: James Watson, 1721).

6 Conclusion

Epilogue: further plague scares

The devastating epidemic of the 1640s was to be followed by several further plague scares of major significance: in 1663–64, when the disease was found to be widespread in the United Provinces, in 1665 when it ravaged London and in 1720, when it spread from the southern French port of Marseilles, reaching the English Channel and even (so it was rumoured) coming as close to Scotland as the Isle of Man. Although on each occasion no outbreak eventuated, the raft of responses – both temporal and spiritual – reveal predominant consistency with those which had been articulated over the previous decades and centuries. There was a brief scare in the mid-1650s, when plague in Holland prompted the Privy Council to issue quarantine regulations which were subsequently implemented in Aberdeen when a vessel arrived in the harbour from Veere whose skipper had been 'removit his lyff in ane suspitious way'.[1] But it was during the following decade that more serious threats from subsequent outbreaks required concerted action.

The first was in 1663–64, when plague broke out in Holland. The complex political machinations of the 1660s meant that by virtue of a shared monarch Scotland was embroiled in England's wars with the Dutch Republic over trading privileges, among other issues.[2] As had been the case in the 1540s with regard to England, the Anglo-Dutch conflict might actually have helped efforts to prevent sources of plague by the obligation of personnel in Scotland's seaports to implement watches of their harbours. While Dutch vessels were to be prohibited from landing due to the hostilities, plague became an additional incentive for this. At the behest of the Privy Council, Aberdeen instigated a watch of the Blockhouse in May 1664 'for taking notice of all schippes from holland coming to this burgh', so that they could undergo 'duw tryall'.[3] Two ships returning home to Aberdeen were consequently 'tryed' before being allowed to land – the *Elizabeth*, which had transported plaiding for the Dutch market,[4] and the *Kook*, which had come from Veere.[5] Despite these instances, and similar procedures being followed in various coastal burghs, the Privy Council was forced in July to call for a complete cessation on trade with the region,[6] because certain mariners had managed to evade detection and had 'come ashoar themselves, without abiding the ordinary tryal of fourty days'.[7] Accordingly, Aberdeen's council discharged its watch at the Blockhouse and employed an individual specifically to ensure that no ships entered the harbour 'without tryall and will of the magistrates'.[8] The following month the crew on an English ship from an unspecified destination arrived in the anchorage and, despite swearing on consultation that they had not been in any 'suspect place', an armed guard was summoned to ensure they remained aboard if they did attempt to dock.[9] Prompted by Privy Council directives, the council repeated its order on several occasions that Dutch ships were to be immobilised or repelled, and further ordered the Blockhouse to be repaired and guarded to facilitate these tasks.[10] This continued until victory was declared in August 1665; the armed guard was now discharged and in its place Johne Andersone in Torry was appointed to ensure that any vessels arriving in the harbour underwent quarantine.[11]

But Aberdeen was to enjoy only a temporary respite from the threat of plague, for within weeks news spread that a severe epidemic was then sweeping through England's capital, London (probably spread to the south of England from the Low Countries[12]). While plague had the previous year been present in a region ostensibly considered hostile, now it was ravaging part of a country with which Scotland was united in the person of the monarch. The response was therefore more compassionate with regard to the possible fate of allies than had been the case with Holland, though the proximity of the disease was of concern. The General Assembly issued an order for a public fast to assuage the outbreak and prevent its spread north, which was acknowledged most promptly by the Kirk Sessions of Speymouth and Pitsligo, as well as by the Presbytery of Dingwall.[13] By the time the fast had been widely proclaimed, with the majority of north-east parishes observing it for the week following 13 September,[14] the council in Aberdeen had identified a Captain Woodwart as having arrived with his family from Northwich and other suspect places in England with a testimonial which was out of date. The house in which he and his family were lodging was immediately enclosed under guard for forty days at his own expense.[15] In accordance with the Privy Council's order, magistrates also refused to allow a ship from Gravesend carrying commodities from London to dock in the harbour.[16] Aberdeen's Kirk Session was forced to postpone for a week its meeting scheduled for 11 September, at which it would most likely have ordered the fast for plague, due to the implementation of 'ane extraordinarie watch' prompted by the arrival of an English frigate.[17] On being consulted by several of the city's governors, the crew pleaded that their vessel had been damaged and was in need of repair, swearing that they had not been in any infected place during the previous six weeks. The council responded by ordering an armed guard to prevent anyone disembarking if the boat did dock.[18] These various responses to plague – both temporal and spiritual – might have been deemed to have been successful, for no further alarm was recorded about the spread of the epidemic that lingered in London for several more months, during which time the Privy Council issued further embargoes on trade with England which were aimed only at ports in the Forth.[19]

Subsequent measures to prevent plague were taken in 1669, when the vessel of Aberdeen captained by John Nicolsone arrived home, having come from New Haven in France which was reportedly infected. The crew members were placed under guard in an unspecified chapel overnight before being allowed to unload their merchandise under supervision.[20] The council might have regretted its relative leniency, as four of those on board – the skipper, two merchants named John Cruikshank and Thomas Robertson, and another crew member called John Nicolsone the younger – contravened the order by trying to return to their homes and were accordingly fined and, in the case of the merchants, deprived of their citizenship. The entire crew was removed to a wooden lean-to constructed beside the Blockhouse and enclosed under armed guard at the merchants' expense.[21] This gave rise to an awkward situation for the baillies, as the consequent delay in unloading the goods on board resulted in them being accused by the merchants of attempted embezzlement. They wrote to two of their colleagues then in Edinburgh requesting that their case should be fairly conveyed to the Convention of Burghs. Their letter provides specific information about how they heard that plague was then present in Holland – 'not only by publict intelligence and news letters but also by privat letters to some of the french traders within this burghe'. It also tells us that the crew was enclosed for a month. They complained that they had dutifully followed the quarantine procedure expected in such circumstances under the supervision of the Collector of Customs (a responsibility stipulated in legislation of 1655[22]), and that because no testimonial had been produced they felt unable to have trusted the mariners' assurances.[23] No further mention was made of the matter, but the example shows how quarantine efforts could leave officials vulnerable to charges of customs evasion.

By the time of the next plague scare, national government had changed fundamentally with the Act of Union (1707) uniting Scotland and England. A severe epidemic spread throughout the Baltic, Scandinavia and the Low Countries, killing at least a third of Copenhagen's population in 1711 and causing 'significant loss' in ports such as Hamburg and Bremen.[24] The Privy Council, now administering government from its base in London, responded by issuing measures which were received by all seaports, including Aberdeen, stipulating forty days' quarantine, the period long in force in Scotland but which now extended the English period by ten days.[25] In August 1720 these were reissued in response to the major epidemic in the southern French port of Marseilles, which would prove to be the last occasion on which plague broke out in pre-modern Europe.[26] The disease was rumoured to have spread from the Bay of Biscay to the Isle of Man, posing a particular threat to settlements on Scotland's west coast. In recognition that plague was most likely to enter the country via seaborne vessels, several missives were circulated to all burghs situated on the coast – including Aberdeen – advising councils on the best course of action in the event of its appearance.[27] One of these was a copy of a letter from magistrates in Edinburgh warning of the inherent dangers of the 'clandestine importation' of susceptible goods (including wine, which was typically packed in straw for transportation, and 'baill goods' such as cloth, paper and silks), and urging other burghs to follow their lead and implement the accompanying orders to enforce the nationwide orders within their own bounds.[28] These orders included copies of two previous Acts of parliament concerning two important aspects of plague management: the actions that ought to be taken to prevent the disease, and the administrative enforcement of such measures. The former was covered by a copy of the third clause of the Rule of the Pestilence (1456), the first nationwide piece of legislation to regulate civic responses to outbreaks and one which was presumably deemed relevant and sufficiently effective over two centuries later. The administration of the orders, should their implementation be necessary, could be overseen not only by 'any other Head Officer of the City etc' but also within each shire by justices of the peace. First introduced during the reign of James VI, and in Aberdeen from 1657, these were effectively local judges with the power to try minor crimes.[29] Their responsibility for the administration of plague legislation was confirmed in 1720 with the reissuing of legislation from 1661, which ordered justices to 'set doun order in the cuntrie for governance in tyme of pleague, and [to] punish severlie the dissobayers of the order appointed by them according to the qualitie of the delinquent'.[30] The particular powers designated to governors and justices in such circumstances were set out in an appended chapter of Michael Dalton's *Country Justice*, an English manual for justices first published in 1618, which the Convention enclosed in order 'that you may likewise see what the practice is in England in such cases and how it is founded'. They were to have the right to enforce enclosure and indemnified from prosecution if force was used, to appoint 'searchers, watchmen, examiners, keepers and buryers' as necessary, and to collect and dispense monies to support the infected and enclosed.[31]

While the Convention's letter of 1720 displayed continuity with existing legislation stretching back centuries, a number of significant amendments were proposed which shed light on the perceived limitations of previous regulations. No 'vile prostitute wenches' were to be employed as cleansers 'as on former occasions' and the care of the sick was to be entrusted to 'chirurgians or other persons of reputation' under the supervision of a physician. These stipulations indicate that any previous failures in the cleansing and care of victims were deemed attributable to the negligence of the workers involved, rather than the particular procedures they followed. It was also recommended that

> instead of shutting up the sound with the sick in such a house, as has been the practice in too many places, that the sick persone be immediately removed into the infirmary and there be duly attended and provided with food and medicines.[32]

Enclosure of an entire household could effectively condemn all its members to death, but had been deemed an expedient way of containing potential infection without burdening the state with the expense and administrative inconvenience of supervising sufferers in quarantine. However, enclosure within houses had clearly failed to prevent the spread of plague in past epidemics and by the time of London's Great Plague of 1665, the practice was being condemned by some English medical writers including Nathaniel Hodges and William Boghurst.[33] In its place, propelled by controversial medical advice from the English physician Richard Mead and in spite of increasing opposition, came a renewed emphasis on quarantine on a nationwide scale, by forbidding foreign imports and apprehending visiting vessels, cleansing cargoes and isolating crews.[34] Even though each of these measures never needed to be implemented, this certainly does not make them inconsequential, for they reveal much about the mindset of officials at the time – particularly concerning the perceived responsibility that the state had to oversee and care for those subjected to the orders – and a continued determination to repel plague based substantially on measures first issued centuries previously.

It continued to be crucial to address the ultimate cause for the current plague scare, prompting an order from the General Assembly for a fast which was observed by many congregations throughout the north-east on 24 November, less than a week after the Convention of Royal Burghs had issued its plague orders.[35] The interpretation of the disease as the manifestation of divine punishment remained the same, as did the aspiration to appease God through a unified display of sincere contrition – 'a consciencious performance of so necessary a duty', as the Chapel of Garioch Kirk Session termed its fast for plague the following month.[36] The subsequent order issued under royal authority on 16 December described how God's 'Arrows are gone Abroad' and were stuck 'fast in the flesh of Multitudes round about us', and implored Him to 'Keep us, whom thou hast hitherto preserved from this contagious Distemper, in Health and Safety' and to continue to show 'the riches of thy Mercy in hitherto sparing, and forbearing us'. 'O let us live', it pleaded, 'and we will praise thy Name, and thy Judgments shall teach us!'[37] During their sermons given in conjunction with such orders, ministers throughout the north-east illustrated the way in which such disasters were calls to repentance by using biblical examples of providential scourges, particularly from the Old Testament. Passages taken from Ezekiel, Isaiah, Malachi, Jeremiah and Hosea were used variously in late 1720 to tell of God's punishment of sinful Israel, which could just as easily signify Scotland, while its chief city might equally be substituted with Aberdeen or Auchterless, whose congregations were assailed with Jeremiah 6:8: 'Be thou instructed, O Jerusalem, lest my soul depart from thee; lest I make thee desolate, a land not inhabited'.[38] The congregation in Chapel of Garioch parish were invited to put themselves in the shoes of the idolatrous ancestors of Israel, about whom God said: 'Though they bring up their children, yet I will bereave them, that there shall not be a man left: yea, woe also to them when I depart from them!'[39] Through the example of

Jeremiah 3:12, the minister informed his congregation of Rothiemay that repentance could avert the danger:

> Go and proclaim these words toward the north, and say, Return, thou backsliding Israel, saith the LORD; and I will not cause mine anger to fall upon you: for I am merciful, saith the LORD, and I will not keep anger for ever.[40]

At the same time, the congregation of Fraserburgh received a similar message through the fate of the Galileans in Luke 13: 'Nay, but except ye repent, ye shall all likewise perish'.[41] Lest the fear instilled by this message should prove overwhelming, lessons were also given to the congregations of Cruden and Strichen on several of the Psalms, including number 91, which emphasised God's role as 'a refuge and a fortress' as well as a destroyer, a God who 'shall deliver thee from the snare of the fowler, and from the noisome pestilence'.[42]

In the event, practical considerations could undermine the ideal of widespread, synchronised contrition through fasting. The greater the body of penitents, the greater the likelihood that God would take notice, listen and respond benevolently. Theoretically, the political union of the kingdoms within the British Isles in 1707 provided the greatest opportunity to order co-ordinated fasts in several realms and bring together as many like-minded penitential Britons as possible. Within the hierarchical structure of the Reformed Kirk, it fell to each presbytery to decide on what day the fast was to take place within the parishes under their jurisdiction and communicate this to individual Kirk Sessions, so that (in theory) there was at least co-ordination within areas.[43] But the logistics of disseminating orders for fasts throughout rural parishes hindered these efforts. Throughout the north-east, just less than three-quarters of parishes with extant records observed the fast of 1665 over the course of three different weeks. Even though this rose to almost 88% in response to the plague of 1720, there were four weeks between the first and last dates of it being acknowledged. It is hard to tell whether observation of the fast went unrecorded in those other parishes, or whether for some reason the minister resisted ordering it. Pragmatic considerations sometimes took priority over worship, with at least one parish in rural Aberdeenshire postponing its fast for plague scheduled for 20 November because it was due to take place on market day.[44] Concessions could be made for such scenarios: sermons as part of fasts for plague were sometimes ordered to take place on weekdays as well as Sundays in the burghs, but in the rural parishes often only on Sundays when worshippers were already expected to attend their regular service.[45]

The threat of plague over the winter of 1720 would not have seemed to contemporaries to have been far away, for the relative remoteness of its actual existence essentially had little bearing on the possibility of it breaking out at the will of an omnipotent God. This was emphasised in Englishman Christopher Pitt's *The Plague of Marseilles: A Poem*, sold by John Aitken from his shop in Edinburgh's Parliament Close in 1721. Pitt emphasised to his readers that the epidemic

> rages in a neighbouring Nation with such an unparallel'd Violence, that it seems to be the immediate Hand of God. And as it makes its Approaches nearer to us every Day, I think it the Duty of every honest Man, to contribute as much as he can, toward the quickning of the Nation to Repentance.

The poem encouraged believers 'Arm'd with the sacred Violence of Pray'r' to seek contrition, 'Till her Repentance wrest away the Rod/And sheath the Sword of an offended God'.[46] John Aitken also sold an anonymously-authored treatise entitled *The Cleanser*, which was an intriguingly updated version of 'The prayer in time of any common plague or sickness' from *A Companion to the Temple*, the most famous work of Thomas Comber, dean of Durham, originally published in 1672. Intended primarily as a devotional aid to reconcile dissenters to the Church of England, it included prayers to be recited in times of adversity. The reworking of the treatise, which fundamentally urged repentance, gave it relevance and immediacy to its readers through several additions and amendments. For example, the final phrase of Comber's call to 'consider the Sadness of the Disease, when it is upon us, after which there remains little Hope of Life, since very few escape', became in *The Cleanser* 'since very few in the late Plague at Marseilles escaped'.[47] Likewise, Comber's warning that the potency of infected air made people 'more likely to fall in cities, where we breathe in a Crowd', had appended to it in *The Cleanser*, 'especially such a Place as our Metropolis of Edinburgh'.[48] While there is no evidence that copies of this treatise reached the north-east, its contents emphasise the way in which older works addressing plague, though amended to fit the anticipated audience, were nonetheless fundamentally considered to remain relevant in Scotland as elsewhere.

Explaining Aberdeen's immunity

Repentant contemporaries would certainly have concluded that the fasts undertaken during the winter of 1720 were successful and that Aberdeen, the north-east, Scotland and the British Isles had been spared from plague by providence. For the city of Aberdeen, this was the continuation of a pattern of divine benevolence which had been broken only on three occasions: in 1514, 1545 and 1647. What additional factors may we consider to explain Aberdeen's remarkable immunity? To answer this question, it is useful to consider what might have accounted for the disappearance of plague from Europe entirely after the Marseilles epidemic (until the emergence at the outset of the twentieth century of what by then was clinically identified as bubonic plague, spread by *Yersinia pestis* bacteria usually via the bite of an infected rodent flea). The modern debate about this focuses on whether responsibility lies fundamentally with human intervention, or whether its disappearance might be attributed to epidemiological factors such as a transmutation of the bacillus, the growing resistance of populations and rodents to strains of the disease, or climate change which influenced the intensiveness of rat epizootics.[49] The pattern of plague in Aberdeen indicates that rats might have played a role in its spread, as each of the city's three outbreaks appeared to dissipate with the arrival of winter, which fits with the modern understanding of the conditions required for bubonic plague to thrive. The clinical identification of past plagues is of use insofar as it may help us to evaluate efforts to prevent them, some of which might be regarded today as being of little or no use. Medical responses such as drinking concoctions comprised of strange ingredients might be judged by us today as entirely pointless (regardless of which disease was actually present), while airing textiles overnight, fumigating properties and cleaning up environments might be seen to have some merit in 'chas[ing] away even the most irascible rats and fleas',[50] if one believed their presence to have played a role in past epidemics. But to come to such anachronistic conclusions would be to miss the point completely: contemporaries were wholly convinced of the rational efficacy of such measures, and that ought to be what matters to us. In any case, the evidence is too imprecise to trace the transmission and mortality rates of any given outbreak throughout Scotland's north-east with the accuracy that would be required to determine whether that concurs with what is known about modern bubonic plague. It would be unwise to assume that rodents were exclusively responsible for each of the region's epidemics; indeed, it is likely that there were often several diseases involved, which influenced population susceptibility to plague (whatever that was) and inflated mortality rates. Not least because of the difficulties in identifying unequivocally the bacteria responsible for a given outbreak, the overwhelming consensus among historians in recent years has been that governmental measures for quarantine were the most influential factor in reducing and eventually eliminating pestilence from European communities, localities, regions and nations.

It is clear from measures passed in response to subsequent threats of plague after the mid-seventeenth century that there became above all else a focus on quarantine in its widest sense as the most effective temporal way to assuage the disease. The initial prevention of sources of infection and their isolation if this subsequently failed were inherently rational responses, and it is unsurprising, therefore, that such measures have been judged by historians to have had demonstrable success, regardless of which epidemiological identification one wishes to attach to historical plagues. Ragusa was the first European port to implement measures for the isolation of suspect goods and people, and it has been argued that this enabled it to have remained plague-free for forty-four years between 1482 and 1526, a considerable feat not least given its exposure to the particularly severe Italian epidemic of 1502. Furthermore, outbreaks that did occur in the city became shorter and less severe.[51] The efficacy of government measures – particularly the imposition of a *cordon sanitaire* around towns, the monitoring of people's movements, and the segregation of new cases as soon as they were identified – have been credited with the decline of plague in the Baltic, the Low Counties, England and Austria.[52] In a Scottish context this has also been deemed true: writing with regard to the burgh of Dumfries, John Ritchie concluded that the monitoring of people and the isolation of cases through enclosure and quarantine were all 'of real value' in eliminating plague.[53]

Can we say with confidence that this was the case with Aberdeen? As with any government order, the success of quarantine measures depends on the ease with which such regulations can be implemented and enforced. Those few historians who have so far ventured an opinion on the incidence of plague in the city have identified two particular factors that might have had a bearing on this. David Hamilton noted that Aberdeen's 'narrow trade routes from the south and a lesser volume of trade with the continent' helped its '[civic] measures [to be] notably successful'.[54] Similarly, David Ditchburn reckoned that Aberdeen's 'ability to withstand the vectors of disease was simply because of its limited exposure to distant markets',[55] while Robert Tyson also felt that the city 'was helped by its distance from other major towns', adding that 'the main explanation for the avoidance of the disease was probably the council regulations to prevent the plague from entering the town'.[56] Likewise, in observing that 'Aberdeen appears to have been curiously immune from the early visitations of the plague', John Comrie attributed this 'in large part' to 'the severe regulations' introduced by the council in the very late fifteenth century.[57] In order to test these theories, we need to consider two main issues: the city's location and the enforcement of its successive governments' plague legislation.

Aberdeen's location

Chapter 1 detailed Aberdeen's relatively isolated position on the north-east coast and its absolute dominance over an extensive rural hinterland. Recent scientific analysis has shown that diseases in the past spread more effectively in 'highly transitive networks', making peripheral nodes (which Aberdeen can be said to have been) more likely to avoid initial outbreaks and less susceptible to exogenous re-infections.[58] Like other coastal places, plague could reach Aberdeen in one of two ways – by sea or by land, in what has been termed 'maritime and internal phases'.[59] It is apparent that the Aberdeen council came to believe over time that the city was more vulnerable to sources of infection arriving from overseas rather than overland. This led to an increasing focus from the second half of the sixteenth century on efforts to monitor the harbour, intercept arriving vessels and impose quarantine on suspect crews and cargoes. After the epidemic of the 1640s the vast majority of efforts to prevent plague throughout Scotland (and, from the early eighteenth century, the British Isles) were focused on maritime quarantine, though this is less surprising given that threats of infection during this time came overwhelmingly from overseas. Though Aberdeen maintained comparatively strong continental links, relatively speaking these may have been insufficient to bring wide-scale plague to the city. It seems entirely plausible that Aberdeen's location aided the council in its efforts to monitor arrivals both by sea and by land, due to the difficulties in navigating the city's harbour and in negotiating the routes which impeded the approach of travellers on foot or horseback. Furthermore, Chapter 4 showed that by the turn of the seventeenth century, networks of communication regarding the whereabouts of plague and measures to prevent it were actively sustained by both civic and ecclesiastical authorities and individual landowners alike, and these would have enabled watchers to be particularly on guard against people and goods coming from infected places. Given the general agreement among historians about the efficacy of implementing watches at the ports and harbour to evaluate visitors and their goods, requiring health certificates before allowing entry, and isolating or repelling possible sources of infection, it may be conjectured that successive governments in Aberdeen were able to use the city's location to implement measures against arrivals from known areas of infection with more ease than was the case in comparatively less isolated towns.

The implementation of Aberdeen's plague measures

So, the city's location is one possible explanation for its immunity from plague. What, then, of the implementation of civic measures? The likely efficacy of orders for the prevention and elimination of sources of infection must be offset against several challenges. To begin with, such measures were not infallible. No matter how rigorous the guards' checks at the city's ports, some sources of infection were bound to have slipped past them. In addition, it was possible to gain entry to the town via unmanned access points; indeed, it could be supposed that the woman who brought plague from Brechin to Pitmuckston and thence into Aberdeen in April 1647 had come over the river Dee somehow unnoticed, most likely under cover of darkness. An unidentified source of infection had likewise managed to enter the city in 1514 and in 1545, and the same was naturally also true for each landed estate, village, burgh and parish in the north-east which was afflicted by plague at some point. Even in rural areas of the region that contained small, scattered settlements, plague was still able to penetrate. Many were situated close to navigable rivers (such as the Dee, Don, Spey and Ythan), which recent scientific research has shown were a prime factor in enabling the spread of plague.[60] Additionally, the communities that were dotted along the region's extensive coastline shared Aberdeen's vulnerability to overseas infection, as evidenced in the severe epidemic of 1600–01 which probably entered at the port of Findhorn before spreading to other settlements in the parish of Elgin. Even without the added complication of smuggling, it would have been practically impossible to have monitored each and every landing point along the north-east coast in spite of efforts by local landowners and their tenants. For officials, the inherently overwhelming nature of the task at hand was further compromised by various challenges in enforcement. The strictest regulations possible could be ordered by a given government body, but they would be bound to fail if they were administered negligently or not met with compliance, while diligent acquiescence, on the other hand, would strengthen the likelihood of their effectiveness. Can Aberdeen's immunity be attributed, at least in part, to civic plague measures being enforced with requisite success?

Studies of civic responses to plague have highlighted the tensions between the measures deemed necessary by a government for the prevention of infection and the adverse effects they are seen to cause for those subjected to them.[61] *Prima facie*, all civic plague measures would inevitably have had a negative impact on the economy and social stability of a given community. The expulsion of itinerant pedlars and chapmen, the cancellation of local markets, the sequestering of crews and cargoes, the destruction of goods, and the placing of limitations on regional, national and international trade were all bound to precipitate economic decline, stymie manufacturing and create an increase in 'extraordinary' poor. The social tensions that abounded within any given community were sure to be amplified by the enforced segregation and identification of individuals, and by the way in which everyday actions such as lodging visitors and leaving back gates open could suddenly become illegal. It might therefore be expected that such measures would be resisted and, indeed, a number of case studies have highlighted the way in which plague could 'augment the opportunities for crime' in cities such as Siena and Orvieto. The Black Death in the British Isles has been judged to have 'likely ... sharpened the ... motives to steal', while in early modern London the fear of infection precipitated disorder by making magistrates wary of trying criminals.[62]

In Aberdeen, the only recorded occasion on which magistrates conveyed their fear about plague heralding social disorder was at the height of the final outbreak in 1647, when society was already in a relative state of chaos as a result of the civil wars. In expressing their concern at the prospect of the city being 'castin loose, and no ordour keipit at all',[63] they may have used deliberately emotive language to appeal to citizens to contribute to the burgh's beleaguered finances. It would appear that the breakdown in law and order that was feared to accompany outbreaks was not particularly manifested in Aberdeen, aligning the city's experience with that of others such as Bologna which remained relatively stable.[64] This may have been helped by the way in which many aspects of plague legislation legitimised social control, by monitoring people's movements between and within settlements, by searching houses, by ascertaining who was deemed to have a legitimate presence within the community, and by forcibly marking out individuals who posed a risk to social health (whether through badging the poor or having a recovered individual carry a white stick). To some extent, these actions may have helped to identify and repress disorder before it could get out of hand; it has elsewhere been argued that 'the increased scale of surveillance' might have had 'the overall effect of reducing the probability of intercommunity spread of the disease'.[65]

The lack of disorder helped to ensure that civic life did not grind to a halt. The burgh and guild courts continued throughout most of the period to regulate commercial and social relations by convicting individuals of a wide variety of offences that imperilled the common weal, from breaches of economic statutes to slander and molestation. During the second epidemic, the flight of wealthy citizens from the town had created a downturn in tax payments and made it difficult for the government to fund the support of the poor and infected, heralding consequent pleas for their return. However, council business continued throughout both this and the city's first outbreak, and there is no evidence during either epidemic that any magistrates themselves fled. By contrast, in early modern London 'the wholesale flight of the city governors left the city prey to any criminal prepared to dare infection ... [and] provided what was seen as an unrestrained licence to crime'.[66] It was only during the final outbreak that government might be said to have collapsed. The council did not convene between May and December of 1647, aside from an emergency meeting in mid-August and the election held that September. We know from his own diary confession that at least one magistrate – Alexander Jaffray – fled the city during those months, and he may not have been the only one.[67] The consequent lack of records obscures what took place in the burgh during that period, but it did not take long once plague receded for urban life to return to relative normality, the ongoing instability occasioned by political and ecclesiastical infighting during these years notwithstanding.

Contravention and compliance

It was certainly the case that a great many plague regulations imposed in Aberdeen were contravened at some time or another. Particular examples of desperation stand out – such as the three residents of the Gallowgate caught trying to hide a death from plague by burying the body in a midden during the first epidemic, or David Spilyelaucht, who was branded on the hand for concealing his child's infection during the second – but there were plenty of other Aberdonians who were also caught defying plague-related laws.[68] They broke these in all sorts of ways: they hosted visitors and engaged in trade without permission; they attempted to leave their home enclosure; they allowed strangers to enter the burgh over their garden wall; they failed in their duty to undertake a watch of their nearest port or to keep their pigs tethered; and they remained in the burgh after being judged undeserving of charity. This incomplete list of misdemeanours highlights the way in which plague created an entirely specialised set of regulations that were ripe to be broken. In this sense, disease exacerbated criminality – but, perhaps, it did so in that sense only. As time passed without plague, the council expressed a concern about residents' 'sluggische cairlesnes' in obeying plague statutes, but there was no discernible rise in convictions for breaking them.[69] Indeed, throughout the period overall, the numbers of individuals who were convicted was not particularly high and masks the vast majority of the community who (presumably) complied with the orders. This was probably not due to the fear of consequent punishment, contrary to Charles Creighton's suggestion that Aberdeen's immunity may have been influenced by compliance due to 'the Draconian rigour' of [the council's] decrees against the plague'.[70] As Chapter 4 showed, Aberdeen's magistrates punished those who broke plague statutes with no more severity than their counterparts; indeed, on occasion they were demonstrably lenient.

Rather, individuals were perhaps willing to comply with plague legislation because, in addition to being fundamentally law-abiding, they recognised that infection was fatal and that the measures put in place were intended to safeguard the health of the common weal in its most literal sense. While people would have disliked the consequent disruption to their movements, relationships and occupations, they acquiesced to the measures, albeit grudgingly. Though the specifics went unrecorded, there were presumably many instances when residents fulfilled their civic duty by joining in a watch or patrol, by removing middens from outside their houses, by cancelling planned travel, and by notifying officers of suspected cases of sickness or illicit lodgers. Each individual within the physical community had a duty to do these things for the benefit of all, just as everyone within a spiritual community had a vested interest in ensuring the moral regulation of its members, because the consequence of not doing so – divine wrath – might be felt widely. An individual act of defying a particular plague regulation, even out of desperation, risked unleashing infection among the physical community and hence violated the ideals of responsible citizenship. The culprit would have been unpopular, to say the least; little wonder, perhaps, that the charge of deliberate plague-spreading levelled against a baker in 1547 hurt him 'bayt in body & mind', and provides an indication of the way in which in Aberdeen as elsewhere plague had the potential to 'inflame old resentments'.[71]

An urban history of the plague: early modern Aberdeen

There are many variables to consider in explaining how plague reached a given community. We cannot be absolutely sure, for example, that a particular action definitely influenced the course of an outbreak. Conversely, a town might have escaped even if human agency had not played a role, perhaps because a stricken individual was no longer infectious or because an infected rat happened not to cause an epizootic on arrival. The eminent plague historian Paul Slack has summarised the situation concisely by pointing out that 'we are dealing with a balance of probabilities, with finite chances of infection'. That balance might be tilted against effective legislation by extraneous factors, particularly war, which 'disrupted administration and increased mobility'.[72] It is perhaps significant that each of Aberdeen's epidemics occurred in the midst of extensive hostilities – war with England formed a backdrop to the outbreaks of 1514 and 1545, while the civil wars of the 1640s caused extensive socio-economic and political hardships for communities throughout the north-east and beyond. Or, perhaps this aspect happened not to be at all significant in the spread of plague to the city on each of these occasions. We will never be able to say conclusively how it was that Aberdeen did not experience plague within its bounds in 1608, for example, at a time when it was causing extensive misery across the short stretch of the Dee in Torry. However, this book has suggested several possible factors that may have contributed to the city's immunity: its location and surrounding topography; its relatively limited overseas contacts; the networks of communication that various groups cultivated; and the measures its councils imposed and to which its inhabitants largely acquiesced. To this list we could even add providence, as contemporaries certainly would have done.

It may be said that for most of the time the essential aspects of life in Aberdeen continued to function in spite of the disruption and death caused by plague, which were in any case felt to a lesser extent than elsewhere. The ability of a government body to remain in power, to continue under trying circumstances to oversee civic affairs, and to implement measures which were for the most part complied with by the community, may be regarded as testament to its relative strength and authority.[73] Successive councils in Aberdeen faced many challenges over the years: power struggles between merchants and craftsmen; outside encroachment from influential rural magnates; and infighting due to competing factional, familial and confessional interests. Nevertheless, it may be conjectured that they were remarkably successful at tackling plague, with or without input from the medical profession or advice received from their counterparts elsewhere, and often through responses formulated independently of the national framework, which enabled them to be responsive and adaptable to local circumstances.[74] These civic responses may have been given consistency by a degree of continuity in personnel, particularly during the sixteenth century. In turn, this might have made successive councils more likely to act in accordance with what some historians have identified as 'the growing tendency to ground argument on the evidence of precedent'.[75] This is not to imply that they were discerning in judging the success of previous measures, but rather that it may have been a naturally rational reaction at the first rumours of plague to reinstate established legislation, which was overwhelmingly underpinned by pragmatism rather than idealism, and experience rather than theory.

Aberdeen's experience of plague offers an interesting dimension to studies of many aspects of early modern life. For the historical geographer, it invites consideration of how successive governments of a relatively major town were able to use regional networks in conjunction with its location and topography to best advantage in the prevention of epidemics, even when the disease was 'neir its doore'. For the historian of medicine, it offers a Scottish perspective to early modern plague theory, and adds to the growing number of case studies which focus on the incidence and effects of epidemics north of the Alps. For the urban historian, it uses the lens of plague to consider the impact of crisis on civic tensions and cohesion. For the religious historian, it indicates how local circumstances could influence the articulation of piety in the face of the perceived manifestation of divine wrath. For the historian of Scotland, it offers a case study in response to Rob Falconer's call for future scholarship on early modern burghs to 'move beyond traditional debates about their origins and functions' towards 'questions that consider burghs as centres of broader human activities'.[76] Plague had the potential to exacerbate social antagonisms, to cause political and economic dislocation, and to bring about human suffering on a scale which may be hard for modern readers to imagine. Nevertheless – as shown by the numerous fasts that were undertaken by contrite congregations across the north-east in response to the threat posed by the disease not only to fellow believers in the immediate locality, but also to those in the region, the nation or even further afield – plague also had the power to unite.

Notes

1 ACR.53/1.472 [2 Jan 1656].
2 Gillian H. MacIntosh, *The Scottish Parliament under Charles II, 1660–1685* (Edinburgh: Edinburgh University Press, 2007), pp. 57–59.
3 ACR.54.520 [23 May 1664].
4 A payment was later recorded 'from Alexander Walker for the Elisabeth to Holland 12 fardells plaiding at 12s the fardel some of them being knitches…'; Louise B. Taylor (ed.), *Aberdeen Shore Works Accounts, 1596–1670* (Aberdeen: Aberdeen University Press, 1972), p. 501 [8 Sep 1664].
5 ACR.54.522 [8 Jun 1664]. The *Kook* was released on 7 July and its captain, Androw Skein subsequently paid duty on the goods he had imported; Taylor (ed.), *Aberdeen Shore Works Accounts*, pp. 501, fn. [7 Jul 1664], 509 [22 Sep 1664].
6 Aberdeen City and Aberdeenshire Archives: CA/12: Aberdeen City: Proclamations, Advertisements, and Notices, vol. I, 1592–1820 [8 Jul 1664, dated at Edinburgh]; RPC.3/1.561–562 [8 Jul 1664]; prosecutions: RPC.3/1.467 [1 Dec 1663], 501 [16 Feb 1664], 534 [2 Jun 1664], 544 [16 Jun 1664], 567 [14 Jul 1664], 568 [14 Jul 1664], 583 [5 Aug 1664], 584 [9 Aug 1664], 594 [18 Aug 1664], 680 [5 Jul 1664], 681 [15 Jul 1664], 688 [5 Aug 1664], 689 [5 Aug 1664], 690 [6 Aug 1664].
7 Aberdeen City and Aberdeenshire Archives: CA/12: Aberdeen City: Proclamations, Advertisements, and Notices, vol. I, 1592–1820 [2 Jun 1664, dated at Edinburgh]; RPC.3/1.534 [2 Jun 1664].
8 ACR.54.620–621 [2 Aug 1664].
9 ACR.54.625 [13 Sep 1664].
10 ACR.54.572–573 [14 Dec 1664]; ACR.54.609 [22 Feb 1665].
11 ACR.54.620–621 [2 Aug 1665].
12 Edward A. Eckert, "The retreat of plague from central Europe, 1640–1720: a geomedical approach", *Bulletin of the History of Medicine* 74:1 (2000), pp. 1–28, at p. 11.
13 Speymouth KS.3.26A [3 Sep 1665], Pitsligo KS.1.5 [2 Sep 1665], Dingwall Presbytery 2.19 [5 Sep 1665].
14 Clatt KS.1.11 [10 Sep 1665]; Dyce KS.1.259 [10 Sep 1665]; Speymouth KS.3.26A [10 Sep 1665]; Ellon KS.2.102 [10 Sep 1665]; Fintray KS.1.11 [10 Sep 1665];

Inverurie KS.1.188 [10 Sep 1665]; Kemnay KS.1.63–65 [10 Sep 1665]; Cullen KS.1.106r–v [10 Sep 1665]; Alves KS.1.206 [10 Sep 1665]; Dyke KS.1.26 [10 Sep 1665]; Elgin KS.7.294 [10 Sep 1665]; Clatt KS.1.11 [10 Sep 1665]; Croy and Dalcross KS.1.76 [10 Sep 1665]; Petty KS.2.7 [10 Sep 1665]; Old Machar KS.3.351–353 [13 Sep 1665]; Urquhart KS.n.p. [13 Sep 1665]; Forres KS.1.225 [14 Sep 1665]; Belhelvie KS.2.287–288 [17 Sep 1665]; Aberdeen KS.9.52 [18 Sep 1665]; Ellon Presbytery 4.42–43 [27 Sep 1665].

15 ACR.54.624 [6 Sep 1665].

16 ACR.54.625 [6 Sep 1665].

17 Aberdeen KS.9.52 [11 Sep 1665].

18 ACR.54.625 [13 Sep 1665].

19 John Booker, *Maritime Quarantine: The British Experience, c. 1650–1900* (Aldershot: Ashgate, 2007), p. 24.

20 ACR.55.140 [21 Jan 1669].

21 ACR.55.140–141 [26 Jan 1669].

22 Booker, *Maritime Quarantine*, p. 20, which was 'well in advance of the English practice'.

23 ACL.4.381–384 [9 Feb 1669].

24 Eckert, "The retreat of plague from central Europe", pp. 19–20.

25 Aberdeen City and Aberdeenshire Archives: CA/12: Aberdeen City: Proclamations, Advertisements, and Notices, vol. I, 1592–1820 [6 Sep 1711].

26 Aberdeen City and Aberdeenshire Archives: CA/12: Aberdeen City: Proclamations, Advertisements, and Notices, vol. I, 1592–1820 [25 Aug 1720].

27 Aberdeen City and Aberdeenshire Archives: CA/8/1/9: Letters: Correspondence Received by the Burgh, 1720–39 [15 Nov 1720].

28 An additional message was handwritten on the copy of the regulations received by authorities in Aberdeen: a note from a clerk in Edinburgh dated three days later, recording that 'we are glad to find the alarm about the pestilence being in the Isle of Man begins to abate'; Aberdeen City and Aberdeenshire Archives: CA/8/1/9: Letters: Correspondence Received by the Burgh, 1720–39 [19 Nov 1720].

29 Gordon DesBrisay, "'Menacing their persons and exacting on their purses': The Aberdeen Justice Court, 1657–1700", in David Stevenson (ed.), *From Lairds to Louns: Country and Burgh Life in Aberdeen, 1600–1800* (Aberdeen: Aberdeen University Press, 1986), pp. 70–90; Johan Findlay, *All Manner of People: The History of Justices of the Peace in Scotland* (Edinburgh: Saltire Society, 2000).

30 RPS: 1661/1/423 [9 Jul 1661]. This, in turn, was a word-for-word reiteration of legislation passed in 1617, which had originally bestowed on them these duties; RPS: 1617/5/22 [28 Jun 1617].

31 J.D. Marwick (ed.), *Extracts from the Records of the Convention of the Royal Burghs of Scotland, 1711–1738*, vol. V (Edinburgh: Convention of Royal Burghs, 1885), pp. 268–269 [17 Nov 1720].

32 Marwick (ed.), *Extracts from the Records of the Convention of the Royal Burghs of Scotland*, pp. 267–268 [15 Nov 1720]: this was reiterated in the 1721 Edinburgh reprint of the measures advocated in 1665 by the English Royal College of Physicians, which advocated that suspect persons should be 'speedily sent away, or kept in some house or houses set apart to receive such persons (with accommodation of necessaries) for forty or thirty days at least, till their soundness might appear'; National Library of Scotland, Special Collections, Ferg.85: *Certain Necessary Directions, as well for the Cure of the Plague, as for preventing the Infection: with Many easy MEDICINES of small Charge, very profitable to His Majesty's Subjects. Set down by the College of Physicians. By the king's Majesty's special Command* (London, 1665: reprinted at Edinburgh, 1721), p. 5.

33 Charles Creighton, *A History of Epidemics in Britain, vol. I: From A.D. 664 to the Great Plague* [1891] (New York: Barnes and Noble, second edition, 1965), p. 672.
34 Marwick (ed.), *Extracts from the Records of the Convention of the Royal Burghs of Scotland*, pp. 269–270 [17 Nov 1720]; Margaret DeLacy, *The Germ of an Idea: Contagionism, Religion, and Society in Britain, 1660–1730* (New York: Palgrave Macmillan, 2016); A. Zuckerman, "Plague and contagionism in eighteenth-century England: the role of Richard Mead", *Bulletin of the History of Medicine* 78:2 (2004), pp. 273–308; Charles F. Mullett, "The English plague scare of 1720–23", *Osiris* 2 (1936), pp. 484–516.
35 Fetteresso KS.2.28 [13 Nov 1720]; Belhelvie KS.5.33 [19 Nov 1720]; Fintray KS.2.55 [20 Nov 1720]; Airlie KS.2.27 [20 Nov 1720]; Maryculter KS.1.8 [20 Nov 1720]; Newhills KS.2.22 [20 Nov 1720]; New Machar KS.3.56 [20 Nov 1720]; Skene KS.1.1 [20 Nov 1720]; Aberlour KS.1.221 [20 Nov 1720]; Deskford KS.1.156 [20 Nov 1720]; Grange KS.6.192 [20 Nov 1720]; Keith KS.1.112 [20 Nov 1720]; Rothiemay KS.4.31 [20 Nov 1720]; Drainie KS.2.297–298 [20 Nov 1720]; Mortlach KS.3.103 [20 Nov 1720]; Banchory Devenick KS.1.169 [20 Nov 1720].
36 Chapel of Garioch KS.1.68 [11 Dec 1720].
37 *The extraordinary parts of a form of prayer, to be used in England, &c. on Friday the sixteenth day of December, being the day appointed by His Majesty for a general fast and humiliation, to be observed in a most solemn and devout manner: for obtaining the pardon of our sins, and averting those heavy judgements which they have most justly deserved; and particularly for beseeching God to preserve us from the plague, with which several other countries at this time are visited. His Majesty's special command* (Edinburgh, 1720), pp. 7, 9.
38 Deskford KS.1.156 [20 Nov 1720] (Ezekiel 9:4); Durris KS.1.6 [24 Nov 1720] (Isaiah 5:24); Mortlach KS.3.103 [20 Nov 1720] (Malachi 7:7); Aberdeen KS.28.322 [28 Nov 1720]; Auchterless KS.1.133 [15 Dec 1720] (Jeremiah 6:8).
39 Chapel of Garioch KS.1.69 [16 Dec 1720] (Hosea 9:12).
40 Rothiemay KS.4.31 [20 Nov 1720] (Jeremiah 3:12).
41 Fraserburgh KS.5.40 [16 Dec 1720] (Luke 13:1–3).
42 Cruden KS.1.305 [2 Dec 1720] (Psalm 91:1–4); Strichen KS.3.42 [11 Dec 1720] (Psalm 43:106).
43 The initial order for a fast issued by the General Assembly in 1720 urged the presbyteries 'to determine the day on which it is to be observed within their respective Bounds'; Fetteresso KS.2.28 [13 Nov 1720].
44 Fintray KS.2.55 [20 Nov 1720].
45 Natalie Mears, Alasdair Raffe, Stephen Taylor and Philip Williamson (with Lucy Bates) (eds), *National Prayers: Special Worship Since the Reformation, vol. I: Special Prayers, Fasts and Thanksgivings in the British Isles, 1533–1688* (Woodbridge: Boydell, 2013), p. 284.
46 National Library of Scotland Special Collections, RB.s.1107: [Christopher Pitt], *The plague of Marseilles: a poem. By a person of quality* (London [reprinted Edinburgh?], Printed for J. Bateman, at the Hat and Star: And are to be sold by John Paton Book-seller at his Shop in the Parliament-Close, Edinburgh, 1721), pp. 5, 20.
47 Thomas Comber, *A Companion to the Temple; or, A Help to Devotion in the use of the Common Prayer*, vol. II [1676] (Oxford: Oxford University Press, 1841), p. 329; National Library of Scotland, Special Collections, Jolly.2990(4): [Anonymous], *The Cleanser; or, the Method How to Behave in Time of Plague, Pestilence, or common Calamity of Sickness: and that with respect either to OUR SELVES or NEIGHBOURS when We or They are Infected* (Edinburgh, 1720), p. 9.
48 Comber, *A Companion to the Temple*, p. 334; [Anonymous], *The Cleanser*, p. 19.

49 To cite an influential early example of the historiographical debate, Appleby's suggestion that rats acquired immunity to the bacillus was refuted by Slack in favour of the efficacy of human action; Andrew B. Appleby, "The disappearance of plague: a continuing puzzle", *Economic History Review* 33:2 (1980), pp. 161–173; Paul Slack, "The disappearance of plague: an alternative view", *Economic History Review*, new series 34:3 (1981), pp. 469–476. The relationship between climate and the incidence of past diseases has increasingly captured historians' interest; see, for example: Bruce M. S. Campbell, *The Great Transition: Climate, Disease and Society in the Late-Medieval World* (Cambridge: Cambridge University Press, 2016); and for a Scottish example, see Richard Oram, "'The worst disaster suffered by the people of Scotland in recorded history': climate change, dearth and pathogens in the long fourteenth century", *Proceedings of the Society of Antiquaries of Scotland* 144 (2014), pp. 223–244.

50 Karl-Erik Frandsen, *The Last Plague in the Baltic Region, 1709–1713* (Copenhagen: Museum Tusculanum Press, 2010), p. 492.

51 Zlata Blažina Tomič and Vesna Blažina, *Expelling the Plague: The Health Office and the Implementation of Quarantine in Dubrovnik, 1377–1533* (Montreal: McGill-Queen's University Press, 2015).

52 Eckert, "The retreat of plague from central Europe", p. 24: 'improved quarantine measures' were responsible for the reduction in the spread of plague via ships between ports of the Baltic and Low Countries after 1640; Frandsen, *The Last Plague in the Baltic Region*, p. 494: the severe epidemic throughout the Baltic in 1709–14 was brought to an end through effective government measures; Mary J. Dobson, *Contours of Disease and Death in Early Modern England* (Cambridge: Cambridge University Press, 1997), pp. 486–487: a combination of quarantine and environmental measures 'could have helped to retard the progression of plague carriers to areas outside the epizootic range and to have minimised any risk of infection via the human flea'; Gunther E. Rothenberg, "The Austrian sanitary cordon and the control of the bubonic plague, 1710–1871", *Journal of the History of Medicine and Allied Sciences* 28:1 (1973), pp. 15–23, at p. 15: 'most important [among the measures] was the exclusion or isolation of humans, animals, and goods suspected of being plague carriers'.

53 John Ritchie, "The plague in Dumfries", *Transactions of the Dumfriesshire and Galloway Natural History and Antiquarian Society*, third series, 21 (1939), pp. 90–105, at p. 103.

54 David Hamilton, *The Healers: A History of Medicine in Scotland* (Edinburgh: Canongate, 1981), p. 14.

55 David Ditchburn, "Locating Aberdeen and Elgin in the later Middle Ages: regional, national and international paradigms", in Jane Geddes (ed.), *Medieval Art, Architecture and Archaeology in the Dioceses of Aberdeen and Moray* (Abingdon: Routledge, 2016), pp. 1–15, at p. 9.

56 Robert E. Tyson, "People in the two towns", in E. Patricia Dennison, David Ditchburn and Michael Lynch (eds), *Aberdeen Before 1800: A New History* (East Linton: Tuckwell Press, 2002), pp. 111–128, at p. 113.

57 John D. Comrie, *History of Scottish Medicine*, vol. I (London: Wellcome Historical Museum, second edition, 1932), p. 217.

58 Jose M. Gómez and Miguel Verdú, "Network theory may explain the vulnerability of medieval human settlements to the Black Death pandemic", *Scientific Reports* 7:43467 (2017) [doi: 10.1038/srep43467].

59 Eckert, "The retreat of plague from central Europe", p. 3.

60 95.5% of outbreaks in pre-industrial Europe were found to have occurred within ten kilometres of navigable rivers; Ricci P.H. Yue, Harry F. Lee and Connor Y.H. Wu, "Navigable rivers facilitated the spread and recurrence of plague in pre-industrial Europe", *Scientific Reports* 6:34867 (2016) [doi: 10.1038/srep34867].

61 Though several scholars have shown that the government of Seville was able to negotiate a balance between medical concerns and economic interests; Alexandra Parma Cook and Noble David Cook, *The Plague Files: Crisis Management in Sixteenth-Century Seville* (Baton Rouge: Louisiana State University Press, 2009); K. W. Bowers, "Balancing individual and communal needs: plague and public health in early modern Seville", *Bulletin of the History of Medicine* 81:2 (2007), pp. 335–358.
62 Trevor Dean, "Plague and crime: Bologna, 1348–1351", *Continuity and Change* 30:3 (2015), pp. 367–393, at pp. 367–368, quoting W.M. Bowsky, "The impact of the Black Death upon Sienese government and society", *Speculum* 39 (1964), pp. 1–34, at pp. 24, 27; É. Carpentier, *Une Ville devant la Peste: Orvieto et la Peste Noire de 1348* (Paris: École Pratique des Hautes Études: VIe section, 1962), pp. 195–196; and Benedict Gummer, *The Scourging Angel: The Black Death in the British Isles* (London: Bodley Head, 2009), pp. 205–206; see also Kevin Killeen, "Powder for padlocks: the rhetoric of thanksgiving and the politics of flight in Caroline plague", in Matthew Dimmock and Andrew Hadfield (eds), *Literature and Popular Culture in Early Modern England* (Farnham: Ashgate, 2009.), pp. 193–208, at p. 199.
63 ACR.53/1.130–131 [11 Aug 1647].
64 Dean, "Plague and crime", *passim*.
65 Eckert, "The retreat of plague from central Europe", p. 26.
66 Killeen, "Powder for padlocks", p. 199.
67 ACR.53/1.133 [22 Sep 1647]; ACR.53/1.138 [22 Sep 1647]; John Barclay (ed.), *Diary of Alexander Jaffray, Provost of Aberdeen* (London: Darton & Harvey, second edition, 1834), pp. 181–182; Alexander M. Munro, *Memorials of the Aldermen, Provosts, and Lord Provosts of Aberdeen, 1272–1895* (Aberdeen: privately printed, 1897), p. 156.
68 ACR.9.518 [16 Nov 1515]; ACR.19.265 [17 Dec 1546].
69 ACR.41.408 [11 Oct 1603].
70 Creighton, *A History of Epidemics in Britain*, p. 371; echoed by John Comrie's opinion noted in reference 59, this chapter.
71 ACR.19.308 [18 Mar 1547]; Dean, "Plague and crime", p. 367.
72 Slack, "The disappearance of plague: an alternative view", pp. 473–474.
73 Ritchie, "The plague in Dumfries", p. 104 attributed the weakness of early plague measures in Dumfries to a lack of sufficient administrative machinery to ensure they were enforced.
74 Booker, *Maritime Quarantine*, p. 17 reckoned that this well-established paradigm of locally-implemented measures throughout Scotland as a whole helped to make them stronger, as they were 'taken more literally and enforced with public visibility at market crosses' in comparison with England, whose national plague measures were relatively in their infancy.
75 Robert Tittler, "Reformation, civic culture and collective memory in English provincial towns", *Urban History* 24:3 (1997), pp. 283–300, at pp. 292–293.
76 J.R.D. Falconer, "Surveying Scotland's urban past: the pre-modern burgh", *History Compass* 9:1 (2011), pp. 34–44, at pp. 34–35.

Bibliography

Appleby, Andrew B., "The disappearance of plague: a continuing puzzle", *Economic History Review* 33:2 (1980), pp. 161–173.

Barclay, John (ed.), *Diary of Alexander Jaffray, Provost of Aberdeen* (London: Darton & Harvey, second edition, 1834).

Blažina Tomič, Zlata and Vesna Blažina, *Expelling the Plague: The Health Office and the Implementation of Quarantine in Dubrovnik, 1377–1533* (Montreal: McGill-Queen's University Press, 2015).

Booker, John, *Maritime Quarantine: The British Experience, c. 1650–1900* (Aldershot: Ashgate, 2007).
Bowers, K.W., "Balancing individual and communal needs: plague and public health in early modern Seville", *Bulletin of the History of Medicine* 81:2 (2007), pp. 335–358.
Bowsky, W.M., "The impact of the Black Death upon Sienese government and society", *Speculum* 39 (1964), pp. 1–34.
Campbell, Bruce M.S., *The Great Transition: Climate, Disease and Society in the Late-Medieval World* (Cambridge: Cambridge University Press, 2016).
Carpentier, É., *Une Ville devant la Peste: Orvieto et la Peste Noire de 1348* (Paris: École Pratique des Hautes Études: VIe section, 1962).
Cook, Alexandra Parma and Noble David Cook, *The Plague Files: Crisis Management in Sixteenth-Century Seville* (Baton Rouge: Louisiana State University Press, 2009).
Comber, Thomas, *A Companion to the Temple; or, A Help to Devotion in the Use of the Common Prayer*, vol. II [1676] (Oxford: Oxford University Press, 1841).
Comrie, John D., *History of Scottish Medicine*, vol. I (London: Wellcome Historical Museum, second edition, 1932).
Creighton, Charles, *A History of Epidemics in Britain, vol. I: From A.D. 664 to the Great Plague* [1891] (New York: Barnes and Noble, second edition, 1965).
Dean, Trevor, "Plague and crime: Bologna, 1348–1351", *Continuity and Change* 30:3 (2015), pp. 367–393.
DeLacy, Margaret, *The Germ of an Idea: Contagionism, Religion, and Society in Britain, 1660–1730* (New York: Palgrave Macmillan, 2016).
DesBrisay, Gordon, "'Menacing their persons and exacting on their purses': The Aberdeen Justice Court, 1657–1700", in David Stevenson (ed.), *From Lairds to Louns: Country and Burgh Life in Aberdeen, 1600–1800* (Aberdeen: Aberdeen University Press, 1986), pp. 70–90.
Ditchburn, David, "Locating Aberdeen and Elgin in the later Middle Ages: regional, national and international paradigms", in Jane Geddes (ed.), *Medieval Art, Architecture and Archaeology in the Dioceses of Aberdeen and Moray* (Abingdon: Routledge, 2016), pp. 1–15.
Dobson, Mary J., *Contours of Disease and Death in Early Modern England* (Cambridge: Cambridge University Press, 1997).
Eckert, Edward A., "The retreat of plague from central Europe, 1640–1720: a geomedical approach", *Bulletin of the History of Medicine* 74:1 (2000), pp. 1–28.
Falconer, J.R.D., "Surveying Scotland's urban past: the pre-modern burgh", *History Compass* 9:1 (2011), pp. 34–44.
Findlay, Johan, *All Manner of People: The History of Justices of the Peace in Scotland* (Edinburgh: Saltire Society, 2000).
Frandsen, Karl-Erik, *The Last Plague in the Baltic Region, 1709–1713* (Copenhagen: Museum Tusculanum Press, 2010).
Gómez, Jose M. and Miguel Verdú, "Network theory may explain the vulnerability of medieval human settlements to the Black Death pandemic", *Scientific Reports* 7:43467 (2017) [doi: 10.1038/srep43467].
Gummer, Benedict, *The Scourging Angel: The Black Death in the British Isles* (London: Bodley Head, 2009).
Hamilton, David, *The Healers: A History of Medicine in Scotland* (Edinburgh: Canongate, 1981).
Killeen, Kevin, "Powder for padlocks: the rhetoric of thanksgiving and the politics of flight in Caroline plague", in Matthew Dimmock and Andrew Hadfield (eds),

Literature and Popular Culture in Early Modern England (Farnham: Ashgate, 2009), pp. 193–208.

MacIntosh, Gillian H., *The Scottish Parliament under Charles II, 1660–1685* (Edinburgh: Edinburgh University Press, 2007).

Marwick, J.D. (ed.), *Extracts from the Records of the Convention of the Royal Burghs of Scotland, 1711–1738*, vol. V (Edinburgh: Convention of Royal Burghs, 1885).

Mears, Natalie, Alasdair Raffe, Stephen Taylor and Philip Williamson (with Lucy Bates) (eds), *National Prayers: Special Worship Since the Reformation, vol. I: Special Prayers, Fasts and Thanksgivings in the British Isles, 1533–1688* (Woodbridge: Boydell, 2013).

Mullett, Charles F., "The English plague scare of 1720–23", *Osiris* 2 (1936), pp. 484–516.

Munro, Alexander M., *Memorials of the Aldermen, Provosts, and Lord Provosts of Aberdeen, 1272–1895* (Aberdeen: privately printed, 1897).

Oram, Richard, "'The worst disaster suffered by the people of Scotland in recorded history': climate change, dearth and pathogens in the long fourteenth century", *Proceedings of the Society of Antiquaries of Scotland* 144 (2014), pp. 223–244.

Ritchie, John, "The plague in Dumfries", *Transactions of the Dumfriesshire and Galloway Natural History and Antiquarian Society*, third series, 21 (1939), pp. 90–105.

Rothenberg, Gunther E., "The Austrian sanitary cordon and the control of the bubonic plague, 1710–1871", *Journal of the History of Medicine and Allied Sciences* 28:1 (1973), pp. 15–23.

Slack, Paul, "The disappearance of plague: an alternative view", *Economic History Review*, new series 34:3 (1981), pp. 469–476.

Taylor, Louise B. (ed.), *Aberdeen Shore Works Accounts, 1596–1670* (Aberdeen: Aberdeen University Press, 1972).

Tittler, Robert, "Reformation, civic culture and collective memory in English provincial towns", *Urban History* 24:3 (1997), pp. 283–300.

Tyson, Robert E., "People in the two towns", in E. Patricia Dennison, David Ditchburn and Michael Lynch (eds), *Aberdeen Before 1800: A New History* (East Linton: Tuckwell Press, 2002), pp. 111–128.

Yue, Ricci P.H., Harry F. Lee and Connor Y.H. Wu, "Navigable rivers facilitated the spread and recurrence of plague in pre-industrial Europe", *Scientific Reports* 6:34867 (2016) [doi: 10.1038/srep34867].

Zuckerman, A., "Plague and contagionism in eighteenth-century England: the role of Richard Mead", *Bulletin of the History of Medicine* 78:2 (2004), pp. 273–308.

Index